IMPOSSIBLE HISTORIES

IMPOSSIBLE

HISTORIES

The *Soviet Republic* of Alaska, the United States of *Hudsonia,* *President* Charlemagne, and Other Pivotal Moments of History That Never Happened

HAL JOHNSON

NEW YORK

For my parents

for starting this whole mess

JOYFUL BOOKS FOR CURIOUS MINDS

An imprint of Macmillan Children's Publishing Group, LLC
120 Broadway, New York, NY 10271
OddDot.com • mackids.com

EDITOR Daniel Nayeri
DESIGNER Tim Hall

ISBN 9781250809674
Library of Congress Control Number 2022034644

Our books are available at special discounts when purchased in bulk for premiums
and sales promotions as well as for fund-raising or educational use. Special editions
or book excerpts also can be created to specification. For details, contact the Macmillan
Corporate and Premium Sales Department at (800) 221-7945 ext. 5442, or send an email
to MacmillanSpecialMarkets@macmillan.com.

First edition, 2023

Printed in the United States of America

10 9 8 7 6 5 4 3 2 1

George Ross tells of the movie magnate who was once asked if he had read H. G. Wells's "Outline of History."

"Naw," he said, "I thought it might make a good picture. But I looked at the ending, and I don't like the way the story comes out."

—Dr. Francis Leo Golden, *Tales for Salesmen* (1951)

CONTENTS

NOTES TO THE READER

History is really big and really long, and it keeps getting bigger and longer. However much you try to write about any historical topic, something will be left out. A history book should be the exact opposite of a mystery novel, with carefully inserted clues and a confession in the last chapter. Even the confessions in history are suspect. Even the corpse in the chalet may not exist.

Every sentence in this book, including this one, should be accompanied by a footnote enumerating the exceptions, the ambiguities, and the points of contention. Each footnote would need its own footnotes, of course. Lewis *"Alice in Wonderland"* Carroll once wrote about a map with a scale of one mile to one mile; it was too difficult to unfold, so people just used the country itself as a stand-in for the map. Similarly, the only really complete history book would be one of the same length and breadth as history itself.

If you're ever tempted to impart moral value to a historical event from before you were born, there's about an 80% chance you're merely indulging in your own prejudices rather than making an impartial moral judgment. If the historical event dates from before the eighteenth century, say, the odds are closer to 99%. There's simply too much backstory and too much context. History is two toddlers *hitting each other back* forever, and the only thing for a historian to do is to tell them, "I don't care who started it . . ."

Even if the facts of the case are clear, the morality often isn't. Attila the Hun lived and died thinking he was a good person, and he was hardly delusional; the other Huns (except maybe his brother, whom he murdered) thought he was a good person, too. Torquemada, head of the Spanish Inquisition, has long been a watchword for cruelty and intolerance, but in the fifteenth century he was a righteous man.

And yet it's so very tempting to make moral judgments about the past! I do it all the time! If my prejudices match yours (I assume you don't like

Hitler or Stalin either), you'll barely notice. When we differ—well, I tried to cite my sources!

England's greatest scholar of his day, the Venerable Bede, wrote in the preface to his history of England that any errors the reader finds could hardly be blamed on poor Bede, for in accordance with the "true law of history," the writer has merely passed along what older books have said. It's the sources' fault!

I encourage you to take any assertion I make with a grain of salt. Check my work and catch me out! In any controversy I tend to side with whoever has the better prose style, and this weakness may have led me astray. I'm sure I made more blunders than Bede, and I have no one to blame but myself.

On a scale of historical time, pretty soon everyone you have ever loved will be dead. So will you, and so will I. The world we lived in, which you may have loved and may have fought and died for, will change and become unrecognizable. This is just going to happen, and it's not my fault.

But I wrote this book, which *is* my fault. In almost every alternate, hypothetical history, you and I will never have been born. Most people on earth would never have been born. Some chapters here involve the death of millions or hundreds of millions of people. This is pretty bad, and I'm sorry. Harder to notice is the fact that if most people alive weren't born, that's over a billion souls snuffed out of existence. I did that.

Is any given alternate history better or worse than our unfortunate, benighted real history? Is whatever chapter you turn to a cautionary tale or an aspiration? Judging these questions is as easy and as hard as deciding whether Attila the Hun was a good person.

For all the deaths I caused, for all the people who never even existed, for the inexorable creep of the apocalypse—my only defense is that all of this, unlike, perhaps, you and me, is make believe.

The real deaths (and there are plenty in history) I blame, like Bede, on someone else.

WHAT DOES IT MEAN FOR SOMETHING NOT TO HAVE HAPPENED?

A philosophical prelude

I.

Everyone's got a pithy quip about history. "History is the autobiography of a madman," wrote the Russian socialist Alexander Herzen. Arnold Toynbee, British historian, complained about "the dogma that History is just 'one damned thing after another,'" while James Joyce wrote, "History is a nightmare from which I am trying to awake."

These are pretty good, but Jane Austen, as was her wont, came closest to the truth when one of her characters sums history up as "the quarrels of popes and kings, with wars or pestilences, in every page; the men all so good for nothing, and hardly any women at all"; she adds, "it is very tiresome."

Whatever else history is, most people would agree that it is an account of *things that happened*. There's an old joke that runs: Two men in a bar are watching a televised baseball game. One man bets the other a sawbuck that the visiting team will win. Sure enough, the home team's outfielder drops a fly ball, and the game ends with the visitors' victory; but when it comes time to collect the man says, "You know what? I feel too guilty to take your money. They're airing a game from this morning, and I saw it live. I already knew who would win."

The second man says, "I saw the game this morning, too. I just thought for sure this time he'd catch that fly."

Whatever that is, that's not history.

II.

Paul Rée is most famous now for being friends with Friedrich Nietzsche—Nietzsche had so few friends that all of them are at least a little bit famous—but in the nineteenth century he was known as a philosopher in his own right. How many friends Paul Rée had is open to debate, because Rée had the annoying habit of going around Europe trying to persuade people they had no free will. No one likes to hear that. People inevitably responded to Rée's claim by saying, "Look, look, I can do whatever I want," and demonstrated their freedom by raising their right arms, always their right arms, to prove their will was free; once Rée spoke to a left-handed man, and he, for a change lifted his left. Rée was unimpressed.

Rée espoused a deterministic view of the world, a view that was somewhat in vogue among depressive cynics of the time. Mark Twain, case par excellence, famously said: "The first act of that first atom led to the second act of that first atom, and so on down through the succeeding ages of all life, until, if the steps could be traced, it would be shown that the first act of that first atom has led inevitably to the act of my standing here in my dressing-gown at this instant talking to you."

I am free to lift my arm, if I will it. But am I free to will it? Philosopher Arthur Schopenhauer (whom Rée had read) pointed out decades earlier that you are free to put a gun to your head and pull the trigger, if you wish to—but it's a rare man who would do it just to prove he was free!

III.

Don't worry about Rée. Just play along for a moment.

Play along as we imagine a coin flip.

When we say a coin flip has a 50% chance of coming up heads, we don't mean it for any one particular flip. Any one flip has either a 100% chance of coming up heads or a 0% chance of coming up heads; we just don't know which one it'll be. Flip a coin a hundred times and about half of those flips will be heads; that's what the 50% means. "Call it in the air!" A hypothetical alien superintelligence capable of perceiving *1.* the force with which the coin was propelled upward, *2.* the speed of rotation, *3.* the wind resistance, *4.* the balance of the coin, *5.* etc., could tell you, before the coin fell, whether it would be heads or tails. In a Rée/Twain universe, a really impressive alien superintelligence could determine, based on your genetic makeup and every stimulus you'd ever received from conception on, including the exact environment you are in right now, precisely how you would flip, and therefore what the result would be, before you even flipped it.

No such superintelligence presents itself, but our limited brains can perceive the result of its experiment. If the coin comes up heads, you were going to flip it heads. If the coin comes up tails, you were going to flip it tails.

"I could have flipped it differently," you say. But you didn't.

Rée would say you couldn't've.

IV.

Arthur Schopenhauer was an interesting fellow. He followed the same precise, self-imposed schedule every day, which included five hours of writing, half an hour of flute practice, and a two-hour walk—regardless of the weather—around Frankfurt. He was one of the world's biggest jerks, and once pushed an old lady down the stairs for making too much noise. He believed the highest virtue was lying down, doing nothing until you starved to death (which of course he never attempted). He enjoyed being miserable perhaps more than any other human being in history, even compared to other nineteenth-century Germans. His famous mental exercise to prove that there is more suffering than joy in the world runs like this: Imagine two animals, one eating the other; imagine the joy of the eater; imagine the suffering of the eaten; which is greater?

Schopenhauer published his magnum opus, *The World as Will and*

Representation, at the age of thirty and declared the book to be the absolute answer to all philosophical riddles, insisting that the Holy Spirit had "dictated" parts of it; no one noticed, and he languished in obscurity for years. His mother was a popular novelist, and Schopenhauer seethed with jealousy over her success. When he yelled at her that his book would be available long after hers had been forgotten, she replied that, yes, his book's entire print run would still be available.

A great zing, but it turns out that Arthur Schopenhauer was right, which is why we're not citing *The Aunt and the Niece* by Johanna Schopenhauer, and neither is anyone else. Arthur Schopenhauer became famous eventually, in part because he won a contest. In 1838 the Norwegian Scientific Society offered a prize for the best essay on the freedom of the will. Schopenhauer's entry won, and it was very nearly the first time anyone had read something he'd written. Schopenhauer later published his "prize essay" bundled with another essay, written for another contest, *which lost even though it was the only entry.*

People would tell Rée: Sure, I lifted my right arm, as everyone does, but I *could have done* something different. And this is what Schopenhauer pounces on. In the winning essay, "On the Freedom of the Will," he compares *could have done* to still water, which may insist it can rise in great waves (as it does in a storm) and can turn into steam (as it does over a fire) and can course rapidly (as it does downhill)—but is currently choosing to stay calm and placid. Thus wills the pond!

Because if we could have done something different from what we've done, why has no one in the history of the world ever done it? If I claimed to be able to levitate even though I had never done so, everyone would laugh at me; and yet we accept the alleged power to deviate from our actions sight unseen.

You say you could have flipped the coin differently, and yet you never have. You never have because you couldn't've. This is a book about couldn't've.

This is a book about things that could never happen. We know that because they didn't.

V.

What if, we ask ourselves, what if Napoleon had not invaded Russia, but rather had gathered his troops and invaded England? We never ask ourselves: What if Emily Dickinson gathered troops and invaded England? It seems absurd to imagine Dickinson organizing such an expedition, but in fact an Empress Emily marching into London is just as likely as an Emperor Napoleon marching into London. Both are 100% impossible.

No one knew, in 1803, that Napoleon's invasion of England was impossible, of course. It worried a lot of people, whereas Emily Dickinson would not be born for another twenty-seven years, and provoked no terror among the British people even after she began existing. Perhaps Napoleon's invasion was impossible because the British had too much naval experience, or perhaps Napoleon's invasion was impossible because the general was simply a better tactician on land than he was at sea. If things had been different, the invasion would not have been impossible— if *1.* Napoleon was a naval genius, for example, or if *2.* a meteor had struck London, or if *3.* all British naval vessels had spontaneously turned into piles of dry leaves, rendering them defenseless. But things were not different, and all three possibilities were, it turned out, equally unlikely. It's just that the British knew *3.* was impossible, and never worried about it; and knew *2.* was unlikely, and never worried about it; and so they fretted about *1.* We imagine ourselves in their position, and we imagine a different Napoleon, or a freak storm destroying the English fleet, or a series of lucky naval battles giving the French control of the Channel. But it's no more likely to have happened than a martial, power-mad Emily Dickinson. It would require a different Napoleon, or *a different world*.

VI.

The first thing that happened was that a meteor hit the earth and wiped out the dinosaurs.

That's not really the first thing that happened, of course. The universe was billions of years old by the time the asteroid hit. But it's the first thing that happened that most people know about.

It wasn't the first meteor to hit the earth, and it wasn't the first mass extinction, nor was it the worst. The worst was two hundred million years earlier, when over 95% of marine species were wiped out, and I can't name any of them. It was the worst day in the history of the earth; the dinosaurs only saw what was probably the third-worst day in the history of the earth.

If previous mass extinctions had not happened, there wouldn't have even been any dinosaurs. Before the dinosaurs, huge long-legged crocodile-like creatures stalked the earth. A meteor (or something) killed half the life on earth, including most of the crocodile guys. Dinosaurs only started flourishing in the wake of that extinction. And then what went around came around.

The ancient Greeks weren't even sure if rocks *could* fall from the skies. They saw it happen on occasion, of course, but Plutarch records the suggestion that meteorites were just rocks from tall mountains, blown aloft by the winds and dropped to the earth like autumn leaves. But rocks sure can fall from the skies, and one fell in the Gulf of Mexico and that was it for the dinosaurs.

"It could have happened differently," of course. The meteor could have missed. We could be living in a world where mammals are mere vermin, and the most intelligent creatures are bipedal, tool-using raptors. Everyone lays eggs. Everyone has feathers. On the backs of specially bred triceratops mounts, raptors armed with bronze spears ride into battle, until, over millions of years, they develop better weapons and better vehicles. They have a long head start on us; they are our warm-blooded, archosaurian future. Their laser flails and ion cannons are literally millions of years more advanced than ours. Flying cars; elevators to orbit; Mars colony. *The Flintstones* is still on the air, but Fred is a velociraptor and he rides to work on a dimetrodon. Out in the suburbs a shrew-like relative of ours skulks about in a terrarium. It could have happened, if only the meteor had missed.

But how would it have missed? What would have made it miss? If you say solar winds could have blown it off course, what would have made these solar winds gust? If you say the moon could have interposed, like the hero from a melodrama leaping in front of a gunshot, then what would have modified the moon's orbit? We say *it could have missed* and then stop worrying about the how, but the meteor still worries about the how. Unless you're really persuasive about why that meteor should violate the laws of physics, it's going to hit the earth, right on a plesiosaur, every time.

This is a book of things that didn't happen, and there will be times, when you read it, when you consider the counterfactual suggestions implausible, when you will say, "That's impossible!" And you'll be right. None of this could have happened. It is all impossible. Richard the Lionheart could not have died at Jaffa, and Vikings could not have sold horses to Native Americans, and Freemasons never could have conquered America. Sleep easily.

VII.

Despite everything he said to support a deterministic universe, Schopenhauer actually thought that his prize-winning essay had proved the existence of free will. He was opposed to it, of course—he was opposed to everything, which makes him sound like a good guy when he was opposed to slavery or vivisection, which he was, and like a king jerk when he was opposed to women or existence, which he also was—but he had proved free will was a fact. "Prize Essay on the Freedom of the Will" is pretty easy to find, if you want to check his work. He's a much better thinker than my crude summaries have made him appear, and everything I've said about him is unfair except the part about being a jerk.

The point is that Rée may be wrong. Ashida Kim (for example) writes:

"What will happen in one's own life is already written, but one must choose to be there. This is the Way of the Ninja." Kim may be right. Schopenhauer may be right, and if he is you're off the hook; everything in this book is possible, or, rather, *was possible*. But if Rée's right, none of it ever was.

This is a book of impossible histories, and you can decide if they simply didn't happen, or if they never could have.

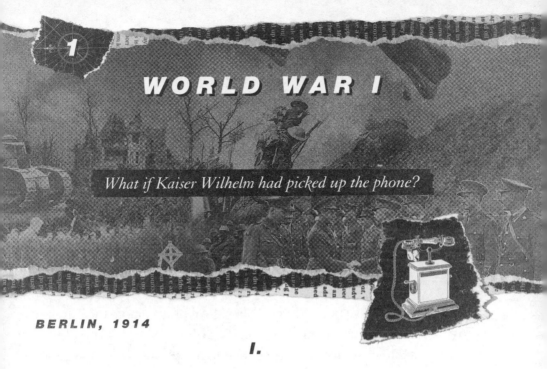

WORLD WAR I

What if Kaiser Wilhelm had picked up the phone?

BERLIN, 1914

I.

Zero people who fought in or lived through World War I knew they were living through or fighting in World War I. When I say that I mean two things:

One: Although World War I has become a watchword for the grimmest, most depressing and terrible of all wars (until the next one), the soldiers of 1914 marched off to war certain that the conflict would be *1*. short and *2*. fun. Everyone wanted a war; Europe hadn't had a big one since the fall of Napoleon in 1815, and, throughout the intervening ninety-nine years, European states were more likely to suffer a revolution than a fight with a neighbor.

It was an era of boy's adventure books, and wars were just another venue for venturesome lads to show their "pluck" or "grit" in various serials and novels: This was true of the American Civil War ("The Blue and the Gray" series by Oliver Optic), the Spanish-American War (*Winning His Commission* by H. Irving Hancock), even the Boer War (*The Young Colonists* by G. A. Henty)—why not WWI?

And so, the high school students from H. I. Hancock's "Dick & Co." series of kids' books (1910–12) got a sequel, enlisting in the war to "smash the Germans." The works of Col. James Fiske (not a real colonel, not a

9

real person; a pen name) sent American boys in search of adventure to war-torn France, Russia, or Serbia. "It's the most exciting thing that ever happened to me!" bubbles one young hero after a battle. "Now that it's all over I—yes, I believe I have enjoyed it!"

Clair W. Hayes's "Boy Allies" series had two strapping American lads, Hal and Chester, and, for a while, their dog, crisscrossing Europe to help the Allied cause in espionage and battle. Over the course of thirteen books (the first one published in 1915) they learn the valuable lesson that "there are adventures to be found in the eastern as well as the western theater of the war."

It was so much fun!

With the spirit of a boy's adventure book, people went into the war and didn't know they were going into World War I.

And *two*: They didn't know they were fighting World War I, because there was not yet a World War II. Just as *Rocky I* would never be called *Rocky I* until *Rocky II* came out, World War I was just called the World War (alternate title: the Great War) until the 1939 sequel. In fact, the assumption was that the World War would never be called World War I because there would never be another war; the "war to end all wars" was yet another name for it. Wherever you live, the odds are that the local World War I monument in your town is much larger and more ornate than the World War II monument. Everyone really got into WWI monuments because they were supposed to be the last monuments ever.

They were not the last monuments ever.

II.

Europe's streak of ninety-nine years without a big war didn't happen by accident. A century of diplomats kept a precarious peace through a non-stop juggling act. By the time the early twentieth century rolled around, peace was preserved by a series of alliances: The great powers, so-called, were divided between the Triple Alliance (Germany, Austria-Hungary, Italy) and the Triple Entente (Great Britain, France, Russia), with smaller countries glomming on to one or the other. Although the rules that bound these countries to each other were complicated and varied, the basic idea was: If you got into a fight with one country, all its allies pig-pile on you. Since all your allies would then assist you in pig-piling back, you would, by necessity, have plunged the world into a gigantic war nobody wanted. It was essentially a threat of mutual assured destruction before the term existed; unfortunately, peace lasted so long that people forgot how bad destruction could be. In his 1910 safari memoir, John T. McCutcheon could complain that for a red-blooded young man, "lion hunting is about the only thing left—except wars, and they are few and far between." How sad, 1910, how sad for you!

"During this quiet time of peace we are fast forgetting the exciting and astonishing events of the Napoleonic wars; and the very names of Europe's conquerors are becoming antiquated to the ears of our children. Those were more romantic days than these etc." Mary *"Frankenstein"* Shelley wrote that nostalgic paean to the bloody old days . . . *in 1829!* That's only fourteen years after Napoleon went down at the Battle of Waterloo! By 1914, people had forgotten the blood and remembered only how romantic it all was.

Fortunately for McCutcheon's red blood and Shelley's romantic pining, 1914 would remind them.

For in June of that year Serbian terrorists tried and failed to assassinate Archduke Ferdinand. When the Archduke headed for the hospital, though, to visit those collaterally wounded in the assassination attempt, his car by sheer chance stalled right in front of one Gavrilo Princip, a teenage anarchist who took advantage of the situation to shoot the Archduke and his wife. Two shots, two kills. Later legend claimed that Princip had stopped to buy a sandwich when the Archduke presented himself, but this is ridiculous—Serbians no more ate sandwiches in 1914 than they ate sushi. Princip was just moping around because no one had succeeded in killing Ferdinand yet.

Anarchists, note, were responsible for the deaths of six heads of state in the years around the turn of the century (including President McKinley, 1901), which is quite a record! Princip wasn't the most ardent anarchist, but then Ferdinand wasn't a head of state. He was merely heir to the throne of Austria-Hungary, but that's close enough for his death to give his country an excuse to invade Serbia.

A dead archduke wasn't a bad excuse, as far as they go, but it was still an excuse. The five-hundred-year-old Ottoman Empire had been falling to pieces of late, and various great powers had been jockeying to fill the power vacuum the Ottomans left. Squabbling over former Ottoman possessions had led to international crises in 1909 (Bosnia) and 1911 (Morocco), but neither of these had come to war. The 1914 Serbian crisis could have gone the same way, negotiated into oblivion; but by poor chance it didn't. A series of missed opportunities and boneheaded choices dominoed the world toward war.

Here's a boneheaded choice: After the assassination, Kaiser Wilhelm II of Germany gave his ally Austria-Hungary a blank check of support and then went on vacation in Norway. While he was gone, Austria-Hungary decided to demand from Serbia a roster of harsh concessions. Serbia conceded to *almost* all of them. That morning, the Kaiser, freshly back from his Norwegian cruise, woke up, went for a morning ride, came back, read his mail, learned that Serbia had caved, and was overjoyed. He wrote to the Foreign Office in Austria, expressing delight that there was now no reason for war.

Wilhelm's letter was a tacit withdrawal of support for Austria's war plan. If the Austrian emperor Franz Joseph had known that his chief ally thought peace necessary, he would have had no choice but to work things out with Serbia.

Unfortunately, by the time the letter reached Austria, around noon that day, it was too late. Austria had declared war on Serbia at 11:10 A.M.

III.

Serbia was de facto allied with Russia. Russia was allied with France. France was allied with Britain. Nobody except perhaps Austria but probably including Austria wanted to enmesh all of Europe in war.

But people didn't *not want it* enough. Wilhelm sent a letter, but frankly, all along he hadn't been acting like someone whose world was on the brink of catastrophe. It was 1914; he could have picked up a telephone.

The war would be short. The war would be fun. Nobody wanted the war, but they accepted it with a bit of a shrug.

Gavrilo Princip, the assassin who started it all, was sentenced to twenty years in prison. He was too young to receive the death penalty. Almost twenty million other young men, though, did receive the death penalty as the result of his actions.

*Kaiser Wilhelm picks up the phone → **THE KAISER STOPS THE GREAT WAR FROM HAPPENING** → Women can't vote → Prohibition doesn't pass → The Mafia is like fourteen people in a basement in Little Italy*

I.

BUT WHAT IF THE KAISER HAD SKIPPED HIS MORNING RIDE and read his mail first? What if he'd picked up the phone? What if he'd singlehandedly stopped the whole Great War from happening?

The most obvious result of no World War I is that twenty million or so people would not have died in World War I. (And, of course, another twenty million would not have been wounded.)

Since WWI led directly to WWII, you would save another eighty million lives from the latter war, which number includes those killed in the combat and those killed by its collateral effects: famine, disease, societal breakdown, deliberate genocide.

But there's more. The mobilization of troops in WWI helped spread the great flu pandemic of 1918—another (high estimate) hundred million who would not have died.

And since WWI toppled Tsarist Russia, ushering in the era of world communism, you can add those murdered by communist regimes—about a hundred million again—to the saved. Without the Great War, three hundred million people would not have died.

Of course, it's not like most of these people wouldn't have died eventually anyway. Many would still have died prematurely. Take the hundred million "saved" in a world without communism—Stalin killed twenty million or so, but the tsars would have killed some of them had tsars still been around. Not twenty million, probably, but also not zero.

Or the Jonestown massacre: The Reverend Jim Jones was a devoted communist who was actively petitioning the Soviet Union to accept him and his parishioners as immigrants; everyone in Jonestown was studying Russian. In 1978, Jones ordered the deaths of a US congressman, three journalists, and 914 other people, including himself, most of them via poisoned Flavor Aid. Jones's last recorded words, as he was dying, were peppered with communist jargon: "We didn't commit suicide. We committed an act of revolutionary suicide protesting the conditions of an inhumane world." These count as communist kills! But would these 918 people have lived if Jones had not been able to embrace communist ideology? Or (more likely) would Jones have found some other excuse to seduce, isolate, and then slaughter the gullible?

So sure, if the Kaiser gets on the ball, some number of people somewhat less than 300M would have lived longer than they did. That's something.

Also, the world would be totally different in every other way, because World War I was the biggest change agent there is.

II.

The historian Barbara Tuchman found the perfect detail to demonstrate how alien the world before the Great War was: President Charles Eliot of Harvard calling a baseball player shamefully dishonest for "making a feint to throw a ball in one direction and then throwing it in *another*." Believe it or not, this was not an isolated incident, but rather part of a debate that worried the sporting community at the time: When one of H. I. Hancock's sports heroes (from a 1910 book) makes a similar deceitful play in football, the heavy-handed fretful narrator steps in to assure the reader that it was not a lie, but "a legitimate ruse, as honest as any other piece of football strategy intended to throw the enemy 'off.'" If you've never worried about the morality of outfoxing your opponent in a children's game, you can thank World War I.

It's easy to romanticize the prewar era as not only pastoral and irenic but also honorable, just, and secure. No era could live up to such a romanticization; but perhaps it gropes toward accuracy. W. B. Yeats wrote in 1921:

> *We, who seven years ago*
> *Talked of honour and of truth,*
> *Shriek with pleasure if we show*
> *The weasel's twist, the weasel's tooth.*

"Seven years ago" from 1921 is 1914—the cusp of the War. By 1921 no weasel talked of honor or truth anymore.

The War marked not only a transition from the "old days" to the modern age; it marked a rupture. The progress of civilization, the improvement of humanity, was not only balked but was exposed to be a sham. This is Yeats again: same poem, same weasels:

> *We pieced our thoughts into philosophy,*
> *And planned to bring the world under a rule,*
> *Who are but weasels fighting in a hole.*

It's no accident I cite a poet for authority. Art is inseparable from any history of the Great War. Every war inspires art: World War II has its novelists and its poets who die young (Richard Spender, d. 1943; Alun Lewis, d. 1944); but World War II is imaginable without these texts, while World War I was so unprecedented an experience it required art to mediate, explain, and interpret it. Where would the War be without the retrospective novels *All Quiet on the Western Front* (Remarque, 1929) or

The Secret Battle (Herbert, 1919), without the modernist experiments of *In Parenthesis* (Jones, 1937) or *The Waste Land* (Eliot, 1922), without the dead poets Rupert Brooke (d. 1915), John McCrae (d. 1918), or especially Wilfred Owen (d. 1918)? Their attempts to explain what life was like is our truest record of the war, with its "shrill, demented choirs of wailing shells" and its "hot blast and fury of hell's upsurge."

"But until peace, the storm / The darkness and the thunder and the rain."

III.

In *The Three Musketeers* (1844), each time D'Artagnan meets a Musketeer, the first thing they do is agree to fight to the death! It happens three times in a row! Chance and mutual respect ("Monsieur, I love men of your kidney") prevent them from killing one another, and soon it's *all for one*, etc.; but first comes the violence, and then comes the friendship. This motif, by the way, goes back to *The Epic of Gilgamesh*, which means it goes *all the way back*.

This was the idea of violence that soldiers took *into* WWI; this was also their idea of war. War was glorious. War was honorable. You may think that you still think war is honorable, but you don't think war is honorable the way the pre-War world thought war was honorable. In one 1910 children's book about young army recruits, *Uncle Sam's Boys in the Ranks*, we learn in chapter 1 that anyone who doesn't support the armed forces is a "brainless anarchist." The chapter is titled "A Lesson in Respect for the Uniform," and naturally the lesson is delivered with fists. Not only is the army an unalloyed good ("unfortunately, few American youths, comparatively speaking, are aware of the splendid training that the United States Army offers to a young American"), but the only vocabulary to name it as good is the vocabulary of violence.

For the century or so before World War I, war, for Western Europeans, simply wasn't that bad. You might die in one, of course, but you probably wouldn't. Europeans generally waged war far away, in Africa or Asia, and against people whose armaments and training were inferior. In Bengal in

1757, Robert Clive brought three thousand troops to fight fifty thousand at the Battle of Plassey, and won decisively—with seventy-two casualties. It just wasn't too hard! These colonial wars tended to endanger only soldiers, who had, after all, volunteered for the danger; their families were safe at home. The whole thing was a lark. Africans and Asians, needless to say, did not experience colonial wars the same way; but for Europeans: adventure!

World War I, in contrast, was simultaneously *1.* miserable, *2.* deadly, and *3.* useless.

Miserable: Instead of marching with bright banners and fifes, Great War soldiers crouched in pestilential water in filthy trenches, breathing into gas masks while machine guns spat death at whoever unkinked his knees. Everyone had lice. Here is Wilfred Owen, so miserable that he is envying (alongside the dead) the "joys" of "microbes":

> *Dead men may envy living mites in cheese,*
> *Or good germs even. Microbes have their joys,*
> *And subdivide, and never come to death.*

Speaking of the dead: WWI casualties came in numbers completely unprecedented up to that time. Back at headquarters, the generals assumed they were simply errors. In one day at the Battle of the Somme the British suffered some sixty thousand casualties—still the bloodiest single day in British history. That's thirteen British soldiers killed and twenty-seven wounded *every minute* for twenty-four hours.

Edward Gibbon, the most quotable of historians, had written in a previous century that "whole generations may be swept away, by the madness of kings, in the space of a single hour"; and the Great War made this hyperbole less hyperbolic. Of the 3,000 students enrolled in Oxford University in 1914, the War would claim 2,700. In France: Young André Varagnac was the only member of his class of twenty-seven lycée students to survive—not just the War, but 1914! The other twenty-six were all killed in five short months! When the war started, a British volunteer needed to stand five feet, eight inches; after three months, the tall volunteers were dead, and the height requirement was reduced to five feet, five inches; *one month later* it was five feet, three inches.

And *useless*: All the death and suffering, all the attacks and battles and gassings—and they achieved nothing. Between September of 1914 and March of 1917, the Western Front barely changed at all. No one gained any territory; no one lost any. The Somme—a million casualties—gained the Allies six whole miles.

Sir Walter Scott wrote in 1807 about the disastrous 1513 Battle of Flodden (where perished the Scottish king and "the flower of Scottish gentility") that "all was lost *but our honour*." Nobody, looking back at the Somme, would ever write that. No one writes that way anymore.

Even after it became clear that the strength of defensive positions—trenches protected by barbed wire, machine guns, mud, and artillery—precluded real success in the War, leaders weren't willing to call it off. In a 1917 speech, French prime minister Georges Clemenceau would still proclaim, "You ask me for my policy. It is to wage war. Home policy? I wage war. Foreign policy? I wage war. All the time, in every sphere, I wage war." A 1916 political cartoon shows death luring a donkey over a precipice with a dangling carrot. The carrot is labeled "victory."

The incompetence with which the war was waged eroded trust in the military. The mendacity of the government propaganda—before the War, the word *propaganda* usually referred unpejoratively to the work of Christian missionaries—eroded trust in government. But most of all, people lost faith in violence. In 1904 the popular children's play *Peter Pan* ran with the line "To die will be an awfully big adventure." In 1915, that line was dropped from performances. The adventure had ended.

The War's survivors were a breed apart, and the new world they were demobilized into reflected their new outlook. In James Hilton's novel *Lost Horizon* (1933), an immortal Tibetan lama remarks to the protagonist (a WWI vet), "My son, you are young in years, but I perceive that your wisdom has the ripeness of age. Surely some unusual thing has happened to you?"

The answer he gives: "No more unusual than has happened to many others of my generation."

The Modern Era had begun.

IV.

Not everything the War brought was bad. The premodern world had been hopelessly classist, and the War helped break that down, slowly, slowly. Pre-war British cemeteries were segregated by class, for example, but the wartime need to bury the innumerable dead quickly led to a jumbling of social strata as well as body parts. In the English-speaking world, the War gave votes to women. At least in England, the War led to women's suffrage in some odd ways.

"Suffragettes" before the war were best known for *raising awareness through vandalism*. In 1914 Mary Richardson took a meat cleaver to Diego Velázquez's painting of Venus in the British National Gallery, e.g., but it was arson that really became associated with the suffrage movement. One 1913 *Punch* cartoon shows a "militant" woman griping, "Now isn't that provoking? Here's a lovely big house to let *and I've forgotten my matches!*" With the War come, suffragettes gave up on domestic terrorism to help with the War effort, and public perception, once so negative, changed enough that in 1918, British women over the age of thirty gained the right to vote. The resolution passed in part because the British government assumed few women would admit to being over thirty, so few would vote anyway.

In the US, where arson was less central to the cause, the fight for women's votes had been creeping, state by state, toward success. Women would have eventually gotten the vote nationally anyway—by the early 1990s, even Switzerland let women vote—but the Great War's overturning of traditional values helped speed it along. Also helping: America's sudden hatred for all things German. But to understand why that matters, we must look at the "other women's issue" that had marched hand in hand with suffrage for decades: temperance.

It's hard to comprehend, from our twenty-first-century vantage, how influential the temperance movement used to be in America. Not everyone (ca. the turn of the century) practiced temperance, but everyone agreed *they probably should.* Back then, "imbibing" was perhaps closest to smoking today: you can do it with like-minded people, and you can even enjoy it, but you know you're risking a lecture when you do it in public.

Charles Sheldon's runaway bestseller *In His Steps* (1896) asks a Christian congregation the then-novel question: "What would Jesus do?"; and the book answers: Jesus would get rid of those three scourges of society: "the whisky element," "the whisky forces," and "the whisky powers." Jesus's opposition to alcohol may come as a surprise to those who remember him turning water into wine (John 2:9); one 1885 tract (*The Water Drinkers of the Bible*) has a solution, though: The wine Jesus made was nonalcoholic!

This may sound unpersuasive. And Alexandre Dumas had already coined the greatest religious objection to temperance in 1844: "The wicked are great drinkers of water," he wrote, "as the flood proved once for all." There was always an undercurrent of eye-rolling about temperance, as there is with any "goody-two-shoes" issue. When Mark Twain wrote a story with a teetotaling hero, he made sure to give him a Siamese twin (!) who was an alcoholic ("Those Extraordinary Twins"). From the trenches in WWI, Lieutenant Colonel F. E. Smith requested that his wife label care packages of cigars as temperance tracts—so no one would open them or steal them.

Outside these grumblers, though, temperance was growing stronger. Many midcentury temperance groups started out patterned after the Freemasons but soon abandoned secrecy in favor of a bigger tent and more followers. Pastor Edwin Noah Hardy declared, in 1899, that "the present is the golden age of temperance in modern times." An 1888 etiquette guide notes that its advice on where to place wine glasses on the table only applies to "those whose conscience will allow them to do so." Alcohol was (according to one popular 1828 play) "the mockery of life, the antipodes of reason."

Temperance was partially a Christian issue, but also partially a women's issue: The influential Women's Christian Temperance Union had a foot in each camp. It was a women's issue because "saloons deprived women not only of the companionship to which they thought they were entitled but absorbed money which the women felt they were entitled to share"—which is a nicer way of saying that men were drunks, and women had few legal ways to earn money on their own. Pre-War literature is filled with long-suffering women driven to penury and/or ruin by intemperate husbands: Mrs. Warden in *Sketches by Boz* (Dickens, 1836), Emma Alton in the story of the same name (Butler, 1850), Jane Trafton in *Robert Coverdale's Struggle* (Alger, 1881), even Alicia Vernon in the above-quoted melodrama *Fifteen Years of a Drunkard's Life* (Jerrold, 1828)—to take four very different interpretations of the word "literature." The titular character of Anne Brontë's 1848 novel, *The Tenant of Wildfell Hall*, manages to flee, son in tow, her sot husband and his addiction to the "rank poison" of "hell broth." "My child must not be abandoned to this corruption: better far that he should live in poverty and obscurity, with a fugitive mother tha[n] in luxury and affluence with such a father."

One thing the dread "whisky element" knew was that women would, if they could, vote their product into the dustbin. Alcohol manufacturers therefore led the crusade *against* women's suffrage. When Tennessee was deciding whether to ratify the Nineteenth Amendment, liquor lobbyists just gave free booze to state legislators until (as former National American Woman Suffrage Association president Carrie Chapman Catt recalled later) "the Legislature was drunk!"—all in an attempt to swing the vote.

One important, and vocally anti-suffrage, sector of the "professional wets" was the brewing industry. The brewing industry was controlled by German Americans. If the idea of a bunch of Huns trying to keep our women down was ever going to fly in America, it was not going to fly in 1918. By 1920, with ratification of the Nineteenth Amendment, women had the vote across the US. Was it time to get revenge on the "whisky element"?

Well, revenge was already gotten. In 1886, as part of an *epic poem in blank verse* about the perils of the demon rum, Samuel Leech wrote:

> *Then let us pray and speak and give and write*
> *And work and vote until, from sea to sea,*
> *The white flag waves, and Prohibition reigns*
> *Law-girt throughout the sisterhood of States.*

Before 1920 hit, Leech's dream had come true.

You'll notice that women's suffrage was ushered in by the Nineteenth Amendment, Prohibition by the Eighteenth. The ordinal numbers tell the tale. It turns out that national women's suffrage hadn't been necessary for Prohibition. Yet by the time the Eighteenth Amendment passed, women could vote in some capacity in twenty-seven states. What had been necessary for Prohibition was simply that women be *sufficiently politically entrenched.*

Women would have gotten the vote eventually anyway, but the push toward women's suffrage happened to coincide with a rising tide of temperance. And suddenly Americans were voting for a law they had no intention of obeying.

V.

Prohibition was a failure, as everyone knows. Mabel Willebrandt claimed (in 1929) that it was succeeding in rural areas, and only failing in the cities—but cities controlled the media, so everyone considered it a failure. Please note, though, that *Assistant Attorney General* Mabel Willebrandt may have been partisan. Under Prohibition, people drank more (Willebrandt said this was false) and there was more public drunkenness (Willebrandt said that was just because intoxication laws were never enforced until Prohibition started).

Edmund Pearson once noted that Prohibition might not have stopped people from drinking, but it certainly stopped people from writing temperance literature. There would be no more epic teetotaling poems in blank verse. (Pearson thought this was a good thing.) Prohibition had killed the industry.

In fact, it killed the whole temperance movement. There is (in the modern world) no more "Blue Ribbon Army"; there is no more Anti-Saloon League. There still is a Women's Christian Temperance Union, but it is hardly the power it once was. These "dry" crusaders made an elementary mistake: They fought for a goal (Prohibition) that was possible to accomplish; once they accomplished it, they withered (now useless) away. Movements nowadays are too cunning to fall into this trap. If you wonder why the government has declared war on *terror*, or why your friends march to end *hate*, it is because these enemies are immortal, and triumphing over them is literally impossible.

Prohibition did not stop drinking, but it did stop temperance.

And what did it bring us? Well, Prohibition didn't exactly make the Mafia—the Mafia's been in America since the 1870s—but by taking a billion-dollar industry and handing it over to organized crime, it *made* the Mafia. People wanted to drink; bootleggers like Al Capone were (his words) "supplying a public demand." And, unlike the Blue Ribbon Army, the Mafia did not go away. Prohibition ended in 1933, but during the previous decade the Mafia had become too rich, too entrenched in too many industries to be wiped out by the loss of one revenue stream. Almost anyone who built anything in New York City in the '80s and '90s, just to take one example, has paid off the Mob. Is anyone in New York real estate clean?

The dominoes that Kaiser Wilhelm's morning ride knocked over have tumbled directly through World War I through women's suffrage through Prohibition to the Mafia. The victims of Mob violence—Jimmy Hoffa (1975), Steven DiSarro (1993), Michael Meldish (2013), twenty miscellaneous assassinations in Philadelphia, 1980–1984, etc., etc.—these are really just the latest casualties of the Great War.

If the Kaiser had used the phone, they'd have died peacefully in old age. Along with a couple hundred million others.

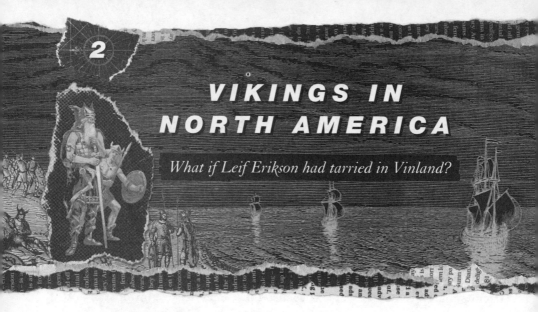

VIKINGS IN NORTH AMERICA

What if Leif Erikson had tarried in Vinland?

NEWFOUNDLAND, ca. 1010

I.

Half a millennium before Columbus, the Viking Leif Erikson left Greenland to set up a camp in North America. Other family members followed in his wake and established a colony, presumably in what is now Newfoundland. It only lasted a few years (estimates range from three to ten), but its existence was one of the most important moments in the history of the world—because of what didn't happen.

Leif only ended up in Greenland because of the Viking criminal justice system. Medieval Iceland had no prisons, so most crimes were punished by fines, but the worst crimes could be punished with outlawry. An outlaw was one who lived outside the protection of the law, and anyone could do anything to him without fear of legal punishment. If you point to a man and tell several thousand Vikings that they can kill him with no consequences—well, most outlaws enjoyed short lives. Some legendary characters managed to survive for a long time by hiding, by being stronger than everyone else, or both. The record was set by Grettir Ásmundarson, who survived eighteen years an outlaw, followed by Gísli Súrsson with thirteen—but Grettir and Gísli were celebrated in sagas as heroes, and were in the end murdered anyway. Most outlaws sensibly left Iceland for its sister-state Norway to ride out their sentence.

24

Around the year 982, Erik the Red, Leif's father, was outlawed in Iceland for three years on a murder charge. Unfortunately, Erik had already been banished from Norway some years earlier (also murder), so Erik sailed west instead, choosing to follow up rumors about a land spotted by a lost sailor a hundred years before. This is more or less as if Billy the Kid, upon fleeing New Mexico, went not to Arizona but in search of Atlantis; in Erik's case the gamble panned out, though, and he spent his three years exploring the land he'd found. He named it Greenland not because it was fertile or clement but because (according to the thirteenth-century *Greenlanders' Saga*) "people would be more likely to settle there if the land had an appealing name." You may not be inclined to follow a double murderer across the open ocean to a strange land, but you are probably neither as brave nor as foolhardy as a Viking, and I didn't see you conquer Normandy. And maybe Iceland was starting to feel overcrowded, with an estimated fifty thousand inhabitants and mediocre farming. Norsemen were always overbreeding and running out of space in their inhospitable homelands; in the sixth century, the historian Jordanes called Scandinavia the "vagina" of nations because its people kept sailing away from their homeland in such great multitudes and conquering places to the south. In Jordanes's day Norse Goths conquered Spain and Italy, and Norse Lombards conquered Italy from them in turn. In later years Scandinavians would take England, Ireland, Normandy, England again, Italy, Sicily, Russia, and Antioch (!), and would colonize the Orkneys, the Faroes, the Shetlands, Iceland, and Greenland.

Leif grew up in Greenland, on his father's estate of Brattahlíð. As a young man he traveled throughout Scandinavia until the Norwegian king Olaf Tryggvason sent him back home to Brattahlíð on a special mission.

King Olaf himself had a life that could have come from a pulp fantasy magazine. The great-grandson of King Harald Fairhair, infant Olaf was spirited out of Scandinavia after his father was murdered as part of a dynastic struggle. He was captured by pirates and sold into slavery in Estonia; after many adventures he became captain of the king's guard in Novgorod and a pirate himself in the Baltic, married a queen in what is now Poland, and, upon her death, another queen in Ireland. When he was in his thirties he returned to Norway in force and claimed the throne. Probably not all of these adventures are true, but this is what the medieval historians claim; they also claim he could catch arrows ambidextrously and throw them back at whoever shot them, so make of that what you will. But certainly, somewhere along the way Olaf had abandoned the Norse gods and been baptized, with the explicit goal of converting Scandinavia to Christianity. Norway had experimented with Christianity before, but Olaf was serious about making it stick this time, strong-arming conversions and enforcing trade embargoes with pagan lands. Using political and economic pressure, as well as a healthy dollop of violence, Olaf managed to convert Norway, Iceland, the Shetlands, the Orkneys, and the Faroes, and he sent Leif to convert Greenland. Technically the king had no authority over Greenland, but he had no authority over Iceland either, and he was, at about this time, taking Icelanders hostage and threatening their families if Iceland did not convert. That was Olaf for you!

Greenland's conversion went more peacefully. Erik the Red was reluctant to abandon the old gods, but Leif's mother was into it; she had a church built, the first in Greenland, and Leif must have felt his missionary work sufficiently progressed that he could trundle off on a self-imposed mission, a mission of discovery.

II.

Sometime around the year 1000, Leif decided to set out from Greenland and follow up on rumor of a land farther west, as his father had before him. He tried to get Erik the Red, who now lived a comfortable life as the chieftain of Greenland, to come along on the journey, but the old man fell off his horse on his way to the ship and interpreted it as a sign he shouldn't go. He would die of disease before his son's return.

Meanwhile Leif headed west and south with thirty-five men and touched land at three places, each a couple of days' sail apart. He named them Helluland (*land of flat stones*), Markland (*land of forests*), and Vinland (usually translated as *land of grapes*). In Vinland his men built houses and settled down. The next year they packed up and returned home.

Where exactly this all happened has been for many years a matter of great controversy. In fact, whether it happened at all was a matter of great controversy—the Middle Ages are filled with stories of people, including King Arthur and St. Brendan, sailing off into the unknown ocean and discovering lands, and it's not immediately apparent that Leif's story should be taken more seriously than these. Although Vinland is referred to obliquely in several old texts, the only ones that give specifics are two Icelandic sagas, *Erik's Saga* and the aforementioned *Greenlanders' Saga*. Both were written two centuries after the fact, both contradict each other, and both contain passages that are either implausible or clearly false. It's extremely unlikely that North America was ever populated by amphibious, one-legged hopping archers, for example, but *Erik's Saga* would have you believe it was; *Greenlanders' Saga*, meanwhile, features a talking corpse and an ominous ghostly woman who appears and disappears without explanation. These are not the best sources, but for centuries they were all we had.

Assuming that Helluland, Markland, and Vinland were real places, pretty good guesses for their locations are Baffin Island, Labrador, and Newfoundland, all in Canada. In the 1960s Norwegian archaeologists Helge Ingstad and Anne Stine dug up pre-Columbian Norse ruins at a site in Newfoundland and called it Vinland. *Vinland* is supposed to mean *land of grapes*, and grapes scarcely grow in Newfoundland, but Greenland isn't green, either, and, most importantly, Ingstad's work proved definitively that whatever the truth of the sagas' specifics—grapes and monopods—the larger point they made was right. Greenlanders clearly stayed on North American soil long enough to build houses and a forge, because houses and a forge were what Ingstad found.

Leif brought back to Greenland word of a warmer and more fertile land that was, most importantly, filled with trees. Greenland had few, small trees, as whatever larger ones that had once grown there had already been cleared away by short-sighted Vikings to make grazing pastures, so most of the Greenlanders' timber came from driftwood—therefore, a nearby Markland (*land of forests*, remember) was very attractive to them.

Attractive enough that Leif's three siblings would all set out on their own voyages to the North American continent, and it was Thorvald Erikson who made first contact between the peoples of the Old World and the New. Thorvald and his men killed the natives they found; then more natives showed up and killed Thorvald.

This is the first encounter between Native Americans and Europeans in recorded history, and it does not go well for anyone. Although the regions of Greenland that the Icelanders settled in had been inhabited at various times before Erik's discovery, no one was living there when Vikings showed up—all the natives in Greenland were far to the north. Estimates of how densely populated the Americas were before Columbus are extremely loose and controversial, but whatever they were, even Newfoundland must have been quiet enough that Leif Erikson could spend months there and not see a stranger. This state of affairs would not last.

Leif's other brother, Thorstein, attempted a trip to Vinland, to fetch brother Thorvald's corpse, but he got lost at sea, floundered back to Greenland, and died of unrelated issues (*it was the Middle Ages!*) before he could leave again. His widow Gudrid, though, did get to the New World, along with her new husband, the Norwegian adventurer Thorfinn Karlsefni, and a group of 160 men and women. They brought along cattle, too, for this was the first attempt to create a permanent settlement in Vinland. Gudrun gave birth there to the first European baby born on American soil, Snorri Thorfinnsson, unless you believe it is too convenient that the leaders of an expedition should happen to be the first to have a child; in any event, Snorri is the first baby recorded, and if any thralls or servingwomen gave birth in Vinland, it's been forgotten.

From that settlement Thorfinn Karlsefni and a small party sailed south of Vinland, exploring the coast. Karlsefni met natives as well, and traded with them at first, cloth and milk in exchange for pelts. The relationship soured, though, and degenerated into combat. *Erik's Saga* singles out fear of further fighting as a reason for abandoning southward expansion. Presumably the number of natives grew the farther south the explorers went.

The sagas are less clear on why Vinland was abandoned, or when. At some point Karlsefni returned to Greenland (and then to Iceland). *Greenlanders' Saga* tells of a further expedition to Vinland, led by Leif's sister Freydis and two brothers named Helgi and Finnbogi. Freydis ended up quarreling with the brothers and then goading her husband and his men into a general massacre of the Helgi-Finnbogi party. When no one else was willing to murder the women loyal to those brothers, Freydis took an ax and dispatched all six of them herself. She then threatened with death anyone who should speak the truth about the massacre, and they all sailed back to Greenland. The saga ends shortly afterward.

Whether anyone else ever returned to Vinland after that, or to the southern reaches Thorfinn explored, no extant source tells us. Records mention trips to Markland, at least, but just to harvest wood, not to settle. Presumably there were too many natives to make settling safe or attractive. Presumably Greenland was not populous enough to lose so many able-bodied explorers.

III.

The people in Greenland lasted several more centuries, and you might think it would make sense for them to continue exploring. Perhaps they did—for a while. But things were not going well in Greenland. The growing season there was always short, and the wood was scarce enough that it was hard to build houses, heat houses, boil water, or, perhaps most importantly, make charcoal to heat and forge iron. So life was hard anyway, although trading ships from Norway brought much-needed supplies in exchange for precious walrus ivory, Greenland's biggest export. But events were conspiring against the survival of the colony.

The so-called Little Ice Age, a cold spell that swept the North Atlantic starting around 1275 is one obvious cause of woe in a country with poor heating supplies. But there were other problems. The Norwegian supply ships grew fewer and finally stopped coming in.

There are several reasons why the ships stopped. The Black Death had swept through Scandinavia, killing half the population in some places, and everyone had more things to worry about than far-flung colonies. The various Scandinavian countries have often merged or conquered one another, and in the late fourteenth century, Norway happened to share a monarch with Denmark, and then later, in a pan-Scandinavian union, with both Denmark and Sweden, and the joint king of all three countries—a native Pole—had little interest in lands beyond the sea. Furthermore, the Crusades, and the ongoing presence of a European outpost in the Middle East, had opened new elephant ivory sources to the West, so walrus tusk was not as fashionable as it used to be.

The last official supply ship reached Greenland in 1368; 1409 marked the last year any ship from Europe landed at Greenland; after that they were cut off, and it was still getting colder.

A collection of medieval Norse mythological poems called the *Poetic Edda* talks of the end of the world being preceded by the so-called Fimbulwinter, a great apocalyptic winter that lasts three years straight and climaxes in the extinction of almost all of humanity. For the Greenlanders, the Little Ice Age must have felt like the Fimbulwinter. More of their meager fuel supplies burned for heat meant less wood to make into charcoal; less charcoal, recall, meant no way to fire the forges; cold forges meant less iron; less iron meant worse tools meant less efficient collecting and preparing of food supplies, at a time when efficiency would have been key.

Less iron also meant worse weapons. There's some debate about the quality of Viking swords, but they, along with iron battle-axes and iron-tipped spears, were clearly superior to weapons of bone or slate, as most often used by the natives who lived in Greenland far north of the Norse settlers. Colder weather was driving them southward, following the seals they hunted, and into increased conflict with the Norse. If Vikings had a chance at holding the natives off, it was going to take iron weapons. In the Icelandic annals we read of a 1379 raid by natives killing eighteen

Norsemen and carrying off three captives; in 1379 the Greenlanders didn't have so many men that they could easily spare twenty-one.

Sometime after that, sometime after 1409, from starvation or violence, every single one of them died.

IV.

The extinct Greenland colony is a footnote in history; its brief subcolony in Vinland a footnote to a footnote. Some people have claimed a somewhat higher pedigree for Vinland, or rather for the knowledge of how to reach there. Christopher Columbus, according to the biography written by his son, visited Iceland in 1477, and throughout the nineteenth century writers averred that he had learned there about Vinland, and been sailing toward it when he reached the Bahamas. The theory has a hard time explaining why Columbus missed Vinland by some two thousand miles, but that hasn't stopped the cranks—the Rev. B. F. DeCosta in 1872, Marie A. Brown in 1887, etc.—from proclaiming Columbus's Viking inspiration.

But even if the Vikings crossed the Atlantic first, just as the innumerable Native Americans had crossed the Bering Strait *first* first, it was Columbus's voyage that made history. After Columbus, the world would never be the same again, while after Leif the world would go on for almost everyone as it always had. Because Leif is a footnote.

Leif Erikson stays in Vinland → Native Americans get Viking iron and Viking germs → COLUMBUS REPULSED BY ARMORED HORSEMEN → No European settlement of the Americas

BUT WHAT IF LEIF AND THE OTHER VIKINGS HAD MADE THEIR stand in Vinland? What if they hadn't packed up and left?

I'll cut right to the chase. If the Eriksons had stuck it out in Vinland a little longer, there would have been no later settlement of the Americas by Europeans.

This is a bold statement, so let's back up a little to see what path of logic leads us to it.

Leif Erikson was the first to set up camp in Vinland, and the first to abandon that camp. It's easy enough to tell him he should stay, but it would probably have been difficult to persuade him. He had a family back in Greenland, and obligations; he didn't know his father was dead, but he knew his father was old, and he himself was heir to the chieftainship of Greenland.

Still, he and his family, in their several attempts at exploring and settling, could have done some things differently. Instead of recruiting from the sparsely populated Greenland, they could have sailed all the way back to Iceland to get settlers—Leif's father had managed to persuade some twenty-five ships to leave Iceland for Greenland, more than ever came to Vinland, and more than Greenland could comfortably lose.

Vikings had succeeded in colonizing lands with much harsher climates than Newfoundland, and all of them were previously inhabited. Iceland, before the Norse arrival, sported a population of Irish monks; the Faroes (according to one medieval source, the Irish geographer Dicuil) had Scottish hermits. You will perceive, though, that these are not very martial figures. The southern coast of Greenland had been inhabited at various times in the past, probably by the Dorset culture, possible relatives of today's Inuit; when Erik the Red landed there, though, everyone else had long since abandoned that part of the island. Only the Orkneys and Shetlands were populous at the time of Norse arrival, and these were also the closest colonies to the Scandinavian homelands. For regions farther afield, as Vinland was, no fighting had been necessary to take possession.

The x-factor in Vinland, therefore, is the presence of natives. It might be worthwhile looking at who these natives were.

The Norse called them "skraelings," a word that in modern Icelandic just means *barbarians*, but was applied indiscriminately by the medieval Vikings to the native peoples of Greenland, Newfoundland, and the eastern coast of the Americas. Many peoples lived along this thousand-mile stretch of mainland, and the sagas do not leave a lot of clues specifying which ones the Vikings encountered where. We do know from archaeological digs in Newfoundland, though, that during the time of the Vinland settlement, the island was inhabited by the Beothuk, hunter-gatherers who had lived there for over a millennium. The last of the Beothuk died in 1829, and most of our information about them comes from centuries after the Norse contact, so it's difficult to confirm the saga account with anthropological knowledge. The Beothuk were skilled with the bow and arrows, just as the "skraelings" near Vinland were—but this is not exactly a unique trait in pre-Columbian North America. *Erik's Saga* depicts the natives as being especially eager to trade for red cloth, and red was a sacred color to the Beothuk. But *Erik's Saga* also locates the site of trading well south of Vinland, so probably well south of the Beothuk.

The brief peaceful moments of trade that *Erik's Saga* describes predictably degenerate into violence, and here the Norse account includes a curious detail that has never been adequately explained. The attacking "skraelings" make use of a catapult-like weapon that throws a blue ball resembling a sheep's stomach, which causes a loud noise when it lands.

No such weapon is known to have been used in North America, but there is a brief, tantalizing passage in Henry Rowe Schoolcraft's enormous ethnographic study *Historical and Statistical Information Respecting the History, Condition, and Prospects of the Indian Tribes of the United States*, published in many volumes and many thousands of pages throughout the 1850s. Schoolcraft writes of a "tradition" among the Algonquin Indians of a weapon used "in ancient times": a boulder sewn tight in an animal skin attached to a long pole, wielded by several men and used to smash small boats, for example. Schoolcraft calls the weapon a "balista," a curious choice of term, as a ballista is really a large siege crossbow; the weapon as described is more like an enormous hammer. But it's also reminiscent of the skraelings' catapult.

Schoolcraft was an important scholar, sympathetic to his subject matter (especially for his time) and wide-ranging in his collection of data. The breadth of information in *Historical and Statistical Information* is staggering, and ultimately deadening to the senses. (Fortunately, the "balista" account is in the first volume.) His wife was half Ojibwe, and her reminiscences, which Schoolcraft published, are among the earliest recorded accounts of the Hiawatha legend and the main source for Longfellow's Hiawatha poems. Nevertheless, Schoolcraft's short and vaguely sourced account of an Algonquin weapon should be taken with a grain of salt. Many people have had traditions of spurious ancient devices. Old Sanskrit texts, for example, send characters around in flying chariots called *vimanas*, but no one would suggest that ancient India actually had aircraft. (Actually, David Hatcher Childress suggested just that in his 2000 book, *Technology of the Gods*, but to say the least, he hardly represents a mainstream view.) Nevertheless, if *Erik's Saga* is correct in its geography, the lands south of Newfoundland that the Norse were exploring would have been home to relatives of the Algonquins, and the circumstantial resemblance between the two listed devices, "balista" and catapult, is undeniable.

But in Vinland, in Newfoundland, the Norse had to make their colony, and if they were going to be fighting anyone for possession of that island, they would be fighting the Beothuk. The question is, could the Vikings prevail?

Jared Diamond won a Pulitzer for summarizing the reasons Europeans, starting in the sixteenth century, were able to conquer so much of the known world: "guns, germs, and steel," he wrote. The Spanish conquistadors, to take one example, were preceded by waves of disease to which they were already resistant, and their steel armor made them all but immune to the weapons of the Native Americans. Add the killing power of their firearms, and you had the recipe that allowed small forces of adventurers to defeat the strongest empires in the New World.

The Norse Greenlanders did not have guns, of course, and out in the hinterlands they may not have had much steel, but they had germs, and they also had iron. Although Native Americans worked in copper and possessed some limited access to iron, they lacked the Norse techniques of forging that gave Vikings their ax-heads, spearheads, arrowheads, and, for the wealthy or particularly martial, swords, helmets, and armor. *Greenlanders' Saga* says that Lief's brother Thorvald was killed by an arrow to the armpit; *Erik's Saga* says an arrow to the groin. Both armpit and groin are traditional weak points in armor, joints that are difficult to cover with metal. It probably strains credibility to imagine that either saga preserves an authentic record of Thorvald's death—remember, one of these arrows was allegedly fired by a monopod, and there's no reason to believe that Thorvald was fully armored for war while exploring the continent—but they do highlight the potential efficacy of armor against stone-tipped weapons. Armpits and groins only. No other Vikings, the sagas say, fell to that hail of arrows.

Horses don't make Jared Diamond's top three reasons for European conquest, but they deserve to be runners-up. We have learned, again from conquistador accounts, that horses were a source of great marvel and fear in the natives, who had no way of knowing that man and beast were not a composite, centaur-like monster. When Pizarro was hard-pressed by overwhelming numbers of Quitu people in a coastal city of what is now Ecuador, for example, one of his men fell off his horse, and the Quitu were so alarmed to see one creature split in two that they fell back in fear, allowing the Spaniards to escape. Although we don't have any record of horses being brought to Vinland, they certainly lived in Greenland, or Erik the Red couldn't have fallen off one; there's no reason a Vinland colony wouldn't have its share of horses.

Bartolomé de las Casas, the Dominican friar who sailed with Columbus in 1498 and lamented the atrocities the admiral and his successors committed, wrote that the horse was the deadliest weapon the Spanish had against the natives; but de las Casas was wrong. The deadliest weapon was disease. At least in part because of the large number of domesticated animals, animals that often wintered right in the house with their masters, people of the Old World were more riddled with disease than people of the New. This meant that the New World had zero resistance to smallpox, measles, chicken pox, whooping cough, leprosy, influenza, scarlet fever, malaria, cholera, and the bubonic plague; the list goes on. You may think you don't have much resistance to the bubonic plague, but the Americas had even *less* resistance. The Vikings in Vinland did not have the plague, of course—it wouldn't reach Scandinavia for another 350 years, when a ghost ship from England, its crew dead to a man, ran aground in Norway and scattered plague-infested rats across the countryside—and they didn't have malaria or cholera, either. They may not have even had smallpox, the deadliest of European diseases brought to the New World—the first recorded outbreak in Greenland is not until 1430 or so. But the Norse, just by dint of having more domesticated animals, certainly had more diseases than the Beothuk did.

Historically, the paradisal disease-free state the Americas enjoyed came to a sudden halt at the end of the fifteenth century, and in the 150 years after Columbus's landing the population of the New World had been reduced by up to 90% because of novel diseases. It's difficult to make comparisons, because the timelines are so different, but only one third of Europe was killed by the plague in the fourteenth century and it caused the collapse of the feudal system and the end of the Middle Ages. The Americas were left with a mere tenth of their former population, leading European observers to assume that the land was almost completely unpopulated, a ghost town on a continental scale.

Clearly the Norse did not remain in Vinland long enough for their European diseases to take hold in the native population, but a longer stay would certainly have had a disastrous effect—perhaps not as disastrous as the Spaniards' arrival, because medieval Spain was much more densely populated than medieval Scandinavia, but disastrous nonetheless. The Norse would not have understood any more than the Beothuk what was happening, of course: The medieval European understanding of disease was based on bad Greco-Roman theories, and it is extremely unlikely that many Vinlanders had even read Aristotle, so they *didn't even have bad theories*. But if Beothuks started falling dead all around them, the Norse would have been quick to fill the niche they left behind.

Although the sagas do not specifically mention the overwhelmingly superior numbers of hostile natives as a reason for the abandonment of the Vinland experiment, any foothold on the New World would certainly require either befriending or defeating the native population, and Vikings don't always befriend easily. With horses and superior armaments on the Norse side, and an ailing population on the Beothuk side, a slightly better-stocked Vinland colony would change the course of world history.

Not because any of the Vikings would survive, of course. Even with a population cut to 10% its original total, the Beothuk could have near-parity of numbers with the Vinlanders, and it would take many years for the population to drop to 10%. Furthermore, Newfoundland is less than ten miles from the North American mainland, the population of which, no matter how ravaged by disease, far outstripped any number of Vikings who would be willing to make the long transatlantic voyage. The Norse would need to learn to trade with the natives, but of course the more they traded the more they traded away their advantages. Even *Erik's Saga* states that the only items the skraelings wanted as much as red cloth were arms. The Vikings, sensibly, were loath to trade these away, but how long would that embargo have lasted? Soon the locals would have horses and iron weapons, and the fighting would be on a more even footing.

The dangers of a strange continent are difficult to overstate: Think of what a famously hard time Plymouth Colony had surviving the New England winter six hundred years later, and four hundred miles south— and with guns. The Norse couldn't survive indefinitely in Greenland; it's unlikely they would have survived indefinitely in Vinland.

But they would have survived long enough.

We've already seen that trade would give the natives iron or even steel weapons, and horses. Adapting their culture to accommodate the ability to smith their own weapons would have taken longer—forges and bloomeries (ovens used to smelt iron) are heavy and difficult to transport, while hunter-gatherers like the Beothuk are nomadic by necessity. But many nomadic Native Americans had expanded into slash-and-burn agriculture that allowed them to travel along predictable routes over the course of several years. There's no reason a similar cultural shift couldn't have built permanent forges, occasionally visited. Newfoundland is a large island—larger than Iceland, after all.

As for European germs, after an apocalyptic century or so of pandemic, natural selection will start to develop immunities to these diseases in the native population. We still don't know how fast the diseases Columbus brought traveled—probably faster in densely populated Mesoamerica than they would in the hunter-gatherer populations surrounding Newfoundland—but it's a safe bet that the novel diseases will spread among not only the Beothuk but also their neighbors, and both populations will then bounce back.

This means a well-armed, disease-resistant native population is eventually ready to fight—or absorb—the Vinland Norse. With a declining Greenland population and dwindling interest from the Scandinavian homeland, the Vinlanders will be on their own, with no natural advantages.

It's difficult to make broad stereotypes about entire people on very little evidence. Actually, it's not difficult—history has shown it to be incredibly easy—but it's difficult to do it with any degree of accuracy. Remember: No one wrote anything down about any of the native peoples involved until half a millennium after Norse contact. We're therefore dealing with long stretches of time where we know next to nothing about the people involved, and if there's one thing dicier than stereotyping, it's stereotyping across centuries. Would anyone have extrapolated modern progressive Scandinavia from the actions of the Vikings? Raoul Wallenberg from King Erik Bloodaxe?

Despite these caveats, let's look at what we know of the Beothuk. Unlike most coastal peoples, the Beothuk tried to avoid contact with the European colonists, generally eschewing trade. In sixteenth- and seventeenth-century Newfoundland, English colonists failed to establish the conventional barter trade for furs that existed elsewhere on the Atlantic Coast, and therefore were forced to develop the rudiments of fur trapping themselves, selling the wares directly to merchants. Newfies were the first Englishmen to professionally trap in the New World, and they only did it because trading was not an option.

Furthermore, the Beothuk never adopted firearms, going so far as to smash, rather than use, any guns they acquired—perhaps a unique practice among Native Americans.

The Beothuk made the decision to avoid contact, trade, and novel weaponry five hundred years after their encounters with the Norse, and we have no way of knowing if the Beothuk of the eleventh century would have behaved similarly. But this is the only information we have to go on, and it does not sound as though the Beothuk would have been people most likely to start trading with a permanent Vinland colony.

All around the Beothuk, though, up and down the east coast mainland, were various Algonquian peoples. By the sixteenth century the Mi'kmaq were the closest geographically, and it's likely that at the very least Algonquians similar to the Mi'kmaq lived near Newfoundland in the eleventh. Algonquians were historically much more open to trade, to receiving new ideas and technologies, than the conservative Beothuk. It's easy to imagine Algonquians acquiring horses and metal spears. The Algonquians' internecine enemies, the Iroquois, formed in the twelfth century a powerhouse union of five (later six) nations that expanded into Algonquian territory, giving the Mi'kmaq (or other Algonquians) ample motive to acquire new weapons, and new weapon technologies—the ability to forge iron, or even steel. Bog iron is widespread on the eastern coast, with large deposits on, for example, Bell Island—right off the coast of Newfoundland.

Of course, the Iroquois may never have formed their confederation had the Norse stayed, because nine tenths of them would have died from disease. But the Algonquians, first struck by Old World diseases, would have been first to bounce back, and they would have bounced back riding horses and wielding iron arms. The small wooden shields that many natives used in warfare were designed to deflect slate weapons, not great iron battle-axes.

An innovation in military technology often allows the innovators to run roughshod over their neighbors. The Macedonians under Philip II and his son lengthened their spears to increase the power of their phalanxes and gave Alexander the epithet "the Great." The Zulu under Shaka shortened their spears to become stabbing weapons and conquered South Africa. At least for a time, the Algonquians would have found themselves unopposable in North America.

Perhaps you are wondering what this has to do with the modern world. Thousands and thousands of battles gave ascendancy to one and then another native peoples in North America over the millennia, and most of these battles and peoples are now completely lost to time. A shift in power dynamics among pre-Columbian Indians may look like it would not affect much of anything. The eventual establishment of European colonies throughout the New World was inevitable, after all, because the Europeans had guns, germs, and steel . . . and horses, too.

Except in a world where the Vinlanders stayed, the New World would have germs, steel, and horses as well.

In the eleventh century the population of North America would have been devastated but it would have *five hundred years* to restore itself before Europeans arrived. Although Central and South America had metallurgical technology superior to North America's, they did not have widespread use of weapons made from metals harder than copper; if news of iron and steel reaches them from the north, this all changes. The Spanish conquistadors would not face sick empires, weakened by disease and inadequately armed: They would face hale, metal-armored, mounted opponents. The Spanish gun would still be a formidable weapon, but as it stood, even with all the advantages the Spaniards had, Hernando Cortés's conquest of the Aztecs was still a close contest, and Francisco Pizarro's conquest of the Incas was a lucky break. Either conquest would have been almost impossible against a better-armed foe.

And North America would not have been depopulated and empty when settlers arrived in Jamestown or Plymouth. Instead it would have had a teeming population of metal-clad horse archers.

The difficulty here is smallpox, which the natives will still not be resistant to no matter how many Viking diseases they encounter. As deadly as smallpox was to Europeans, with a 30% fatality rate, it was much deadlier to the natives. You can get a hint of this from the fact that European names for the disease trivialize it—*smallpox* in English, *la petite vérole*, the diminutive Spanish *viruela*—while the Aztec term, *huey zahuatl*, means "big rash." Smallpox specifically, above all other diseases, was the biggest killer in the New World, and it would probably still be in our counterfactual history. And yet—smallpox was still new to many parts of Europe in the fifteenth century (e.g., Sweden, possibly Germany), so the hypothetical Algonquian Empire, with a cocktail of other European diseases in its blood, will not be far behind the European invaders. After all, it's not like nine out of every ten Swedes died from smallpox in the fifteenth century.

We know that European technology allowed little England to conquer the subcontinent of India in the eighteenth century, so the Americas would not be completely safe. In their southern regions, where the lure of gold gave great incentive to face the harshest odds, Spain could have used its island bases in the Caribbean—disease resistance and new technology will hardly spread to the Bahamas, where Columbus first landed—as staging grounds for conquest. But small, imperialistically held colonies are very different, and less permanent, than the waves of immigration that reached especially North America from Europe, supplanting the native population. The New World would remain native, just as Hong Kong, after a hundred years of British rule, remained Chinese.

Without colonies in the New World, Europe suffers through a completely different history. There will be no ascension of Spain, fueled by American gold. Britain has to look eastward for its colonial designs, and it will not have had a powerful English-speaking rival (and then ally) across the ocean. That means that World War I and World War II will be fought without American intervention. The various American nations can intervene as they like, of course, but they will not automatically be intervening on Britain's side. No United States also means a much-reduced African diaspora. And no atomic bomb, no jazz, no rock and roll, no comic books.

Meanwhile, the American nations, perhaps still led by the sovereign state of Algonquia, will have their own contributions to world history, their own atrocities to cover up and pop culture to export. They may stretch Algonquia from sea to shining sea. They may stagnate in a series of endless wars for dominance on the continent. Or they may settle, like Europe, into many small nations coexisting in relative and tentative peace.

More than almost any change in this book, this small change would change everything. Every aspect of your life would have been different if a few Vikings had, one thousand years ago, just hung tough a little bit longer.

ALEXANDER THE GREAT

What if Alexander had married Barsine?

DAMASCUS, 333 BC

I.

Here are some facts about Alexander the Great, from various sources.

In the 1880s the Hunza chief Safder Ali Khan claimed that "great kings," such as himself and Alexander the Great, never left their home countries.

A sixteenth-century Ethiopian manuscript recording the history of the world says Alexander reigned as king for fifty-six years and died at the ripe old age of seventy-two.

The fourteenth-century English poet John Gower wrote that Alexander was the son of the last pharaoh of Egypt, Nectanebo, who had traveled to Macedon "thurgh magique of his sorcerie."

A version of the West African oral epic *Sundiata* collected in Guinea proclaims that the rulers of Ghana were all descendants of Alexander.

None of these sources is in the least bit correct. They also come from places Alexander the Great never visited, except by reputation. He left his home country of Macedon while barely out of his teens, and never saw it again; he died in Babylon at the age of thirty-three; neither Nectanebo nor the kings of Ghana are any relation.

This much is true: During his short life, Alexander conquered more land than anyone else in history except Genghis Khan: Asia Minor, Egypt, the Levant, Persia, parts of India and modern Afghanistan. He made Macedon—his backwater kingdom hovering on the barbaric fringe of the Greek lands—a world power. He belongs to that exclusive club of generals who never lost a battle. Hannibal, who knew a thing or two about generalship, called him the greatest general of all time. Alexander left behind not only an empire but also a dream of unity, of one law extending over Europe, Asia, and Africa.

But the dream of unity was brief. When Alexander died in 323 BC—either of malaria or drunkenness or (some have alleged) poison—he had no legitimate heir. There was an illegitimate son named Heracles; a half brother, who appears to have been mentally handicapped; and two wives, one of whom was pregnant.

The Edwardian wit Saki wrote, "Where there is no heir there are many, may not be a proverb, but it has all the qualifications for one." And among the people very aware there was no heir to Alexander's empire were a circle of friends who had followed Alexander from Greece to India, who had watched history's greatest general in action and learned from him everything they could, and who had grown accustomed to conquest and victory. For this, the largest empire in the world, to remain intact, one of them would have to step into Alexander's shoes.

Alexander prophesied that his friends would hold "funeral games" for him, and indeed, these games were to prove the largest and deadliest the world had seen. The winner would be the most powerful man alive; the losers, of course, would die. Let's meet the players:

- **Perdiccas:** When Alexander's father, King Philip, was assassinated in Macedon (336 BC), Perdiccas was one of the men who chased down and slew the assassin. Years later, on the way back from India, when Alexander took an arrow to the lung, and no physician dared cut the arrowhead out, for fear that his hand would slip and he would kill the king, Perdiccas, fearless, made the cut. He was one of Alexander's seven bodyguards and stood at Alexander's bedside when the conqueror died.

- **Ptolemy:** Another of Alexander's seven bodyguards. Later legend held that Ptolemy had been abandoned as an infant, and only survived because an eagle brought him food. He was one of Alexander's oldest friends, and had once been exiled from Macedon for standing up to King Philip on his buddy's behalf.

- **Lysimachus:** A third bodyguard. Impetuous in the hunt, he had slain a lion in Syria single-handed, getting himself mauled in the process. The mauling hardly made him cautious; later, in Sogdiana, he was about to set off after another lion when Alexander himself pulled open Lysimachus's cloak, exposing the scars from his last mishap, to convince Lysimachus to back off.

- **Antipater:** An old general of King Philip's generation, Antipater had stayed in Macedon, taking care of the place while Alexander went off on his crazy adventures. His young son • **Cassander** was an object of fun, because he had never managed to make a kill on a boar hunt and so could not recline at the dinner table (as was Macedonian custom). Cassander would get his revenge on all those who'd laughed at him . . .

- **Antigonus the One-Eyed:** Another of Philip's old generals, Antigonus had been tasked with protecting Alexander's supply lines in Asia Minor. He was a great bear of a man, huge in stature and girth, with a towering appetite and a bellowing laugh. And his son • **Demetrius**, everybody's favorite character, was known for facing each crisis with courage, industry, and magnanimity; unfortunately, when the crisis passed, Demetrius invariably sank into drunken lecherousness and vice—which tended to get him into trouble, such that at the inevitable next crisis he would once again prove courageous, industrious, etc.

- **Eumenes:** Alexander's personal secretary. Eumenes was not Macedonian but Greek, which meant almost no one else on this list liked or trusted him. But he was clever enough to earn a seat at the table; also, via Alexander, he had dirt on everyone.

Add to these • **Queen Olympias,** Alexander's terrible mother. Only two of these players would die peacefully of old age in bed.

II.

Immediately after Alexander's death, his generals gathered to decide what to do. Alexander's only instruction for the future of his empire was that it should go "to the strongest," which you will perceive is not very useful.

Alexander's admiral, Nearchus, suggested that they simply legitimize Heracles, the illegitimate little son of Alexander and his concubine Barsine. Alexander's senior taxiarch (brigadier), Meleager, suggested that Alexander's half-witted half brother Arrhidaeos should be named king. But Perdiccas, player #1 from the above list, suggested that no decision be made until Alexander's pregnant widow Roxana gave birth. She might, after all, have a legitimate son.

Alexander's inner circle—the bodyguards and the generals—supported Perdiccas's plan, for perhaps selfish reasons. An infant son meant a long regency, and a long regency meant the inner circle would keep holding the reins of power. But the infantry favored Meleagar's. They loved that half brother Arrhidaeos! They may have thought he was touched by the gods; they certainly agreed with him in longing to return home. Goaded by Meleager, they took up arms in defense of their candidate, and, chanting his name, broke up the council, seeking to slay them as traitors to the royal blood of Arrhidaeos. It was the Greek secretary Eumenes who got everyone to calm down, brokering a compromise whereby the empire would be jointly ruled by Arrhidaeos (rechristened Philip Arrhidaeos) and Roxana's hypothetical unborn son (named, on the spot, Alexander). Perdiccas would be the kings' "guardian."

Nearchus's candidate, Heracles, was not part of the compromise, so the admiral slunk away to write a book about all the places he'd sailed to, places no Greek had ever seen before. The infantry was satisfied, but Perdiccas was not. He soon arranged to have elephants trample any infantry rabble-rousers, while orchestrating Meleager's murder in an unrelated incident. Also murdered, perhaps by poison, was Alexander's second wife, Stateira; she was just a complicating factor in a situation that was already complicated enough.

And then everyone got to be a satrap—a regional governor, more or less. Lysimachus got Thrace, Antigonus One-Eye got several regions of Asia Minor, etc. The ever-unpopular secretary Eumenes got Cappadocia and Paphlagonia, two regions in Asia that were as yet unconquered, and it must have seemed like quite a joke. Go conquer them, Eumenes, if you want to play with the big boys. Old Antipater remained in charge of Macedon. And Alexander's boyhood pal Ptolemy, in the single cleverest move in the whole game, specifically requested Egypt.

But Perdiccas had no satrapy; he stayed in Babylon with the two kings—for the infant Alexander, born and hale, was no longer hypothetical. Although Athens, predictably, tried to revolt (unsuccessfully), overall the empire was unified and at peace. But actually, everyone was eying one another suspiciously; and especially everyone was eying Perdiccas.

And then the uneasy balance of power tipped. Queen Olympias sent a letter to Perdiccas suggesting that he might make a fine husband for her daughter Cleopatra—Alexander's sister. Perdiccas (like Ptolemy) was already married to one of old Antipater's innumerable daughters, as Olympias well knew. She hated Antipater (the two of them had locked horns in Macedon while everyone else was adventuring in Asia) and wanted to bring herself closer to Perdiccas, who was, after all, her grandson's guardian.

Even the suggestion that the regent might marry into the royal family was just too much. There was war. Antipater, Lysimachus, Antigonus, and Ptolemy formed a coalition against Perdiccas, while Eumenes alone remained loyal. Perdiccas invaded Egypt to try to take Ptolemy off the board, while Eumenes held off the rest of the coalition at his rear. Egypt, however, as history shows us time and time again, is not so easy to invade: Specifically, the Nile Delta is marshy, treacherous, and teeming with crocodiles. Perdiccas's armies never got to fight Ptolemy; they just got stranded among the shifting labyrinth of the Delta, drowning as they wandered among *really* so many crocodiles. They were well aware that most of the known world had turned against them, and that their flank was protected by Eumenes, a bookish Greek who knew nothing of "shield and spear" but only of "pen and paper." Small wonder they decided that the whole expedition was doomed, and, in frustration, murdered Perdiccas in his tent. They were unaware that Eumenes had scored a great victory near Cappadocia; when word came, two days later, that their side was actually winning the war, it was too late, and Perdiccas's men had already gone over to Ptolemy. They even offered Ptolemy the regency, but he preferred to stay in Egypt.

You should all cross Perdiccas off your lists. Now that he had been removed from the board, peace returned. The two kings, one impaired and the other still a baby, were sent to Macedon; Antipater would be their guardian now. The coalition against Perdiccas condemned Eumenes to death in absentia, and Antigonus One-Eye set off to hunt him down. Eumenes would prove to be a wily prey, eventually ensconcing himself in the impregnable Cappadocian fortress of Nora. While Antigonus set up a siege, Antipater, back in Macedon, sickened and weakened. He was in his late seventies. His son Cassander assumed he'd take over for his father, but a dying Antipater (cross him off!) named as his successor another septuagenarian, the undistinguished old general Polyperchon. A disappointed Cassander immediately contacted Antigonus One-Eye with a secret proposal that they team up against Polyperchon. Antigonus abandoned his siege, and a now free Eumenes decided to throw his hat in with Polyperchon. Eumenes always sided with the kings, and the kings were in Macedon with the old general; in return, Polyperchon declared (by means of a letter ostensibly endorsed by King Philip Arrhidaeos) Eumenes commander of all the empire's armies and master of all the empire's gold.

It was war again. Lysimachus and Ptolemy joined Cassander and Antigonus. Polyperchon fought them in Europe, while Eumenes fought them in Asia. In Macedon meanwhile, the royal family fell out over the new regency. Queen Olympias, speaking for her grandson, favored Polyperchon, while the wife of King Arrhidaeos, a warrior woman named

Eurydice, said her husband favored Cassander. The two factions met in battle; Eurydice led her troops dressed in full armor. Queen Olympias came unarmed.

The Secret History of the Mongols insists that the only things Genghis Khan ever feared were his mother and "to a lesser extent" his wife. Well, Alexander didn't fear Roxana, but he must have feared his mother. *Everyone* feared Queen Olympias. When Eurydice's troops saw Alexander's mother riding toward them, they turned on their leader. Eurydice and Arrhidaeos fell into Olympias's hands, which were not hands you wanted to be in. Remember that Arrhidaeos was only half brother to Alexander the Great; he was not Olympias's son. The dowager queen must have felt that her young grandson had shared his throne long enough. Olympias executed Arrhidaeos and sent Eurydice, as a hint, a poisoned cup, a dagger, and some rope. Cross them off, cross them off. Olympias, with no one left to rein her in, started settling old scores, purging the Macedonian court of all rivals.

This was the worst thing that could have happened to the aged Polyperchon. Suddenly his whole cause appeared bathed in blood. One king was dead, the other in the hands of a madwoman. He fled, his army evaporating, and Cassander marched into Macedon easily. The dangerous Olympias he put to death. The baby, King Alexander IV, was now in his control.

In Asia, meanwhile, Eumenes found that the king who had declared him master of armies was dead. But he took his letter from Arrhidaeos— always a name to conjure with—and moved east, collecting money and troops from distant satrapies that had not yet heard of the Macedonian massacres. Soon Eumenes was riding back west with a large army and a boatload of treasure. He and Antigonus One-Eye each called himself Lord of Asia, and now they were fighting to see who was right.

In the end, Eumenes proved impossible to defeat on the battlefield. Antigonus and he fought each other to a standstill time and time again over the course of nearly three years, until Eumenes's men got sick of risking their lives with no result. Eumenes was never very popular anyway. They betrayed him and handed him over for execution to Antigonus One-Eye, who now truly was Lord of Asia (not literally, obviously; China is just one of the places that had never heard of Antigonus). Antigonus got the treasury. Antigonus got the armies.

Whenever one player gets too powerful, you can bet there'll be a coalition against him. Antigonus One-Eye now had more men, more money, and more land than anyone else on the board. Polyperchon (who'd been in hiding) declared himself for Antigonus. Against the Lord of Asia, Cassander in Macedon, Lysimachus in Thrace, and Ptolemy in Egypt joined forces—alongside newcomer • **Seleucus**, one of Alexander's generals, who had received the undistinguished satrapy of Babylon. Seleucus had himself abandoned Babylon, fleeing before Antigonus One-Eye. But he wanted Babylon back, and he joined the coalition.

The fighting continued in Greece and throughout Asia. Ptolemy sent an army out of Egypt into Syria, and Antigonus's son Demetrius fell upon it, capturing seven thousand soldiers and the general, Cilles. Demetrius sent all the prisoners safely back to Egypt, for at war he was the most magnanimous of men. Seleucus sneaked back and recaptured the great city. The war went on and on.

All such coalitions were of course provisional and temporary, because the surviving players (Ptolemy aside) wanted to control all of Alexander's empire. They didn't want to share. But—and this is important—at least in theory they were not fighting to be king. Young Alexander IV was king! It may be hard to believe, but all this time they were fighting merely to be *regent*.

Perhaps it was too hard to believe. Cassander finally got tired of the fiction. He murdered the young Alexander and his mother, Roxana; soon he would be openly calling himself King of Macedon. With Alexander IV dead, everyone was doing it: King of Thrace, Pharaoh of Egypt, etc. Antigonus One-Eye's son Demetrius freed Athens from Cassander's yoke, and the Athenians proclaimed him not only a king but a god—in fact, the only true god, because all the other alleged gods were absent, or deaf, or uncaring, while Demetrius had come when they called for help.

Predictably, Demetrius in Athens started behaving badly, inviting whores into the Parthenon and wasting city funds on elaborate parties. Since they'd already deified him, it was difficult for the Athenians to call him out on these excesses.

It was not in Greece that the contest would be decided, though. The final showdown was in Asia Minor, at the Battle of Ipsus, 301 BC. Everyone was getting older—Antigonus One-Eye was in his eighties—and everyone wanted the affair to be settled. The aged Antigonus was the best living general, and perhaps the coalition would not have prevailed against him; but they had elephants.

Where did those elephants come from? It turns out that all these years of warfare had hardly been good for the empire. Over in India, a man named Chandragupta had risen from humble origins to carve out his own empire, conquering most of India. Parts of India, of course, were still part of Alexander's empire, and Chandragupta's expansion brought him into conflict with Seleucus. The eventual peace treaty ceded the far eastern satrapies to Chandragupta in exchange for five hundred war elephants. This proved to be a solid bargain for Seleucus. At Ipsus the elephants drove through Antigonus's lines. Antigonus died on the field; it was the only battle he ever decisively lost. Demetrius managed to escape.

Once again, things settled down. Ptolemy ruled Egypt, the richest part of the empire; Seleucus, Asia, the most powerful; but Cassander had Macedon, the homeland, and therefore the most prestigious. Lysimachus in Thrace had kind of the short end, but he received part of Asia Minor for his courage at Ipsus. And then there was Demetrius . . .

What do you do if you are a dashing and charismatic king with no kingdom? Naturally, Demetrius became a pirate king and the scourge of the Mediterranean. He was so successful for so long that his old foe Cassander died of consumption, and when Cassander's sons squabbled over the inheritance, Demetrius sailed in like a peacemaker and became king of Macedon.

The dream of a unified empire had not quite died, but it was sleeping. Perhaps there would have been peace, but Demetrius, once he became king, had to make a pig of himself. When Lysimachus decided to invade Macedon, the Macedonians were too disgusted with their king even to prepare a proper defense. Facing the prospect of another exile, Demetrius's long-suffering wife, Phila, committed suicide in despair; but Demetrius never despaired. He went back to piracy, raiding the territories of Lysimachus, Seleucus, and Ptolemy in turn. Finally, though, he decided to march to the far eastern satrapies, as Eumenes had before him, and here his fortune failed. A pirate king should not travel so far inland, and on the march he took sick and became delirious. His army abandoned him; finally, he turned himself in to Seleucus. Fortunately for everyone, Demetrius was probably just as happy drinking himself to death as a prisoner in Babylon as he would have been drinking himself to death as the king of Babylon. Lysimachus offered Seleucus two thousand talents for Demetrius's head, but Seleucus refused. He had once told his Persian subjects that he had come to bring them not Greek laws, but only the universal law: that what the king does is right. And perhaps he wanted to live by this maxim.

Lysimachus, king of Macedon, Thrace, and Asia Minor, was vexed that Demetrius lived (not for long; he really did drink himself to death). Now there were only three players: Ptolemy, Seleucus, and Lysimachus; and then Lysimachus fell in with bad company. This was Ptolemy's son, known as • **Ptolemy the Thunderbolt**, kicked out of Egypt by family squabbles. The Thunderbolt, keen to make himself heir to the throne of Macedon, somehow managed to frame Lysimachus's son for treason. Lysimachus dutifully executed his own son, but this atrocity was too much for the people of Lysimachus's triple kingdom. They invited Seleucus to come avenge the death of their prince, and he started marching through Asia Minor, hailed as their salvation. Lysimachus, with Ptolemy the Thunderbolt as his lieutenant, marched to face him. They met at Corupedion, in Asia Minor—the last major battle in Alexander's funeral games. There Lysimachus fell, and the Thunderbolt was taken captive. Seleucus treated his captive generously; he had good reason to. Although he had not quite unified the empire—nothing was going to drive Ptolemy or his dynasty from Egypt—he had finally, in 281, yoked Asia and Europe. What the king does is right; so Seleucus magnanimously treated the Thunderbolt as a prince, and let his captive accompany him as he crossed from the Bosporus on his triumphant march toward Macedon . . .

. . . and the Thunderbolt stabbed him to death as he set foot in Europe. Ptolemy the Thunderbolt declared himself king of Macedon.

That was the end of the funeral games. History, of course, kept moving along. Seleucus's son inherited the holdings in Asia, and the Seleucid dynasty ruled a vast empire that kept getting whittled down by a resurgence of native Persian power. Macedon was overrun by barbaric Gauls, who took out the Thunderbolt; it would be Demetrius's son, the knock-kneed philosopher Antigonus Gonatas, who finally established a Macedonian dynasty, under the protection of his patron god, goat-legged Pan.

Eventually all of it—Macedon, the tiny Asian remnant of the Seleucids, and Egypt—would be absorbed by Rome. The famous Cleopatra was the last of Ptolemy's dynasty, and the last Macedonian to rule a part of the once great empire.

It was Ptolemy, incidentally, who died of old age peacefully in bed. Antipater was the other one.

III.

Alexander the Great left quite a legacy; it's just not always clear what that legacy is. The philosopher G. W. F. Hegel claimed that two men spelled doom for Greece; one was Socrates, but the other one was Alexander. And yet Alexander is everywhere. Ethiopia, England, Guinea. He appears in the Quran (sura 18) under the sobriquet Dhul-Qarnayn, "the two-horned one"; one thirteenth-century Egyptian text glosses that although it's possible Alexander did have horns on his head, probably the name just means he ruled over the "two horns of the sun," the east and the west.

A 1528 etiquette manual, *The Book of the Courtier*, tries to enumerate "the thousand other things that could be told in proof of the benefit that his victories conferred upon the world," but it is noticeably light on specifics. It does mention that Alexander taught people not to marry their siblings, which sounds like a spurious claim, as Ptolemy's son married his own sister.

No more plausible is the claim, made by an anonymous seventh-century Syriac Christian, that Alexander had constructed giant copper gates behind which the forces of Gog and Magog mill ceaselessly; only at the end times will they burst forth and conquer the world. Needless to say, this is unlikely.

The nineteenth-century moralist Jacob Abbott asserted that Alexander "was simply a robber, but yet a robber on so vast a scale, that mankind, in contemplating his career, have generally lost sight of the wickedness of his crimes in their admiration of the enormous magnitude of the scale on which they were perpetrated." That's getting closer.

Alexander conquered and then he died. Oh, he had a lot of additional plans. Some of them were simply bizarro crazy, such as carving Mount Athos into a statue of Alexander himself, holding in one hand a city, pop. 10,000, in the other a bowl with a lake inside. Others made more sense, like attacking Carthage. With Greece and Persia under Macedonian sway, Carthage, in North Africa, was the only remaining great power in the Mediterranean. Diodorus mentions a projected campaign against Carthage; Arrian adds that the plan was to catch Carthage in a pincer, with a fleet sailing all the way around Africa and entering the Mediterranean through the Pillars of Hercules to catch the Carthaginians from the west, while Alexander's land force approached from the east. This plan would have been difficult to coordinate, especially since Africa extends about three thousand miles farther south than Alexander would have expected; but Alexander did a lot of things that sounded impossible at the time.

> *The Persians will be blamed no more.*
> *One can forgive the cattle who run from the lion . . .*

. . . Posidippos wrote a century later. Who knows what he might have accomplished had he lived?

Alexander marries Barsine → *His son Heracles ascends to the throne with zero civil warring* → **ALEXANDER'S EMPIRE LASTS A THOUSAND YEARS** → *You speak Greek and are very wise*

I.

THESE FUNERAL GAMES SHATTERED ALEXANDER'S EMPIRE, leaving each fragment vulnerable. The dream of a universal empire that yoked Europe, Africa, and Asia would be short-lived. But Alexander could have avoided funeral games altogether. What if sometime around 333 BC, perhaps in Damascus, he had married his mistress Barsine, so that their son, Heracles, had been legitimate?

Prince Heracles is still a toddler when his father dies, but he is a toddler well known to the army, who always supports the Macedonian bloodline, and to Alexander's generals, many of whom are childhood friends of the late king. They may find it harder to betray a child they saw Alexander play with than an embryo Alexander never met. Young Heracles is king, Perdiccas is regent, and the empire remains at peace.

Actually, it *cannot* remain at peace. It is too jam-packed with soldiers. Alexander had been recruiting from all over for his burgeoning army, and if they have no one to fight, then the countryside is going to be flooded with unemployed but heavily armed young men. Ptolemy, in our history, arranged for an expedition into Carthaginian territory in 308 BC just to keep the lads "out of trouble." Perdiccas will find that sending the army off to fight someone on the borders of the empire is the best way to keep the peace.

Carthage is an obvious target—Alexander had planned to take it, and Ptolemy actually (albeit in a half-hearted fashion) tried. The Greek states of the west, such as Sicily or the coast of Spain, are another. And then there's Rome.

The Roman historian Livy was the first to ask what would have happened if Alexander had fought Rome. Unsurprisingly, Livy thought his people would hold the conqueror off; but actually, Rome had severe troubles even forty years later when fighting Alexander's kinsman Pyrrhus. Fresh from victory, with Alexander's most talented generals at their head (Perdiccas would, of course, want to keep the generals busy), Rome falls to the Macedonians. Carthage falls to the Macedonians. These soldiers had balked once at heading too far east, far from the things they knew, but they could conquer to the west all the way to the Atlantic Ocean and still be mingling with Greek colonists, people whose language and customs were familiar.

II.

How long could the Macedonians have kept it up? Rome expanded to make the Mediterranean a "Roman lake," but not, as they say, in a day. Heracles grows old and fathers an heir. The task of conquering the Mediterranean coast may take generations.

The Romans had a method for keeping conquest going: They made their conquered people into Romans. The Macedonians, however, were so jingoistic they could not accept a Greek—Eumenes's problem—despite the fact that the Macedonians were *really closely related* to the Greeks. It's hard for a foreigner to tell the two peoples apart! Although Alexander made some efforts to incorporate Persians into his government, it was an unpopular policy, and did not survive his death. The Macedonians were frankly too racist to make an enduring empire.

Except under Heracles. Heracles was only half Macedonian; his mother was half Persian and (on her mother's side) half Greek. King Heracles was a cosmopolitan by blood. His own wife could be a Carthaginian princess, his son- or daughter-in-law an Etruscan. The heirs to the throne of Alexander would be less and less Macedonian by blood, although they would all speak Greek and read Homer.

And so, we see something like the Roman Empire, its borders extending from the Atlantic to India—some forty-five hundred miles in length. It would take six months or more to traverse the empire by land in the best of circumstances, so there's a strong motivation to construct something analogous to the Suez Canal, perhaps connecting the Nile to the Red Sea.

The empire may fall eventually, as Rome fell. Its borders are vast, and filled with barbarians. Or the danger might come from a civilized foe: An Indian with the talent of Chandragupta sweeps west like wildfire, the way Alexander swept east.

When it falls, it leaves a dark age, much as the fall of Rome does. But look at how different these dark ages are. They darken a much larger area, for one. Also, while Rome granted two languages to two halves of the empire—Latin to the West and Greek to the East—the Alexandro-Heraclean Empire gives only Greek. Although vulgate languages still exist, Greek serves as a lingua franca.

Even after the fall of Rome, in our world, its empire's borders marked the lands medieval geographers were familiar with. In the ninth century, Alfred the Great of England made a pilgrimage to Rome; in the tenth, Gerbert d'Aurillac, a French monk, studied in Spain, taught in Germany, and became Pope in Italy; by the eleventh, French knights were conquering Jerusalem in the former Roman province of Judea. John Mandeville's fourteenth-century travel book is full of marvels and miracles throughout, but things don't get really weird until he passes beyond the Holy Land—Rome's eastern border—whereupon it's nonstop cyclopes, griffins, sixty-foot-tall giants, women with gem eyes and a death stare, gold-digging ants, and the face of the devil under a stone. The Roman Empire remained as a kind of comfort zone for the medieval mind.

The Alexandro-Heraclean Empire is simply that much larger. Medieval troubadours can wander from India to the Atlantic, singing in Greek. A hypothetical monk like Gerbert d'Aurillac can now study in Babylon, teach on the banks of the Indus, and become high priest at the feet of the Egyptian sphinx.

Trade routes are easier because even after the empire falls, people within the old pale share so many cultural norms. China is outside the borders of the empire, but it's not *far* outside the borders of the empire.

In our world, Marco Polo tried to describe thirteenth-century China to Italians and everyone called him a liar. If Alexander had married, sixteen hundred years of Marco Polos would have made China as familiar to Italy as Denmark or Russia. Nothing in the Old World, except perhaps sub-Saharan Africa, would be truly alien to any other part. It would be a much smaller world, and this is the irony of Alexander's enduring conquest: The more land the Macedonians conquer, the smaller the world they conquered seems.

H. G. Wells would come to call the memory of Alexander's conquests a "grisly parasite" that "bored into the human brain . . . and filled it with disordered thoughts and violent impulses." And yet surely Wells, of all people, would see benefits from a more unified world.

In our history, the first-century philosopher Apollonius of Tyana proclaimed, "The whole earth is mine, and I wander through it at will" while crisscrossing the known world from Spain to India. Everywhere he went he interviewed the wise, for it was specifically wisdom Apollonius sought. Two thousand years later, G. R. S. Mead would call Apollonius "one of the greatest travellers known to antiquity" while also hailing him as one of its greatest philosophers—and surely the two accomplishments are related.

Imagine a world in which Apollonius's travels are not unusual, in which the wisdom he painstakingly gathered is available . . . not to just *anyone* (travel is for the rich), but to more than just this one peripatetic. Wells's grisly parasite in the human brain is not a dream of conquest but a dream of wisdom.

4

THE INCA EMPIRE

What if the emperor Atahualpa set his brother free?

I.

As a boy, the poet Robert Penn Warren once asked his father "whose side" you should take when reading a history book. His father said you should take the side of whomever you were reading about. This is a useful policy, and one I've tried to follow. You can root for William the Conqueror as he sails to Hastings to claim his crown, and you can root for Harold Godwinson as he races the length of England to Hastings to defend his. Winston Churchill wrote that Harold was "unconquerable except by death, which does not count in honour," while Jacob Abbott insists that William, "by his personal accomplishments and his bravery, . . . won all hearts, and was the subject of every body's praises." Kind words all around.

The tragedy of Francisco Pizarro is that he won no hearts and was the subject of no one's praises. No one has ever rooted for Pizarro.

In 1847, at a time when Columbus was still being hailed unironically as a hero and a mensch, William Prescott called Pizarro's conquest of Peru "one of the most atrocious acts of perfidy on the record of history!" A quarter century later, John S. C. Abbott carped on Pizarro's "cruel, faithless, and treacherous character." Lawton B. Evans, writing for a younger audience, is scarcely more sympathetic, introducing Pizarro with the words "Francisco Pizarro was a Spaniard of low birth, and was so ignorant that never in all his life did he learn to read and write"; Evans's account gets worse from there.

Pizarro will long be remembered as one of the villains of history, but he also achieved a remarkable record in the (not mutually exclusive) annals of conquest. He doesn't necessarily look like one of the all-time greatest conquerors, but this is only because of convention. By convention, we grade conquerors by the number of square miles they conquer: Genghis Khan therefore holds first place, while Alexander (called the Great) and Cyrus (called the Great) and Timur (called, cruelly, the Lame) bicker over who's number two. We could, if we wanted, grade them on the *number of people* they conquered or the number of square miles conquered per year, etc., and it would throw the rankings all out of order. For square miles conquered by year, Hitler is going to move up a lot further toward the top spot.

Well, if by chance we decided that what made a great conqueror was *efficiency*—that is to say, square miles conquered per individual in the conquering army—then Pizarro would be a contender for world champion conqueror. With 167 men, Pizarro conquered over 772,000 square miles. Although estimates on Mongol troop strength vary, this metric still makes Pizarro somewhere between twenty and fifty times as good a conqueror as Genghis Khan.

But nobody likes him. His first cousin is one of our primary sources of information about Pizarro's conquests, and even with a partisan primary source, nobody likes him. After conquering the Inca Empire and making his fellow Spaniards rich beyond belief, Pizarro was murdered, in 1541, by his own countrymen.

He was just a rotten human being.

II.

In 1526 (before the Inca business) Francisco Pizarro was a reasonably successful conquistador. He had traveled with Vasco Núñez de Balboa when he adventured across Panama and "stared at the Pacific." He possessed a homestead in Central America, and a comfortable fortune. The one thing he did not possess, though, was *fabulous wealth and power beyond his wildest dreams*. Five years earlier, stout Cortés had conquered the Aztec Empire in Mexico and in a stroke become one of the richest men in Spain. Pizarro wanted to pull a Cortés. It was too late in Mexico, of course, but there were rumors of another native empire to the south. With his partner Diego de Almagro, Pizarro organized a private corporation (the profits would be in conquests!), confirmed the existence of the Inca Empire, and gained permission from the queen of Spain to conquer it. While Almagro stayed in Panama rustling up more money and troops, Pizarro traveled down the west coast of South America with what they'd been able to raise. A few small clashes with the natives, but Pizarro was mostly unopposed as he marched inland, up into the mountains, to the city of Cajamarca. Accompanying him were his half brothers Hernando, Juan, Gonzalo, and (mother's side) Francisco Martín; the dashing young cavalier Hernando de Soto, who had brought a company of reinforcements; a Dominican friar; 106 foot soldiers; 56 more horsemen; and a few noncombatants. Cajamarca was empty when the Spaniards reached it, but its emptiness was a trap: The city was quickly surrounded by tens of thousands of Incan warriors. There would be no escape for Pizarro, but he learned that the Incan emperor Atahualpa was camped among the armies surrounding the city. So Pizarro invited the emperor to dinner. This dinner was a trap within a trap.

The position these outnumbered and surrounded Spaniards were in was so clearly hopeless that Atahualpa must have believed he had nothing to fear. He controlled not only the tens of thousands of crack troops in the immediate vicinity but also the hundreds of thousands of troops, and indeed the millions of people throughout the empire. "The very birds in my dominions," he once bragged, "would scarcely venture to fly contrary to my will." With a retinue of some five thousand nobles, borne on an enormous litter, the emperor entered the deserted city, expecting to dine. The entourage was so numerous that they had to squeeze in tight just to fit in the town square. After a brief theological discussion (the friar attempted to persuade Atahualpa to become *1.* a Christian and *2.* a subject of the Spanish crown, both unsuccessfully), Pizarro gave the signal, and the Spaniards attacked.

For 168 soldiers to attack 5,000 sounds suicidal, but it is precisely the suicidal nature of the ambush that let it work. Atahualpa was so unthreatened by the Spanish invaders that he and his thousands of men came dressed for dinner. They were unarmed.

Even unarmed, twenty men should be able to pull down one, but the Spaniards had some other advantages. The first blow of the attack was a battery of cannons, mounted and concealed ahead of time, fired directly into the crowd. The Inca had never encountered gunpowder before; the cannons' roar was possibly the loudest noise any of them had ever heard, so even those Incas not harmed by cannonballs plowing through their ranks had to have been struck with terror. The cannons were followed by a volley of shots from the Spanish arquebuses (primitive rifles). Even large crowds have proved ineffective at fighting back against hails of gunfire: think St. Petersburg in 1905, the Vorkuta mining gulag in 1953, or Tiananmen Square in 1989; and the victims there *knew what guns were.*

Also, the Spaniards had steel armor, which was proof positive against the Inca's stone or bronze weapons—which, again, they had not brought to dinner. The Inca were so confused by steel that they figured the Spaniards' arms were made of silver. Pizarro's brother Juan Pizarro would be killed by the Incas in 1536, but it was a two-step process: First they managed to hit him in the jaw with a sling stone. His swollen jaw would not allow him to buckle on his helmet, so the next day he fought bareheaded, and another stone cracked his skull open. He died (after lingering delirious for two weeks), but you will perceive that this is a very inefficient way of dispatching Spaniards.

It's possible to overplay the inutility of Incan weapons against Spanish armor. Not every fight in the Incan lands would be as lopsided as the massacre at Cajamarca. The Incas got their licks in, and gradually, especially under the leadership of General Quizo Yupanqui, they learned to use the uneven terrain of the Andes to their advantage: Bolas, traditionally used to hunt deer, they repurposed to throw around the legs of the Spanish horses. The Aztecs had possessed weaponry no better than that of the Inca, and Bernal Díaz, who marched with Hernando Cortés into Mexico, quotes experienced soldiers in his company as saying that the Aztecs were deadlier fighters than the French or the Turks. Cortés's first attempt at Mexico ended in a rout, with the defeated Spaniards only barely escaping total annihilation.

The Incas got their licks in, but not at Cajamarca. There, the thousands of Incan nobles were packed too tightly into the square to allow them to disperse. The narrow exits were soon blocked by the dead, and what few Incas survived only escaped when the press of bodies became so great that a city wall *crumbled before it*. The slaughter ended with the fall of night. Pizarro was the sole Spaniard wounded that day: He received a cut on his hand when he batted away a conquistador's sword, to prevent it from striking Atahualpa.

Pizarro needed Atahualpa alive. The Incan emperor, a prisoner amid the mounds of his dead subjects, did indeed dine that night with the Spaniards.

III.

Civilizations (you probably learned in grade school) rise up in fertile river valleys. The four earliest centers of civilization—in Mesopotamia, Egypt, northern India, and China—owe their existence to the Tigris and Euphrates, the Nile, the Indus, and the Yellow River, respectively. The pattern is pretty obvious: Civilizations can spread far beyond river valleys, but they need a river valley to start.

Just look at the New World: There are two centers of advanced civilization—Mesoamerica and the Peruvian coast—and there are also two of the world's great river valleys—the Amazon and the Mississippi.

Unfortunately, the Amazon and the Mississippi are nowhere near Mesoamerica or Peru. Like most theories, this one was great until it wasn't. New World, new rules.

There along the Peruvian coast, several civilizations—their histories made ambiguous by the years—rose and fell and spread and tussled, until they were all conquered at last by the Inca. The Inca boasted the largest empire in the hemisphere—actually, it was the largest empire in two hemispheres: the Western (definitely) and the Southern (probably; no one seems certain of the exact extent of the Majapahit Empire in Indonesia). It's easy to view vanished civilizations with rose-colored glasses, and perhaps when William Prescott testifies that "no government could have been better suited to the genius of the people; and no people could have appeared more contented with their lot, or more devoted to their government" than the Incan subjects—well, either the word "appeared" has to do a lot of labor, or we should take the whole sentence with a grain of salt. But it does seem that the Inca Empire was like the Roman Empire, ca. AD 150: reasonably safe, reasonably stable, reasonably contented.

But the Inca managed to do something the Romans never did: They *conquered the known world*. Obviously they did not conquer the whole world; no one has since Kaïumarth, in the sixth generation after Adam— at least according to legend. But they conquered every civilized people they knew of. Their borders contained nothing but barbarians, who neither built cities nor organized themselves into states. Other non-barbarian peoples did exist in the Americas, of course, but to the Incas they were rumors at best. The Romans may have conquered all of civilized Europe, but the world they knew teemed with other unconquered civilized peoples—Persians, Ethiopians, Indians, etc. Alexander the Great is said to have wept because he had no more worlds to conquer, which is nonsense; but the Incas really could assume they had completed the job.

Also, they were fabulously rich.

Richer than they knew, even, because gold was simply not as rare in the Inca Empire as it was in, say, Europe and therefore not as valuable. An Inca would have done well to trade gold for its weight in iron, a fool's bargain in almost any other situation. The Inca had ornaments of gold, statues of gold, washtubs of gold. In the imperial pleasure gardens, imitation stalks of maize, with golden ears and silver leaves, swayed among the plants.

The omnipresent gold is really the least impressive part of the Incan achievement. More impressive were their cyclopean architecture; their roads and relay systems; their skill at harvesting, storing, and distributing food; and their mastery of organization, all accomplished without a true writing system. Only the ancient Indus Valley civilization managed to cover such a large area without access to writing, and the Indus civilization was never as advanced as the Inca. Indeed, anthropologist Edward P. Lanning once suggested with a straight face that the lack of a writing system benefited the Inca, because it prevented the bureaucratic inefficiency of red tape, allowing their government to stay lean and nimble.

All of this is a much greater testament to the Incan legacy than the happenstance of vast gold deposits. But not, of course, to Pizarro.

IV.

There would be other battles, but it was the "Battle of Cajamarca"— actually, massacre plus kidnapping—that decided the war. Atahualpa was the leader of the Inca Empire, and Pizarro controlled Atahualpa. Buoyed by an air of invincibility, Pizarro quickly mopped up the remaining native resistance. From that point on, the Incas could rebel (and they did), but they were rebelling against an entrenched power structure. The Spaniards would spend more time fighting one another than fighting the natives.

Atahualpa, meanwhile, took steps to protect himself. He offered a ransom for his freedom, the greatest ransom in history. First, he walked into a large room in one of the buildings in Cajamarca that served as his prison and said he would fill it with gold as high as he could reach. That's about three thousand cubic feet of gold. Then he offered to fill a smaller room with silver, twice over.

Offering such a ransom was a terrible idea. Pizarro was not going to be satisfied with a mere three thousand cubic feet of gold. There was probably no theoretical upper limit to the amount of gold Pizarro wanted. Also, "cruel, faithless, and treacherous," etc.

The room never quite got full of gold; maybe it never could have. Eventually, Pizarro got tired of waiting and predictably killed the emperor. He had to do it while Hernando de Soto was away on a mission, because de Soto, for all his flaws, was still not base enough to kill a captive who was paying his ransom. This was the de facto end of the Inca Empire; there would be more emperors, but they would all be puppets.

Atahualpa did something else while he was a captive, though: He ordered his half brother killed.

Pizarro was a wildly successful conqueror, but his success was due to timing as much as anything. The First Crusade (as we'll see) would have failed had it not happened while Turkish forces were divided; the Muslim expansion (as we'll see) would have faltered had it not swept across lands exhausted from a long and bloody war; and in 1524, the Portuguese adventurer Aleixo Garcia actually invaded part of the Inca Empire, coming from the Atlantic, but he was repelled; 1524 was the wrong time; 1532 was the right time.

Because 1524 was before the civil war.

V.

The Inca Empire was not very old when Pizarro overthrew it. It's only around 1400 that the small Inca state began to grow, and only in its last half century of existence did it become the universal empire Pizarro encountered. The obvious analogy is, again, Rome, which sat as a little city-state for four centuries, then spent another century or so expanding in Italy before exploding all over the north coast of the Mediterranean in the second century BC, the first of three centuries of Roman expansion. The Inca explosion had barely begun when it encountered the Spanish counterexplosion.

Atahualpa's father, Huayna Capac, added the area around Quito (in modern Ecuador) to the empire. Then he caught smallpox. Smallpox had been inadvertently brought to the New World by Columbus's second voyage and had slowly spread outward from the areas of Spanish colonization. Around 1527, smallpox hit the Incas, and the effect was as dramatic as the bubonic plague in fourteenth-century Europe. The pestilence would have been the greatest calamity in Incan history even if everything else had gone well, but Emperor Huayna Capac, as he was dying, did the thing you should never do. He split the empire between his sons.

What happens when you split an empire? In 817 Louis the Pious (Charlemagne's successor) split his empire among three sons—and immediately there was civil war. In 1103, the kingdom of Norway was split among dead King Magnus Barefoot's three sons, and—well, that turned out okay (much to my surprise); but after Magnus's three heirs died, his grandson and his illegitimate son divided the kingdom, and there was civil war. Alexander the Great's generals carved up his empire, and we've already seen what happened. Never split the empire.

The Incas had no established method of succession; there was always a scramble and a civil war when an emperor died. Huayna Capac may have thought he was nipping a succession crisis in the bud when he split his land between his legitimate son Huascar (who got the south) and his illegitimate son Atahualpa (the north). Instead, he just gave each son a ready-made power base from which to conduct their unavoidable civil war. Atahualpa won the war; Huascar got captured while fleeing a battlefield. The inevitable massacres followed, Huascar forced to watch as his family was murdered in front of him: first his wives and children, and then extended relatives. Prescott notes that the scale of the atrocities betrayed "an appetite for carnage unparalleled in the annals of the Roman Empire or of the French Republic"; but also, that most of the atrocities are probably fiction, conjured up by Huascar's latter-day partisans and spread by Spaniards eager to present their own reign as the just and sober one. We'll probably never know how many relatives Atahualpa had killed.

Except one. We know about one. He killed Huascar.

Inca emperor Atahualpa frees his brother → New Inca emperor Huascar kills Pizarro and the would-be conquistadors → **INCAS HELP SCOTSMEN SETTLE A BUFFER STATE IN PANAMA** → The west coast of South America speaks Quechua, not Spanish

I.

WE KNOW THAT ATAHUALPA KILLED HUASCAR, AND WE KNOW why he did it: He was afraid that his own captivity would delegitimize him as a ruler, letting Huascar serve as an obvious rallying point for the six to ten million Inca subjects not yet slain by the conquistadors. In retrospect, such a rallying point seems like not a bad idea, but Atahualpa did not have the benefit of retrospect, and ordered his brother's execution.

It would have been very easy for him not to. In fact, you probably would have expected him not to. Take a moment to ruminate over this story by Harvey Kurtzman from a 1951 issue of the comic book *Weird Science*; it may sound familiar:

A scientist (Professor Harlow) contrives a scheme to end all war. He notes that people tend to stop fighting when faced with a larger outside threat: For example (these are his examples), two brothers fighting over a girl will team up when they learn she's actually dating a third guy (to beat up their joint rival); similarly, all squabbling Americans forgot their quarrels on December 7, 1941, and worked with unity of purpose to stop the Japanese. So Harlow builds an ersatz Martian missile and launches it at "the sleeping town of Middleburg," faking the trajectory so it appears to come from Mars.

Wars end. Planetwide peace. Faced with the prospect of interplanetary bombardment, the nations of Earth pool their resources to fight off the Martian menace. Instead of fighting among ourselves, we put all our efforts into launching our own missiles at Mars.

Because this is a comic from EC, a company known for its *Twilight*

Zone *avant-la-lettre* twist endings, it turns out, horribly, horribly, that Mars is populated, and instead of bringing world peace, Professor Harlow has started interplanetary war. He dies in the first Martian counter-salvo. But don't worry about that last part. They say that every story has a happy ending if you end it too soon; if you end the story of Oedipus early, it's a fairy tale (wanderer defeats monster, saves town, marries queen). Cut the last page of this *Weird Science* story: a happy ending.

The story may sound familiar because it's a lot like a 1963 episode of *The Outer Limits* ("The Architects of Fear"); it's also a lot like a 1959 Jack Kirby comic from *Tales of Suspense* #2. It's also the plot of *Watchmen* (book and movie). It's also (of course, of course) the story of Atahualpa, who faced an invasion of mysterious strangers with wonder weapons from beyond the known world, and responded by . . .

Well, Atahualpa went off script. He killed his brother.

Here's Ronald Reagan, speaking at the United Nations in 1987: "I occasionally think how quickly our differences worldwide would vanish if we were facing an alien threat from outside this world." Or: In the early days of the Civil War, Secretary of State William H. Seward suggested Lincoln start a war with France or Spain to unite the divided country. It didn't happen, of course; but probably Seward—as well as Professor Harlow, and Messrs. Reagan, Kurtzman, Kirby, et al.—was insufficiently cynical. Perhaps it's more characteristic of human nature to respond to an outside threat by scrambling to grab what one can in the chaos. But we're imagining that Professor Harlow is right. We're imaging that Huascar survives.

Huascar was clearly not the best choice to fight off a Spanish invasion; if he was so good at fighting, he would've been emperor! But with Atahualpa out of commission, he was the best chance the Inca had. Atahualpa could as easily have sent word to free Huascar as he did to kill him. He could have sent, as well, a firsthand report of the strange Spanish weapons; their armor; their horses; their cannon.

Atahualpa was captured by Pizarro a mere seven months after he himself had captured Huascar. The vast empire must have been still mobilized for war in many places; all it needed was a leader. Unity between Huascarite and Atahualpite factions could be achieved through massacres and terror, sure, but it could also be achieved, if Professor Harlow is right, by a common enemy.

Even with a leader, the Inca would have a hard time driving off the Spanish. The civil war weakened them; the smallpox epidemic had weakened them even more, and that was still boiling around the empire (and would continue to boil until the 1940s). The Spaniards had their horses and their steel. At one point during the Inca rebellion of 1536, the death toll stood at ca. three thousand dead Incan subjects against thirty-five dead Spaniards. But especially during the earliest days of the conquest, the conquistadors were vulnerable. There were only 168 of them. They were stuck up in the mountains, far from the coast. If the Inca had just refused to feed them, the Spaniards probably would have died with their horses.

Atahualpa was hardly going to suggest starving the Spaniards out— his heart on a stick would have been Pizarro's first meal, metaphorically if not literally; but if he passes the baton to Huascar, this strategy will probably suggest itself. Atahualpa dies, then, but Pizarro and his men die as well. Weakened from hunger and harassment, they try to fight their way to the coast. The Inca, of course, have local area knowledge and block every pass. Pizarro wanders in circles in the mountains until large rocks fall on his head.

That will hardly be the end of the Inca's troubles. Pizarro has some troops he's stationed closer to shore; a surprise attack might take them out. Diego de Almagro is trying to whip up reinforcements in Panama, remember, but if Pizarro's venture has zero men returning—reinforcing a debacle will hardly seem attractive. If Spain were to launch an all-out attack on the Inca lands, it would win, of course, but Spain's not about to do that. Any attack on the Incas would be conducted by ragtag bands of adventurers. The Incas can't fight off all of Spain, but all they'll ever have to fight off are Spanish pirates. Pizarro could only find 167 willing men to attack the great empire the first time; the second time, Almagro is going to have a rough go.

To make things worse, the supply line for Spaniards to reach the Inca Empire was hardly a simple one. Although Magellan had discovered a way around the southern tip of South America, it was stormy, wild, and mostly untried. Supplies would have to be transported across Panama and then down the long west coast.

Time was on the Inca's side, at least in the sense that they could hardly be less prepared for attack than they were in 1532; every year would make them more prepared. Diplomatic relations with curious Spaniards could only benefit them. They had plenty of gold to trade for swords, armor, horses, and guns. Every encounter with Spanish goods and techniques would also be a learning experience. One thing they may learn from Spanish explorers: the presence of the culturally advanced Muisca people to their north. The Inca promptly conquer them.

After a while, though, time might turn against the Inca. The supply line grows shorter as Spanish settlements spread along the Pacific. The vast resources of the Inca can only grow more enticing every day.

(Also, the smallpox isn't going away: Although eventually the surviving Inca would have a tolerance similar to the Spaniards', that tolerance could never be very good, because Europeans' tolerance was never very good. For centuries, Europeans would express fear of cities because the crowded streets were a haven for smallpox; in 1774, for example, two of Connecticut's delegates to the First Continental Congress refused to go to Philadelphia, lest they catch the disease. It's not always easy to understand why some smallpox outbreaks are deadlier than others. In 1769–70, up to one third the population of Bengal was slain by the disease, and Bengal had known smallpox for centuries by then. So the best the Inca can hope for is that the smallpox keeps killing Spaniards while it is at the same time killing them.)

But every year that the Inca Empire exists side by side with the Spaniards adds to its appearance of legitimacy. If the Inca permit Catholic missionaries to come within their borders, it will be difficult for the Spanish crown to justify invading its territory. Since there are no civilized-but-oppressed peoples around the universal empire of the Inca, there is no one to team up with and "liberate" as a casus belli.

And so the two sides sit: The Spanish wanting the Inca gold but unable to take the wild risk of seizing it from a wily and prepared opponent; the Inca seeking through diplomacy and a show of strength to keep the Spanish at bay.

It remains a standoff until some third force comes to disrupt things in the area. How long would that take?

Let's say 167 years.

II.

Europeans who came to the New World, they all had their reasons. Hernando de Soto came because his prospective father-in-law, Pedro de Avila, wanted to kill him. De Soto did not flee to the Americas to escape Don Pedro, as you might imagine; Pedro de Avila had been appointed governor of Panama, and he intentionally brought de Soto along with him when he sailed from Spain to *1*. keep him away from his beloved daughter Isabel, and *2*. send him on enough dangerous missions that death would find him before the wedding. But no matter how many suicide missions de Soto went on, no matter how many duels (egged on by Don Pedro) he fought, de Soto always came back. It was Don Pedro who sent de Soto to Peru to reinforce Pizarro. (De Soto survived that, too, and returned to Spain to wed Isabel; he later died near the Mississippi, vainly seeking another empire to conquer.)

Pizarro and Almagro traveled to the Americas because they were poor, illiterate, and illegitimate; opportunities for them anywhere else were slim. Add: the religious motives of the Pilgrims and Puritans; Walter Raleigh's (genuine but futile) quest for El Dorado; Ponce de León's (completely made up but also futile) quest for the Fountain of Youth.

And then, in 1699, came the Scots, inspired by (I quote the great Victorian historian Lord Macaulay) "dangerous fits of passion and delusions of the imagination." Perhaps these delusions were no more delusional than the search for "the golden Temple of Doboyba," or "the golden sepulchres of Zenu" (both Spanish goals in the New World)—but they ended just as badly.

The fits and delusions started with William Paterson, a Scottish financier who claimed he knew of a secret place in the New World that the Spaniards had forborne to settle, notwithstanding its salubrious climate and fertile soil. Such a place would be the perfect spot for a colony he had in mind: a colony that would span from the Atlantic to the Pacific, a colony that could become a mercantile center, passing goods from Asia on one end to Europe on the other, and vice versa. Control of the Asian markets would make the colony fabulously wealthy, enriching, as well, anyone with the foresight to invest. A true patriot, the Scottish-born Paterson decided to offer the good people of Scotland this exciting investment opportunity: Incorporate the Company of Scotland Trading to Africa and the Indies; shares were £100 each. The Scots quickly invested £400,000, which may not sound like so much, but this was the 1690s and Scotland was not a rich country: The sum amounted to nearly one fifth the cash in Scotland. A mania had seized the Scots, and they hailed Paterson as a kind of religious prophet, set to lead them to a Promised Land.

There were several problems with Paterson's scheme. The first that anyone noticed was that Paterson's "secret location" could only be the Isthmus of Darien, in Panama, and it just so happened that Spain, even if it had not settled there, nonetheless claimed it. If a coterie of Scots moved into Spanish territory, the result could only be war with Britain, which the English parliament understandably did not relish. It would be England, after all, that would be footing the bill and fighting the war that Scotland's nonexistent navy could not participate in. The British East India Company, meanwhile, balked at the idea of losing their monopoly to some Scottish upstarts. Although the English tried through legal and economic means to prevent the continuance of the scheme, the perfervid Scots were not to be dissuaded. Denied English ships to take them to Darien, they purchased three from Holland and Hamburg.

In 1698 William Paterson and twelve hundred Scotsmen sailed for the New World.

And there they found the second problem with the scheme. Far from being the paradise Paterson had fancied, Darien was a pestilential death trap. There was a reason the Spanish had decided not to build settlements there. Paterson had spent his youth in Jamaica, and perhaps he assumed all tropical climates were as pleasant. Not Darien, though. Waves of disease swept through the colony. Although more and more ships came, swelling the colonists' numbers to ten thousand, the reinforcements merely increased the ranks of the dead. Soon almost everyone had either died or given up and fled back to Europe. The hangers-on were struggling just to survive when the Spanish arrived, in force, and surrounded them. Quickly, all sides came to the conclusion that the Scots would be best off departing Darien forever.

The Darien Scheme was a disaster; not only was there the death and humiliation, but Scotland could not afford to lose such a huge investment. The seventeenth and eighteenth centuries saw their share of New World investment disasters, but the Darien calamity was unique in what a huge percentage of a country's population and wealth was implicated. Not until 1996, when two thirds of Albanians invested in Ponzi schemes, would a bubble "burst with a more lamentable explosion." A crippled, paralyzed Scotland could only consent to union with England.

This is what happened when a small group of Scots chose to surround themselves with hostile Spanish subjects. To the north of them was Spanish Mexico. To the south of them was Spanish Peru. When things got bad, there was nowhere to go but home.

But if there was no Spanish Peru, things might go differently.

The Scottish colony of Caledonia is the third force in the Inca-Spanish standoff. Of course, no foreign colony could flourish in the heart of Spanish Panama, but depending on how far north the Inca had extended their domain in the last century, Paterson's narrow isthmus might be located in the no-man's-land between the Inca and Spanish Empires.

Eager for a buffer state and doubtless desperate to find a European ally, the Inca roll supplies and assistance into the struggling Caledonian colony. Although the Scots are ill-prepared for the rigors of the climate—their supply ships were full of periwigs and woolen garments—a little advice from advanced and experienced neighbors goes a long way. Caledonia survives, and then flourishes.

Paterson's idea had mostly been stupid insofar as it would inevitably lead to the death or expulsion of everyone involved. It had also been stupid because transporting goods from ocean to ocean across Darien is a fool's game. Darien is mountainous jungle interspersed with swamps. But if the Inca learn from the Scots that cross-continental transport is what's needed—well, to go around the pestilential swamps to the south, someone would have to figure out a way to build roads through the Andes Mountains.

Raise your hand if you're a representative of a culture with long experience building roads through the Andes Mountains.

This is the Inca's key to sustained independence. The British are willing to forgive a harebrained and quasi-legal scheme if it brings the wealth of Asia that much closer. Tea comes from Asia. The British Pacific fleet and Atlantic fleet each dock at Incan ports, doubtless with a Scottish harbormaster to negotiate. The Spanish cannot invade the Inca Empire now without starting a war with Britain. Their colonies to the north are cut off from their Rio de la Plata colony (in modern Argentina) and the Portuguese colonies in Brazil.

In our history, in 1780, a prophecy spread around South America that the British would bring the native Inca back to power (this prophecy proved false); perhaps in a history where Huascar returns to the throne, Inca power is instead preserved by the British.

By the twenty-first century, the Incan Republic of Tahuantinsuyo (as the Inca styled it) is the second-largest state in South America, after Brazil. No one has ever written a book calling Pizarro cruel, faithless, or treacherous. No one remembers who he was.

FREEMASONRY

What if William Morgan stopped drinking?

YOUNGSTOWN, NEW YORK, 1826

I.

The Freemasons pretended to be an ancient secret sect for so long that they are now, at last, actually an ancient secret sect. Everything about their history is provisional and mingled with myth. Almost everything written about them is crazy and clearly false.

In the late eighteenth century, American Founding Father Thomas "Common Sense" Paine wrote: "It is always understood that Free-Masons have a secret which they carefully conceal; but from every thing that can be collected from their own accounts of Masonry, their real secret is no other than their origin, which but few of them understand; and those who do, envelope it in mystery." Actually, by the late eighteenth century, probably no one alive knew the true story of their origins. I sure don't.

The party line, more or less, is that during the construction of King Solomon's temple, the stonemasons laboring on this prodigious edifice developed a series of passwords to keep the right worker on the right job, or to make sure each mason was paid the correct amount—or even to hide access to forbidden lore. Perhaps a certain password is also a word of power, or a secret name of God. Hiram Abiff, the master architect, is assaulted by three lesser masons, who demand all the passwords. He refuses, and they kill him. Further passwords resurrect him. May any mason who betrays the trust have his "t t ot @ br i ⊣ sd % ⊣ s at lw w mk wh ⊣ t ebs @ fs twc i tf hs"! This is cryptic Masonic shorthand for "tongue torn out and buried in the sand of the sea, at low water mark, where the tide ebbs and flows twice in twenty-four hours."

Solomon's masons, they say, learned their secrets from even older sources—the masons who built the Tower of Babel in some accounts, or from Enoch, Noah's great-grandfather, who ascended to heaven (Genesis 5:24) and brought back hidden knowledge. Enoch inscribed what he learned on two indestructible pillars, called Boaz and Jachin, which survived Noah's Flood. Solomon set these pillars in front of his Temple (2 Chronicles 3:17), and *thus* did the masons of old acquire literally antediluvian knowledge. Which they passed down through three thousand years to the men who are still called Masons today, in honor of their origins. They gather in Lodges across America, and the world. When they're not sharing ancient wisdom with one another, they run charitable blood drives.

Paine quite rightly debunks these claims—not the blood drives, the Solomon's Temple stuff—and then goes on to claim Masons are just druids, hiding their religion behind a secret society for a thousand years to avoid persecution—which is just as bananas. Everyone's got a bananas theory. Occultist Manly P. Hall traces Masonry back to the fire-worshippers of Atlantis. Only slightly less eccentric authors link Masonry to the Knights Templar, who guarded the secrets of Solomon's Temple (hence the name *Templar*). In 1307, the Templars were outlawed and, largely, executed. The survivors went underground in Scotland, where their occult wisdom burbled up into the Freemasons.

The last grand master of the Templars was Jacques de Molay. Today the Freemasons' junior auxiliary is called DeMolay International. *Coincidence?*

Back in the real world, you flat-earthers, back in the *round world*, the Freemasons most likely started as a guild of actual masons somewhere in Britain. Such guilds were a product of the Middle Ages, and they were always shrouded in secrecy. In the same way that American labor unions were, strangely enough, created to prevent immigrants from getting jobs, medieval guilds were created as a form of protectionism. Not just anyone could become a mason in medieval Europe, because the techniques of building were strictly protected. In those days you couldn't just google up "how to masonry videos"; methods for building an arch were discovered and then forgotten again and again through the millennia; unless you invented a technique yourself, you had to be told of it by a mason. And they weren't telling unless you were in the guild. They knew you were in the guild if you had the password.

Exactly how "say the secret word and learn about bricklaying" morphed into "say the secret word and learn the secret teachings of the ages" is anyone's guess. But clearly it happened.

We have the Mason Word and second sight,
Things for to come we can foretell aright . . .

. . . Henry Adamson wrote in 1638. By 1670, a roster of master masons in Aberdeen showed only ten actual stone masons, while the other thirty-nine members either were "gentlemen" or belonged to other professions. You will notice that this was no longer a guild of masons. Somewhere along the line they had become the Freemasons.

One way of looking at the Masons is that they were simply men "of good character and reputation" bound together in fellowship to share wisdom. This wisdom they shared need not be sinister: A 1953 anthology titled *A Treasury of Masonic Thought* contains poems and aphorisms from an utterly typical roster (Shakespeare, Poe, Longfellow) of canonical writers, some of whom (Emily Brontë, Marcus Aurelius, Confucius) were 100% definitely never Masons; but that's okay, because, the introduction says, "the principle tenets of Freemasonry are so fundamentally universal that they belong to all men in all times and all nations." A typical selection from the volume (this one by Edwin Markham) runs:

He drew a circle that shut me out—
Heretic, rebel, a thing to flout.

But Love and I had the wit to win:
We drew a circle that took him in!

This quatrain is so anodyne that it could appear in an AA bulletin, or on a counted cross-stitch pillow sold at a church bazaar. It is threatening only to people who have poetic standards. I'm not saying it's not wisdom, just that if this is Masonic wisdom, Masonic wisdom is utterly safe.

Yet Masonic wisdom has often appeared unsafe: not because people have analyzed it and found it subversive, but simply because it is secret. The Masons encoded it in rituals and symbols. They refused to explain anything to the uninitiated. This secrecy was one of Freemasonry's selling points. In the 1740s, Freemason John Coustos told the Portuguese Inquisition that Masons' secrecy "excited curiosity" and served to swell the ranks of people clamoring to join. Certainly, the secrecy was exciting to the Masons; they crowed about it in their songs, such as

The world is in pain
Our secret to gain,
And still let them wonder and gaze on,
They ne'er can divine
The word or the sign
Of a free and an accepted mason.

So, one way of looking at it is *fellowship and wisdom*, but another way of looking at it is that men *conspiring in secret* are up to no good.

Why, you may have found yourself asking a few paragraphs ago, was John Coustos testifying before the Inquisition in the first place? It turns out there's only one reason anyone testifies before the Inquisition. It's not a reason you'd want to experience yourself.

John Coustos survived "unparalleled sufferings" of "the most cruel tortures ever invented by man" to write an account with those phrases as part of its very title. His book, from 1746, was one of a small cottage industry of books about the martyrdoms of Freemasons. Indeed, in some parts of Europe, Masons had "for centuries been objects of a bitter persecution, and . . . large numbers of them have suffered death in defence of their principles" (to quote an 1880 Masonic martyrology).

In the United States, though, Freemasons hardly needed to worry about persecution. George Washington was a Mason. Ben Franklin, the Marquis de Lafayette, and both Lewis and Clark were all Masons. Americans were more likely to be suspicious of Catholics than of Masons. American as apple pie.

And then William Morgan messed it up for everyone.

II.

William Morgan was a shiftless drunkard; or at least there have been many who wished to present him as one. In 1825, despite his lack "of good character and reputation," he became a Mason in upstate New York, and in 1826 he threatened, perhaps in a drunken rage, to publish an exposé of Masonry's deepest secrets. Then he disappeared. Thirteen months later a body was discovered in Lake Ontario that may or may not have been William Morgan. He may or may not have been kidnapped and murdered by Freemasons.

We are two centuries too late to solve this crime. I have no idea what happened to William Morgan, but the people in Niagara County were pretty darn certain. Four Freemasons went to prison for the crime; but this proved to be only the tip of the iceberg. America had smelled blood, and that blood was Masonic.

To call the resulting fracas a witch hunt for Masons might be overstating the case (witches got *hanged*!), but it's notable that America's first national "third party" was 1828's Anti-Masonic Party. Its candidate in the 1832 presidential election managed to get only seven electoral votes, but the Anti-Masons did better in Congress, electing forty (!) national Representatives between 1827 and 1839, mostly from New York and Pennsylvania. William H. Seward, later secretary of state, and Millard Fillmore, later president, started their political careers as Anti-Masons.

Anti-Masonic fever, to no one's surprise, was a catastrophe for

Masonry. Members quit, or simply stopped attending meetings. In 1830 Maine had thirty subsidiary Masonic Lodges; in 1837 one; in 1842 none. The rest of the country may not have experienced a decline quite so extreme as Maine's, but it's not far off the mark.

The Freemasons bounced back, of course. The Anti-Masonic Party got absorbed into the Whig Party, and mostly forgot its origins; Henry Clay, the greatest Whig, was a Mason. The aftermath of the Civil War saw a growth in Lodges, perhaps as veterans sought to re-create in peacetime the fellowship they'd enjoyed in their military companies. By the twentieth century there were more Freemasons in America than ever before. Their numbers peaked in 1959. The mystery of William Morgan probably remains unsolved.

What would have happened, though, had a soberer Morgan never fallen into the lake/spilled the secrets? What if there had been no crime, no scandal, and no anti-Masonic backlash? The swell of Masonic adherents up to 1959 is impressive, but would Masons have experienced a greater swell if their membership upswing had never been checked? Masonry in Europe, as we have seen, was too bound up with religious rivalry; in America alone could it thrive, in a Morganless world, without worrying about the swaying fortunes of sectarianism. And what if it had?

William Morgan stays sober → He never floats facedown across Lake Ontario → Millard Fillmore and his pals love the Masons → THE FREEMASONS TAKE OVER THE US GOVERNMENT, FOR REAL THIS TIME

I.

LET'S SAY THAT WITHOUT MORGAN, MASONRY HAS NO precedent of an 1830s, and therefore a 1960s, downturn. Let's say that Masonry just becomes more and more entrenched in American life. Unchecked, Masonry becomes the norm. Think about the norm, because the norm is very powerful.

It's already been noted that Washington, Franklin, etc., and even Henry Clay were Masons. Clay's arch-rival, Andrew Jackson, was a Mason. William "Buck" Travis and Jim Bowie, who both died at the Alamo, Sam Houston, and Stephen F. Austin—that's half of Texas history right there—were all Masons. Buffalo Bill Cody, Mark Twain, Henry Ford, and Irving Berlin were Masons. Nearly one third of all presidents have been Masons (Gerald Ford was the last). The dollar bill's eye on the pyramid is only one of many Masonic symbols tucked secretly into innocent Americana; get out a dollar, draw a star of David around the pyramid, and you'll see the points of the star point to the letters *A*, *S*, *M*, *O*, *N*—an anagram for MASON. Some occult historians (*it's always a bananas theory*) have noted that, like most of the British command in America, General Charles "Surrendered at Yorktown" Cornwallis was a Mason, and may have "thrown the match" to his Masonic brother Washington for secret Masonic reasons.

You don't have to believe the Cornwallis thing to believe that Freemasons have been important in American history; even crazier sources claim that George Washington's identity was usurped by notorious Bavarian Freemason Adam Weishaupt; you don't have to believe that either. Freemasons were still important in American history, Weishaupt or no Weishaupt. But saying that Freemasons have been important in American history is not the same as saying that Freemasonry has been important in American history. Five of the last nine presidents have been left-handed, but a treatise on the role of *sinistrality in American politics* would just be silly. Cody, Twain, Ford, Berlin, Truman, and all the other famous Americans who embraced Masonry after the Morgan incident would have built just as many cars and written just as many *Huckleberry Finn*s without Masonry. It may appear that America with more Masons or with fewer Masons would look just about the same.

Freemasonry is not just a secret society, though. Masonry is an entire method of leisure. And that's what will turn out to be important.

II.

In 1935, P. Hal Sims wrote, "One of the greatest problems confronting the average American family today is that of finding some method of entertaining children. Let me strongly advise you to teach your children to play Pinochle."

Sims was a pinochle expert who wrote pinochle guidebooks, so his advice may not be impartial, but he has a point. You've got to entertain children. More importantly, you've got to entertain yourself. You've got leisure time, and you've got to do something to fill it: the remote in one hand, your game controller in the other. But in Sims's 1935, it was not so easy. And before 1935, before you even had a radio, it was harder still.

Leisure time is nothing new, of course. Even medieval serfs had long winter nights when there was nothing to do in the dark but pray, talk, and make more serfs. Their music was homemade and their stories, polished from endless retellings, became the basis for fairy-tale collections. The Industrial Revolution would have cut down the amount of leisure some people had, simply because factories can stay open during winter months that farms cannot. But, the new manufacturing processes also swelled the ranks of the middle class and led, overall, to more people with more free time. "How do ye vary your vile days and nights?" Leigh Hunt once asked a fish, but it was becoming a question more humans had to answer, too.

The publishers of one 1895 collection of elocution pieces claimed that "no entertainments are more universally popular" than (I'm not making this up) listening to children recite poetry. This sounds like hell itself to any modern ear, but they had a book to sell, and may have been exaggerating. But such "entertainments" existed. Although people could, by necessity, spend the vile days and nights of 1895 reading any number of books and newspapers, they still, by and large, had to make their own entertainment.

And if your idea of entertainment did not involve kitschy "uplifting" poetry recitals by Sunday school children, then in 1895, as in 1795, as in

1695, you might want to retreat to a place where there were no children. If you were a gentleman, you could retreat to a gentlemen's club.

Nowadays a gentlemen's club is a euphemism, a club for people who are anything but gentlemen, but in the eighteenth and nineteenth centuries, gentlemen's clubs were chaste and exclusive. Readers know them well from their appearances in literature: Phileas Fogg leaves for his trip *Around the World in Eighty Days* from the Reform Club (a real club); Mycroft Holmes belongs to the Diogenes Club, Bertie Wooster to the Drones Club (both fictional).

Holmes and Wooster are gentlemen, of course, but the idea of an exclusive club is hardly class specific. In his 1869 novel, *Mark the Match Boy*, Horatio Alger tries to depict a club attended by disreputable young men who drink "hot whiskey" and smoke cigars, but as usual his imagination fails him and the bad boys literally spend their time singing opera arias; afterward, at least, there is a little card playing and a fist fight, and then the authorial voice intrudes to hector readers that this is a "very poor way" to spend an evening. Amen.

The Masons did not originate as a gentlemen's club, but they evolved into something *like* a gentlemen's club; yet they offered things that a gentlemen's club never could. Secrecy. Ritual. Perhaps not actual occluded and clandestine power, but the hint of occluded and clandestine power. Masonic fellowship runs deeper than the mere coincidence of belonging to the same club. Edward S. Ellis collected two volumes (1907–1912) of "striking and truthful incidents illustrative of the fidelity of Free Masons to one another in times of distress and danger." In one anecdote he shares, a tuberculous Union veteran is found hemorrhaging by a Confederate veteran shortly after the Civil War's end; both are Masons, as is revealed by secret signs. The Confederate cannot bring himself to speak to the Union man, but he cannot refuse a Mason in need, and so in silence he wraps his coat around the sufferer and bears him to the nearest doctor.

The Masons were scarcely alone in offering secrecy, ritual, etc. In the flat America of the screen, Fred Flintstone and Barney Rubble are members of the Loyal Order of Water Buffaloes, Ralph Kramden and Ed

Norton are members of the International Order of Loyal Raccoons, and Amos and Andy are members of the Mystic Knights of the Sea; but the real America has abounded in Masonic alternatives as well. The Knights of Columbus are a specifically Catholic analog of the Masons, designed to appeal to Catholics who wanted to experience everything about Masonry except the excommunication. The Odd Fellows, moribund today, once rivaled the Masons in popularity (their mission: to "visit the sick, relieve the distressed, bury the dead and educate the orphan"). Somewhat less secretive is The Benevolent and Protective Order of Elks; much less secretive is the Rotary Club. Even more secretive are the Rosicrucians. Manly P. Hall, who, you'll remember, confidently proposed Atlantis as the source for Masons, is so uncertain about the role of the Rosicrucians that he offers four contradictory possibilities: one of them is that the Rosicrucians do not exist; another is that the Rosicrucians are spiritual beings of great power from another world. Among those who have *called themselves* Rosicrucians is Sirhan Sirhan, assassin of Robert F. Kennedy. Anything can happen.

When the fraternal anti-immigrant Order of United Americans merged with the fraternal anti-immigrant Order of the Star-Spangled Banner in 1852, their one million secret members influenced the American government in the most boring way—by electing candidates. This was the origin of the anti-immigrant "Know-Nothing" Party (so-called because when asked about their secret organizations, members inevitably answered "I know nothing"), a political force that swept in and nabbed a fifth of the seats in the House of Representatives in 1854 only to fade away a few years later.

They faded away because of the Civil War, of course, which made immigration look like less of a big scary deal by highlighting bigger, scarier deals. And the crucible of the Civil War produced its own secret political organizations, all on the fraternal model. While the Order of the Heroes of America lobbied for peace (i.e., subverted the war effort), the pro-Confederate Sons of Liberty committed sabotage and random acts of arson throughout the North, and robbed a bank in St. Albans, Vermont.

One bank robbery is small potatoes: the Bolsheviks, in comparison, financed their revolution through a string of bank robberies that Lenin and Stalin coordinated, and John Dillinger robbed a dozen banks in a year. Soon after the Sons of Liberty evaporated, though, the sinister motives attributed to Freemasons came to fruition in the "invisible empire" of the Ku Klux Klan, everybody's least favorite American fraternal organization. The Klan started as something akin to the Shriners, a secret club for drunken revelry and pranks. Klansmen would dress like ghosts in white sheets and ride their horses pell-mell through upper-class garden parties of the postbellum South, where disaffected young men, disappointed in war, had little to do beyond mischief. While dressing like ghosts and acting like drunken jerks was fairly widespread in the nineteenth century, the Klan soon discovered a serious purpose, and turned from pranking to terror and murder. Their whimsical start is preserved in the jocular misspelling of "clan" and the ludicrous (Grand Cyclops, Grand Wizard) titles.

The Klan, you will perceive, is unique. Not unique in being racist and violent—this is America, after all—but unique in being a secret fraternal organization that grew powerful enough to influence public policy. The Know-Nothings went aboveground before they influenced much of anything, and the Sons of Liberty were too small to accomplish much, more bogeymen than a real threat; they did not outlast the Civil War. But the Klan, in various incarnations, has lasted, and has wielded real power. In a history without Morgan's scandal, in a history of more widespread Masonry, we can expect to see *more of this*.

III.

We can see something adjacent to *more of this* in one surviving legacy of Masonry in America: the college Greek system.

Wonder Woman in her early years was helped by the "Beeta Lamda" sorority. Her fourth case, in 1942, involved handing a Nazi spy over to the sorority girls, who blindfolded her and spanked her until she repented— one of the weirder moments in a generally weird run of comics stories.

But in the days since 1942, fraternities and sororities have spent less time catching spies and more time building a reputation for vandalism, rape, and occasional manslaughter. Collecting a roster of hazing deaths (at Penn State's BΘΠ in 2017; Baruch's ΠΔΨ in 2013; Cornell's ΣΑΕ in 2011; Cal Poly's ΣΑΕ in 2008; Alfred U.'s ZBT 2002; Cal State LA's AKA in 2002 [two dead], etc., etc.) is too easy to be interesting and too depressing to be fun, but it is not the killing that interests us.

Fraternities and sororities offer a glimpse at what happens when you expand the basic ideas of Masonry to a new context. They have the secrecy; the ritual; the mysterious initiations; the focus on "tradition" and on "fellowship." Masons are dedicated to the virtue of fraternity, and fraternities preserve this in their very name. They have everything except the ancient Solomonic wisdom.

More of this, too. Expect more of this.

IV.

No one trusts secrecy. The Inquisition told John Coustos, with no small degree of irony, "that inviolable secrecy can be observed in such things only as are of a criminal nature"; and perhaps you and I would not agree with the Inquisition on most subjects. Yet doesn't this sound right?

Democracies are nominally transparent, and although some decisions are made by secret cabals far from prying ears—the decisions to make the atomic and later the hydrogen bombs, for example—they are made by people who should, in theory at least, be held accountable. The KKK, in its heyday, was accountable to no one, because no one knew who ruled this "invisible empire." Not until 1975, when the Khmer Rouge conquered Cambodia but refused to tell the world who they were or who was in charge, would another group so powerful and notorious lack any kind of public face. (The twenty-first century may offer its own examples.)

Imagine, though, that belonging to a secret society in the years after 1826 slowly became de rigueur. Especially in the corridors of power, everybody is a Mason, or if not a Mason then possibly a Knight of Columbus or an Odd Fellow. In history as we know it, the conflicts over slavery's expansion that led ultimately to the Civil War in 1861 were debated openly: on the floors of Congress as well as in newspapers and pamphlets. Imagine if the resolution was debated in secret, by men who had sworn great oaths not to reveal what they were debating, lest each have his "tongue torn out by the root, and buried in the sand," etc. Imagine, then, that every great event in American history—every war, every reform—is a decision over which the voting public has no say, or even awareness.

This is a paranoiac's fantasy come true. Many people would say that the government is run by secret and unelected forces: If you're crazy, the forces are the Rosicrucians or the Rothschilds; if you're only slightly less crazy, they're something nebulous and perhaps Hegelian called the "Deep State." Call it *bureaucracy + inertia* and even if you're not right, you at least sound sane; you *might* be right.

But when we imagine a deep state, or a "vast right-wing conspiracy," or a Babylonian Brotherhood, we usually imagine one group pulling the strings. The philosopher Karl Popper points out that conspiracy theory "comes from abandoning God and then asking: 'Who is in his place?'" But there's no reason to assume that a pantheon of fraternal organizations need be monotheistic.

It's a little weird that America's most powerful terrorist group modeled itself after fraternal organizations (including the UNC fraternity Kuklos Adelphon)—weird enough that subsequent terrorist groups in our history would take different paths—but in a world where fraternal organizations are more commonplace, in a world where the KKK's fraternal background does not seem strange, the KKK would not be opposed by a federal government; it would be opposed by another fraternal order. And the two would vie for power not only at midnight in the South: They would vie for power in the Capitol.

In shadowy corridors and star chambers, Freemasons face off against Odd Fellows. Lions prey on Elks. These are specifically fraternal, as opposed to sororal, orders, but perhaps the Daughters of the American Revolution can throw their hats into the ring. Rosicrucians against all.

And suddenly American history disappears. History is what is written; what happens before writing is prehistory. American history as written becomes a shadow play, performed to keep the masses distracted. What actually happens is unwritten. What actually happens is post history.

Close the book, then. In this timeline there is nothing more to write.

6

SIGMUND FREUD

What if Freud read more Sophocles?

I.

Martin Amis once remarked that Vladimir Nabokov could have written another novel ("or two") in the amount of time he spent hating Freud; and Nabokov is hardly alone. There's a cottage industry of authors vying with Nabokov in their level of vitriol for "the Viennese quack"—or, more soberly, simply critiquing Freud, Freudianism, and the whole psychoanalytic apparatus. Frederick Crews's *Freud: The Making of an Illusion* may be the most thorough of a spate of similar books. It's a good read if you want to develop a contempt for Sigmund Freud the man, but a Freudian may object that many of the revelations this and like volumes contain are not really material criticisms of the science of psychoanalysis. Freud's penchant for plagiarism, his cocaine addiction, his tax evasion, his paranoia, his philandering, his autocratic demeanor, his cocaine addiction (mention it twice! it was quite an addiction), his, yes, even his (alleged) incest (!) should perhaps be mere footnotes to the study of the great man and his thought. But there's also the inescapable problem that Freud fudged his data. Serial fudging. Of all his lifelong vices, fraud was Freud's most damning.

The scandal of the early years of psychoanalysis was that Freud, even as he touted his new science, cured no one. His nascent medical practice simply did not attract many patients; he often had no one to cure. He therefore had to construct his theories *at best* without very much data. In fact, much of his information on the human psyche seems to have been extracted solely from introspection, which means that most of what would be passed off as revelations of the mind's inner workings are just revelations of Sigmund Freud's mind's inner workings. Certainly, no other human in history has dreamed about castration as much as Freud did.

In one of grift's greatest fake-it-till-you-make-it schemes, Freud blundered through a decade in which he satisfactorily cured *zero patients*, covering up this failure with statements that range from misleading to full-on mendacious until he was famous enough that his patients started faith healing from just being in his presence. The great composer Gustav Mahler claimed Freud cured his impotence during a brief discussion while strolling through Leiden; this is all very good for Mahler, but it's not exactly an endorsement of the techniques of psychoanalysis, which never even claimed to be applicable to short, perambulatory conversations. If the problems are all in your head, then believing in Freud, however irrationally, can cure you. Psychoanalysis as placebo; this was the only way Freud could successfully treat a patient.

Freud eventually became so big that the idea of his influence spread beyond the bounds of what he said or did, the way ancient poems used to get credited to Homer by default. The novelist Louis Auchincloss attributed to Freud's theories the idea that we are responsible only for our actions, and not for our thoughts or desires; I think Adam Smith or even Moses would be better sources for this idea, but the point is that Freud had had such an impact on the world that by the late 1960s (when Auchincloss was writing) anything current could be Freud's doing, because *everything current* was in some way Freud's doing.

This is perhaps an error, but it's hard to blame Auchincloss for the error when I'm going to make it myself several dozen times in the next few pages.

II.

Freud's writings became famous for several reasons, but one of them was simply that they were salacious. Freud wrote about subjects that were taboo, and in some places illegal to publish; "It's okay, I'm a doctor," Freud could say, though, and we all read with clean minds and pure hearts a book about a man who wanted to strap a bowl full of live rats to his butt.

The Oedipal complex was not necessarily the aspect of his theoretical framework that Freud primarily stressed in his writings, but it's the one that most captured the popular imagination. It's *designed* to capture the popular imagination. It's based on a story that's been sensational for twenty-three hundred years, after all.

Freud learned about Oedipus the same way all educated Austrians of his time would—from reading Sophocles's play *Oedipus the King*. The plot you well know: A horrified King Oedipus of Thebes discovers that years ago he had killed his father and married his mother. His wife/mother, Jocasta, hangs herself. Oedipus gouges out his eyes with her brooch. The king's compound crime of parricide and incest had brought to the city of Thebes a plague, which presumably ends when the guilty king shuffles off into the sequel, *Oedipus at Colonus*, to die. If you haven't read it, you should, although I did just spoil the twist ending.

Oedipus's story is strange as well as sensationalistic. It demands an explanation; or at least, many people over the years have tried to come up with one. On a basic level, it's clear the ancient Greeks, like a lot of us, had strict taboos against incest and parricide. Oedipus's is merely a cautionary tale.

Incest, like parricide, is a fairly standard taboo, the Ptolemies notwithstanding. The anthropologist Claude Lévi-Strauss dragged a *very different* meaning out of the myth, which is only germane here insofar as when he wrote his analysis—1958—he mentioned that every recorded version of the Oedipus myth must be studied; including, he insisted, the Freudian one. Freud's take on Oedipus had become so widespread that no academic, even one far outside the field of psychology, could ignore it.

And just what is Freud's take on Oedipus? If I say that Freud sees the Oedipus myth as an echo of the Oedipus complex—a universal desire of children to kill one parent and marry the other—a Freudian might say this is oversimplified. And it is! But the versions of Freud's theories that reached the public were always oversimplified. Parents become obstacles children must overcome. Parents become objects and victory conditions. In one of his novels, Mark Leyner offers as a formula for success: "Everything you do must be an act of patricide. You must always kill the father. Every song you sing, every sentence you write, every leaf you rake must kill the father." Leyner is joking, but the best jokes aren't far from the truth.

Here's a counterproposal, from the Finnish folklorist Edvard Westermarck. In the 1890s he hypothesized, as a source for incest taboos, ancient Greek or otherwise, that children simply never become sexually attracted to people they live near in their earliest years. This hypothetical "Westermarck effect" explains several problems. In general: Why don't you want to have sex with your siblings? More specifically: Why did the Israeli kibbutz system, which raised children communally, sibling-like, fail to produce marriages within the kibbutz, despite the twin incentives of convenience and societal pressure? The Westermarck effect prevented kibbutzniks from thinking about the other people in their kibbutz as anything other than family. They didn't want to marry family members, so they had to look further afield to find potential mates; they had to marry people from other kibbutzim.

The Freudian theory seems to be in direct opposition to Westermarck's. But Steven Pinker has pointed out that Freud had had, as any upper-class Austrian would, a wet nurse and a governess, and he may have done all his Westermarck-style imprinting on his nannies instead of his own mother. It's possible that if you asked Freud about being sexually attracted to a governess, he would have told you that was a sick and vile thought.

Freud always called his governess his "second mother."

III.

I once heard Freud invoked as one of the four horsemen of modernism—the other three being Darwin, Marx, and Einstein. Modernism is sometimes branded as a Jewish movement, and of course three quarters of the horsemen here are Jewish—but they're not *very Jewish*. Einstein said he could not be a Jew because Jews believed in free will and he was a determinist; Freud didn't even bother getting his children circumcised; Marx, worst of all, was baptized a Lutheran! Certainly, some of the antipathy toward Freud has traditionally been simply displaced (!) anti-Semitism. The Nazis, never ones to displace their anti-Semitism, harried Freud out of Austria, and he died (like Marx) in exile in England. So just to be extra careful, let's take a moment to drive home what a fraud and a fake Freud really was.

Before there was the unconscious, there was cocaine. All of Freud's early work was done while high. But Freud was not only a coke addict; he was also a pusher. He sent cocaine samples to friends and family. He endorsed its use for cases of depression or heart disease. He produced the first scientific paper on the drug, written only two months after being introduced to cocaine (but nevertheless implying a long and fruitful acquaintance), extolling its virtues. Freud believed cocaine was a miracle cure for many afflictions, but most of all for morphine addiction. He trumpeted his success in using cocaine to break the morphine cravings of his friend Ernst Fleischl von Marxow, but the trumpeting was premature—which is what happens when you write a paper about a drug two months after learning about it—and actually his novel treatment just got Fleischl addicted to morphine *and* cocaine. Fleischl in fact developed such a coke habit, and ordered such quantities of cocaine from the pharmaceutical manufacturer Merck that Merck assumed he was using it as part of a medical study. It was actually all for Fleischl's use, but Fleischl couldn't admit that; he pretended to be a researcher in collaboration with Dr. Freud—and Freud played along. He had no choice, really; he'd been delivering lectures in which Fleischl's "morphine cure" was the centerpiece, and if Fleischl was revealed to be an addict, those lectures would lose their bite.

Well, Freud did have a choice, actually. But he chose to lie. It was a lucrative choice: Soon Freud was actually working for Merck itself. He continued, not coincidentally, to sing paeans to the wonder drug his employer was selling. He wrote popular articles in several countries encouraging their citizens to start taking cocaine. All the while he watched his friend Fleischl, who was now injecting his cocaine subcutaneously along with his morphine, sicken and die.

It was a different time back then, of course; it was the 1880s. Cocaine was perfectly legal, and nobody knew it was dangerous. One reason they didn't know it was dangerous was that Freud, the international face of cocaine, kept lying about its side effects. But as the popular tide turned against the drug, Freud realized the cocaine gravy train might not carry him forever. He'd need something else.

That something else was the unconscious, but it's not the unconscious as Freud eventually presented it. Freud's original scheme involved dredging up repressed memories from his patients' infancies. These memories, as curated by Freud, always seemed to reveal a history of violent childhood molestation. When "recovered memories" had a second wave of faddishness in the 1980s, it led to a spate of implausible accusations of "Satanic ritual abuse." Well, Freud spent the waning years of the nineteenth century digging up similarly unbelievable stories and attributing their widespread and ludicrous details to what he called the "remnant of a primeval sexual cult . . . a primitive devil religion with rites that are carried on secretly." Needless to say, the primitive rites of "Moloch" were all in the head . . . of Freud's patients, perhaps, but of Freud himself especially. When Freud presented his Moloch theories at a lecture to the Viennese Circle for Psychiatry and Neurology, he was greeted with incredulity. The great Richard von Krafft-Ebing dismissed Freud's lecture as a "fairy tale"—perhaps because its conclusions were so silly, and perhaps because the data was so clearly shoddy. There simply wasn't very much of it.

At his presentation, Freud claimed he had eighteen cases' worth of evidence; but a month before, he had admitted to his friend Wilhelm Fliess that he had "not finished a single case." As late as 1897 Freud would confide in Fliess that in eleven years in the practice, he had *never success-fully completed a patient's treatment.*

IV.

Freud's friends and colleagues presented him, on his fiftieth birthday, with a medallion inscribed in Greek: "He divined the famous riddle and was a most mighty man"—a line from *Oedipus the King.* Oedipus divined the famous riddle. Oedipus was a most mighty man.

Make of *that* what you will.

V.

Here's a puzzle for you (I don't know the answer): How do frauds get it right? The Brothers Grimm faked all their research and then lied to cover it up—and yet their collection of fairy tales is a masterpiece of world literature—the bestselling German-language book in history.

Similarly: If Freud was, at best, confessing his own secret desires obliquely, and at worst just making things up, how did his model of the unconscious prove to be such a useful one?

Let's look at an earlier writer who had his fair share of psychological insights. Let's see what St. Paul says about a divided consciousness: "If then I do that which I would not," he says, "then it is no more I that do it, but sin that dwelleth in me" (Romans 7:16, 17). There's been a lot of ink spilled over the meaning of this passage, but the clearest meaning is that the will or the self is simply not divided; if it appears to be divided, this is because of what sin wills, and not because of what *I* will.

St. Augustine is often (justly) lauded as the greatest psychologist of the ancient world, and he spent his fair share of time puzzling over Paul's passage in Romans. In his *Confessions,* he asks how it is that we can fail to do things we want to do (such as, you know, avoiding sin). We are free to tear out our hair and bang our head against the ground if we choose to (these are his examples), because the body obeys the mind; but we cannot choose to change our mind, because if the mind were to tell itself to choose something, it would already be chosen! The mind cannot obey the mind any more than the mind can disobey the mind; the mind obeying the mind is redundant. Augustine explains this "monster" (his word) of a situation by positing that there are two wills (*duae voluntates*) and neither one is complete, for if either were complete, it would simply do what it wants to do.

This is better—I don't say more accurate, because I have no idea what the will or the self is really like, but *more useful*. Augustine's model works pretty well to explain people's actions, and it's all anyone had for a millennium and a half.

Freud's model, of drives in tension, shuffled around by an unconscious that seeks to appease as many of them as possible without letting the conscious mind know what's going on and thereby spoil the game— isn't this *much more useful*? Doesn't that explain things better than Augustine? If you've ever accused someone of rationalizing, or of being passive-aggressive—if you've even found these pop-psychology concepts apt—you have implicitly affirmed a structure of the psyche that divides against itself, Freud-like. Every time you've picked a fight with a loved one over some minor point because the real issue was too upsetting to bring up—if you weren't aware you were doing it, that's Freud's model working in your head.

The great insights of the twentieth century's great thinkers would be inconceivable without Freud. When Eric Hoffer writes that missionaries proselytize not because they are certain their religion is correct, but because they are uncertain and need to convince themselves; when René Girard writes that we seek something not because we desire it, but because we want to grow closer to another person who also desires it; they are building on a foundation that Freud laid.

Yes, yes, of course this foundation as presented above is just an oversimplification of Freud's model, but an oversimplification is all you need to explain a lot of the world. To be fair, that was an oversimplification of Augustine's model, or Paul's model, as well; I'm not a philosopher of mind here—and neither is the average American, who's learned about Freud from magazine articles or internet quizzes. The point is that Freud helped a lot of people see the world, and themselves, more clearly, which is puzzling if he was a total fraud.

And if the Oedipal complex is just Freud's own mental problems made public (and what is more Freudian than accidentally exposing your own weird family dynamics to the world while convincing yourself you're just "doing science"?), why is the second half of the twentieth century so . . . Oedipal?

The answer to the first question may lie in Freud's habitual plagiarism. The unconscious was neither discovered nor invented by Freud; it was a useful idea whose time had come by the late nineteenth century, and Freud jumped on its bandwagon. His first bandwagon, cocaine, had proved an embarrassing nonstarter, so on his second try he got the unconscious.

Among Freud's more obvious precursors in plumbing the unconscious was the German philosopher and self-styled psychologist Friedrich Nietzsche. Freud simply popularized some of Nietzsche's insights until they became conventional wisdom. Nietzsche was a deeper thinker than Freud, but he was the polar opposite of a popularizer, writing in a playful, difficult, aphoristic style. "In the mountains the shortest way is from peak to peak," he wrote, "but for that route thou must have long legs." He meant that his writing offered, to those few who were long-legged enough to handle it, the opportunity to travel from the highest idea to the highest idea, with no nonsense slogging around in the valleys in between. By definition, this is not for everyone. Freud repeatedly claimed he had never read Nietzsche, but the evidence shows he was lying; he may have been lying to himself. As Nietzsche wrote: "'I have done that,' says my memory. 'I cannot have done that'—says my pride, and remains adamant. At last—memory yields."

Freud the popularizer is clearly a success in a way that Freud the doctor was not. Sigmund Freud was, and remains, the paradigmatic psychologist, as surely as Houdini is the paradigmatic escape artist. When the paradigmatic advice columnist Abigail "Dear Abby" Van Buren wanted to position herself as knowledgeable on psychological matters, she consulted with Franz Alexander, who was, she boasted, "a student of Freud." For the heart of America, there is no imprimatur like Dear Abby's.

Meanwhile, Freud's theories seeped into first fine arts and then pop culture. The 1945 Hitchcock thriller *Spellbound* featured a Freudian treatment, complete with the analysis of a dream sequence designed by Salvador Dalí. In 1955 EC started a comic book titled *Psychoanalysis*, which depicted, rather dryly, characters lying on couches talking. By 1959, Charlie Brown's nemesis Lucy had a booth offering "psychiatric help." By 1964, Batman could suffer from an "inferiority complex" (Superman's diagnosis) because he is not as bulletproof as other heroes. If the term "inferiority complex" doesn't sound like specifically psychoanalytic jargon, that's only a measure of how deeply such jargon has permeated popular discourse.

By the 1950s, psychologists were just expected to make sweeping generalizations about American culture. Fredric Wertham insisted that Batman comic books were making children gay. Edmund Bergler theorized that '50s high fashion was a "gigantic unconscious hoax" by homosexual men, who wanted to humiliate women with ludicrous outfits. Dr. Benjamin Spock, in a somewhat less ridiculous vein, "conceived the idea that someone going into pediatrics should have psychological training" (his words); Spock studied Freud, and America studied Spock.

This iron grip Freudian analysis maintained on the popular consciousness explains the pervasiveness of the Oedipal complex as well. As St. Paul says, "I had not known sin, but by the law" (Romans 7:7b); and no one had known to kill that father, but by Freud. To put it another way, by the 1940s, every educated person in the West knew that children "should" or "would" develop along Oedipal lines. For the first time in history, a generation was raised by parents who just assumed their children were filled with Oedipal lust and rage.

Very few children born in the '40s murdered one of their parents—Charles Whitman did, but he had a brain tumor—and even fewer married one. But every single one of them knew on some level that *it was expected of them.* As early as 1954 psychologist Erik Erikson fretted that psychotherapy might have become a cure for the few, but a disease for the many.

The hoods of the 1950s and the hippies of the 1960s implicitly or explicitly sought to overthrow the achievements of their parents. You cannot kill the father literally, but you can unmake his civilization; you can make him despair. It would be trivial to dig up testimonials of the scandal, outrage, and despair Baby Boomers evoked from their parents. Since I have my Dear Abby clippings handy from the Franz Alexander example above, let's see how she characterizes this generation: as "using X-rated language and wearing ragged clothing, long hair, and unkempt beards—and looking for all the world as if they were on their way to a meeting to overthrow the government." If you can't see overthrowing the government as a stand-in for overthrowing your parents, you should probably read more pop psychology.

Dear Abby is being unfair, of course; but perhaps it will be fairer to talk about music. Here's a quick metric for how important music was to "youth" identity in the late '60s. It involves Archie comics.

In 1966, Archie Comics Group published *1.* a bunch of monthly titles about Archie Andrews and his teenage friends; *2. She's Josie,* about the slightly older gang in Midvale; and *3. Mad House,* a surreal humor comic. *None of the characters were musicians.* By 1969, *1.* Archie and the gang had formed The Archies, a band that produced a *Billboard* number one hit single ("Sugar Sugar") despite being fictional; *2. She's Josie* had been retitled *Josie and the Pussycats,* another fictional band whose singles, although better than "Sugar Sugar," did not chart; *3. Mad House* had abandoned surreality and begun chronicling the adventures of a rock band called the Mad House Ma-ads (later the Mad House Glads); and *4.* a new series, *That Wilkin Boy,* sprang up, its titular character right from the beginning (issue 1) a member of the band the Bingoes. Neither the Ma-ads nor the Bingoes released singles. For the next two years Archie would publish *zero comics about characters who were not in a rock band.*

Music was a key part of youth culture long before 1966 of course; it just usually takes Archie comics a decade or so to get with the times. The music of Boomers' youth was rock and roll. Chuck Berry sang about studying for math tests ("School Days," 1957); the Coasters sang about doing chores for allowance money ("Yakety Yak," 1958). These are not grown-ups' concerns. No genre of music not sung by a puppet has ever been so resolutely targeted toward a youth market.

In other words, no genre of music has been so resolutely designed to irritate one's parents. This is the music Oedipus would have played, if Oedipus had had a radio. The lyrics are easiest to quote in this regard, but the form of the music is more important. Loud, thumping, simple, ambiguously ethnic, it's everything mainstream America feared and hated.

Rock and roll was not just obnoxiously Oedipal; it was designed from the get-go to be faddish (a new series of dance steps!), ephemeral, constantly replaced with a new driving hit. It was designed to kill the father not once, but *constantly*. Before rock and roll, parents and children listened to the same kind of music. The very idea of a generation gap was created in the wake of rock and roll. The phrase didn't exist before then!

Pop culture as we know it now is just the shadow of rock and roll projected onto the cave wall. Everything pop is designed to be absorbed and replaced. Fads were not invented by the Boomer era, but fads were formalized by the Boomer era. From the 1950s on, culture would no longer be a steady accumulation of "the best which has been thought and said"—it would be an eternal now, endlessly replacing the discarded corpse of yesterday.

No matter what the memes say, this is not a Boomer issue, but an ongoing process. Hippies of the '60s sought acid trips and mellow vibes, so punks of the '70s went straight-edge in a violent mosh pit. Every generation seeks to unseat its predecessor.

For Boomers, who set about killing the father in apparent unconcern that they would ever ("don't trust anyone over thirty") be in a paternal position themselves, this prospect eventually became terrifying, and they spent their waning years trying to make sure that the Beatles would forever be the best band in history. See: any list.

In 1998 Tom Brokaw put out a bestselling book called *The Greatest Generation* in praise of Baby Boomers' parents. In a fit of Oedipal rage, Boomer Leonard Steinhorn cranked out *The Greater Generation: In Defense of the Baby Boom Legacy* in praise of his peers. If you don't want to read Sophocles's *Oedipus*, just imagine Leonard Steinhorn clambering into his mother's bed while screaming, "I'm the one who belongs here! Me!" and you'll get the idea. If you don't want to read any history of the latter half of the twentieth century, just imagine the same image.

This is our world, and all this Freud wrought.

Freud reads more Sophocles → He bases his theories not on Oedipus *but* The Trachiniae → Adults love the ginchiest new tunes → OUR WORLD SHEDS ITS ANXIETY AND WE LEAD FRUITFUL, HAPPY LIVES

I.

IT IS A RARE PRIVILEGE TO BE PERMITTED TO REMAKE THE world. Freud did it, but he had a model provided by the ancient Greek playwright.

Oedipus the King is Sophocles's signature play. Samuel Taylor Coleridge declared that the three "most perfect plots ever planned" belonged to *The Alchemist* (1610), *Tom Jones* (1749), and *Oedipus* (since the plot of *Tom Jones* also concerns the protagonist sleeping with his mother, one wishes Freud could analyze Coleridge on his tastes in literature). But Sophocles is no one-hit wonder; *Antigone* may be his altogether greatest work; his finest individual passage is the monologue on time from *Ajax* ("thus the snow-strewn winters yield before fruitful summer" etc.).

And then there's *The Trachiniae*.

It's no one's pick for Sophocles's best play. The German critic August Schlegel claimed it was "so very inferior to the other pieces of Sophocles which have reached us, that I could wish there were some warrant for supposing that this tragedy was composed . . . by his son Iophon, and that it was by mistake attributed to the father." This, too, is a statement a Freudian could have made much of.

The Trachiniae tells the story of the last day of Hercules. It ends with the hero begging his son Hyllus, "Son, you've got to kill me and marry my mistress Iole" (that is not a quote but an accurate paraphrase). Hyllus dutifully arranges to have his father immolated; he agrees to take his father's place in Iole's bed. As he himself points out, doing anything else would require him to be a disobedient son. It's a tragedy, because Hercules dies, and yet Hyllus comes out of it pretty well: He's got a wife lined up; his father is dead, but the gods don't blame him.

You may notice some parallels here to Oedipus the King. You may also notice how different the two plays' endings are. Sigmund Freud, who knew his classics well, in a lifetime of writing about Sophocles, Sophocles, always Sophocles, never once mentioned The Trachiniae. He chose not to.

But of course, he could have. What if, instead of an Oedipus complex, Freud had proposed a Hyllus complex?

A Hyllus complex could maintain the dubious but crowd-pleasing concept of a childhood desire to kill or marry one's parents (Iole isn't Hyllus's stepmother, technically, but as his father's mistress she plays a similar role). But look at Hyllus—there's no anxiety. Oedipus ends his play dark and comfortless, poking his own eyes out; Hyllus ends his on his way to a wedding. Get me to the church on time.

Roughly speaking, the project of the 1960s was to remake society. Remaking society can be a fine idea; change is painful but often necessary. "Standing water," William Blake writes, "breeds reptiles of the mind."

And change was coming anyway. Two world wars had made that certain, and the sheer demographic power of postwar Boomers meant that the change would happen "on their watch," so to speak. The only question was how the change would be played out.

What followed was less an indictment of Boomers than an indictment of America for handing over its entire worldview to a drug-addicted foreigner.

For, to remain true to Sophocles, the project of the 1960s had to end with participants blind and wailing, or (later) lying dead in Colonus. You can call dead-in-Colonus an accurate summary of the 1970s if you want to be a wiseacre, but the point is that the Boomer youth movement was, as Thomas Carlyle said about *anarchy*, not only destructive but *self-destructive*. Its representatives cast out the reptiles of the mind, but they did so by getting America hooked on drugs. They freed themselves from the bondage of familial obligations by exploding the nuclear family. Their reaction to higher learning was to set the student union on fire. In this they had no choice. *They were raised in an Oedipal world.*

The decades that followed the 1960s reaped the whirlwind of the willful and deliberate ignorance sown during these heady years. In the 1960s, when Boomers' parents were still a market force, Hemingway and Faulkner would make the bestseller lists; in the 1970s, Solzhenitsyn and Bellow. By the 1980s, as Boomer spending took over the book market, the bestseller lists had become overwhelmingly movie tie-ins, Jackie Collins, Sidney Sheldon, and thrillers. Thrillers aren't necessarily bad, but they are, necessarily, escapist; after the Boomers had finished killing the father-as-literature, no attempt at treating books as anything other than shoot-em-ups or bodice rippers would survive.

It is a little unfair to blame a generation for its ignorance, when the tide of ignorance had been swelling at least from the Great War. A popular 1881 etiquette manual (*Gems of Deportment*) contained a section of books that *everyone should read* simply for general knowledge ("books you've gotta read before you die" is how we'd phrase it): After a long list of great authors that includes Dante, Goethe, and Kant, the book goes on to admit that although most of these books should be accessible even to "boys and girls," maybe a couple of them will prove challenging "the first time," and then serves up an alternate list for dummies, which starts with—the first name on the list—David Hume. Probably no etiquette book in the twentieth century, and certainly no etiquette book since the

1920s, had prescribed Kant-but-if-you're-dim-Hume. But the long, slow decay *really started showing its bones* sometime in the 1960s.

Case in point: Helen Gurley Brown's 1962 bestseller, *Sex and the Single Girl*, doesn't look, from the title, like it's going to be the smartest volume of the year; but Brown was born in 1922, so she still valued appearing intelligent. In *the first seven pages* of her book, Brown drops references to Proust, Flaubert, and Stendhal. Brown would take over the editorship of *Cosmopolitan* magazine a couple of years later, and during the three decades of her tenure she would, it is needless to say, stop citing classic French literature. At the beginning of the twentieth century, *Cosmo* had included fiction by Edith Wharton and George Bernard Shaw; by the end of the century, the only fiction it contained was literal pornography: 1962 was Proust's last waltz. Never again would the contributions of the past look nonthreatening enough to treat as anything valuable. By 1970, the Harvard Classics' perennially popular "five-foot shelf of books"—fifty volumes designed by Charles Eliot to bring the Western canon and a liberal arts education to every American's home—would be out of print.

Every generation looks like the end of the world, because every generation is the end of a world; the world that was; the world of the previous hegemony. Every generation displaces the prior, like Zeus castrating Cronus.——Of course, I only believe something this Oedipal because I live in post-Freud times and think post-Freud thoughts.

II.

Hyllus, meanwhile, is happily getting married.

This is the alternate history of the twentieth century, one in which Freud is more enamored of *The Trachiniae* than *Oedipus*. Rock and roll still rises up, like the barbarian at the gates, to overthrow the decadent complacence of fifties crooners. That's what barbarians are *for*. But rock and roll, like the Visigoths in Rome, settles down quickly. There is none of the martyrdom that rock seemed to demand. Johnny Ace, rock's first martyr in our Oedipal history (†1954), does not need to shoot himself accidentally in this Trachine history. Maybe Buddy Holly still dies—a plane crash is willed by no one, and even Glenn Miller went down that way—but Janis Joplin and Jimi Hendrix and Mama Cass survive. If anyone's going to die young, it will be for the old Romantic reasons—Shelley in the deeps, Byron in the war. The Rolling Stones' Brian Jones drowning in his swimming pool is a poor parody of Percy Bysshe Shelley fighting the storms of the Tyrrhenian Sea in a tiny skiff.

Hippies (stereotypes tell us) became, fifteen years later, yuppies. *Any Oedipal society will be unsustainable.* But a Trachine society would be under no such stricture. Hercules gets killed by his son, sure, but he arranges it so that there's a peaceful transfer of authority. The Trachine generation would aim to reform society more cautiously; that society, then, would not be abandoned, nor overthrown in its turn. Oedipus never looks to the future; Oedipus is *blind.* Shortsightedness is also the great vice of modern times. But Hyllus needs to plan ahead. He's got a family to look after.

To put it bluntly: There's no need for Trachines to assassinate political leaders (JFK/MLK/RFK). They know that leaders will step down when the times comes. At the right moment, Hercules climbs onto the pyre.

III.

We are so steeped in an Oedipal worldview that this change, a change in the very way we think, is the most difficult to imagine. In a Hyllus world we would all have different brains. Only dimly can we perceive a more stable, less anxious society, where every step toward the New Jerusalem is not followed by two steps away.

The old definition of comedy is a play that ends in a marriage; so, for Hyllus, hand in hand with Iole, the tragedy *Trachiniae* is literally a comedy.

Imagine generations growing up under the wake of the Hyllus complex. Imagine the twentieth century as a comedy. Imagine people happy.

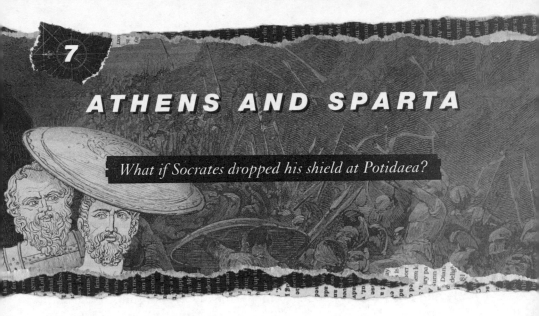

7

ATHENS AND SPARTA

What if Socrates dropped his shield at Potidaea?

POTIDAEA, 432 BC

I.

Hollywood keeps making movies about historical events, and then everyone else keeps writing articles pointing out how the movies get everything wrong. But we rarely mention Hollywood's most common blunder, which is its insistence (Liz Taylor is Cleopatra! Clark Gable is Fletcher Christian!) that history is made by attractive people. Movie stars are hardly a representative sample of the modern populace, let alone of the people of a bygone era—who lived before orthodontia, so their teeth were snaggled, before vaccines, so their skin was pocked, before proper nutrition, so their stunted bodies shuffled about on gouty feet. Also (with some exceptions) they never bathed.

To be fair, one must admit that if you go back far enough, people did not have cavities—at least in Europe. Their gnarled teeth may have been *damaged*—Don Quixote irritated people enough that some shepherds knocked out "three or four of his cheek teeth"—but they never rotted out, because sugar was rare or unobtainable. Medieval skulls, in contrast with skulls from the eighteenth century, are filled with gleaming, pearly teeth. But cavities aside, there's no reason to believe everyone was attractive.

Of course, history is *sometimes* made by attractive people. Kings and queens are always getting flattered, so we can be suspicious even when one is singled out for beauty: King David of Israel (1 Samuel 16:12), say, or Queen Zenobia of Palmyra ("the most lovely as well as the most heroic of her sex," says Edward Gibbon) or King Magnus Sigurdsson ("more handsome than any other man who was then in Norway," says Snorre Sturlason) or Marie Antoinette ("glittering like the morning star" says Edmund Burke, who at least saw her with his own eyes). But when history claims that a commoner or even a minor noble is the best-looking person around, perhaps then we may believe it. After all, *someone* has to be the best-looking in any time period.

Sir Everard Digby was known as the handsomest man in England in 1605. He tried to kill his own king, James I, with a gunpowder bomb. John Wilkes Booth, the celebrated actor, was billed as "the handsomest man in America." Everyone knows what *he* got up to. And then there was Alcibiades, the handsomest man in ancient Athens, who never tried to blow up his own king, or shoot his own president, but you get the feeling he would have liked to. It's the kind of thing he would have done, if he'd had access to gunpowder.

Alcibiades was one of history's greatest rascals. Dante imagined Brutus and Cassius trapped at the lowest point of hell because they betrayed Julius Caesar. That's only one betrayal! But Alcibiades betrayed everyone, one after another. And his good buddy Socrates saved his life at the Battle of Potidaea, which, oddly enough, made Europeans hate the concept of democracy for two thousand years.

II.

Democracy got a bad name because of one moment in one battle in one ancient war: the Peloponnesian War, a generation-long conflict between the two greatest cities of ancient Greece, Athens and Sparta. Usually when we read about things that happened in a distant country almost two and a half millennia ago, we read neutrally and dispassionately; but no one has ever read about the Peloponnesian War without taking sides. Americans have tended to root for Athens, a democracy that fights against a monarchy. The British have also tended to root for Athens, a sea empire (and democracy) that fights a more militaristic state with a larger army but smaller navy.

And actually, *everyone* in recent centuries has rooted for Athens, because by all the rules of narrative they look like the good guys. Sparta spent all its time thinking about war; Athens spent all its time thinking about art. It doesn't hurt that our image of ancient Greece is shaped by Athenian writers. Name an ancient Greek writer and you have about a 75% chance of naming someone who lived in Athens: Plato, Aristotle, Sophocles, Aeschylus, Euripides, Aristophanes, Herodotus, Thucydides, Xenophon. The other 25% you might have named (Homer, Hesiod, Sappho) weren't Athenian, but they all lived before Athens was a great power, or even a democracy.

Lord Macaulay claims that "all the noblest creations of the human intellect"—he specifically mentions works of Shakespeare, Dante, and Cervantes as examples—are "directly or indirectly" descended from the genius of Athenian letters; while Sparta (Macaulay continues) has a governmental system so bonkers that it looks like something out of *Gulliver's Travels.*

One of those writers Macaulay loved so much is in fact our chief source about the Peloponnesian War: the Athenian general Thucydides, whose account of the war is the Western canon's most influential history book not written by Herodotus. Thucydides was not necessarily pleased with his home country during the book's composition, as his history was written while he was in exile—exiled for incompetence in the field, probably, although since our best source on this is, again, Thucydides, you can see why he'd keep the details vague. But his hometown biases can't help but seep through into the history. Even our name of the war is taken from Thucydides, and represents his point of view: This war was only a "Peloponnesian War" from the perspective of Athens; the Spartans, who lived on the Peloponnesian peninsula, probably called it the "Athenian War."

You'll notice that the list of famous Athenian writers above did not include Socrates—by necessity, as he was not a writer. He taught that the invention of writing had made people stupider, and he never wrote anything down himself, leaving the task of recording his thought to his students—just as other great teachers in history did, such as Buddha or Pythagoras or Jesus or the father of modern linguistics, Ferdinand de Saussure. Socrates's most famous student was Plato (whose most famous student was Aristotle, whose most famous student was Alexander the Great, who had such an educational pedigree he was able to *conquer the world*), but Socrates had many other famous students, including (and this will be important) that handsome rogue Alcibiades.

In the fourth century BC, Greece was divided up into innumerable independent city-states, each pretty much free to follow its own course—in theory. In actuality, a great many Greek cities were tied up in alliances— generally, in the fifth century, with Athens or Sparta, the polar opposites of the Greek world. And then in 435 BC, something went wrong in a remote city far up the west coast of Greece, in what is today Albania. In later years, Romans would find the city's name unlucky—it looks like *damnum*, the Latin word for damage or loss (and source of our word *damnation*)—and rename the place Dyrrachium, but to the Greeks it was Epidamnos. What "went wrong" was just an internal squabble between two Epidamnian factions, which history would scarcely have noticed, except that each faction called upon the aid of another city, Corcyra and Corinth.

Corcyra was allied with Athens, Corinth with Sparta.

The Peloponnesian War is often compared to World War I, and this is the first reason: In both cases *1.* a series of alliances and treaties lets *2.* an obscure conflict in a peripheral state *3.* drag the great powers into a drawn-out war. The great powers here were Athens and Sparta, and Corcyra and Corinth dragged them, somewhat reluctantly, into war.

III.

Although the Athenians started the war with the advantage of vast wealth, a navy, and a trans-Aegean empire, the Spartans started the war

with the advantage of being Spartans. They were the most feared warriors in Greece, because while most Greek cities filled their armies with
part-time conscripts, the core of the Spartan army were the Spartiates, a
eugenically crafted, carefully trained caste of warriors.

I don't say "eugenically crafted" lightly, by the way; the Spartans
raised only the strongest of babies. Calling this practice *eugenics* may be
an anachronism, but Ernst Haeckel, the nineteenth-century German
Darwinist who influenced Hitler's eugenic schemes, singled out for praise
Sparta's propensity for infanticide, crediting it with their "rough heroic
valor (for which they are eminent in ancient history)."

The Spartiates were exclusive. You could not *become* a Spartiate, you
had to be born one, born to a family of Spartiates. The Spartan constitution contained no provisions for creating new Spartiates, although it did
feature plenty of provisions for demoting cowardly or disgraced families.
Throughout Spartan history, Spartiates were a dwindling resource (both
from demotions, and because warriors tend to die in battle), and even
in the fifth century, when they were still near their maximum capacity,
they were still rather rare; most people in Sparta were slaves, or serf-like
semi-slaves.

Spartiates might have been rare, but they were terrifying. Most Greek
soldiers cropped their hair short, so no one could grab it in hand-to-hand
combat, but the Spartans wore it long, as a sign of contempt for their foes.
All other major Greek cities were walled, but Sparta's buildings sat out in
the open, and the Spartans bragged that their only wall was their Spartiates.

While the Athenians were great talkers, the Spartans gave us the
word *laconic* (after Laconia, the region Sparta is located in) because they
eschewed prolixity. Herodotus provides this illustration: In the sixth century, exiles from Samos came to Sparta and delivered a speech asking for
assistance: a long, flowery speech, as was the custom at the time. When
the Samians finished speaking, the Spartans said they had already forgotten the first half of the speech and could not understand the second.
The Samians reconvened to discuss strategy, and the next day returned

to the Spartans and held up an empty sack. "The sack needs grain," they said.

The Spartans had one critique. "There was no need to say 'the sack,'" they pointed out. But they assisted the exiles anyway.

So the Spartans had the army and the Spartans had the laconism. Pit that against the Athenians' economic and naval power, and it turns out you have roughly a draw. After a decade of Peloponnesian fighting, both sides were exhausted; the Athenian general Nicias brokered a peace; everyone decided there was no reason to fight anymore.

Everyone except Alcibiades.

IV.

The Greco-Roman biographer Plutarch tells a revealing story about Alcibiades's youth. About to be pinned in a wrestling match, Alcibiades bit his opponent and thereby slipped the hold. Understandably incensed, the opponent accused Alcibiades of fighting like a girl. Alcibiades corrected him: He had fought *like a lion*.

Alcibiades came from a famous family, and when his father died, the boy was raised by the great Athenian statesman Pericles himself. That celebrated beauty of his brought Alcibiades many admirers from among the greats of the day, but the main influence on his life was Socrates, his mentor and (probably) lover. Socrates, remember, had saved his life at the Potidaea. He also tried, we might say, to save the younger man's soul. Socrates believed that philosophy could show one how to be just and happy. He attempted to teach Alcibiades virtue (Alcibiades appears in several of Plato's dialogues, most notably the *Symposium,* and two, perhaps apocryphal, are even named after him); but Alcibiades was a wayward student. "In his boyhood," wrote Bion of Olbia, Alcibiades "drew the husbands from their wives and as a young man the wives from their husbands." Socratic virtue was never going to be his specialty.

In those days philosophers were expected to live their teachings. When King Nicocreon of Salamis condemned the philosopher Anaxarchus to be killed in a giant mortar and pestle, the philosopher laughed at the idea that mere destruction of his body could hurt him. "You can pound the sheath of Anaxarchus," he told the king. "Anaxarchus himself you cannot pound." Incensed, Nicocreon ordered the philosopher's tongue cut out, so Anaxarchus obligingly bit it off and spat it at the king. Such should be a philosopher's contempt for worldly power!

Worldly power was precisely what Alcibiades did not hold in contempt. He was ambitious, unscrupulous, impious, and impulsive. His life of ostentatious debauchery scandalized the Athenians. But withal he was so generous, so brilliant in his oratory, so successful in diplomatic missions for the state, so unprecedentedly victorious at the Olympics—his horses swept first, second, third, and fourth place in the chariot races (although other ancient sources say only first, second, and fourth, which is still not bad)—that the Athenians justified his excesses as boyish high spirits. In order to get his house decorated, he imprisoned the famous painter Agatharcus inside until he had painted the walls; but then he released Agatharcus with a great reward for his services, and everyone treated it as a prank, not a crime.

War is a great opportunity for ambitious men, and Alcibiades was counting on the Peloponnesian War as his chance for greatness. He was just starting to make a name for himself when Nicias proposed his peace. Peace would thwart all Alcibiades's plans for glory, and he lobbied hard against it. In fact, when that lobbying failed, and the Peloponnesian War ended, Alcibiades persuaded the Athenians to start a new war on the faraway island of Sicily.

Sicily and Greece don't seem so distant to us, but travel was a lot harder in those days. The *Odyssey* is an epic poem about a guy trying to get from the Dardanelles to Ithaca, a few hundred miles away, and it takes him ten years; the *Aeneid* is an epic poem about a guy trying to get from the Dardanelles to Italy, which only goes a little better. Sicily was on the frontier of the Greek world; not the most far-flung Greek colony—there were Greek cities as far as modern Spain—but still one to two weeks' sail from Athens by the fastest boats and under optimum conditions.

Even Alcibiades couldn't invent a war out of whole cloth, but he didn't need to. An Athenian ally on Sicily, the city of Segesta, was already at war with Syracuse, Sicily's most powerful city-state, and the Segestans turned to Athens for help. Segesta offered Athens a vast sum of money—more than the city actually possessed, it turned out—and the inducement of practicality: Syracuse was a Spartan ally, Syracusan dominion over Sicily could throw the balance of power over to the Peloponnesians, in which case peace would not last.

General Nicias, predictably, spoke against the enterprise. Athens had just finished a long decade at war, and there was no need to throw themselves in for another round. But Alcibiades used his considerable charisma to argue that a small fleet to Sicily offered Athens great gains with little risk. The depleted Athenian treasury could definitely use the Segestans' money, and the strategic importance of checking Syracuse's expansion was worth danger to a few ships. Once the Athenians landed, Alcibiades predicted, the rest of Sicily would rise up and join them in battling Syracuse, so most of the actual fighting would be done by others. Despite Nicias's naysaying, the Athenians listened to Alcibiades and voted to send a small expeditionary force. Nicias and Alcibiades were to share command.

And then Nicias pulled one of his patented boneheaded moves. Although by all accounts a skilled general and an honest man, he had a weakness: He kept trying to manipulate people to achieve his own goals, and the attempts kept backfiring. Back in 425, when his rival Cleon had criticized Nicias for failing to capture a band of Spartan soldiers trapped on the island of Sphacteria, Nicias had said, "Well, if you think it's so easy to do, why don't you do it?" He thought this would shut Cleon up, but Cleon went ahead and captured the surviving soldiers and brought them back to Athens. Nicias was humiliated, but he had brought it on himself. And yet he would try such tactics again and again, and always they would blow up in his face.

So as Athens prepared to sail to Sicily, Nicias spoke up at the Athenian Assembly and tried one last time to talk them into calling it off. He painted a bleak picture of the fleet's chances. He spoke of the vast power of Syracuse, whose soldiers would be fighting on their home ground. He pointed out that the tiny force the Athenians were sending would be helpless against the Syracusan cavalry. Finally, one of Alcibiades's allies, Demostratus, challenged Nicias: If the current expedition was too small to fight Syracuse, what size did Nicias consider sufficient? Nicias gave a deliberately inflated answer—double the number of ships, with concomitant increases in soldiery—assuming the Athenians would give up in despair. Instead the Athenians agreed with him. Nicias found himself sailing off in joint command of an armada of a hundred triremes, with five thousand hoplites (heavy infantry), and a much larger number of light infantry. It was not the last such blunder in Nicias's career.

The generals had scarcely reached Sicily when Alcibiades learned he had been recalled to Athens. In Greece in those days, boundaries were marked with sacred posts called *herms*, on which the head and genitals of Hermes were carved, and shortly before the fleet sailed, someone had broken the genitals off some Athenian herms. Evidence (perhaps trumped up; it's hard to conduct an investigation so many centuries later) pointed to a night of drunken vandalism by Alcibiades and his friends, and the general was being recalled to stand trial.

Now, the Athenians were not always merciful to generals brought to trial. Thucydides, remember, had been exiled. Only a couple of years earlier, when the court announced a verdict, the convicted general Paches (in the words of Plutarch) "drew his sword in the very court-room and slew himself" rather than face a sentence. A few years later in the war, six generals would be executed en masse for their failure at the Battle of Arginusae. Alcibiades may have feared that he would not get a fair trial, with his friends and allies busy in Sicily. He may also have been guilty. In any event, he dutifully set sail back to Athens, and then secretly changed course for Sparta . . .

. . . where he offered his services to the Spartan king. All the Spartans had to do to triumph over Athens, he told them, was put him in charge— Alcibiades, the great general!

Alcibiades would indeed prove to be a great general—but, and this is what is amazing, when he arrived in Sparta he was not a great general yet. His victories had all been diplomatic. Militarily, his only leadership position had been on the Sicilian expedition, and that was just getting started. He was just an attractive traitor with a high opinion of his own merits.

An even greater monkey wrench in Alcibiades's plan was that Sparta had no reason to give even a great general sanctuary, as Athens and Sparta were still at peace. But peace, you will recall, was anathema to Alcibiades. He tried to rile the Spartans up against Athens, telling them that the Athenians' Sicilian expedition was not a simple contest with Syracuse: It was step one in a secret plan to conquer Carthage and southern Italy, creating a western Athenian empire to match its empire in the East. Athens would then, Alcibiades claimed, use its even greater wealth and manpower to come back and crush Sparta once and for all.

None of this could be even remotely true. Alcibiades was the one who'd pitched the war with Syracuse, and even if he had secretly intended to expand it to include the Carthaginian empire (which would probably have been suicidal), he sure hadn't told the rest of Athens that plan.

Whether the Spartans believed Alcibiades or not, they just couldn't help liking that dashing rogue. Alcibiades grew his hair long to fit in, began eating plain meals like a Spartan, and adopted all the simple habits of the city. And although the Spartans did not, as he encouraged them to, launch a large-scale operation in Sicily, they did send one ship to check up on what the Athenians were up to.

Not much, it turns out.

V.

Everyone wants to follow the madcap adventures of that dashing rogue Alcibiades, but we need to take a moment to pursue the sorry fate of that poor, honest schmuck Nicias.

Without Alcibiades, Nicias was left in senior command, and Nicias didn't even want to be in Sicily in the first place! Under his leadership, the Athenian fleet sailed around Sicily, looking impressive—but accomplishing nothing. The fleet was so large that cities Athens had assumed would be friendly were instead intimidated, and barred the ships from their harbors. Nicias (predictably) tried negotiating with Syracuse, instead of attacking it—with little success. He didn't seem comfortable in his command. Sailing across the Mediterranean on a madcap mission was much more an Alcibiades thing; for all his skill, Nicias couldn't perform effectively when he was acting against his nature.

Finally, after about a year of ineffective actions, Nicias settled down to besieging Syracuse at last. The Athenians surrounded the city's harbor and began building a wall around the city, to prevent supplies or reinforcements from arriving.

Fighting alongside the Athenians at the siege of Syracuse were soldiers of the allied city-state of Argos, and they managed to pressure Athens into sending some ships, in return, to help Argos harry the coast of its ancient enemy, Sparta. Just a few ships. A small operation, but a significant one, because it violated the peace. The war was back on, and this time Alcibiades would be fighting for the Spartans.

And that one ship that Alcibiades had encouraged the Spartans to send to check out the situation in Sicily? It happened to arrive just as the Athenians had almost completed their wall to seal the Syracusans in. The force the Spartan ship brought was negligible, but its effect on the morale of Syracuse was profound. The newly arrived Spartan general rallied the exhausted local troops and managed, in a few skirmishes, to seize the Athenian supply depot and treasury. This delayed Athenian operations long enough for a fleet to arrive from Corinth, another Syracusan ally. The Athenians had come within a hair of taking Syracuse, but now they found themselves outmaneuvered and outnumbered.

Nicias wanted to give up and return to Athens while he still could. But he knew, as Alcibiades had, how unforgiving the Athenians could be to an unsuccessful general. He decided to try one of his patented tricks again, sending a message back to Athens describing the dire straits the Athenian army was in. He said that Athens should either send a whole lot of reinforcements or recall its forces. He was confident that the Assembly would vote for the recall, in which case the dishonor of abandoning the plan would be on the people of Athens, not on Nicias.

It didn't work out that way, of course. The Athenians voted to commit more ships. Nicias had done his best to describe how bleak the situation in Sicily was, but the Athenians must have been confident that they could fight their way back to victory. They sent seventy-three more ships—the bulk of Athens's remaining navy—to Sicily, with five thousand more hoplites and three thousand more archers.

But the tide had turned against the Athenians. Sparta was sending its own reinforcements to Sicily; after all, the two cities were now at war again, and they may as well fight on foreign soil as on Greek. Nicias was ill, and failed to coordinate well with the incoming generals. The next seven months would see the Athenian forces trying desperately—not to conquer Syracuse, but merely to stay alive. In the end, they failed even at that. The great Athenian expeditionary force, together with its reinforcements, lay dead on the battlefield. The survivors were worked to death in the Sicilian silver mines, a long, agonizing, and humiliating death. Nicias himself was executed by the Syracusans, although their Spartan allies wanted to take him alive to Sparta in chains.

What few Athenians escaped managed it by a novel method. The plays of Euripides were popular in Sicily, but his latest works had not made it across the Mediterranean yet. Many of the Athenians had seen the newer plays performed before they sailed. By reciting or acting out scenes from new Euripides productions, some Athenians were able to buy their freedom from Syracuse, along with transport home.

VI.

The disaster in Sicily shook the Greek world. Athens lost its army and navy and was practically defenseless, with a handful of ships and a depleted treasury. Surely Athens would fall! But Athens had its famous unbreachable city walls, it had its overseas holdings, and soon it managed to build a new fleet. Sparta seemed at last to be realizing it had no way to win this war, no matter how many Athenians they killed.

But Sparta had Alcibiades, who knew Athens's weak spots. He knew, for example, that its empire was resentful of being bled dry in this long war. Soon he was traveling through the Athenian empire with a Spartan fleet, persuading cities to rise up in rebellion against their Athenian overlords. Every city he visited was one less ally for Athens, one more for Sparta. It turned out, perhaps to no one's surprise, that Alcibiades was really good at convincing people to betray their allies. At a time when Spartan morale was at an ebb, Alcibiades was there to turn things around for them.

But as much good as Alcibiades did for Sparta, he could not count on their protection forever, because Alcibiades would not be Alcibiades if he was not biting the hand that fed him. During his time in Sparta he'd been having an affair with the Spartan queen, and she had given birth to a son she'd taken to calling Alcibiades. The Spartan king was not pleased and tried to arrange Alcibiades's assassination.

Since Alcibiades was wanted dead by both sides of the conflict, he decided to defect from Sparta to Persia. This was not so great a leap: Persia was nominally allied with Sparta, and Alcibiades himself had helped negotiate the alliance, through the Persian satrap Tissaphernes. Now Alcibiades insinuated himself with the satrap, who controlled most of western Asia Minor, and quickly became his favorite. Tissaphernes even renamed his beloved pleasure park for the Athenian. Alcibiades was technically still on the same side as the Spartans, but he spent all his time with Tissaphernes. After four years of Spartan living, he wanted to enjoy the luxuries of Persia. Also, he needed to get a secret message off to Athens.

Athens, meanwhile, had been having a bad time of it, but despite a massive loss of manpower, despite the slow disintegration of their empire, they were still in the game. And then select Athenian noblemen got word from Alcibiades that he was looking to let bygones be bygones—and more importantly that he could bring Persia into the war on Athens's side. It must have been a huge relief to the beleaguered Athenian nobles. All they had to do, Alcibiades suggested, was overthrow the Athenian democracy that had condemned him and institute an oligarchy—Persians would never deal with a democracy—and Alcibiades would come sailing to the rescue, backed by the might of Persia.

There was no way Alcibiades could do this, of course. Tissaphernes might name a park for Alcibiades, but even if he had the authority to go to war for him—which was doubtful—doing so was, to put it mildly, a lot more to ask of a friendship. The nobles of Athens did successfully overthrow the democratic government, just as Alcibiades asked, mostly by assassinating a bunch of democrats, and they set up an oligarchic regime called the Four Hundred after the number of oligarchs. But when it had become clear that Alcibiades could not deliver the Persian forces, they abandoned him. They'd had their coup without him.

The Athenian forces were now divided: Athens was in the hands of the oligarchs, but the rebuilt Athenian navy, docked at Samos, was still ruled by democrats. And there was still Sparta to reckon with! Athens seemed doomed.

But Alcibiades saved the day. No one knew of his secret role in instigating the oligarchic uprising, so he passed himself off as the savior of democracy. He came to Samos with promises (all false) of imminent Persian intervention and took control of the Athenian forces. The Athenian navy wanted to sail directly to Athens and oust the oligarchs, but Alcibiades persuaded them that a civil war in the middle of a larger war would be suicidal. Nevertheless, his arrival, his speech, and his empty promises about the Phoenician fleet started a chain reaction. The Four Hundred oligarchs panicked at the idea of having to fight off Alcibiades and plotted to betray the city by opening the gates to Sparta first. The Spartan army, invited by the Four Hundred, came so close to Athens that the citizenry panicked in turn, and rose up against the four hundred oligarchs; it wasn't much of a fight, as there were a lot more than four hundred Athenians. Before Sparta could get into the city, the Four Hundred were no more. Soon Athens was a democracy again; the new government rubber-stamped Alcibiades's stewardship of its navy. Alcibiades had betrayed himself full circle, and was now fighting for his homeland again. All he had to do was win this endless war.

He put in a solid effort. Off the coast of Abydos, near the Bosporus, he led a small fleet up to a battle in progress, feigning that his ships were Spartan reinforcements and only at the last minute hoisting the Athenian flag, sending the Spartan navy into a panic and winning the day for the Athenians. At the naval battle off the nearby the city of Cyzicus, Alcibiades split his forces and with a few ships lured the Spartan fleet into an ambush. This battle was even more decisive: The Spartan admiral Mindarus was killed, and Spartan forces were driven from the area. Since the Bosporus was the route of Athens's food imports, these victories, securing Athenian control of the straits, were of vital importance. On land Alcibiades defeated a Persian army once near Abydos and again near Chalcedon.

At the siege of Byzantium, Alcibiades pretended to give up hope and sail away with his entire army, only to sneak back at night and take the city by surprise. Byzantium fell to Athens. At the siege of Selymbria, Alcibiades, due to a confusion of signals, found himself inside the city walls with only thirty men, facing off against the entire Selymbrian army. Alcibiades bluffed, acting as though the rest of his army was elsewhere in the city, and demanded that the Selymbrians set their weapons aside and parley. The Selymbrians, believing no one who was this heavily outnumbered could be so brash unless he had the upper hand somehow, agreed to talks. Alcibiades was persuasive, and when he left, Selymbria was an Athenian ally with an Athenian garrison.

It was an impressive string of victories. Partway through them, Alcibiades stopped back to see his old friend the satrap Tissaphernes, only to find that things had changed in Persia. Tissaphernes had fallen into disfavor with the Persian king Darius II, known as Darius the Bastard, who blamed the satrap for the entangling and fruitless alliance with Sparta. To get back in the king's good graces, Tissaphernes arrested his favorite and imprisoned poor Alcibiades in the city of Sardis. According to legend, Sardis was impregnable on three sides, because the ancient king Meles had carried a lion around it; but he could not carry a lion on its south side, which was a steep precipice, and so the south side was both a strong natural defense and Sardis's one weak spot. This is just a legend—but Sardis was nevertheless notoriously inaccessible and difficult to conquer. If Sardis was hard to get into, it was also hard to get out of. It took Alcibiades thirty days. Somehow he slipped his jailers, snuck out of Sardis, stole a horse, and rode to freedom. Nothing could stop Alcibiades.

VII.

But Alcibiades was the victim of his own good press. He'd spent so much time persuading the Athenians of his phenomenal skills and his Midas touch that every result that fell short of perfect was seen as a deliberate sabotage. The Athenians didn't trust Alcibiades, but they trusted his genius, and when even his genius was insufficient to bring the war to a swift conclusion, they grew suspicious: If Alcibiades had not already triumphed, it was because he did not want to triumph. And the Spartans were receiving gold and supplies from Persia now, while the Athenian treasury had long since been depleted, and so Alcibiades had to spend as much time sailing around the Aegean scrounging up donations as he did fighting.

Finally, one day Alcibiades's deputy Antiochus, ignoring Alcibiades's instructions to stay put while he was away, started a fight with the Spartan fleet and lost. The Athenians blamed Alcibiades, who had not been present on the occasion; in fact, they blamed him *because* he had not been present on the occasion. Just where had he been?

Rather than answer, or face the possibility of another fall from grace, Alcibiades left the Athenian side again. And rather than rejoin any of the other parties, he took a mercenary company and led them against the Thracian barbarians to the north. Perhaps the Thracians were the closest thing to a neutral force that Alcibiades could find: They were the only people he had never previously helped or betrayed. For two years he made himself wealthy (once again) fighting in Thrace. Eventually, he had a castle and a band of Thracian horsemen loyal to him.

The Athenians, meanwhile, had carried on the fight without Alcibiades. By 405 BC they had the whole Athenian fleet near modern Gallipoli, trying to egg the Spartans into a decisive naval battle. And who should show up suddenly, like a surprise guest star, but Alcibiades. He said that he had been nearby and couldn't help but notice the Athenian position was poor; the site the Athenians had chosen for battle was potentially disastrous. He offered the services of his Thracian cavalry and the gift of a plan he'd come up with to take the Spartans by surprise—motivated, purely, no doubt, by love of his homeland.

They didn't believe him, the Athenian generals. Instead they insulted Alcibiades and drove him away, and we can understand why. But maybe they shouldn't have, because the next day they had their battle and they lost horribly. The Athenian navy was sunk, its sailors captured and executed. Athens was starved into submission, and six months after the battle, Spartan troops were marching through the Acropolis. The war had lasted twenty-seven years and had ended with the complete defeat and humiliation of Athens, now under a Spartan-backed puppet government, the Thirty Tyrants, one of whom was Socrates's pupil Critias. You'll notice that thirty tyrants are, by definition, an oligarchy, the kind of government Spartans prefer.

Plutarch wrote that Alcibiades was like the soil of Egypt, from which spring both medicinal herbs and deadly poisons. In the end, the Athenians could not tell one from the other. His country in shambles, Alcibiades retired to the Persian Empire, hoping to live out the rest of his days in peace (or to lure the Persian Empire into war against Greece; who knows?). But Alcibiades was too dangerous a loose end to leave dangling, and one of his many enemies (probably the Spartans) arranged his assassination. The assassins set Alcibiades's house on fire, and when Alcibiades managed to grab a sword and leap through the flames, none dared stand and face him. They kept at a distance and shot him down with arrows.

While he lived, Alcibiades could turn on the charm and persuade people that his tricks were in some way lovable. But after his death, all that was left were the bare facts of his résumé: He had single-handedly embroiled Athens in a disastrous war, betrayed it not once but twice, and abandoned it to perish. All of that is bad enough.

But to make matters worse, five years later, Athens, having thrown off its Thirty Tyrants and yet again reinstated democracy, put Socrates on trial.

VIII.

Socrates was still the wisest man in Greece (the oracle at Delphi had proclaimed him as such) when it happened. He'd spent the last half century annoying Athenians, as a "gadfly" does, and gotten away with it. But then in 399 BC, after everything had settled down, he was formally accused of impiety—also, of corrupting the youth, but this seems to have meant corrupting them to impiety, so it comes out the same. It was potentially a capital charge, but then most crimes in Athens were potentially capital charges. The case against Socrates had been building for a long time.

In the Athenian court, the defendant spoke in his own defense. We have two accounts of Socrates's speech to the jury (each titled *The Apology*), one by Plato and one by Xenophon (another of Socrates's students, most famous today for his memoir about his days as a mercenary captain in Persia). The accounts agree on almost nothing, which is Business As Usual for ancient speeches, and probably each is a later, idealized version of his speech. In Plato's *Apology* (the better, and therefore more famous, version), Socrates suggests that as a punishment for his crimes he be given free food for life by Athens (but then he backs away from this suggestion, and instead proposes that he be fined thirty minae). Perhaps annoyed by the free-food jape, the jury gave him the death penalty.

There's also a purported surviving copy of the prosecutor's speech, the speech Socrates was ostensibly rebutting, recorded by a contemporary Athenian rhetorician, Polycrates. The prosecution harps upon Socrates's relationship with Alcibiades, the arch-traitor, the desecrator of herms, the would-be tyrant. Socrates literally corrupted this youth (is the allegation), and we know it because this youth was corrupt.

Six hundred years after Socrates's death, the Roman writer Aelian said that if you take Socrates as your model, you will become wise, but if you take Alcibiades as your model you will become conceited and crooked. And yet we know that Alcibiades took Socrates as his model. It's a difficult paradox to unravel.

It turns out that while Socrates had not been very popular in Athens, it wasn't his incessant questioning or simple lifestyle that people found most galling. It was the fact that his students—not just Alcibiades, but especially Alcibiades—were so bad for Athenians.

So bad for Athenians that they killed him.

IX.

Just to be fair to attractive people, I should point out that the handsomest man in the Greek army during the Persian Wars, Callicrates, did not try to betray anyone. He fought and died loyally for Greece.

Socrates lets his shield slip → *Alcibiades dies* → *No one bollixes the whole frammis, and* **SPARTA CANNOT CONQUER ATHENS** → *Socrates lives a long and healthy life* → *Democracy's shining name keeps kings out of Europe for two thousand years*

I.

SOCRATES SAVED ALCIBIADES'S LIFE AT THE BATTLE OF Potidaea. But what if he hadn't? What if he'd been a moment too slow to deflect the spear thrust with his shield? (We don't actually know *how* Socrates saved Alcibiades, but it's easy to imagine a cinematic moment like that.) Alcibiades lies dead on the field of Potidaea, age eighteen. What do we get then?

Democracy. A dead Alcibiades means a short Peloponnesian War, and a long-lived Socrates, and, finally, a democratic Europe.

To understand how a short Peloponnesian War and a long-lived Socrates could lead to democracy in Europe, you need to understand how very influential, and for how long, the Peloponnesian War and Socrates were.

Thucydides insists that the Peloponnesian War is the most important of all wars; but in most ways it doesn't look important from a distance. Its political changes were rapidly undone. After the conquest of Athens, Thebes (a Spartan ally) wanted the city torn down and plowed under, but the Spartans refused. According to Plutarch, while the victors debated Athens's fate someone started quoting apposite lines from Euripides (always Euripides!) and the Spartans dissolved in tears and decided to spare Athens. But probably they also worried that a power vacuum in Greece would allow Thebes to wax in might, giving Sparta another rival.

It was a valid worry: In the next century, Thebes would develop an army made up entirely of pairs of male lovers, who would fight with especial bravery to impress those they loved and who would, of course, never retreat and leave their loved ones to die; this army, the Sacred Band, vanquished Sparta's forces in 371 BC, and Thebes became the dominant military power in Greece. (Until Alexander the Great defeated it, tore Thebes down, and plowed it under. What goes around comes around.) Instead of Thebes's harsh suggestion, the Spartans decided to institute a puppet government, and even that, as we've seen, didn't last long. Soon Athens was back on its feet, rebuilding its fleet and therefore its empire. Everything was back to normal!

When Constantinople fell to the Turks, it meant the permanent cessation of a millennium and a half of Roman rule; an end of Greek cultural dominance in Eastern Europe; the replacement of Greek language, culture, and religion with Turkish language, culture, and religion. None of that happened after the Peloponnesian War. It was not the Peloponnesian War that humbled Athens from its status as a great power, but later events, namely the Macedonian and the Roman conquests.

II.

Remember that the Peloponnesian War is often compared to World War I, and this at long last is the second reason: After World War I,

Germany's borders were only a little different from its borders before the war. Germans still spoke German, were still ruled by Germans. The maps didn't look so very different. But the culture of the Western world had changed.

There is a passage from Thucydides's history that *everyone* quotes. It asserts that during the war "the meaning of words had no longer the same relation to things, but was changed by them as they thought proper. Reckless daring was held to be loyal courage; prudent delay was the excuse of a coward; moderation was the disguise of unmanly weakness; to know everything was to do nothing. Frantic energy was the true quality of a man. A conspirator who wanted to be safe was a recreant in disguise. The lover of violence was always trusted, and his opponent suspected . . . In a word, he who could outstrip another in a bad action was applauded, and so was he who encouraged to evil one who had no idea of it."

A certain gentlemanly conduct had governed, at least in theory, the wars of the Greeks before the Peloponnesian, and by the end of the war that all went right out the window. Massacres and atrocities increased on a scale never before seen in Greece. The Spartans developed a new policy to kill all prisoners captured at sea, whether they were allied with Athens or simply neutral, and were not averse to killing all prisoners taken on land, either, as at Hysiae in 418 BC, for example. But the Athenians—the ostensible good guys, remember—now started racking up their share of atrocities as well. Let's list some!

At Scione in 421 BC and then at Melos ca. 415 BC, they killed the entire male populations of the conquered cities, selling the women and children into slavery—and Melos wasn't even on Sparta's side! It had been trying to stay neutral! Similarly, when Athens liberated the city of Thyrea from is Aeginetan occupiers, there was once again a massacre of all captives. Athens intercepted Spartan ambassadors to Persia in 430 BC and executed them without trial (not accepted practice with ambassadors). At Mycalessus in 413 BC the Athenians lost control of a group of Thracian mercenaries they had hired, and the Thracians went on a killing spree, murdering everyone they could get their hands on, even killing pack animals in their blood lust; Thucydides's grisly account of this particular atrocity even has the Thracians bursting into a school full of young students and . . . well, you can imagine what happens next. In the later years of the war, the Athenian admiral Philocles, in emulation of Sparta's procedures, had ordered all captives cast into the sea to drown, and Philocles got a taste of his own medicine after the war's final battle. Not only Philocles but pretty much the entire Athenian navy was captured and put to death by Sparta. That's how the war ended, with an atrocity.

"War," Thucydides writes, "is a most violent master." By *master* he means *teacher*.

Religious customs also broke down by the end of the war. For the first time, a living man (the Spartan general Lysander) was worshipped by Greeks as a god. Readers of Greek mythology will remember what used to happened to mortals who compared themselves to the gods "in the old days": Arachne was turned into a spider, Marsyas was flayed alive, and Niobe lost all her children and then got turned into a stone; Bellerophon got pitched off Pegasus and killed just for trying to *visit* the abode of the gods.

The Greeks had been scandalized by the Persians' tendency to venerate their leaders: There is a story that when the Theban ambassador Ismenias sought to petition the Persian emperor, he was told that he must first bow before the emperor in worship; in order to avoid worshipping a mortal, Ismenias surreptitiously dropped a ring in the presence of the emperor, and got down on his hands and knees, bowing his head, only to retrieve it. In this way Ismenias fooled the Persians but avoided blaspheming. At one time, Greeks bowed only to their gods.

But now Lysander was openly worshipped in Samos, and he was only the beginning. A century later, as we've seen, the people of Athens deified the Macedonian general Demetrius, and quickly regretted it.

This orgy of bloodletting and blasphemy culminated in the execution of Socrates, 399 BC.

The fifth century BC was the golden era of Greek culture, and in the fourth century it all fell apart. This has been the conventional reading of Greek history for centuries, but it's important to remember that the Greeks had no idea that they were moving from the fifth to the fourth century. These dates were assigned to events much later. To us the death of Socrates in 399 looks like the tidy end of an era—but Socrates would have no way of knowing it was 399! The orator Demosthenes, in the fourth century BC, looked back in regret at the greatness of Athens in the previous century—but he didn't know it was the previous century! Dividing history up into epochs by century may always be arbitrary, but at least Napoleon knew he was ushering in the nineteenth century with his 1799 coup in Paris, just as Freud knew he was ushering in the twentieth with the 1899 publication of *The Interpretation of Dreams*. Dividing Greek history into ex post facto centuries is *even more arbitrary than that*.

But even if the Greeks couldn't know that killing Socrates was a watershed moment, many Greeks knew it was at least an *important* moment. They knew it because they were Socrates's students.

Part of this probably reflects an antidemocratic circle sympathetic to Sparta that flourished around Socrates. Alcibiades and Critias are extreme examples, but even his student Xenophon was exiled for being too pro-Spartan. Ancient literature preserves some encomiums to democracy—Pericles's funeral oration, for example—but it preserves a lot more criticisms of it. And those criticisms became a lot more plausible after the world's most powerful democracy became a loser. Athens lost to Sparta and then, just as they were starting to recover, they lost to the Macedonian kings. For two thousand years, Athens is the archetype of a democracy, and look what happened to them. And look what they did!

For the next two thousand years, people would know only one thing about democracies: A democracy killed Socrates.

III.

The ancient world, and specifically Athens, and most specifically Socrates, were *a big deal* to future generations. For centuries, students of rhetoric, as a standard classroom exercise, used to compose *their own defenses of Socrates.* Nietzsche called Socrates "the turning point and vortex of so-called world history." Everyone was talking about Socrates!

In 1625 Francis Bacon dictated (from memory, while lying sick in bed) his *Apophthegms*, which Lord Macaulay once called "the best collection of jests in the world." Most of the humorous stories in the book concerned ancient Greece and Rome, with five of them specifically dealing with Socrates. In the thirteenth century the Syrian divine Gregory Bar-Hebræus (despite the name, he was a Christian bishop) wrote his own jokebook, *Kethabha dhe-Thunnaye Mighaizjzikhanl* (*The Laughable Stories*), and this, too, is chock-full of Socrates jokes. One example:

"A man saw Socrates eating tree roots, and told him, 'If you would only get used to flattering the king you wouldn't need to eat such humble fare.' Socrates replied, 'If you would only get used to eating such humble fare, you wouldn't need to flatter the king.'"

The point is, Socrates is all over the art and literature of the next two millennia. In Dante's *Inferno*, he dwells in Limbo with the other virtuous pagans. Farid ud-Din Attar's twelfth-century Sufi epic, *The Conference of the Birds*, contains the (apocryphal) dying words of Socrates. In Chaucer's *The Canterbury Tales* he gets urine dumped over his head by his shrewish wife. To quote: "Xantippa caste pisse upon his heed."

Although the West in the Middle Ages didn't have access to much of the works of Plato or Aristotle, they had access to *some* of the works of Plato and Aristotle, and that sampling was enough to impart a reverence for Socrates. And everyone was angry at a people who killed him.

They probably should have been angry at Alcibiades, but instead they were mad at Athens.

IV.

Monarchy was the default political system in Europe during the Middle Ages, and in a way this is surprising. In the Bible, the Lord specifically warns the people of Israel against taking a king (1 Samuel 8), and the history of Israel under a monarchy is ambiguous at best: after one king, civil war; after three kings, a divided kingdom. The Romans for their part were fanatical in their distrust of kings; Julius Caesar was assassinated because of fear he would take the title of king (*rex*), and the title of emperor (*imperator*) was essentially invented to keep the fiction that Rome was not a monarchy. Since medieval European thought was pretty much one half Roman and one half biblical, the widespread occurrence of kingship is surprising. Of course, many European peoples had native monarchies, and while they were willing to replace their native religions with Christianity and their native illiteracy with the Roman alphabet, they weren't about to replace their native kings with a democracy. Their new knowledge taught them: *Democracies kill Socrateses.*

Throughout the long Middle Ages and Renaissance, when Europeans struggled for power, they struggled between kings and barons, or kings and clergy. When there were elections (the Holy Roman Emperor was an elected position beginning in 1376; by that date, Polish kings were already being elected), the elections were held by small groups of nobles. The election of a Holy Roman Emperor was about as democratic as the College of Cardinals electing a pope. Even the most democratic of medieval states, the Republic of Venice, was in practice an oligarchy. Oligarchies, we recall from Plato, are less dangerous than democracies. *Democracies kill Socrateses.*

Those few times when the common people made a bid for power, such as the 1381 Peasants' Revolt (also called Wat Tyler's Rebellion) in England, kings, barons, and clergy put their differences aside. The contemporary poet John Gower called Wat Tyler's soldiers "violently ignorant onagers and asses" as well as "monsters," "dogs," etc. What the peasants said in turn is almost completely forgotten, except for one rhyme:

> *When Adam delved and Eve span,*
> *Who was then the Gentleman?*

Predictably, Wat Tyler was killed while negotiating peace, and his followers beheaded without trial.

It may not be the case that when Europeans were sitting around trying to work out what kind of government to have, some cautious fellow would pipe up, "Not a democracy, please! Socrates and all." But it had to be in the back of everyone's mind. Despite biblical and Roman injunctions against monarchy, despite the heavily democratic leanings of the early Christian church, democracies were rare in Europe before the eighteenth century—the Swiss being one notable exception.

Well . . . there were also the Stedinger, a group of swamp-living Dutchmen who had developed a kind of representational government by the twelfth century. Unfortunately, their representative government decided to stop paying taxes to the County of Oldenburg, part of the Holy Roman Empire, which led to thirty-one years of warfare. The Stedinger did well at first, so Oldenburg accused them, on questionable evidence, of heresy and idol worship, which persuaded the pope and the Holy Roman Emperor to muster the forces of Christendom against the Stedinger. They were rooted out and put to the sword, every man, woman, and child that were found, which may not have been what Oldenburg had had in mind: You can't collect taxes from corpses.

So the Stedinger were fairly democratic, but they paid for it. Iceland, on the rim of the world, was at the very least a proto-democracy. But aside from such edge cases, Europe was for a thousand years mostly a collection of autocratic monarchies, shading into oligarchies of strongman barons whenever the king was weak. "King rules or barons rule," T. S. Eliot has the common people, the women of Canterbury, say. "We have suffered various oppression."

People came around to democracy eventually. Starting in the seventeenth century and flourishing in the eighteenth, political theorists looked to the past for positive models of democracy; often this meant Rome, but James Harrington in his *System of Politics* (ca. 1660) used the Old Testament Israel of Judges as a democratic model. In 1681 Algernon Sidney launched a defense of Athens, explaining away Socrates's death as brought about by perjury, and asserting that any government might have been similarly bamboozled. This is special pleading, but it gets the job done. Yet it was a long time coming. By the time Sidney was writing, Athenian democracy had been a whipping boy for over two thousand years. *Democracies kill Socrateses*. But they only kill Socrateses because of Alcibiadeses.

Well, *Alcibiades*, singular. As Archestratus wrote, "Greece could not have endured two Alcibiadeses."

Because none of this happens if Alcibiades dies at Potidaea. Without the machinations of Alcibiades, Athens is no longer the loser that murdered philosophy; and that makes all the difference. A redeemed Athens isn't a sufficient condition for widespread democracy—plenty of places that had never heard of Socrates, such as Japan and the Inca Empire, opted for monarchy. But with Athens as a model instead of as a warning, democracy would have bloomed in Europe much earlier. What would such a world look like?

Everything would be different. There's a lot to talk about.

V.

Let's say that by the late Middle Ages, Europe has become a continent dominated by democratic governments. They're not necessarily democratic nations—nothing in that era was a nation in the modern sense—but they are groups of people who are ruled by public assemblies or representatives they elect. Not all are alike. Athens was unusual in being much more democratic, in many ways, than most modern countries. Most of the Athenian government was not even elected—it was chosen at random from the populace, which sounds like a nutty system, except that many countries use it for jury selection. Athenian government policies tended to be determined by massive plebiscites. This was a governmental system designed for a city, and would probably be too unwieldy for a larger body; fortunately, the example of the Roman Republic would have offered the option of representative democracy to larger entities like England and France. Regardless of the different systems different parts of Europe adopt, all that matters is that they start out early on as, in some sense, democracies or republics.

You might think that the first thing to be different would be that the poor peasants would have a voice; but there's no guarantee that the lowest classes would be allowed to vote. If you grumble that no democracy is a true democracy unless it offers universal suffrage, remember that universal suffrage is far from a precise term. In the US in the early twentieth century, suffragettes marched under a banner reading "Universal Suffrage," and they meant they wanted votes for women; but when Congregational minister Henry Ward Beecher delivered a sermon calling for universal suffrage (its title was, indeed, "Universal Suffrage") in 1865, he didn't mean women at all. He meant that the vote should be extended to, as he put it, "the Anglo-African" male. In 1915, Alice Duer Miller published a collection of quotations from the likes of Benjamin Franklin, Charles Eliot, and Lord Macaulay, writers who opined about universal suffrage, never thinking it applied to votes for women. Theoretical voting rights were made practically enforceable after the 1965 Voting Rights Act—but this was still not universal suffrage. Eighteen-year-olds couldn't vote nationally until the Twenty-Sixth Amendment in 1971—and this, too, was not universal suffrage. *Universal* is a really broad category, and covers infants, felons, foreigners, cats, rocks, Saturn, etc. All of these are part of the universe, and none of these are allowed to vote. *Universal* in *universal suffrage* just means "all people we think should be enfranchised," and is therefore circular.

You're welcome to laugh at the suggestion that cats should vote, but the Athenians would have laughed at the suggestion that women should vote. The Athenians thought everyone who should be allowed to vote was allowed to vote. Americans in 1920 (when women got the right to vote) thought that now everyone who should be allowed to vote was allowed to vote. Americans in 1965 thought that now everyone who should be allowed to vote was allowed to vote. Americans in 1971 thought that now everyone who should be allowed to vote was allowed to vote. That's what we always think. "This time we got it right. Mission accomplished." Right now, the US is at something like "the set of all eighteen-year-old non-felon citizens," which is still a far cry from "universal."

Aristotle himself defined as one of the fundamental principles of democracy that officials were elected from all by all. There is no way in heaven or earth that Aristotle meant by *all* "all."

So yes, some peasants may be out of luck. But you can't disenfranchise *too* many people in a democracy, because if you do, you become an oligarchy by default; still, the Middle Ages were not known for their tolerance. Even if serfs got the vote, Jews never would.

But even if many of them were disenfranchised, peasants—and everyone else—could see a benefit from an increase in medieval democracies. The "democratic peace theory," an extrapolation of a genuine historical trend, holds that democracies *will not fight* one another. Since there's no hard-and-fast definition of a democracy (North Korea claims to be a "democratic republic") or of a war (the US Congress claims the Vietnam War was not a war but a "conflict"), it's hard to prove that democracies never war against democracies, but we do know that democracies fight democracies less often than they fight dictatorships, say, or than dictatorships fight one another. It comes down to this: The voting public generally does not like having its sons and husbands die, so unless the elected officials are *really certain* the war's going to go great, they have a large incentive not to start it. Otherwise they'll get voted out.

It's not like having democracies could bring about an increase in the number of medieval wars. Europe had nowhere to go but up. Democratic Europe would not necessarily have experienced perpetual peace, in part because modern democracies are better at pax than medieval democracies, for specifically modern reasons—free trade, for example, or the cosmopolitan mingling of populaces—and perhaps because it could still be attacked by nondemocratic outside forces—Attila the Hun doesn't care about your silly democracies! But Europe would certainly experience *more peace*. Peasants often didn't fight in medieval wars—kings were afraid to allow peasants access to weapons, lest they get all Wat Tyler on them—but peasants certainly *suffered* in medieval wars, as their villages were plundered and pillaged by knights. Peace could only help them—as it could only help most people.

War isn't the only source of violent death democratic regimes have to worry about less. The political scientist R. J. Rummel coined the term *democide* in the late twentieth century to describe the act of murder performed by a government—not *killing*, but specifically *murder*; which means that killing people in a war doesn't count as democide, because soldiers are not murderers. Capital punishment doesn't count as democide, because the hangman is not a murderer. But massacres, purges, show trials, orchestrated famines, extermination camps, unchecked lynchings, and pretty much any indiscriminate killing of civilians do count—and democide, so defined, killed more people in the twentieth century than war did. In fact, twentieth-century democide killed about as many people as might be expected to die in a nuclear exchange—it just took longer.

Democracies commit a lot less democide than authoritarian regimes. As Rummel says in the first paragraph of *Statistics of Democide*, "the more democratic a regime, the less democide." According to Rummel's count, the top five democidal regimes of the twentieth century were (in order): *1.* the USSR, *2.* the People's Republic of China, *3.* Nazi Germany, *4.* Nationalist China, and *5.* Imperial Japan, followed by *6.* the Khmer Rouge, and, the first true democracy on the list at *7.* Turkey. Number seven's not a great ad for democracy, but it's better than the autocratic regimes at one through six (Nationalist China has been a democracy at some points in history, but it wasn't at the time it was racking up its democide numbers). The next few regimes on Rummel's list are not exactly teeming with democratic governments, either: *8.* Vietnam, *9.* the Polish Soviet satellite state, *10.* pre-1988 Pakistan, *11.* Tito's Yugoslavia, and *12.* North Korea. Democratic governments certainly do commit democide (*all* governments commit democide), but they simply cannot keep up with their autocratic neighbors.

As you can imagine, democide was a huge problem in the Middle Ages. Massacres were a common feature of medieval warfare—there were no POW camps back then, so if you didn't kill your prisoners, you were probably lopping off their hands or putting out their eyes so they couldn't fight you again. As the Middle Ages wore on, you can add to your democidal scenarios the persecutions of the Inquisition, pogroms against Jews, and nonstop witch trials—by the fifteenth century, some German cities were executing an average of two witches per day. James VI of Scotland, later and better known as James I of England, was the king of the witch hunters. He had sailed through storms on the way back from a trip to Denmark, and had been alarmed to learn that Danish witches had confessed (under torture) to responsibility for the poor weather. Soon James was deep into the theory and practice of witch hunting, penning a handbook, *Daemonologie*, for all would-be witch sniffers in 1597. The assiduity that James brought to ferreting out witches made Scotland and witchcraft synonymous in the popular imagination: This is one reason Shakespeare included three witches in *Macbeth*; in his source material (*Holinshed's Chronicles*) the Weird Sisters are not witches but "nymphs or feiries," but nymphs weren't Scottish enough. Just to be clear: All of the convicted witches were innocent. None of them had the power to conjure up storms at sea.

James murdered witches as a religious duty, but Christian Europe hardly had a monopoly on witch hunting. According to the *Heimskringla*, a medieval history of Norway, pagan King Erik Bloodaxe burned eighty "warlocks," one of whom was his half brother (!), in the early tenth century: *"Ok var þat verk lofat mjök"* ("and that work was much praised").

This barbarous act was pretty typical of Norse kings, and of the Middle Ages in general. No one wants to slog through a long depressing list of democides from the period, so we'll briefly just name-drop three of the most famous: the massacre of Verden (forty-five hundred Saxons killed by Charlemagne in 782), the massacre of the Latins (sixty thousand or so Catholics killed by the Byzantine Empire in 1182), the St. Bartholomew's Day massacre (some ten thousand Huguenots killed by France in 1572). These three stand in for a much longer list of equally bad atrocities we know of—some of which can be found elsewhere in this book—and an even longer list of atrocities that have been forgotten to time.

There was another big problem in the Middle Ages, which was general lawlessness: bandits or barbarians sweeping through lands too weak to hold them off. This is a problem whether your government is a democracy or not, and would not change when we change models; it might mean that life in the Middle Ages sucked regardless of what your government looked like.

But even if life sucked, life under a democracy, with less war and less democide, would probably suck a little less. A Europe not constantly murdering itself would have a very different history. Part of the reason the US was dominant in technology in the mid-twentieth century is that it was the only major power not ravaged by war. Had there been no WWII, it's likely that France would have developed nuclear energy in the 1940s, under the oversight of Frédéric Joliot; but Hitler invaded France, Joliot joined the French Underground, his assistants fled to the Anglosphere, and nukes were innovated in the US, a country that had not been recently invaded.

Maybe a peaceful Europe would pour its resources into an unprecedented series of artistic and scientific triumphs. Or maybe it would turn its aggressions outward earlier, starting the Crusades the moment Jerusalem falls to the Muslims (AD 637). Or maybe it would be weak and backward in its military preparedness, and get conquered by Attila (probably not Attila, Attila was too early, probably some other invader).

Whatever it was doing, though, it would not be doing it at the behest of "the madness of kings." When Socrates fails Alcibiades at Potidaea, he saves not only his own life but also Athens's signature form of government.

VI.

Also, the Disney princess franchise would be the Disney senator franchise instead.

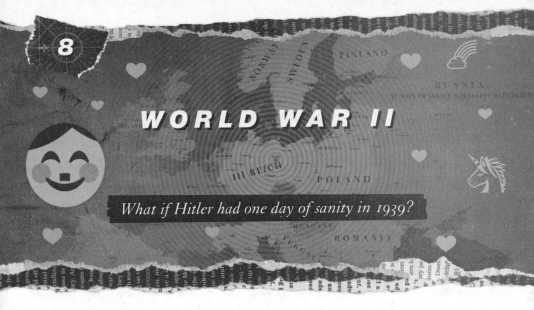

WORLD WAR II

What if Hitler had one day of sanity in 1939?

SYLT, 1939

I.

Hitler winning the war: We all want to think about this one (I'm no exception), which is weird, because to imagine the world after Hitler wins the war, you have to figure out *how* he could win the war. And such knowledge is dangerous, perhaps, because a time traveler could bring the information back to the 1930s, and suddenly retroactive Nazis are goosestepping through Philadelphia. Nevertheless, let's look at the war, and what Hitler might have done differently. It's going to be a close race, regardless of how well the Führer plays his hand.

Here's the basic paradox: The steps Hitler would have had to take to win the war would have required a sane Hitler, and a sane Hitler never would have gotten into the position where he could rule Germany. Hitler has to stay crazy until 1939, and then suddenly snap into sobriety.

Sebastian Haffner points out that for the first forty years of his life, Hitler failed at everything he tried. For the next twelve years, he succeeded as few have succeeded, triumphing in every endeavor. And then, for his remaining four years, he failed at everything again. Suicide in an underground bunker while his life's work collapsed all around him, leaving behind the most ignominious reputation the world has known—has anyone else ever failed so miserably?

In the middle of Hitler's first round of failures—between his failure to become an artist or get a job and his failure to overthrow the German government—Hitler served in the First World War, and although in one sense he failed (his side lost), he was not a bad soldier. He was not bad at being a soldier. The First World War set the stage for all his successes. Before we figure out how to reverse his final four years of failure, we need to see how the world conspired to give Herr Hitler a successful second act.

II.

Right at the beginning of the First World War, a London publisher put out a humorous poem called *Swollen-Headed William* (a parody of the popular nineteenth-century German children's book *Shock-Headed Peter*), in which the spoiled Kaiser Wilhelm is bitten by a dog (symbolizing France); the book promises that "soon" the French dog "will eat / The finest banquet ever known." The banquet, in an accompanying illustration, is helpfully labeled "indemnity," just in case the reader misses the point. Although swollen-headed Wilhelm was not defeated as easily as the book predicted, he was indeed defeated, and the Allies, including that French dog, demanded that banquet! This was the draconian Treaty of Versailles, one of the greatest blunders in history. Not only was Germany stripped of the territory it had seized from France in the previous century, not only did it lose its overseas colonies, not only was it saddled with a crippling debt of reparations—that part marks the banquet—it was also forbidden to build up a competitive military. Germany would never be a danger again!

It didn't work out that way, of course. This is the law of unintended consequences. The first thing the treaty did was ruin the German economy. By the 1930s, everybody's economy would be in shambles, but Germany's economy was in shambles first, with inflation on an almost parodic scale. In 1920, one US dollar could buy you four German marks; bring the inflation; by the beginning of 1924, it would buy you *over a trillion* marks. In three years, German currency had become worthless. Elias Canetti, who fled Austria to escape the Nazis, once theorized that this experience—the experience of watching the number of marks required to buy a loaf of bread spiral upward so extravagantly that wheelbarrows of cash are trundled to the market—numbed the German people to the concept of large numbers, so that the huge body counts slaughtered in concentration camps seemed like comparatively little to them.

Hitler tried to ride the economic discontent to power, staging a failed revolution (the famous "Beer Hall Putsch"). He went to jail. It was all, predictably, a failure.

Once out of jail, Hitler and his party decided to (in Hitler's words) "hold our noses" and focus on seizing power by more or less legitimate methods—in other words, enter politics. At this, too, they failed—until the Great Depression ruined the German economy again. Hitler was by this point the master and high priest of failure, and he knew how to offer the German people scapegoats for all their own failings. It was the Jews' fault. It was the Treaty of Versailles's fault. It was the fault of the Weimar Republic—Germany's current government.

Hitler was a lifelong failure, but he had, as we say, skills. He was a good organizer, and he was persuasive. Soon (1933) Hitler was the head of the Weimar Republic. Then (1934) there was no more Weimar Republic. There was only Hitler.

This rapid rise of an obscure little felon baffled the world. Hitler seemed like a joke. His party was a party of gangsters and thugs. Bertolt Brecht would write a play (*The Resistible Rise of Arturo Ui*) allegorizing Hitler's career by depicting the crimes of a Chicago mobster, and it was hard to see a difference between Hitler and Capone. The head of state of a major European nation was a crooked clown.

And then to make matters worse, Hitler started doing a good job.

Now, Hitler doing a good job is different from Hitler being a good guy. He never really stopped the violent assaults on dissent, or the anti-Semitism. But the Nazis self-consciously coded themselves as *cartoonish supervillains* so assiduously (the death's-head lapel pins, the torchlight rallies) that we need to remind ourselves that, at first, they were not *cartoonish supervillains*; at first they were just villains. Hitler did as good a job in Germany as a villain could, meaning that some people suffered cruelly, and more people lived in fear, but most Germans prospered. Hitler's economic policies cut Germany's massive unemployment to a pittance. They reinvigorated the German economy. Hitler had vowed to spill so much blood upon taking office that the little blood he was spilling looked like clemency. There was still the general thuggish-ness and the Jew-baiting speeches, but Hitler had not yet started murdering Jews; he called for a one-day boycott of Jewish businesses instead, which was, compared to the millennial history of pogroms and massacres against European Jewry . . . less bad. And the Huns, as a whole, were no longer hungry. For several years, Hitler's Nazi Party looked, on the balance sheet, like a positive force for Germans. And when the Treaty of Versailles got in the way of his plans, Hitler just flouted it.

Frankly, the Treaty of Versailles had been too much, and, what is worse, everyone knew it was too much. Even if the Allies couldn't come out and admit it, they must have known they'd been pushing things, which is why they kept failing to enforce the treaty. Meanwhile, Germans had for twenty years considered the treaty humiliating and hobbling. It was the worst of all worlds: a treaty cruel enough to breed resentment and too cruel to actually be enforced.

And so it wasn't enforced. And now Hitler was building up the military, constructing submarines, bringing back the draft—all things the treaty had deemed verboten. Versailles declared that Germany was not allowed to merge with Austria—a clause apparently included just because the Allies had learned that Germans wanted to do it—but in 1938 Hitler's Germany absorbed Austria. And then there was the Rhineland.

The Rhineland, by the terms of the Treaty of Versailles, and the subsequent Pact of Locarno, was sovereign German territory, a strip of German land along the Rhine on the border of France. It was also a demilitarized zone. No country, the treaties said, was allowed to move troops into it. No country was allowed to build fortifications in it. That included Germany. It was a buffer between Germany and France, and for German forces to enter it was an act of war. In 1936, Hitler brought in the troops. A small number of troops—Germany had started rearming, in violation of Versailles, but it had a long way to go—but the meaning of the action was clear. France and its ally Britain had no choice but to invade the Rhineland and drive the criminal German troops out.

But they did nothing. It was an international game of chicken, and the Allies blinked. General Maurice Gamelin, commander in chief of the French army, refused to order his troops to fight, for fear of starting another world war. British prime minister Stanley Baldwin said that peace was "worth taking almost any risk." Gamelin and Baldwin—and most famously Baldwin's successor, Neville Chamberlain—remembered the carnage of World War I. In 1936, along the Rhine, French forces were overwhelmingly superior, and German troops could have been driven back almost without loss of life. The outgunned Germans were in no position to fight, and probably would have slunk away in retreat. Such a humiliation would have brought an end to Hitler's reign. But peace, the Allied powers said, was worth any risk, so Germany armed its border with France, and no one did anything.

Hitler had insisted, in speech after speech, that his Germany had no territorial ambitions. Then he started demanding territory. He wanted the Sudetenland. The country of Czechoslovakia had been kludged together after World War I from pieces of the dissolved Austro-Hungarian Empire, and part of it, the Sudetenland part, ended up with a population that was ethnically German. "The shame of Versailles has only made more imperative the rise of the German people to fulfill their destiny," explained Hitler. That meant he had to have the Sudetenland. Anyone who kept it from him would be causing a war!

It would not be easy, though, for Germany to just take the Sudetenland. The Czech border was well defended, Maginot Line–style. The terrain was mountainous and difficult to move in. Worst of all, France was bound by treaty to protect the integrity of Czechoslovakia's borders. Hitler met with representatives of France and Britain (and not of Czechoslovakia!) in Munich to see if they could work out a compromise. They did come to a satisfactory compromise: They would give Hitler everything he wanted. He could straight up have part of Czechoslovakia.

Having betrayed his allies to a madman, PM Chamberlain returned to London pleased as punch, bragging that he had brought "peace for our time."

In October of 1938 German troops annexed the Sudetenland. In March of the next year, German troops just went ahead and annexed *the rest of Czechoslovakia*. Chamberlain sat stunned. That wasn't part of the deal! It had all happened so fast, and the Czechs had had no way to resist: All their defenses had been on their former border, in the Sudetenland. Chamberlain had essentially unlocked the front door and invited a burglar in, only to be surprised when Hitler roamed at will through the rest of the house.

Fortunately, the absorption of Czechoslovakia was, no joke, Hitler's final and ultimate desire. Hitler wanted no more mischief. "Here was a man who could be relied upon when he had given his word," Chamberlain said, without irony. So Hitler kept Czechoslovakia, and no one went to war.

Then Hitler invaded Poland.

What would the Allies do about this act of unprovoked aggression? Chamberlain had an idea: break Britain's treaty obligations to Poland and do nothing at all. When he proposed this idea to Parliament, two MPs *literally vomited* right then and there. Chamberlain's plan was not going to pass muster. And so, Britain declared war. France declared war. Then they did nothing, while Germany and the Soviet Union (suddenly fast friends) invaded Poland from two sides. For eight months, the Allies did nothing, or almost nothing (they dropped propaganda leaflets; there were skirmishes), while Hitler conquered not just Poland but also Denmark and Norway. It's usually called the Phony War, but we would also have accepted the Sitzkrieg or the Bore War. Technically England and France were at war with Germany, but there was very little evidence. There weren't a lot of battles.

Then all of a sudden Hitler conquered France. The French thought they were secure behind the long, fortified Maginot Line, which skirted the French-German border. General Maurice Gamelin huddled his troops in apparent safety behind the line, while the Germans . . . just went around it. They went around it. In six weeks in 1940, Hitler accomplished what his country had failed to do during the four years of World War I. France had fallen. So, incidentally, had the Netherlands and Belgium (and Luxembourg).

Hitler then offered to make peace with Britain, but the British refused. Hitler didn't care. He perfidiously invaded his ally Russia. The Russian troops melted before his onslaught. Small wonder—Stalin had recently, in a paranoid fever, purged the best of his officer corps, including the highest-ranking marshal and best military strategist in the Soviet military, M. N. Tukhachevsky; the rumor that Tukhachevsky and his fellow generals were traitors had in fact originated with German intelligence. Furthermore, Stalin had forbidden even defensive troop buildup on his western border, for fear of antagonizing his buddy Hitler. Hitler was bombing London on one side and vanquishing Stalin on the other. The rest of Europe was either a German ally or a (frequently German-friendly) neutral. Hitler was winning the war.

Then, suddenly, he wasn't. Suddenly he was back to failing. In December of 1941 his Russian invasion was turned back at Moscow. Almost simultaneously, after the Japanese attack on Pearl Harbor, Hitler declared war on America. His two-front war, stagnating on both fronts now, had just added another antagonist. After that, his fate was sealed. It took another three and a half years, but there was no longer any way for him to avoid his fate: Bullet in the head in a lonely bunker.

Hitler wakes up sane → He accepts Neville Chamberlain's final olive branch → HITLER CONQUERS THE USSR AND THEN THE REST OF EUROPE → Uh-oh

I.

IN RETROSPECT, HITLER'S ATTEMPT TO FIGHT PRETTY MUCH the entire world simultaneously was crazy; but what if Hitler hadn't behaved so crazily? What if he had woken up sane one day?

It's hard to *stay* sane, but if Hitler managed it, one thing he could do is sit back and wait. He's building up his military faster than anyone. Winston Churchill points out that, while 1930s German workers were laboring at a furious pace to prepare for war, France universalized the forty-hour workweek. Every year, every month, adds to Hitler's advantage. His Czech adventure got him not only all of Czechoslovakia's troops (thirty-six divisions already mobilized, with the possibility of much more, of course) and armaments but also the Czech Skoda Works, an industrial center that matched, in the first year of German oversight, the entire output of British armament manufactory from the same period. Time was on Hitler's side.

Hitler was crazy, and he became convinced he was going to die young, so he did everything really fast. But if he was saner, he could have waited. In fact, if he was saner he could have waited forever, and died of old age under a revitalized German Empire that dominated the continent. It would be a good life, and he'd be remembered as Germany's greatest leader. His thuggish anti-Semitism (which in 1939 was arguably less pronounced than anti-Semitism in contemporary USSR or Hungary) would be an embarrassment that everyone wanted to forget, like George Washington's slaves.

But we have to assume that sane Hitler still wants to achieve his evil dreams, including the conquest of Europe. And we have to assume that he isn't going to wait ten years to do it. Sane Hitler is still evil, and sane Hitler is *impatient*. What should sane Hitler do?

Clearly, sane Hitler can easily nab Poland, Denmark, and Norway without a problem. He can conquer France and the Low Countries without breaking a sweat. Crazy Hitler did it, and sane Hitler could do no worse.

But now, sane Hitler must think. From now on, he must play it cagey.

The first thing that must be done is *avoid a two-front war*. That means Britain must either fall or sue for peace. This is a hard nut to crack, because Great Britain is 1. an island; 2. possessed of the world's greatest navy; and 3. possessed of history's largest empire, which it can use to funnel goods, by means of the world's greatest navy, to its island fastness. Hitler had written in *Mein Kampf*, way back in 1925, that he would offer the "renunciation of a German war fleet" to forge an alliance with England; he could have added his right arm, and it would have been worth it.

Hitler's basic plan throughout the war had been to "break the spirit" of the British, which wasn't necessarily a bad plan. Although we now think of the wartime British as indomitably unified bulldogs who "keep calm and carry on" in the face of the Blitz, defeatism and despair were actually rife in Britain at the time—which makes sense, frankly, because for a while Britain stood alone against the triumphant Axis. In May of 1941, George Orwell predicted that in two years England would be conquered, either by Germany or the Soviet Union. Submarine warfare threatened Britain's supply line. Hitler wasn't demanding surrender from Britain— he was just demanding peace.

But Hitler had missed his big chance to break the Britons' spirit in May of 1940. The British Expeditionary Force had been fighting for their allies in France, and had, of course, been losing. The remnant retreated until they found themselves in the port of Dunkirk, surrounded by the Germans, their backs to the English Channel. All the Germans had to do was drive their tanks in and kill or capture everyone; but Reichsmarschall Hermann Goering somehow persuaded the Führer that if the German army struck the deciding blow, the generals would hog all the credit. Better to wait till the Luftwaffe could move in and finish the British forces off from the skies. Not coincidentally, Goering was commander in chief of the Luftwaffe.

Commander in Chief Goering deserves an Allied medal for this terrible advice. The German tanks halted before Dunkirk. While the Germans waited for the Luftwaffe, 224,585 British and 112,546 French and Belgian troops successfully evacuated across the narrows to Britain. The "miracle of Dunkirk" was spun into a victory by British PR, with the notion of little English fishing boats making the perilous trip back and forth to ferry desperate soldiers a key element in the resistance myth.

Thirty thousand British soldiers died in the defense of France. Imagine, now, if the British had lost *nine times that many* in the first few weeks of fighting. All told, throughout the war Britain lost about 380,000 soldiers. Could they have handled three fifths of that total dying almost immediately?

Sane Hitler wouldn't fall for Goering's cruddy advice, of course. Dunkirk is toast. But it doesn't matter if sane Hitler breaks the British spirit right then, or if he has to bomb the British air force into submission so he can invade. He just has to take Britain out of the equation. This is easier said than done—the British Royal Air Force fought hard and well. Airplane duels over Britain were a sucker's game, because if an RAF pilot was shot down, he parachuted to the loving arms of mother Albion, and was back in the air the next day, while any Luftwaffe pilots shot down went to jail. Germany was going to run short of pilots before Britain was. The whole reason Hitler decided to terror-bomb cities is because he could do it at night, and from a safe height, as no precision is necessary to hit a target the size of London. Anything to avoid the losses he suffered at the hands of the RAF. But this is sane Hitler's task, difficult as it is; he cannot make his next move until he removes Britain from the equation. Pour all your resources into Operation Sea Lion (the code name for the aborted invasion of England), sane Hitler. Take Gibraltar, Britain's outpost on the Mediterranean, even if it means violating Spanish neutrality. (Violating neutrality is not exactly a strong taboo for Hitler.) Perhaps try nighttime bombing of British airfields, so planes have fewer places to take off or land from. Whatever it takes. We'll assume he gets it eventually.

The next move, of course, is Russia.

Germany invaded Russia in June of 1941, later in the year than Hitler had originally planned, because he had to take time out to help Mussolini conquer a recalcitrant Greece. Mussolini deserves an Allied medal as well, for slowing down the timeline, because winter in Russia is brutal, and thanks to him the Germans were going to have to face it. But sane Hitler won't be invading Russia in 1941. Sane Hitler knows that Stalin is completely unprepared, and will continue to be; time is on sane Hitler's side, and 1941 is the year to take Britain out. In 1942 he invades Russia.

In 1942, Russia did not actually border any independent country on the European mainland; the Soviet Union did, though. Between the Russian Soviet Socialist Republic and the rest of Europe lay other Soviet Socialist Republics: Ukraine, Belarus, Moldavia, the Baltic states. The only common element among the people of these political divisions was that they all *hated Russia*. The Germans moved across all of them, and because you cannot escape from who you are, they behaved, as they advanced, reprehensibly. The Nazis could have arrived like liberators, but they behaved like conquerors, and any welcome they received in Ukraine or Belarus they wore out immediately. Since their whole plan was to export so much food from these areas that "many millions of persons will be starved to death" (this is from a German government memo of the time), the Germans couldn't have kept a friendly face up for long, but they didn't even try.

This is the thing about Russia, though. It's really, really big. You can pin the British and French forces against the sea, but it's hard to pin the Russian army against anything; Russia's an infinite staircase: There are always more steppes behind them. Hitler, like Napoleon a century and a quarter earlier, drove into Russia and then found himself overextended. There's no way to take a country this large by traveling over scorched earth. You have to make sure of your position every step of the way.

If sane Hitler secures the cooperation of the Ukrainians, the Belarusians, the Lithuanians, etc., he'll be halfway to Moscow already. Since in 1942 he's not held up by Greece, he times things so he doesn't get snowbound at the gates of Moscow. Since he has no British second front, he can commit more troops. Invading Russia is never going to be easy, but Hitler should be able to grab enough Soviet infrastructure that the Russian army, falling back inland, cannot outproduce him. Slowly he can absorb as much of Russia as he wants, and then make a treaty with Stalin, perhaps at the Volga, perhaps at the Urals. The Ukrainians et al. will be aware that the liberator has no intention of leaving; but by this point it will be too late for them.

The only problem left is the US. When Axis Japan bombed Pearl

Harbor in December of 1941, Hitler stood by his allies like a big boy, for once in his life, and declared war alongside the Japanese. This was a huge mistake. He should have sent a fervent letter denouncing the criminal act and affirming his undying friendship with America. By December of 1941, if sane Hitler is lucky, Britain should have already negotiated a peace, so there wouldn't actually be a war in Europe to enter into, but, if the British are still in it, there's every chance President Roosevelt will want to come to their aid. Hitler then needs to use all his charm to persuade the American people they have no reason to fight. The Japanese won't like it, but Hitler's not in this business to make friends—except for the Americans; he must make friends with the Americans. Then, when he invades Russia a few months later, he can remind the US that he is fighting the Bolshevik menace.

By 1944 or so, Hitler controls all of Europe except for three neutral states (Ireland, Sweden, and Switzerland), four allied states (Italy, Finland, Spain, and Portugal), and a handful of client states (Vichy France, Bulgaria, etc.)—with Britain being either a fifth ally or a client.

French prime minister Paul Reynaud, in his last broadcast before the surrender to Nazi Germany, succinctly described what will happen next. "If Hitler wins," he told his people, "it would be the Middle Ages again, but not illuminated by the mercy of Christ."

II.

Sane Hitler could achieve a lot, sure, but he'd have to stay sane *a long time* to do it. Keeping Hitler sane for so long strains credibility. He clearly didn't have it in him. How short a time could Hitler stay sane and still win the war?

One moment is all it would take, provided that moment was in August of 1939. And all because of Neville Chamberlain.

III.

The theory of forest fires is that in a state of nature small forest fires frequently burn through the underbrush. Twentieth-century firefighters sought to combat all forest fires and quickly extinguished these small fires. The forests built up a thick supply of underbrush kindling. Finally, when fires erupted, there was so much kindling in the forests that the conflagrations burned out of control, climbing up to the tree canopies and felling even old trees, burning so hot they sterilized the soil. These mammoth fires were so bad, we would have been better off not fighting forest fires in the first place.

Prime Minister Neville Chamberlain sought to prevent any wars, anywhere, of any size. He kept the peace for a while, but when war broke out, it was literally the largest war the world had ever seen.

In retrospect this seems foolish, but perhaps we can say that Chamberlain was like one of those benighted firefighters, doing what seemed like a good idea at the time.

How hard did Chamberlain strive to prevent a war? Do we even know everything he tried?

This is true: In August of 1939, seven British industrialists met secretly with Hermann Goering on an island in the Baltic. What exactly they talked about is a matter of contention. According to Lord Aberconway, the last surviving member of the delegation (he died in 2003), they went to warn Germany that an attack on Poland would lead to war; this was Britain's avowed, official position, so it's hard to see why the meeting had to be secret, but sure. Maybe it was a threat meeting.

According to the historian Andrew Roberts, who studied Aberconway's papers, the meeting was actually another of Chamberlain's gambits: an offer to Germany to give it part of Poland in exchange for maintaining peace. A second Munich, as it were. Peace for our time, once more with feeling.

Even if Chamberlain had sent a delegation to cave in about Poland, Hitler was not about to accept the caving. He wanted a war! He'd been annoyed that Czechoslovakia hadn't brought him one. But here's where everything could fall into place for Hitler. All he needs is one lucid moment, one moment of caution. What if he'd woken up, that summer morning in 1939, sane? What if he'd taken (assuming there really was an offer from Chamberlain) Chamberlain's offer?

Stalin wanted eastern Poland, and had signed a nonaggression pact with Germany in part to let him take this prize. If Hitler slid into western Poland with the full contrivance of England and France, could he not clandestinely suggest to Stalin that the time was now ripe for the Soviets to seize what should be theirs?

And so, the Soviet Union invades Poland in 1939. At that moment, Germany borders the Soviet Union. But still Hitler sits there peacefully, waiting for May of 1940 (or even, if he manages to be cautious, 1941).

It will still be an invasion of Russia, and Napoleon will tell you that invasions of Russia are always dicey—but now it's a one-front war. Now he has no reason to fear American involvement. No one's going to march to war to help out Stalin! As Harry S Truman said in a 1941 interview, "If we see that Germany is winning, we should help Russia and if Russia is winning we ought to help Germany and that way let them kill as many as possible"—but "help" here would only mean supplies, and if Hitler had not attacked England or France, or any other "good" countries, the USSR might not even get that. If Hitler ever could have won a war with the Soviet Union, this would be his chance, with no distractions on his western border. Stalin is still unprepared. Germans could be in Moscow by September.

After that, the German Empire, now the world's largest country by area, could take over France if it wanted. It could do what it wanted. The thousand-year Reich.

"Mr. Chamberlain," G. K. Chesterton wrote, "said that the war was a feather in his cap and so it was: a white feather." He was writing about Neville Chamberlain's father, but the quip is apt, in our history, for the son; and how much more in this counterfactual world.

This would have been Chamberlain's legacy. Not only the man who brought Europe to war (which he was), but the man who let Hitler win it.

JULIAN THE APOSTATE

What if Julian put his armor on at Samarra?

SAMARRA, AD 363

I.

The story of Julian is the story of a man with a dream, a dream to reverse the relentless march of history.

Julian was the nephew of the Roman emperor Constantine the Great, who was famous for doing three things: moving the capital of the empire from Rome to Byzantium (renamed Constantinople for the occasion); legalizing Christian practices throughout the empire; and (related) converting to Christianity himself.

Christianity, despite a growing popularity, had been more or less illegal in the Roman Empire for the last three centuries. Persecution of Christians had started under Nero and continued, with greater or lesser vigor, through the good and bad emperors following. It's important to note that *persecution* here doesn't mean "can't get a good job" or "neighbors don't like you"; it means "murdered by the state." Nero is particularly known for his delight in murdering Christians, but Nero is also known for his delight in murdering everyone. The Venerable Bede, scholar and saint of the eighth century, said that the persecutions under the emperor Diocletian were "more prolonged and monstrous" than any preceding. The more lenient emperor Trajan, on the other hand, is on record as ordering that Christians should not be actively hunted down by his officials, and that any Christian brought before the courts should be offered the chance to recant—only those who refused should be put to death. So speaketh tolerant Trajan.

Even with edicts like this, Christianity was nevertheless a booming demographic in the empire when Constantine ended the centuries of futile persecutions and began a tacit encouragement of the religion. At his death he left the empire to three of his sons, all Christians as well. The entire imperial family was raised Christian, including young Julian, son of Constantine's half brother. Although the majority of the empire at the time was pagan—estimates vary, but probably around 90%—Christians now controlled the reins of power and were growing quickly, perhaps by as much as 40% per decade. Christians were the future of the empire, and this was the future that Julian was to stand athwart, yelling, however briefly, stop.

By the time Julian was a boy, the three brothers who ruled the Roman Empire had been reduced to one, the others having died like Romans, i.e., fighting themselves or would-be usurpers. Constantine's son Constantius (the *whole family* had names like this—Constantius's dead brothers were named Constantine II and Constans) was sole emperor and wanted to stay that way. If he was nothing else, Constantius was cautious. The historian Ammianus Marcellinus, his contemporary, said that the emperor was terrified of being assassinated, implying, if not actually stating, that he would only let his daughter shave him, lest a barber slit his throat (actually, Constantius was childless). Barbers must have been a source of anxiety in the ancient world—the emperor Commodus used to *burn his beard* off, so great was his fear—but perhaps a healthy dose of paranoia was practical. Julius Caesar is only the most famous of a host of political figures knifed or poisoned, or strangled in the bath. According to Plutarch, the Persian queen Parysatis assassinated her daughter-in-law (who happened to be Alexander's second wife, Stateira) by coating one side of a knife with poison. She cut a piece of "bird" in two and herself ate the half from the unvenomed side of the knife. Her daughter-in-law, seeing that Parysatis was eating too, assumed the bird was safe; she ate the other half, the half touched with poison, and died. Such cunning must have kept Constantius up at night.

Only the emperor was permitted to wear purple clothing, and Constantius worried that another of Constantine's bloodline might "seize the purple," as they used to say. A fearful Constantius was a proactive Constantius. He arranged to have most of his other family members, including Julian's father, done away with, and when the purge was complete the only other living male relatives of the late Constantine the Great were now Julian and his older brother Gallus, both Constantius's cousins. They were not yet teenagers.

Julian's adolescence was a time of fear. He had every reason to assume he would be killed, as so many of his relatives had been, at any moment. He spent many years under veritable house arrest. There was nothing for him to do but read, but fortunately Julian had access to large libraries, including one particularly impressive collection belonging to Bishop George of Cappadocia.

Obviously, Bishop George was a Christian. Everyone around Julian was a Christian. Julian himself was a Christian. And so, the core of his reading was, of course, the Bible. The Bible is, among other things, a "best of" anthology of several centuries of Jewish literature's greatest hits, including philosophical and poetic texts (such as Job or the Song of Solomon) and historical accounts alongside the "straight" religious books, combined with a sampling of the earliest Christian writings. Julian also had access, thanks to George, to centuries of the best Greek classics. Why Julian became disenchanted with Christianity and enamored of paganism is a riddle that is probably too personal for historians to ever unravel, but it started in this library. Essentially, Julian decided he liked the flower of Greek literature more than the flower of Judeo-Christian literature; he preferred to the Bible the philosophy of Plato, the poetry of Homer, the histories of Herodotus and Thucydides, and the religion of his ancestors.

II.

The Roman Empire of the fourth century was huge, and unwieldy for one man to rule. It had been divided into smaller units with independent rulers several times in the past, with mixed results; but Constantius was not about to share power. However, starting in the first century there had been a custom for imperial heirs to be given a smaller rulership role, a sort of vice-emperor. The Romans called the junior partner *Caesar*, while preserving for the emperor proper the title *Augustus*. Constantius experimented by naming his cousin Gallus, Julian's brother, caesar over the eastern provinces.

This was a very bad idea, as the power went to Gallus's head and he began killing people, including—and this was a big mistake—two ministers the emperor had sent to Antioch to check on the caesar. Such an insult to the emperor's authority could scarcely be tolerated. So Constantius beheaded Gallus.

Next the emperor tried Julian—his sole living male relative—as caesar in the West. The western province of Gaul had seen two major rebellions in the last five years, and Constantius thought the presence of his cousin as caesar might keep the Gauls in line.

Constantius could not have expected much from his cousin. Julian was a bookish twenty-three-year-old who'd spent much of his life under house arrest. He wanted nothing more than to study philosophy. At a time when most Romans went clean-shaven, Julian affected the long beard that marked a philosopher. He ate moderately, eschewed carnal desires, slept on the hard ground, and studied constantly. He cared nothing for wealth, pomp, or luxury. He had learned from the Stoic philosophers the importance of bearing hardships with equanimity; he had learned from the Cynic philosophers the importance of simple living. Diogenes the Cynic threw away his cup when he saw a child drinking water from his hands. One thirteenth-century German poet insists that Diogenes grew to regret this action, but if there's an earlier source for this regret, I have not found it. Julian didn't seem to think Diogenes had repented. Julian sought to live as simply as Diogenes.

Such a character may have been a long shot as a military commander, so the emperor planned to keep Julian in Gaul mostly as a figurehead.

The army would be controlled by experienced generals who would give lip service to the caesar, but would take orders only from the augustus, Constantius. This may not sound like an ideal setup, but remember: Julian was literally Constantius's last chance. Everyone else was dead, and Constantius had fathered no children of his own.

There's an old anecdote about Diogenes the Cynic, the philosopher without a cup, that Julian would have known. When Alexander the Great entered Corinth, he was courted and congratulated by many philosophers, but not by Diogenes. Alexander sought the Cynic out and found him basking in the sun. "Is there anything I can do for you?" Alexander asked, and Diogenes asked him to "step to one side and stop blocking the sun." No one dared speak to the conqueror that way, but Alexander left impressed with the philosopher's fearlessness. "If I were not Alexander," he remarked, "I would wish to be Diogenes." Several ancient sources tell this story, and it may or may not be true, but it was famous throughout the Roman world, and Julian would certainly have read it in Plutarch.

Well, like Alexander, Julian just wanted to be Diogenes, really; he wanted to live simply and study philosophy, but this was not a life permitted of a caesar, so he decided if he could not be Diogenes he would be Alexander. And nobody tells Alexander that he is a mere figurehead for someone else's army.

Soon Julian was leading his troops into battle personally. In a weird adumbration of the twentieth century, Gaul was at the time under constant attack by invading German barbarians, and over the course of five years Julian had to fight them up and down the Rhine. To everyone's surprise, Julian proved to be a spectacularly successful military commander. He'd done his homework, after all, studying Julius Caesar's *Gallic Wars* to learn about battle tactics. After several early victories, Julian had to deal with the Germanic leader Chnodomar of the Alemanni, who led an alliance of seven German kings into Gaul. Chnodomar had defeated several Roman legions some five years earlier, and must have thought the young Caesar would be easy pickings. The German alliance outnumbered the

Romans by about two to one. When the two forces met at modern-day Strasbourg, the battle was a rout. The Germans were soundly defeated, Julian's men suffered light casualties, and Chnodomar was taken captive and sent back east in chains. Julian then advanced across the Rhine into the forests of Germania proper. The German barbarians had grown used to Romans stopping at the river, and the presence of Roman troops beyond Roman borders so terrified them that they sued for a ten-month truce. The power of the Alemanni was broken, and they would later be conquered by, and absorbed into, the Franks, the Germanic tribe that would, centuries later, successfully conquer France. They're the reason we call it *France* instead of *Gaul*, as the Alemanni are the reason the French call Germany *Allemagne*.

His successes, his personal bravery, his administrative policies—he worked to keep taxes low throughout Gaul—and even his luck, for Romans loved a lucky commander, endeared Julian to his armies. You can imagine that these developments pleased Constantius not a whit. A little help in the West was welcome; a lot of help was a threat.

But Constantius was in no position to move against Julian. Because, although the western empire was safer from invasion than it had been in decades, the eastern empire was suffering a series of setbacks from the neighboring Persians. The Romans and the Persians had been squabbling over their common border, somewhere around Mesopotamia, for the last four hundred years (and would continue to do so for the next three hundred), and Constantius had fought Persian troops himself, in the days of Constantine the Great. The two empires had been at peace for a good decade, though, when war broke out again, just as Julian was mopping up Gaul. Although the war ostensibly started because of a breakdown in negotiations over the status of pieces of Armenia, really this was a pretense. Rome and Persia were pretty much always at war. Constantius had been busy fighting barbarians in the Balkans, but now Rome had a more dangerous opponent. The emperor resolved to lead the war in the East himself.

Constantius had gained the reputation of being lucky in battle during civil wars—and he'd faced his share of usurpers already—but unlucky against foreign opponents. A reputation for bad luck can be a self-fulfilling prophecy, as tepid, half-hearted troops win few battles. If he was going to defeat the might of the Persian king, Constantius was going to need all the help he could get. And here's where Constantius may have seen the Persian campaign as an opportunity. It gave him the excuse to call for reinforcements from among Julian's troops. These men, mostly native Gauls, were therefore ordered to make the long trek across Europe and the Levant to fight on the empire's eastern border. In this way, Constantius could cripple his caesar, reducing the threat he posed through reduction of his forces (by as much as two thirds—Constantius wanted a lot of men!), while simultaneously increasing his chances against the Persians. Two birds with one stone. But it didn't work out as he'd planned.

Julian's troops had enlisted under the stipulation that they not be required to serve outside of their home territory. Specifically, Julian had promised them that they would never have to cross the Alps—and far beyond the Alps the Persian frontier certainly lay.

When the Gauls heard that they were being summoned to some distant shore for a dumb war they cared nothing about, leaving, therefore, their own homes and loved ones only lightly defended from barbarian attack . . . they mutinied. Julian went out to talk the angry mob down and found himself seized by the crowd. Far from harming him, though, the soldiers lifted him up on a shield and proclaimed him Augustus— Emperor of Rome. After all, their trusted general would certainly treat them better than the distant emperor had.

"Spontaneous demonstrations" (the phrase comes from George Orwell's *Animal Farm*) were commonplace in countries like Stalinist Russia or Maoist China, but they have rarely been truly spontaneous; and although Julian protested his innocence, it's certainly possible that he orchestrated the army's plan. He insisted, for the rest of his life, that if he had not accepted the title of emperor, the army would have killed him on the spot. Believe it if you will. Regardless of how much or little he had to do with the proclamation, once it went through, he had no choice but to shoot the moon. Constantius had killed men for less; many, many men. Julian would have to be augustus or die trying.

Although he wrote his cousin conciliatory letters (of the "hey! we can both be emperors!" variety), Julian began planning to fight. First came a final raid across the Rhine to terrify the unruly barbarians. If he was going to march east, he needed his power base in Gaul to be safe from any mischief in his absence. This raid was another victory for the Romans, and for Julian's reputation. Julian advanced deep into German territory across the Rhine three times in total—Julius Caesar himself had only done it twice—each time humbling and pacifying the Germans. The historian Tacitus once wrote that the Romans bring desolation and call it peace, but from Julian's point of view, a desolate frontier beat a frontier teeming with rapacious Germans.

Constantius, meanwhile, was proving unlucky in the East. So after some sound defeats he decided to leave the Persian war in the hands of his generals, and turned around to head for Gaul. He'd always had better luck fighting Romans than Persians. His cousin had to die, and Constantius would manage it personally.

In this way, for the fourth time in fifteen years (and tenth time in thirty), the Roman Empire was again torn by civil war.

As soon as he learned that his cousin was coming for him, Julian began his march. And here Julian was able to use not only the military experience he'd gained fighting in Gaul but also the temperate habits he'd learned from reading philosophy. He could travel fast because he could travel light, and he was used to sleeping on the ground. The speed of his march took him to Illyricum before the loyalist prefect there could arm; the prefect fled ignominiously. Constantius's commander Lucillian was preparing to stop Julian at Bononea, but the would-be emperor arrived, as befits a philosopher, *early in the morning*, before the commander had even woken up. A befuddled Lucillian was forced to welcome and legitimize Julian. Seeing how well the upstart was doing, cities began throwing open their gates, welcoming the new emperor. Julian made it all the way to Thrace having scarcely shed any Roman blood.

You will notice that Thrace is well past the Alps, but presumably his Gaulish army was too excited by the successes of its emperor to care.

As successful as Julian was, though, he was in a precarious position. In his haste he had left behind him people and troops whose loyalty was either to Constantius or to whoever looked to be stronger at the moment. At Aquileia, in northern Italy, troops ostensibly pledged to Julian switched sides and barricaded themselves in the walled city, declaring it for Constantius. And the elder emperor had the larger army, and more battle experience. So it was going to be a close fight.

Except it wasn't, because Constantius abruptly caught a fever and keeled over dead, long before his forces faced Julian's. With the exception of his father's, Constantius's reign had been the longest of any emperor since Augustus. News spread slowly in those days, but one by one the provinces of the empire realized that they now had only one emperor, and there was no point fighting.

Anticlimactically, and almost accidentally, Julian had sole command of the entire Roman world.

III.

An opportunity like the imperial purple does not come along often, and Julian was not about to squander it. He had two plans. One was to march into Persia like his hero Alexander the Great and conquer this pestiferous foe once and for all. The other was far more ambitious. Julian had converted to paganism some time before, but had had to keep his faith secret to stay on his cousin's good side. Now he proclaimed his paganism openly, sacrificing oxen to the Olympian gods in celebration of his imperial title—and revealed his intent to make Rome pagan again.

This plan might not have sounded so very hard. It had not been long since Christians in the empire were the minority. Rome had only had two Christian full emperors, Constantine and Constantius. The Roman Senate, of limited political but great symbolic power, was still over-whelmingly pagan. The last ten years or so had seen an astonishing rate of conversion, so now Christians made up a little over half the empire's subjects, but they were divided by sectarian strife. Constantius followed the heretical teachings of Arius, who declared that Christ the Son was not coeternal with God the Father; Constantine the Great had favored the contrary teachings of the Nicene Council.

Trying to understand what people in the fourth century thought about Jesus can be confusing. In the 1940s, American newspaper syndicates would not allow *foreign words* to appear in comic strips; it's unclear to us, eighty years later, why this should have been such a big deal. Similarly, some of the ancient hairsplitting analyses of the nature of the Trinity are real head-scratchers to us today. The Nicaeans believed Christ to be *homoousious* (of the same substance) with the father; Arian heretics believed Christ to be *homoiousious* (of a similar substance) with the father. This one small letter and slight shade of difference were *very important* to Christians of the fourth century.

We now freely call Arians "heretics," but at the time it was unclear who represented heresy and who represented orthodoxy. In 1609, John Harington wrote

> *Treason doth never prosper—What's the reason?*
> *Why, when it prospers, none dare call it Treason.*

Similarly, heresy that prospers is orthodoxy by definition. And Arianism was prospering, having captured the fancy of a recently dead emperor.

From Julian's point of view, these divisions were weaknesses that could be exploited. Constantine the Great, aware of the power of a unified doctrine, had allowed religious tolerance throughout the empire—except for Arians, whose writings he burned. Julian, in contrast, declared an amnesty against all Christian sects. Ammianus Marcellinus says that Julian believed that Christians were more dangerous to one another than "*infestas bestias*"—wild beasts—and would tear one another apart with little provocation. But Julian had another problem: The pagans were hardly unified either.

Rome had long espoused religious pluralism. The Romans borrowed heavily from foreigners; their own traditional gods had had Greek myths grafted onto them, sometimes awkwardly—although we often say that Mars "is the Roman name for" Ares, the two gods are very different in temperament, and the whiny Ares of Homer's *Iliad*, humiliated by imprisonment in a jar or fleeing from the mortal Diomedes, hardly matched Mars, the disciplined ancestor of Rome. The goddess Cybele was brought to Rome from Asia Minor (in the form of a black stone, presumably a meteorite) in the third century BC after a prophecy stated that only this way would the city be saved from Hannibal. Later, the secret practices of Mithras worship, imported with some changes from Persia, swept the Roman military: Ten Mithraic temples have been discovered as far away as Britain.

So part of Julian's trouble was defining exactly what paganism *was*— Mars, Cybele, Mithras, or what. He decided that paganism was more or less synonymous with the entire traditional culture of the Roman world, the inheritance of Greece and Rome—in a word, Hellenism. One of the laws he passed to promote paganism was therefore an injunction forbidding Christians from teaching the basic disciplines of rhetoric, philosophy, and grammar—and by extension the literature that we would now call "the classics." If paganism was synonymous with culture, there was no reason for Christians to teach Plato or Homer.

This was a relatively mild law—Julian wanted to appear mild, and preserve at least the pretense of religious tolerance—with far-reaching implications. Christian thought and literature had been born in the crucible of the Hellenistic tradition. The opening verses of the Gospel of John borrow their vocabulary from Neoplatonism. Paul's letters not only were written in Greek but also betray a mastery of classical rhetorical methods. Early Christian apologists, such as Marcus Minucius Felix, cast their works in the form of Socratic dialogues. Christianity had spread through the empire at least in part due to debate and reasoned argument. In a stroke, Julian sought to remove Christian influence from the highest academics. He would divest Christians of their ability to train in arguing persuasively.

For Julian knew that three centuries of persecution had not destroyed Christianity. He was going to have to try subtler means. Julian therefore commanded that government offices and higher military ranks should preferentially go to pagans. This was discrimination, true, but it was a far cry from Nero or Diocletian. On the other hand, when a pagan mob tore to pieces a Christian bishop—it was the same Bishop George of Cappadocia whose library had inspired the young Julian—Julian did not punish anyone for the murder . . . but he did admonish the locals not to take the law into their own hands again.

From the Christians' point of view the emperor levied fines on their churches; from Julian's, he was merely demanding repayment of grants and subsidies given by the last two emperors. He ordered Christian communities that had torn down pagan temples to rebuild the edifices at their own expense. Julian somewhat facetiously said that when he taxed Christians he was helping them out; did they not teach that the poor would inherit the kingdom of heaven?

Because some Christians believed the Bible stated that the Jewish Temple in Jerusalem, destroyed for a second time in the year 70, would never be rebuilt, Julian ordered work to begin on its reconstruction, hoping to disprove scripture with a magnificent new building. (Natural disasters, sabotage, or, if you wish, miracles, prevented work from progressing, and after two millennia there is still no standing temple.)

In order to prevent sects of pagans from falling at one another's throats like Arian and Nicaean Christians, Julian started implementing a state religion with the emperor—himself, naturally—as so-called pontifex maximus, or high priest. *Pontifex maximus* literally means "greatest bridge builder"—the pontifex builds a bridge between men and the gods—and the term had over the years lost its specific religious connotations and become just another honorific of the emperor, so that even Christian emperors used it (and would continue using it for a few decades after Julian). Julian wanted to restore himself to the head of the pagan priesthood, and indeed he led so many animal sacrifices that his subjects jokingly called him "the butcher" (to be fair, probably the most benign reason a Roman emperor was ever called a butcher). Later the word *pontifex* would be attached to the Christian Pope, the Bishop of Rome, which is why he is known as the *pontiff.*

When he wasn't plotting to restore the empire to paganism, Julian was plotting to restore it to its humble origins. Julian was a philosopher, remember, and despised the glitz and decadence that had built up over the imperial court. The Romans of the Republic had been hardy, plainspoken, simple folk. When the new emperor Julian first arrived at the imperial palace in Constantinople and asked for a barber, the man who answered his summons was so tricked out in ostentatious regalia that Julian said, "It is a barber that I want, and not a receiver-general of the finances." Told that this was indeed the imperial barber, filthy rich from his exorbitant salary, Julian dismissed the man—along with the palace cooks and any number of courtiers and hangers-on. Under its new emperor, the court of Constantinople would live more spartanly than it ever had—at least for a little while. For Julian would not stay long in his imperial city. He was on the march.

Because Julian's other audacious plan, if you will recall, was to conquer Persia.

IV.

Eight hundred years before Julian's time, the Persian Empire had twice tried to conquer Greece. A hundred years later, under Alexander the Great, the Greek-speaking Macedonians overran Persia and kept control of it for over a century. The Persians rose again, of course, but Julian believed he was going to be the one to stamp them out once and for all. Where Alexander had conquered, Julian could conquer. Had he not outdone Julius Caesar in Gaul? Had he not stupefied the Roman Empire with his march on Constantinople? Six months after assuming the purple, Julian left for Antioch to gather forces for the invasion. Further religious reforms would have to wait for his triumphant return.

There had been skirmishing on the Persian frontier throughout his reign, but the army Julian had assembled marked a significant new force, sixty-five thousand men—the largest any Roman had led into Persia. Julian took pains to use it wisely, confounding Persian spies by ordering supply dumps on the northern road from the Roman town of Carrhae, only to feint with his army briefly before wheeling around and taking the southern road along the east bank of the Euphrates River. Meanwhile, a second force of thirty thousand, under the generals Sebastian and Procopius, marched to Armenia to pick up reinforcements. They were to meet up with Julian at the Persian capital.

The emperor fanned his army out to make it appear even larger than it was and instill terror in the locals—a trick he had learned from reading his histories of the general Pyrrhus, who had fought long ago against the Roman Republic. The Persians in every town he passed either surrendered, fled, or agreed to remain neutral. The Romans pushed over two hundred miles into Persian territory without a fight.

And when they fought, they fought like Romans, under their brilliant commander. At Ozogardana they defeated a Persian force; after a brief siege, the city of Pirisabora surrendered; the larger city of Maozamalcha fell to the sword. Everywhere Julian was in the thick of battle, braving dangers alongside his men. When ten Persian assassins slipped into camp and two charged the emperor, he fought them off, slaying one personally and holding another at bay until his bodyguards could come to his aid. Outside Maozamalcha, Persian troops hid in caves, refusing to come out to fight but threatening the Romans' rear if they marched past. Julian contrived for dry brush to be burned in front of the caves; he smoked the Persians out. A Roman fleet had been towed down the Euphrates, and Julian had an ancient canal dug out, allowing it to pass over into the Tigris. Ctesiphon, the capital of the Persian Empire, lay right before them.

The first battle outside Ctesiphon was another Roman triumph. The historian Ammianus Marcellinus, who accompanied Julian into Persia, claims that the casualties were twenty-five hundred Persians to seventy

Romans, which sounds a little implausible—but he was there, and we were not. The Persians had to retreat within their city walls. Everything was going great.

Julian assumed the main Persian host would show up to save the capital and he could meet them in a final decisive battle. He assumed that Sebastian and Procopius were due any day now with reinforcements from Armenia. He assumed that his army could live off the rich land teeming with grain. Based on these assumptions, and against the advice of both counselors and soothsayers—a good pagan general traveled with soothsayers—Julian burned the Roman fleet.

In the days of Julian's grandfather, when the Romans had temporarily lost control of Britain, the general Julius Asclepiodotus led an expedition to the island and burned his ships behind him, lest his men be tempted to flee. Asclepiodotus reconquered Britain. But burning your own navy is not always the best idea. The Ottoman bey (and so-called Barbary pirate) Oruç "Barbarossa" Reis scuttled his ships before he attacked Béjaïa, and he lost both the battle and an arm; Hernando Cortés sank his ships before his first attack on the Aztec Empire, and he ended up retreating with heavy losses. Julian's navy was both his supply line and his means of emergency escape, and he set it on fire.

As soon as they saw that Julian had cut himself off this way, the Persians torched their own fields.

That was the move Julian had not anticipated. He was still undefeated in battle. The Persians attacked several times, and each time the Romans emerged victorious. Julian knew how to win a fight; it's just that with all the crops burned, he had no food! A siege of Ctesiphon was out of the question. Sebastian and Procopius were nowhere to be seen. Low on supplies, Julian began marching, hoping to find some forage. Everywhere he went the Persians had already destroyed. They harassed the Romans with hit-and-run tactics, harrying a foe they could not defeat. They knew that hunger would do what their weapons could not.

Finally, one day, in one stupid minor encounter at the Mesopotamian city of Samarra, Julian rushed into combat rashly with no armor on—he had not had time to prepare as he would have in a conventional battle. A spear passed through his side, and that was the end of Julian.

V.

In the middle of enemy territory, the Romans quickly elected a new emperor, who made an ignominious peace and saved the army by trading large swaths of Roman land for safe passage home. The new emperor, Jovian, was a Christian, as every Roman emperor would be for the next thousand years.

Julian's dreams died with him. In thirty years, paganism would be de facto illegal in the empire. The next generation would be Christian. The only large-scale harm Julian did to Christians lay in conducting such a disastrous campaign against Persia that Middle Eastern cities with growing Christian populations, such as Nisibis, were taken over by Persia. The Persians expelled all Christians from Nisibis.

Emperor Julian puts on his armor → *He survives to* **SNUFF OUT CHRISTIANITY** → *Europe embraces a syncretic mystery religion* → *The Ottoman Empire goes through the Renaissance and conquers Europe*

I.

BUT WHAT IF JULIAN HAD PUT HIS ARMOR ON AT SAMARRA? First thing: A spear thrust rebounds from his breastplate harmlessly. Julian and his dream live on—his dream to roll back history and return Rome to pagan glory.

The conquest of Persia is off, of course. Julian is not going to achieve it that day, and it is unlikely that any Roman commander would have been able to. But it doesn't have to be a *disaster*. Even with Julian wounded the Romans had managed to drive off the Persian assault; even with Julian dead the Romans had managed to make a treaty and get safely home. A brilliant commander like Julian could have done no worse. This one accident aside, neither Julian nor his men had to die in Persian territory. Nisibis stays Roman.

The real question for Julian is not whether he can recapitulate Alexander, but rather whether he can repudiate Paul.

When he brings his troops back to Carrhae, he will have been humiliated. The Romans have not necessarily lost the war, but they have failed in their objectives. It was the custom for Christian writers of the time to "spin" the failures of their opponents as expressions of the displeasure of God. When an adviser of Julian's (also named Julian) sickened and died right before the Persian campaign, St. Ephraem of Syria rejoiced in the providence of the event in one of his religious hymns, and this was hardly an unusual practice. As late as the eighth century, the medieval British writer Aldhelm celebrated in poetry the disgusting way that the heretic Arius died "while the fetid innards of his belly / He repulsively discharged, the intestines having burst from his anus"—Aldhelm pulls no punches here, and just gets more toilet-centric as he goes on. Thus does the Lord requite schismatics.

Hey, Isaac Newton of all people wrote a tract in 1690 claiming that Arius actually died in a much less disgusting way, and that the whole "fetid innards" story was a myth. Choose your sides.

So the Christians will interpret Julian's failure in Persia as a result of his apostasy—but they hate Julian anyway! His failure can hardly make him less popular among Christians. Worse is the fact that pagans, Jews, and fence-sitters now see him as unlucky. If Julian is seeking to influence the course of history, a reputation for luckless, ineffective adventurism is hardly a good start.

Fortunately for Julian, what happens in Persia sometimes stays in Persia. There is ample precedent for emperors fudging the results of distant wars. A century before Julian, the Roman emperor Philip (known to history as "Philip the Arab") had ceded territory and an enormous indemnity to Persia and then declared victory back in Rome, issuing coins celebrating the peace. Long after, Napoleon Bonaparte would begin his career with a humiliating defeat to the British in Egypt—but Bonaparte fled Egypt on a fast ship, reached Paris before news of his defeat, and proclaimed the Egyptian expedition a victory. By the time the truth reached France, Bonaparte was already in charge of things.

Even in the presence of so many witnesses, it should have been possible for Julian to gloss over his failures and play up his (admittedly numerous) victories. But would Julian, the principled philosopher, have been willing to do something this dishonest?

Well, in all probability he already had. Julian claimed in his own writings that the Roman successes in Gaul, starting with the reconquest of the city of Cologne from the Franks, were all his own doing, owing to his brilliant generalship. The Romans did in fact retake Cologne when Julian was in Gaul, but it was during his early months, when he had not yet assumed command of the army. It's very possible that the whole reason we think Julian was such a brilliant commander is that our primary sources for the period are Julian himself and one of his loyal soldiers, Ammianus Marcellinus—neither a neutral party.

It's always important to be suspicious of first-person accounts. Numbers 12:3 says that "Moses was the humblest man on the face of the earth"; according to tradition, Moses is himself the author of the book of Numbers; think about that for a while.

Even with the western frontier safe, and the eastern frontier protected by a hypothetical armistice with Persia (which Julian has to concede in order to get home), the Roman Empire still would have its fair share of troubles. Julian's successors had to deal with even more civil wars—the rising of Procopius, whom Julian had sent to Armenia, for example—as well as more barbarian invasions, and Julian's reign, had he lived, would probably have been just as hectic. But in all probability, he would have had enough free time to work on his plan for paganism. But what is that plan?

II.

Julian has always *meant something* to the people who wrote about him; he's always a *symbol*. In his time, he was either a traitor or a traditionalist;

in later years he starred as a rational hero to the Enlightenment, while Romantics such as the British poet Algernon Swinburne recast him as a brilliant rebel, a Lord Byron locked in dashing but hopeless combat with the forces of convention. Digging through the accumulated advertisements and mythologies of a historical figure is always difficult, but especially so when it is a figure that no writer has even written neutrally on.

Although "classicism" is often used as a shorthand for a balanced, rational, humanistic tradition, in the vein of Stoics such as Marcus Aurelius and Seneca, this is not the tradition Julian championed. Julian started his studies reading in the philosophical schools of Stoicism and Cynicism, but his true loyalty lay elsewhere, in the teachings of Neoplatonism.

The school of Neoplatonism is descended from the writings of Plato, but seven centuries separated the death of Plato from the life of Julian, and things had changed. At least one thing remained the same, though: Platonists and Neoplatonists were anti-materialists in the sense that they said the physical world wasn't *real*. Plotinus (the godfather of Neoplatonism) refused to have his portrait painted, because the resulting work would just be "a copy of a copy": the second *copy* in that phrase being his actual physical body, which was a mere copy of the "idea" of Plotinus.

Julian was especially drawn to the more mystical recesses of Neoplatonic teachings, and he believed in and encouraged magicians and wonder-workers, at least one of which, Maximus of Ephesus, accompanied Julian to Persia. The ancient world had several mystery cults, whose teachings were secrets only revealed to initiates in strange ceremonies, and Julian was initiated into the greatest of these—the Eleusinian Mysteries—as well as the more recent Mithraic Mysteries. In addition to being a frustrated Alexander, Julian was a frustrated mystic.

While Cynics and Stoics would often admit their own ignorance or uncertainty about certain aspects of their doctrine—the origin of things, or life after death—Neoplatonists, like Christians, had a totalizing system that offered to explain everything, with no part left out. In this way Neoplatonism presented a challenge to Christianity that other philosophical schools did not. How well, under Julian, would that challenge have done?

Gaetano Negri, mayor of Milan, wrote (in *his* book on Julian) that Christianity would have died out earlier if Nero hadn't started his persecutions. Nero perversely saved Christianity from extinction. Certainly, brute force can wipe out a religion—in the thirteenth century, for example, the church waged the Albigensian Crusade against Cathar heretics in southern France, and you will note a distinct lack of Catharism in France today. But it doesn't work as easily as you might expect.

As a less violent example we can look at the treatment of the Christians in Egypt after the Muslim conquest in AD 641. Instead of extermination (which probably would have been impossible anyway, the Muslims being so badly outnumbered), the conquerors opted for centuries of discrimination, most notably in the form of a special tax. Frustration with this state of affairs led to several large uprisings of the Christian natives, especially in the eighth and ninth centuries, which were, of course, violently put down, but the sectarian violence was the exception and not the rule. Eventually, Muslims held the majority in Egypt that they enjoy today.

Julian's scheme was more Egyptian than Albigensian. Generally clement in his temperament (especially for a Roman emperor), he tended to respond to recalcitrant subjects with his pen rather than with his sword. But his pen was sharp! Christians were his usual whipping boys, but he'd write against any Roman citizen he thought disloyal, decadent, hypocritical, or lacking in the Roman virtues—which was a lot of people! "I am at this moment preparing a treatise," Henrik Ibsen imagines Julian (in *his* book on Julian) haranguing his subjects in Antioch. "And would you know against whom it is directed? It is directed against you, citizens of Antioch." As you can imagine, outside a situation where he was delivering nonstop victories (as in Gaul), Julian simply wasn't very popular. He wanted everyone to live a simple, ascetic life, and he lashed out at anyone who was either soft or (depending on your point of view) fun.

In a word, Julian lacked the character or the charisma of a universalist. This is a large stumbling block in his goal to establish one pagan church with him at its head. He couldn't even get the pagans behind him!

But even if Julian can't achieve all he dreams, that doesn't mean he must completely fail, his legacy discarded instantly as it was after he died in Persia. Julian arrives on the scene at a tipping point, with the empire only a little over half Christian; the continued reign of Julian would have been a check on Christianity's momentum. If part of Christianity's appeal was its continued success, the setback of a reigning pagan emperor would be a powerful counterargument.

Another thing Julian can do, especially given a long reign, is fill the seats of power with pagans. Although Julian has no heir himself (his wife died when he was in Gaul, and he generally believed philosophers should live chastely, so he never remarried), it was common enough for Roman emperors to choose their successors, and Julian can ensure a pagan dynasty. Twenty years after Julian's death, the Senate was still pagan, and begged the Christian emperor Valentinian II to let them have a statue of the goddess Victory in the Senate building (he forbade it). A longer reign for Julian can similarly pack other government institutions, keeping Christians in the minority.

Steps like this are not going to resolve Julian's problem; they merely push the decision back. The Roman world will remain in a kind of crisis, with two opposing religious systems, Christian and pagan, vying for supremacy. Although premodern societies have existed with multiple faiths, the situation rarely ran smoothly for very long, even in places like East Asia, where we're used to seeing different religions coexisting in apparent harmony. In ninth-century China, the Taoist Emperor Wuzong sought to drive foreign influences out of the country by persecuting Buddhists, Christians, and adherents of other religions; in fourteenth-century Korea, anti-Buddhist Confucian rebels overthrew the Buddhist-majority government; in nineteenth-century Japan, Buddhist priests were forcibly converted to Shintoism as their temples were burned down. Certainly, when Buddhist temples in Japan were not being burned down by Shintos, they were being burned down by rival Buddhist monks.

Although the Roman Empire had maintained multiple religions in the past with some degree of peace, no two had been at such odds as Christianity and Neoplatonic paganism. Even without violence erupting (alas, George of Cappadocia!), the jockeying for power of different cliques would be, to say the least, inefficient for the operations of the empire.

Societies under pressure can remain under pressure for only so long. Something, as we tend to say, has to give. But was the Roman Empire doomed to the eternal feuding of equally matched forces?

III.

There is a history of religions bubbling up out of turmoil that offer a kind of compromise between opposing visions; such religions are called syncretisms. Islam is a syncretic religion that incorporates the history and teachings of both Judaism and Christianity with certain pre-Islamic rituals; Sikhism is a syncretic religion that seeks to unify the truths of Islam and Hinduism; Baha'i is a syncretic religion that emphasizes the partial unity of many world religions. Followers of any of these religions may point out that these brief descriptions are oversimplified, but they're broadly true. Certainly, Islam was first preached in a society where Christians and Jews offered differing alternatives to indigenous Arab religions; Islam's answer was that everyone was part right. We've already seen how Christianity blended aspects of Neoplatonism with Judaism.

There was, in fact, a certain syncretic religion current in Julian's time, the cult of Theos Hypsistos—a phrase that simply means, in Greek, *the highest god*. The highest god was sometimes worshipped under this generic name, sometimes under the name of Zeus Hypsistos.

During the reign of the emperor Tiberius, a mysterious voice at the seaside was heard crying out that "Great Pan is dead!" Later Christian writers said the voice referred to the death of Christ (because *pan* means *all*, and Christ is the Alpha and the Omega), and Jesus was indeed executed under Tiberius. But at the time, pagans who had never heard of a Jewish prophet worried that the voice referred to the death of their god Pan, Hermes's son. What if the Olympians were dying off? It was becoming harder to preserve the old beliefs of multiple gods with distinct personalities, but many skeptical pagans, rejecting Pan, still clung to the worship of Zeus, chief of the gods, as the only real god. Apollo and Aphrodite and all the rest were relegated to a supporting role, like angels or saints, and as early as the first century BC Cicero could call myths of the gods "fictions" by "madmen" while holding out hope for the existence of an "omnipresent and omnipotent" Zeus. "Who now believes in Hippocentaurs and Chimæras?"

So Theos Hypsistos was a name for the one god Zeus, but Theos Hypsistos was also used for the Jewish god in Greek writings such as the Septuagint (the Greek translation of the Torah). Although Christians employed the term less often, its use was not without precedent, and it appears in a similar form several places in the New Testament (such as Luke 8:28).

In this way it was difficult, even in ancient times, to know whether a worshipper of Theos Hypsistos was a pagan, a Jew, or a Christian. Gregory of Nazianzus, Archbishop of Constantinople under Emperor Theodosius, said that the followers of Theos Hypsistos were Christians "in all but name"—that is to say, their character and customs were the same as Christians'.

How much modification would it take to expand the syncretic appeal of Hypsistos to gain more Christian followers? It would take a prophet, but history is never short on prophets. Syncretic Islam swept across lands that had been comfortably Christian for centuries and lands that had been comfortably Zoroastrian for millennia. How much harder would it have been for a version of Hypsistarianism to sweep across lands that had only been Christian for decades? A little brake on the rise of Christianity, a little push toward paganism, would suffice to let it take off.

A world where Julian lives to push back on Christianity is a world with a Hypsistarian Empire, and then a Hypsistarian Europe.

IV.

It's impossible to overestimate how much of the culture and custom of even secularized modern Western society owes to Christianity. Weekends, the Emancipation Proclamation, and saying "God bless you" to a sneezer wouldn't exist without Christianity. Similarly, Christmas in America is not merely a Christian ritual; it is the anchor of the entire retail economy. Black Friday, the first day of the Christmas shopping season, gets its name because it is only after this day, with the year 91% over, that most stores see a profit (or are "in the black"). An economy without Christmas is a very different economy.

Of course, cultures with no history of Christianity have retail economies and can come up with concepts like weekends, too. A church of Hypsistos that preserved the Jewish idea of a sabbath would pass weekends along to the modern world. How closely a Hypsistarian world hews to ours will depend on how much of Christianity gets incorporated into this syncretic religion. It will have to be enough to make it appealing to Christians. Probably it will be more Arian than Nicaean because the less the emphasis on Jesus being the same as God, the better the religion would look to strict monotheists. Islam has always accepted Jesus as prophet, along with the miracles and the virgin birth—just not the co-divinity that most Christian sects (not you, Unitarians!) emphasize.

A world in which Theos Hypsistos overwhelms all competition as thoroughly as Christianity did will nevertheless differ from ours in key ways. First, let's look at what wouldn't change. Nothing that leads to the decline and fall of the Roman Empire will be prevented; barbarians are happy to loot Rome regardless of its religion. A post-Roman "dark age" will still have the unifying element of a shared liturgy; Constantinople will still be the jewel of Europe. Many of the factors that helped spread Islam in the seventh century—the potential energy of the Arabs, the weaknesses of the Roman and Persian states after a particularly long bloody war—will still be in place, even if the crucible that Islam sprang from is somewhat different.

We can guess the nature of Hypsistarianism by noting that one aspect of paganism that the emperor Julian was clearly fond of, and that he doubtless will try reviving, is its mystery. Remember, Julian was initiated into more than one mystery cult. No one knows exactly what initiates learned from the mysteries—that's why they're called mysteries—and the teachings were successfully kept from outsiders and never fully written down. We know that the Eleusinian Mysteries dealt with the goddess Persephone, who was kidnapped and taken to Hades, and her mother who sought for her—but not much else. The Egyptian goddess Isis had her own mysteries, imported to Rome. In the humorous second-century Latin proto-novel *Metamorphoses*, aka *The Golden Ass*, the hero is transformed into a donkey, turns back into a human, and thereafter becomes an initiate of Isis's. The author's description of Isis's rites is the most thorough to have survived to the present day, which means our best source on this religion is a fiction book about an intelligent donkey.

One of the most popular mysteries in Rome, especially among the army, was the cult of Mithras, previously alluded to. Mithras was a dying and reviving god, and the parallels with Christianity are obvious. Early Christian writers such as Tertullian and St. Jerome complained that Satan had plagiarized the true church in coming up with Mithraism. The nineteenth-century historian Ernest Renan famously prophesied that "if Christianity had been arrested in its growth by some mortal malady, the world would have been Mithraistic." Whether or not Renan's money was on the right horse, we will imagine that even though Theos Hypsistos was not a mystery cult, an increasing syncretism would have brought mystery aspects into it. If you're going to graft the most popular aspects of different religions onto yours, you won't want to miss one that the emperor loves and the people still queue up for.

Although the lips of Mithraic priests are still locked concerning their hidden teachings, David Ulansey has argued persuasively that the secret they guarded was the astronomical fact that the stars, called the "fixed stars" by ancient scientists, were not in fact fixed, but moved—not simply moved in their steady orbits around the earth as though they were embedded in a vast, rotating crystalline sphere, but actually *moved*, relative to one another and to the orbits of the planets. All modern astronomers recognize this as true, but until relatively recently the stars were *fixed*. Milton contrasts the Sun with "the fixt Stars, fixt in their Orb," and Shakespeare evoked the apocalyptic nature of the fall of Troy by suggesting that "little stars shot from their fixed places." To a Roman, who saw the stars as eternal and immutable, the idea that they could change position must have been mind-blowing, and dangerous enough that a whole sect grew up around it—to conceal this explosive concept from the masses. Imagine if Charles Darwin, instead of publishing the theory of evolution, had created a secret brotherhood, and only explained natural selection to those who demonstrated their worthiness.

Many religions have had their secrets. The Druze, a religion that traces its origins to tenth-century Islam, has traditionally kept its core beliefs secret from the majority of its adherents, who are therefore uncertain what the tenets of their own religion are—many early Druze immigrants to the US ended up members of Protestant churches, because the services seemed similar and there were not enough Druze around who knew the actual dogma. Mandaeanism, an even older religion that follows the teachings of John the Baptist (but not Jesus), reveals its secrets only to its priests, which caused a problem in 1831, when *every single Mandaean priest* died of cholera. Priests had been required to ritually drink untreated river water, and in the nineteenth-century Middle East, where Mandaeanism was centered, that custom proved deadly. (Ultimately, two enterprising deacons traveled around gathering every stray scrap of Mandaean lore any layperson knew, from which they attempted to reconstruct the lost Mandaean beliefs; the Mandaean church today owes its continued existence to their efforts.)

To return to our secrets: Medieval Christians attended services in a language they didn't understand (Latin) spoken by a priest who kept his back to them, which is not exactly a model of transparency. It's doubtful that most medieval peasants understood the niceties of Christian doctrine. Indeed, much of Christianity was locked up by the simple fact that in many parts of premodern Europe almost no one except clergy was literate: In the twelfth-century Norman poem by Béroul celebrating the romance between Sir Tristan and Queen Iseult, the lovers need convenient monks to write each other billets-doux. In a sense, the idea of a mystery is inherent to Christianity: The Greek word for "sacrament"—Christian rites such as baptism or communion—still used in the Eastern Orthodox Church, is *mysterion*; and the Catholic mass in English still includes the words "the mystery of faith."

But let's not overemphasize the secret aspect of Christianity. Sure, the Benedictine abbot Ælfric argued in the tenth century that translating the Bible into Old English would be very dangerous because men might want two wives after reading the story of Jacob. And, yes, there was a time in history when producing such a translation was punishable by death; William Tyndale paid with his life in 1536 to prove it. (In 1428 John Wycliffe was burned and his ashes scattered on a similar charge—but as he had already been dead for almost fifty years at that point, and his skeleton had to be dug up for the burning, it wasn't so bad for him.) Yet this kind of secrecy, unlike the secrecy of mystery cults, was always a controversial stance, not so much a core tenet of faith as an attempt to stop the spread of certain heresies, such as Protestantism. People kept translating the Bible, and no one could stop it—while no one ever spilled the secrets of Mithras.

Indeed, the Christian denominations that most emphasized secret teachings—such as certain Gnostic sects—were supplanted by orthodox Nicaean, and even Arian, Christians; and the Christian tenet that survived and flourished was one of preaching the "good news" rather indiscriminately. "Go tell it on the mountain," as the spiritual goes, "Over the hills and"—emphasize this part—"everywhere." The Jesuits (for example) were founded to spread the faith and to teach the students at Loyola University, not to whisper in secret the discoveries of Copernicus.

But such is not the case in a world where Julian encourages the ancient mysteries, where a mystery-inspired version of Hypsistarianism-with-Christian-bits mash-up is the common faith in Europe. Now, any scientific discoveries such as Copernicus's get folded into a Mithraic-style secret order. This order is going to be really good at astronomy! But—and this is the problem—scientific progress thrives on the dissemination of knowledge. One of the main causes of the scientific revolution that came out of the Renaissance was the newfangled printing press, which let knowledge spread much faster than laboriously hand-copied books ever could. With science locked away behind complicated initiations, knowledge never spreads.

V.

In 1533, word of Copernicus's theory that the earth orbited the sun reaches Pope Clement VII. Imagine that in 1534, Ignatius of Loyola gathers six friends and proposes the founding of the Jesuit Order to guard this, the latest revolutionary theory of the heavens. Kepler and Galileo would never hear a word of it. Copernicus's revolution would be stillborn.

For a thousand years, the Hypsistarian world is very similar to the one we know. But it cannot have the rapid expansion of scientific innovation that defined the next demi-millennium. It's a Middle Ages with no Renaissance.

If Europe never underwent a scientific revolution, if Europe never industrialized, if Europe never used its newfound knowledge to colonize so much of the world, who would?

Well, the Ottoman Turks, encouraged by their success conquering Constantinople in 1453, could have had a Renaissance of their own.

During the Middle Ages, various Turkish peoples swept from their homeland, somewhere north of China, westward across Asia, carving out huge empires. The vestiges of these empires are obvious throughout western Asia today, which is why the east end of Turkmenistan is two thousand miles from the west end of Turkey—and Turkmenistan is far from being the farthest Turkish-speaking nation. One group of Turks conquered the Byzantine Empire and later extended their dominion as far west as Algiers and as far north as Ukraine. This was the Ottoman Empire.

The Ottomans were in a unique position. They had access to the ancient Greek texts by virtue of conquering Constantinople, where the books were located, and therefore they could have read Aristotle in Greek, if they wanted to. They also had access to the Muslim scientific tradition, which had been expanding on ancient Greece's discoveries for centuries. At a time when ancient Greek science was neglected in Christian Europe, Arabs—and later Persians and other Islamic peoples—passed around translations of Greek scientific, mathematical, and philosophical texts. The extent to which medieval Muslim writers were obsessed with the Greeks is hard to overstate. To take just one example, if you read the *Tarikh al-Hind* (*History of India*) by al-Biruni, an eleventh-century Persian from Afghanistan writing in Arabic about India, you will find that the author can't stay on topic because he can't stop bringing up Plato!

Historians interested in the proximate cause of the Renaissance sometimes mention the influx of Greek texts from the Byzantine Empire into Italy, brought by monks who were fleeing the Turks. It is *precisely these texts* that the Ottoman Turks have the opportunity to read. And because they have access to Arabic and Persian commentaries on the Greeks, they actually have more immediate insight into these classical writings than the Italians did.

Because the lands of Turkic-speaking peoples (whom the Ottomans were sometimes at war with but always were trading with) stretch to India and China, as well as Central Asian sites of learning such as the Ghaznavid Empire, the Ottomans have easier access to the knowledge of the rest of the known world.

This means that the explosion of scientific knowledge that came out of the Renaissance will benefit the Ottomans, and not the Italians—or Western Europe in general.

The advantage that Western Europe acquired from a renewed interest in science allowed small countries from a small continent to impose direct or indirect conquest on much of the globe. The Turks, armed with nothing but scimitars and recurved bows, had already proved their ability to conquer Asia, and they would go on to conquer Eastern Europe. Imagine if they had the technological advantages Europe had—and if Europe didn't.

The Ottomans will certainly move on to take much more of Europe.

The forests of Germany that had stymied the Romans would also be no good for the Turks' traditional methods of fighting—riding around on horses and shooting your enemies from a distance—but that was before Turkish engineers and scientists innovated new modes of warfare. In our history, Ottomans adapted their combat techniques to fight the knights of medieval Europe; science-Ottomans would adapt faster and more successfully.

Just as the knowledge from the Renaissance and the subsequent scientific revolution radiated out from Italy throughout Europe, so the Ottoman Renaissance will galvanize the Turkish peoples who control Central Asia and northern India. While the Ottomans drive into Europe and across North Africa, these people will expand their already sizable empires. Turks had controlled the Middle East only a couple of centuries before, and Iraq and Arabia will fall to them again. Only seventy-five years after the fall of Constantinople, in our world, Turks conquered India *anyway*. Imagine what they can do with greater scientific knowledge. The Ming dynasty in China falls to horsemen from the steppes, just as the Jin and Song dynasties had fallen to the Mongols two centuries earlier. Russia, still weak and paying tribute to the Mongols, becomes a Turkish province. Central Asia is locked in internecine war as different Turks fight for control of the city of Samarkand. It may take four hundred years, but most of the Old World is a string of Turkish colonies, owing allegiances to various sultans and khans.

Art, meanwhile, one of the proudest monuments of Renaissance Italy, stagnates. Assuming that something resembling Islam has risen up in opposition to the Hypsistarians, the Ottomans will have embraced it; and a traditional Islamic injunction forbids depicting the human form. Consequently, Ottoman art is primarily nonrepresentational, and the discoveries of perspective and chiaroscuro that made the paintings of Leonardo da Vinci and Michelangelo wonders of the world would mean nothing to them. Although many Islamic peoples have ignored this injunction, the Ottomans tended to prefer calligraphy to illustration, and to render even their illustrations abstracted: humans with flowers for heads, or simply limbless, headless trunks. If perspective shows up, it will have to be elsewhere, such as in the Turkish Mughal Empire, where artists, in defiance of Islamic custom, excelled at drawing complicated scenes full of people.

One advantage the Turks do not have, though, is the advantage of geography. As the Turks push westward through Europe, Europeans will in turn be looking for somewhere to flee to. The Hypsistarian Jesuits, sole and mysterious gatekeepers of the knowledge of certain aspects of the heavens—and therefore of navigation—will have ships exploring in the Atlantic. There's no motivation for exploration quite as effective as the motivation of *imminent conquest*. One of the traditional reasons for the Turks heading west in the first place is a desire to avoid conquest by the Mongols. Even if no Columbus had had the geographical cockiness to set out in 1492, by 1592 or 1692 the Jesuits would have the knowledge, the drive, and the motivation. As the Ottomans sweep across Europe, the Jesuits are busy in the Americas carving out a series of kingdoms. Desperate European settlers sail to Florida and the Carolina coast at a far greater rate than our world saw. Stiff resistance from the Aztecs in Mexico may keep out the waves of settlers for a while, but North America won't be as lucky. Jesuit mystery–Europe may have a largely medieval technology, but much of the northern continent has a stone-age technology—and Old World diseases are already killing them.

By the time the Ottomans mop up the fighting in Spain, subduing the farthest point in southern Europe, a series of Jesuit-backed colonies have transported the remains of several European kingdoms and city-states to the New World, where their medieval infrastructures keep a precarious toehold against the natives.

Turks have rarely been great mariners; the Ottomans are the closest our world saw, and they did vie for control of the Mediterranean for a time, but that was unusual for a Turkish nation, and even they never sailed on the open ocean. Crossing the Atlantic to continue conquest would sound less appealing than moving on to Britain, or inland Africa.

The world is therefore divided. The Old World is a series of Turkish colonies. Africa is partitioned between Ottomans and Mughals, the two most powerful Turkish states. There are not enough Turks to actually settle China or Western Europe, so client states with varying degrees of autonomy send tribute and owe allegiance to Istanbul, or Samarkand, or any of the other Turkish capitals.

All Turks consider their only true rivals to be other Turks. Even when at peace along their actual borders, proxy wars in Indochina and South Africa—the limits of their empires, where holds are least secure—are common.

The New World, meanwhile, sees toward the south the Incas and Aztecs—unconquerable by medieval European technology—expanding toward each other's borders, while in the north a series of religious-based Jesuit states tries to export feudal Europe to a new continent. They are restricted to the coastline, living in mutual suspicion with their neighbors, mostly Algonquian, Iroquois, and Muscogee peoples. Although French, Italians, and Spaniards—maybe even the English—have separate colonies, the Jesuit order keeps them mostly at peace. Their great hope is that the Turks will wear themselves out by constantly fighting one another, and the exiled Europeans can return to reconquer the lands their relatives still toil in.

Meanwhile, knowledge of a heliocentric solar system, jealously guarded by the Jesuits, becomes common knowledge in the various Turkish empires. Some of them try to teach modern science to the natives of their client states. Somewhere in Krakow, Poland, a Turkish scholar lectures the native Poles about the latest astronomical discoveries in the very halls where Mikolaj Kopernik made the same discovery, half a millennium earlier. The name Copernicus is forgotten, but his discovery is no longer a secret.

10

VICE PRESIDENT HENRY WALLACE

What if the DNC chairman lost his gavel?

CHICAGO, 1944

I.

American presidential elections are ruled by custom as much as law. There's no federal or constitutional requirement preventing you from voting for a Republican president and a Democratic vice president, for example, although every state now sets its ballot up to make it difficult to do so. Or: It is now the custom to give major-party candidates only one chance to run for the presidency, but this is a relatively recent custom; the last candidate to lose a bid for president and then run a second time was Richard Nixon: Defeated in 1960 by JFK, he went up again in 1968 and won.

No defeated candidate, at least not from the Democratic or Republican Party, has gotten a second chance since then—but people used to do it all the time! In the late nineteenth and early twentieth centuries, William Jennings Bryan ran as a Democrat three times (he always lost); Henry Clay and Charles Cotesworth Pinckney are both earlier three-time losers, while more recent times saw the Republican Thomas Dewey (the last major candidate to sport a mustache) and Democrat Adlai Stevenson try twice and lose both times. Most famously, Grover Cleveland won his first election, lost his second, and then won his third, to become the twenty-second and twenty-fourth US president. If anyone sought to try that now, his party would shoot it down, simply because it is against custom. Al Gore fared very well in the 2000 election, but the Democrats didn't put him up again in 2004. Nobody wants a loser to run! But this is merely convention, and the Democrats could put Al Gore up again and again if they wished.

Or: George Washington, as everyone knows, stepped down after two terms, setting a precedent that presidents should serve no more than eight years. Washington was inspired by Cincinnatus, the (possibly legendary) ancient hero who was granted dictatorial power over Rome twice during times of crisis, and each time gave up power as soon as the crisis passed, returning to his life as a humble farmer; Washington also returned to farming when his time of service was up, and for over a century afterward every president followed his model and retired after two terms. If this had not been the custom, if Washington had not set this precedent, then Teddy Roosevelt would have been the Republican candidate in 1912, which sounds great—everyone wants more Teddy—except he would have gotten the US into World War I in 1914, bogging US troops down in the trenches during the bloodiest days of the war, which sounds like a terrible idea, at least for America.

FDR was the first (and only) president to serve more than eight years, and people were so scandalized by his decision to run again and again (until he finally died in office) that they *changed the Constitution afterward* to make sure it would never again happen. But if FDR was the first president to overturn Washington's term limit custom, he was the *last* president to do something that was once not uncommon (Lincoln did it; Grant did it): He switched vice presidents between elections.

Technically, it was not FDR who made the switch, but the Democratic party. *Technically,* presidential candidates do not decide who gets to run for vice president, and *technically,* the only president ever to come right out and choose his vice president was Richard Nixon, who picked Gerald Ford after Vice President Spiro Agnew resigned—but even Ford had to be ratified by Congress. Typically, though, even when the party is choosing, presidential candidates get to weigh in, or even have the primary say, over the VP selection process (although in 1956 Adlai Stevenson expressed no preference, and let the Democratic Party bosses choose as his running mate Estes Kefauver, a senator best remembered to history for whining that comic books were too scary).

Roosevelt's vice president for his first two terms (1933–41) was Texas congressman John Nance "Cactus Jack" Garner, and Garner refused to run for veep a third time in the 1940 election—because he hoped to be the Democrats' presidential candidate if FDR didn't run. Roosevelt thought Garner was a terrible choice for president, being far too conservative to carry on the Roosevelt administration's progressive New Deal policies (conservative Southerners were often Democrats in those days, an attempt to get revenge on the Republican Party for electing Lincoln). Some people say that Roosevelt only decided to run for a third term because all the Democratic frontrunners were, like Garner, insufficiently loyal to the New Deal. On the other hand, FDR's son Elliott once said, "Pop has tried for twenty-five years to become President, and he is going to keep on being President as long as he can."

Whatever his motives, FDR ran for a third term, and since his second-in-command of eight years had already bowed out, he was forced to choose a new vice-presidential candidate. Against the wishes of perhaps every major Democratic Party leader, Roosevelt settled on his secretary of agriculture, Henry Wallace. When the Wallace option was floated at the Democratic National Convention in Chicago, that toddlin' town, that somber city, the delegates booed; they then proceeded to boo Wallace's name every time it was mentioned, in every speech. Roosevelt had to threaten to withdraw his own candidacy if Wallace was not accepted.

Henry Wallace was hardly a hated man—most of the Democrats probably admired him—but he was an odd choice for the vice presidency. Wallace was a political novice who had never held elected office; his only experience in government was eight years in Roosevelt's cabinet. He was most famous for innovating ways of applying statistics to corn farming, one of the most boring but most useful qualifications a secretary of agriculture has ever boasted. He also pioneered the technique of crossbreeding strains of corn to make hardier, faster-growing crops that increased corn production in America by 50% in fifteen years, and with the use of less land. As secretary he had been indefatigable in his efforts to maintain food production and keep farm prices at sustainable levels during the Great Depression. He was generally seen as unpretentious and honest, but strange.

Roosevelt, in selecting Wallace for the vice presidency, focused on two things. *First*, Wallace was loyal to him, in a way that Cactus Jack Garner, for example, hadn't been. When FDR had run into trouble in 1937 with the Supreme Court striking down some of his programs, he had proposed, in one of his more nakedly brazen schemes, that he should be allowed to appoint extra Supreme Court members until justices who agreed with him were in the majority. Garner had criticized this as executive overreach, but Wallace had, however tepidly, defended it as necessary. (It didn't happen, of course; the Supreme Court still has nine justices, just as it has since 1869.) *Second*, Wallace was healthy. Roosevelt was by this time almost completely confined to a wheelchair, and the vigorous Wallace, a nonsmoking teetotaler who used to climb the 898 steps of the Washington Monument every time he passed it, helped to "balance the ticket" as far as appearances went.

Wallace had a tireless curiosity that led him to research the aerodynamic properties of boomerangs, say, or experiment on his own body with different crazy diets (only strawberries and corn meal: ca. 1909; only corn and dairy: 1917; soybean milk: 1934; only corn: ca. 1939; vitamin drinks: ca. 1940). He was always trying to figure out how things worked, a trait that served him well when he was developing new ways of growing corn. But it also led him to try to plumb the mystic secrets of the universe, which meant he fell prey to different charlatans, most notably the Russian-born Nicholas Roerich. A decent painter and possibly not a spy (for either the Soviets or the Japanese), Roerich presented himself as a spiritual guide whose artwork contained hypnotic and healing powers. Wallace fell for this story hook, line, and sinker, addressing Roerich as "guru" in a series of creepily fawning letters that are alternately hilarious and cringe-inducing.

Roerich and his wife ended up rooking the US government into paying for an alleged botanical expedition in Central Asia, a trip that produced little of scientific worth but allowed Roerich to follow his own secret plans, which apparently included fomenting vaguely utopian peasant uprisings in the steppes. Wallace (and Roosevelt, who had originally supported the expedition) withdrew funding, and tried in vain to get back monies that Roerich had claimed for undocumented expenses. In the end, Roerich, like so many gurus after him (the Maharishi, the Bhagwan, Sun Myung Moon, Jim Jones, etc.), was accused of tax evasion. He never returned to the US, preferring to live and die in Central Asia, his mysterious goals unknown.

Republican officials who acquired Wallace's letters found them so startling that in 1940 they briefly considered using them to humiliate the Roosevelt/Wallace ticket. (In the end, the Republicans didn't do it, at least in part because their own candidate, Wendell Willkie, had his own skeleton, viz. a mistress's, in his closet.)

How did the Republicans get the letters in the first place? The great guru Nicholas Roerich (or his proxies) sold them to his protégé's political rivals. This was the kind of amoral trickster that Wallace could be duped by, and it would not be the last time he was duped.

II.

Some people are too honest for politics. The British general Charles George Gordon became private secretary to Lord Ripon, governor general of India, in 1879. He sailed all the way from England to India, and on arriving found that one of his duties would be to reply to correspondence with boilerplate statements such as "Lord Ripon has read your letter with interest." Gordon knew well that Lord Ripon was *not in the habit of reading much of anything*, and naturally he refused to tell a lie, so after three days on the job he resigned and left India. Gordon was good at fighting, but he was too honest for politics. Wallace was good at farming, but he was too honest for politics. Assistant Attorney General Norman Littell compared Wallace's arrival in Washington to "a child . . . walking into a sawmill among a lot of flying buzz-saws." Roald Dahl, the eventual author of *Charlie and the Chocolate Factory*, spied on Wallace for the British Secret Service during WWII, and said that Wallace was "a lovely man, but too innocent and idealistic for the world."

So when, as vice president, Wallace feuded with Secretary of Commerce Jesse Jones, it was inevitable that the cynical, cunning Jones would emerge victorious. Jones managed to maneuver Wallace into criticizing the administration "on the record," and FDR could not forgive such a lapse in loyalty.

Nevertheless, Wallace struggled to hold on to the vice presidency for FDR's fourth term. Officially, FDR stated that the Democratic National Convention should choose his running mate, a hands-off policy that was a far cry from his 1939 push for Wallace. Unofficially, Roosevelt was angling behind Wallace's back for new blood. On the first day of the 1944 DNC in Chicago, Wallace's supporters had actually managed to whip up a pro-Wallace frenzy, and Florida senator Claude Pepper charged the podium to call for a vote to nominate Wallace, a ballot he may well have carried; but Democratic insider Robert Hannegan, allegedly under orders from Roosevelt, got the session chair, Samuel Jackson, to adjourn the session just as Pepper was reaching the podium. By the time the delegates reconvened the next day, Wallace's momentum had been broken, and Wallace found himself bounced from the ticket in favor of the truculent Missouri senator Harry S Truman.

Three months after Truman was sworn in as VP, President Roosevelt died, and Truman took over a job that would have been Wallace's if he had stayed on the ticket.

Truman's time in office is marked by two decisions that were to define most of the rest of the twentieth century. Truman's dropping of the A-bomb on Hiroshima and Nagasaki ushered in the "atomic age," and his hardline stance against Soviet influence, especially in Korea, brought the US into the Cold War. Wallace the mystic was always more trusting of the USSR than Truman, and more of an advocate for pacifism. But finishing the War in the Pacific and standing up to Stalin were jobs that would fall to Truman, and not to him.

Robert Hannegan, who had the session adjourned out from under Wallace's nose, later proposed, as his own epitaph, "Here lies the man who stopped Henry Wallace from becoming President of the United States."

*Samuel Jackson is slow to bang his gavel → Henry Wallace becomes VP, then POTUS → **THE US DROPS NO ATOM BOMBS ON JAPAN** → Northern Japan and much of Europe become Soviet client states*

I.

BUT WHAT IF HANNEGAN'S COMMAND HAD BEEN TARDY, AND Jackson had brought his gavel down a moment too late? What if Pepper's motion had carried, and Wallace had stayed on the ticket? There was no way Roosevelt was going to lose the 1944 election, regardless of whom he was running with. What if Wallace had been VP when Roosevelt died, ascending to the presidency in 1945?

He'd face the two big decisions President Truman had had to face in his first year in office: what to do with the atomic bomb and what to do with the Soviet Union.

According to Truman's victory speech, "the spirit of liberty" is what won the war with Japan, but the atomic bomb gets the real credit. It's hard to view the bombings of Hiroshima and Nagasaki without the lens of future events, but the Cold War, *Dr. Strangelove*, LBJ's "Daisy" ad, "Ban the Bomb," the "Star Wars" Strategic Defense Initiative, and mutual assured destruction are all things that no one had an inkling of in 1945. What people did have an inkling of, what Truman feared and what Wallace would have feared, was the prospect of American casualties as the war with Japan continued.

By 1945, Japan was obviously losing the war in the Pacific. The Japanese had been defeated in New Guinea, the Philippines, many smaller islands such as Iwo Jima, and (most recently) Okinawa. General MacArthur's "hit 'em where they ain't" strategy had successfully isolated many Japanese troops on Pacific islands where they languished, unable to contribute to the war effort. The next step for Allied forces was to invade the Japanese homeland. The success of the invasion was a foregone conclusion. Japan had every reason to surrender. The problem was that Japan had not surrendered.

Not surrendering was something the Japanese excelled at throughout the war. Traditionally, in European wars, a troop that loses one fifth of its strength, killed or wounded, capitulates. In other words, for every one casualty, four soldiers give up. The Japanese, though, had been suffering much higher casualty rates without surrendering. In the North Burma campaign, for example, Japanese troops experienced on average 99.2% (!) casualties and fought on. In some battles, the only Japanese who were taken prisoner had been knocked unconscious during the battle and *couldn't* keep fighting.

Japanese POWs often requested to be put to death: "But if your custom does not permit this, I will be a model prisoner," one is quoted as adding. And they were! Because Japanese soldiers were not supposed to be captured alive, they received no training on what to do should they become prisoners—while American troops in the same situation had been instructed to provide only name, rank, and serial number. American forces were surprised to find hardliner, patriotic Japanese willingly handing over information about troop placements and strengths. They'd never been told not to!

The tenacity of the Japanese gave the Allies cause to worry. The Battle of Okinawa had been a bloodbath, with around 14,000 Allied troop deaths—for an island less than five hundred square miles in area. Add to that over 100,000 Japanese and up to a third of the island's native population, about 150,000 Okinawan civilians, killed. Now scale those numbers up for the Japanese heartland and it makes for a daunting prospect.

Japanese kamikaze pilots were particularly terrifying to the Allied command, and had been very effective in Okinawa, sinking thirty-six ships and damaging over three hundred others. And Japan was innovating kamikaze-style submarines, "manned torpedoes" called *kaiten* subs. At a time when torpedoes' guidance systems were primitive gyroscopes, a torpedo that could steer had a huge advantage, even if the pilot could only use it once.

And Japan had also succeeded in creating and testing a combat jet in an era when almost all planes, and all planes in the Pacific, were propeller driven. The Nakajima Kikka jet plane was in production (but still half-assembled at the factory) when the war ended.

If that wasn't bad enough, remember that US forces had still never faced the largest part of the Japanese army. That's because the Japanese army was in China, conquering its east coast. Even if Allied forces seized the Japanese islands, they would then need to go on and invade a China defended by well over a million battle-hardened Japanese veterans.

Truman announced, and steadfastly maintained, that Allied troops—overwhelmingly American—would sustain half a million deaths invading the Japanese homeland.

II.

That estimate may have been high. Islands like Iwo Jima tend to have relatively few harbors and beaches, allowing Japanese defenders to concentrate their forces; Honshu, the central Japanese island, is the seventh largest island in the world, bigger than Great Britain, Cuba, or Iceland, with many attractive beaches for invaders to land at. Japan lacked the manpower to defend them all in depth, meaning the initial landing, at least, should go smoother than earlier Pacific battles. Admiral Ernest King put the number of casualties at closer to thirty-five thousand, obviously much lower than Truman's estimate.

Had Wallace been president, he would have heard King's thirty-five thousand number. He also would have known that Japan was depleted of resources, its cities suffering under a constant and merciless bombing campaign, its infrastructure in tatters. American planes had dropped mines into Japan's major harbors to disrupt shipping (the US Navy's "Operation Starvation"). With vital calories shunted to key military personnel, hunger was endemic among Japanese civilians, and outright famine always a looming presence.

General Douglas MacArthur thought the Japanese were about to give up—but of course MacArthur *always* thought the enemy was about to give up. In the Korean War, when most people thought UN forces under MacArthur were *losing*, the general called for North Korea to surrender unconditionally (North Korea didn't). MacArthur, incidentally, estimated over a million US casualties should there be an invasion.

Some lower-level Japanese diplomats had made overtures at a peace deal, either through the Soviet Union, which had no interest in helping, or Sweden, which did; but these overtures were hampered by a lack of support from the Japanese government. When people with actual power in Japan finally came around to looking into surrender, they insisted on a string of conditions, while the Allies had called for the unconditional surrender of Axis powers.

The phrase *unconditional surrender* may have entered wartime policy by accident. In a 1943 press conference, FDR quipped that the Civil War general Ulysses Simpson Grant had been called, after his initials, "Unconditional Surrender" Grant; he then casually mentioned the need for an unconditional surrender of the enemy in this war. The use of the term *unconditional* appears to have been an ad lib, but Roosevelt realized the propaganda power of the phrase and ran with it, trotting it out deliberately from then on. And there were valid reasons to demand an unconditional surrender. World War II was a direct extension of World War I, and World War I had ended with an ambiguous negotiated surrender. In the intervening years, this had become a potent Nazi propaganda tool, the idea that the Germans had never really surrendered, they had just been "stabbed in the back" (by the Jews, of course; this was Nazi propaganda, after all) at the negotiating table. In order to avoid a third world war, the Allies had decided to make sure that there was no confusion about who had surrendered to whom.

The Japanese demands included keeping their emperor, exempting their military from war crime trials, and preventing an Allied postwar occupation of Japan—which was never going to carry. But the demands were implicitly negotiable, and it's possible that Japan and the Allies, or at least the US and Britain, could have negotiated a peace acceptable to both. It's unlikely that the Allies would have ever done away with occupation or trials, yet clearly they did eventually accept the emperor. This was not necessarily an inevitability; Hirohito was constantly being linked to other Axis leaders in popular discourse. Woody Guthrie's 1944 propaganda song "Sally, Don't You Grieve" promises to "send Hirohito and Hitler, too," back to America (presumably to stand trial); one 1942 comic book offered readers a "daily reminder" to "give Benito and Hirohito a kick in the seato"; and Dan Gilbert's apocalyptic 1944 book, *Emperor Hirohito of Japan: Satan's Man of Mystery Unveiled in the Light of Prophecy*, declares that the "arch-murderers Hirohito and Hitler ought to be hanged together." Hirohito appeared alongside other Axis leaders in innumerable propaganda images, such as Arthur Szyk's famous cover to *Collier's* magazine (in which the three are pirates with bloody hands), as well as this 1942 ad campaign:

LET'S MAKE HITLER
AND HIROHITO
LOOK AS SICK AS
OLD BENITO
BUY DEFENSE BONDS
BURMA-SHAVE

Keeping Emperor Hirohito in power sounded as far-fetched as keeping Hitler in power. A June of 1945 Gallup poll indicated that a third of Americans (including Dan Gilbert) wanted Hirohito executed for war crimes; another 11% merely wanted him imprisoned for life. After World War I, only one of the Central Powers had been allowed to keep its head of state (the Ottoman Empire), and the Japanese were less popular in America in 1945 than the Turks had been in 1918.

The historian Ronald Takaki has proposed that the primary reasons for dropping the atomic bomb on an already faltering nation were two-fold: One was the desire to cow Stalin with a demonstration of the new superweapon; the other was President Truman's need to look like a decisive tough guy, both to the American people, who saw him as a junior-grade replacement for the imperial FDR, and to his hawkish tough-guy advisers, such as Secretary of State James Byrnes and Manhattan Project director General Leslie Groves, who went ahead and scheduled the bombing of Nagasaki while Truman was still dithering about whether to drop a second bomb.

Especially the first motive is often bandied about as the decisive factor. Just as China's chairman Chiang Kai-shek has been accused of refusing to put up much fight against the invading Japanese throughout World War II because he was stockpiling arms for a later fight against the real enemy that he feared more—Mao Zedong—so the US by 1945 may have worried more about the Soviet Union than moribund Imperial Japan. (For the record, Mao drove Chiang out of China, and the Japanese didn't, so Chiang was right in prioritizing his fears.) On the other hand, former national security adviser McGeorge Bundy writes that no evidence has ever surfaced that consideration for the Soviets entered any US discussions about dropping the bomb, well-documented as they were.

Wallace had a reputation for being soft on Communism. Former DNC treasurer George Allen once wrote that if Wallace became president he would rename the US "the Soviet States of America" and pass a bill requiring that fat southern Democrats be rendered into soap for "unwashed comrades" in the USSR—but Allen was at least partially joking. Certainly, Wallace went out of his way to say that he was not pro-Soviet, but pro-American. Yet in the same way that Roosevelt and later Truman were pro-American but broke toward Britain when conflicts between the British and the Soviets came up, Wallace made clear, time and time again, that Britain and the Soviet Union were roughly equal in his eyes. Wallace didn't like the Soviets' opposition to all religions, including his own unique mysticism; he didn't like Britain's imperial holdings in Africa and Asia. This is why the British had Roald Dahl spying on Wallace; they were very worried about a Wallace presidency and what it might mean for their empire. (Spoiler: They lost their empire anyway, without any help from America.)

Let's say, then, that Dahl's worst fears have come true and Wallace is now president. He may not be pro-Stalin, but he is less inclined than Truman to frighten Stalin. He also doesn't need to impress the hawks: Wallace never cared what other people thought of him; if he cared, he probably would have combed his hair. Wallace, unlike Truman and many of his advisers, had not fought in the trenches of World War I and had no visceral fear of a prolonged, fruitless war. If any American politician has been idealistic enough to believe Japan would surrender with no bomb, it's Wallace. So he doesn't drop it.

And then—Japan doesn't surrender. While the war rages on, while the Japanese and Chinese are fighting it out on the Chinese mainland, while B-29s drop conventional bombs on military and civilian targets daily, Japan doesn't surrender.

Ichiro Hatano, a teenager living in wartime Japan, wrote in his diary (his diary was published in English in the 1960s, which is why we can read it) that Japan was going to lose the war but it would never surrender. He wrote that entry on August 13, 1945—*after* Hiroshima and Nagasaki had been bombed.

Of course, Hatano was just a teenager, and just one guy. He didn't even get to vote about Japan's surrender. The people who did get to vote on Japan's surrender, though, Japan's Supreme War Council, also could not bring themselves to give in—*even after* Hiroshima *and* Nagasaki. Too many members wanted to "lure" the Allies onto mainland Japan, as though it were a trap, and fight them on their home soil. Emperor Hirohito had to step in to break the deadlock, demanding that they agree to capitulate and himself recording a message of surrender. At this point Major Kenji Hatanaka led members of the Imperial Guard and Ministry of War in an attempted coup d'etat. They sought to take over the imperial palace, overthrow the emperor, win over the army, execute the current and former prime ministers, locate and destroy the emperor's speech, and *never surrender*. The only goal they succeeded in was taking over the palace and holding it for six hours. The ringleaders then committed suicide.

So then, after two atomic bombs, a tie-breaking emperor, and a failed coup, Japan surrendered. Except Japan was still bad at surrendering. Small putsches sprang up across Japan as ultranationalists tried to gain enough power to keep the war going. The most successful managed to seize control of the city of Matsue for a few hours, which was not, all told, *very* successful. But then a group of diehard pilots at the naval airbase of Atsugi planned a kamikaze strike on the US battleship *Missouri* with General MacArthur and Admiral Nimitz aboard, come to Tokyo Bay to accept Japan's surrender. Only a last-minute appeal by the emperor's brother, Prince Takamatsu, who traveled to Atsugi in person, managed to persuade the pilots not to launch their planes.

"We will never surrender" is the kind of thing you say in a war. Winston Churchill, for example, said it, in those very words. It never does you any good to tell your opponents, "I'm almost ready to give up, just keep pummeling me a little longer." You always want them to assume that taking you down won't be worth the trouble.

Biologists have found something similar in what is called "agonistic behavior" in animals. The famous arched-back threat display of a cat is a good example: Two cats will face each other with their backs arched and their ears flat and their tails frizzed out, hissing and spitting, and then suddenly one of them backs down (if neither one backs down, they fight, of course, but usually one backs down). The submissive cat doesn't slowly de-arch its back. It keeps it fully arched until the moment it decides to give up, at which point the back goes down. This is common among animals who make agonistic displays: They go full throttle without wavering until the moment they decide to surrender. A cat who lets its back start to fall slightly—that cat is telling its opponent, "I am near the end of my rope; keep it up a little longer." Better for the cat to maintain its bluff.

What I'm saying is that if you are facing off against an enemy and you start backing down a little, *science says you are doing it wrong.*

So, when teenage Ichiro says he'll never surrender, he could have been bluffing. When the Japanese government said they would never surrender, they could have been bluffing. But you'll notice that Japan's *stated preference* of fighting to the bitter end matched its *revealed preference* pretty well.

Japanese pockets of resistance, soldiers on isolated islands who refused to surrender, were not uncommon up through the 1950s. One man, Hiroo Onoda, a Japanese lieutenant in the Philippines, refused to believe his country had surrendered and remained on active duty, carrying out a one-man guerrilla war against what he assumed were the Allies—the Filipino people, government, and police—until *1974*! He killed several people, burned crops, and slaughtered farm animals in acts of sabotage. His old commanding officer, long since retired from the military, had to fly out to the Philippines to persuade Lieutenant Onoda to turn himself in.

Meanwhile, in Brazil, which was and is home to a large Japanese expatriate community, many Japanese-Brazilians also didn't believe that the homeland had surrendered. A secret terrorist organization, Shindo Renmei, which boasted over fifty thousand members, began assassinating Japanese newspaper editors who did not publicly declare Japan victorious. For two years after the war, Shindo Renmei ran wild, killing at least fifteen Japanese-Brazilians and wounding twenty-one others for their lack of faith in Japan's victory—unreported incidents are probably much higher—before Brazilian police managed to break up the ring. As late as 1955 a rally of a hundred believers protested at the Japanese consulate in Brazil, insisting that history was wrong, and Japan would never surrender.

This is what Wallace will face when he decides not to drop the bomb. Perhaps he will elect to starve the Japanese into submission. Remember, Japan's already on the brink of starvation. Even before Pearl Harbor the Japanese government had seized so much food for military uses that there were civilian food shortages. Three years later, every day the war lasts means more deaths from starvation or malnutrition. Blockades and embargoes always sound like a nicer option than bombings and invasions, a peaceful, merciful option—win without firing a shot!—but blockades and embargoes always affect women and children and other noncombatants disproportionately, as the minimal food available is claimed by soldiers and politicians. US sanctions against Iraq after the invasion of Kuwait, for example, killed an estimated one hundred thousand *children* per year—and those sanctions were mild compared to the embargo Japan was facing. Under Wallace's blockade plan, famine and pestilence sweep Japan.

The famine doesn't last for too long, though, because even if the US was worried about the deaths caused by invading Japan, there's someone else who's less concerned with massive casualties. Joseph Stalin has wrapped up his plans in the European theater, is looking east, and has a long record of little or no regard for wasted soldiers' lives. Japan had humiliated Tsarist Russia in 1905, defeating its navy and claiming some minor Russian territories. Stalin certainly wants his territory back, but that's probably not all he wants.

After President Truman bombed Hiroshima, the Soviet Union declared war on Japan and invaded Manchuria. In fact, Stalin was so excited by the bombing that he moved the date for mobilization up by several days. Soviets fought Japan for less than a week before the Japanese surrender—at which point Stalin demanded the Allies split Japan as they had Germany, into spheres of influence governed by a council representing the different Allied powers. MacArthur, who was already in Japan at this point, brushed the demand aside, and even though a council was eventually formed, MacArthur ignored its decisions. Wallace would have been less likely to push back on Stalin this easily even if he'd been in a position to do so, and if the Soviets got into Japan first, a multilateral council would be the best Wallace could hope for.

III.

How bad would this scenario be for the Japanese? Let's do some math (Wallace loved to do math). Estimates for the number of Japanese who died at Hiroshima and Nagasaki tend to vary widely—not only were many records destroyed, but radiation killed people over long stretches of time, and it's not always clear whose cancers to count (many people would have gotten cancer anyway). In both cases, loss of life was exacerbated by the Japanese not being called to air-raid shelters: The small number of planes involved were insufficient to warrant sirens. (The Nagasaki bomb, though, landed some two miles from its target, in the Urakami Valley, which spared much of the city.) A good median estimate for both bombs combined is 150,000 dead, most of them civilians. This sounds terrible, and in part that's because war is always terrible, and bombs are always terrible. On March 9, 1945, conventional (non-nuclear) bombs dropped on Tokyo killed an estimated 100,000 Japanese, with around *1 million* rendered homeless.

If Wallace doesn't drop two nuclear bombs, that's 150,000 Japanese who don't die. But how many die in an invasion?

A quick note: We tend not to compare the deaths at Hiroshima and Nagasaki with other war deaths. Secretary of State John Foster Dulles believed that Stalinist propaganda had been at work persuading people that the atomic bomb was not just quantitatively different but qualitatively different from other weapons. Take anything Dulles says with a grain of salt, but the fact remains that the deaths at Hiroshima and Nagasaki are often set aside, out of context of the war around them. Wallace, like Truman, will not have had that luxury, so we won't take it either.

So, the invasion: Admiral King projected thirty-five thousand Allied casualties in invading the Japanese homeland, and Japanese casualties were always higher than Allied casualties in World War II. If the ratio of Allied to Japanese casualties from Okinawa held, that would mean 250,000 Japanese killed or wounded in an invasion. That's *if* King's estimate was accurate; but King had an incentive to pitch the count low. Military leaders tend to want to lead any major operations, and a low casualty estimate is like a low contract bid—more likely to get you the job. Remember that King was the commander in chief of the US fleet, and it would be his ships that would fight their way to the Japanese homeland.

202 • IMPOSSIBLE HISTORIES

King's projected thirty-five thousand Allied casualties sounds low for the invasion of Japan when you realize that only a third again more than the number of US casualties as in Iwo Jima (and far fewer than in Okinawa); in fact, estimates for casualties for this hypothetical invasion are so all over the place that you can pretty much pick one you like and find a source to back you up (that's what Truman did). If King's estimate, which is on the *very* low end of the spectrum, is too low, then 250,000 Japanese casualties is also an underestimate. If Truman's estimate is accurate, that's over *3 million* Japanese casualties from the invasion. If MacArthur's estimate: *6 million*!

And that's *if* the invasion took place right away. It's hard to find the number of Japanese who were dying per day from hunger at the end of the war, because people are much more likely to write about the famines the Japanese caused, in China and Vietnam, than the famine they suffered under. But by 1945 about a quarter of Japan's civilians would have been undernourished, with a concomitant increase in vitamin deficiency diseases, such as beriberi. Infant mortality was soaring. And every day it was getting worse.

And that's *if* the US led the Allied invasion. As any country in Eastern Europe will tell you, an invasion by Soviet troops leads to a vastly different level of casualties than an invasion by the US. Every army murders and rapes, but the Soviet army, in 1944, murdered and raped a lot more than most. Estimates of the number of German *civilians* killed by Soviets at the end of World War II range from half a million to two million. There's no reason to assume Stalin would be gentler on Japanese civilians.

The Soviets can enter Japanese territory from Sakhalin, without even buying a boat, and from there it's only twenty-five miles across the strait to the Japanese island of Hokkaido. When Stalin rolls into Japan, though, he encounters tough resistance. The Japanese, weakened and low on resources as they are, have spent the last year organizing a civilian militia, armed with bamboo spears when better weapons are not available. We now know that Japan had estimated that twenty-eight million citizens could swell the ranks of these militias. The Japanese had also studied, over the last year of the war, how to fight guerrilla style, harassing the enemy and withdrawing into the countryside. Soviet invaders discover that the Japanese know their home countryside best of all, and although they're poorly armed, the Japanese guerrillas far outnumber the invaders.

And the Japanese have a secret weapon—that's another secret weapon in addition to the jet planes, the kamikaze subs, the resources of China, and the twenty-eight million guerrilla fighters. They have what is called "the honorable death of the hundred million."

This was Japan's last-ditch plan in case of invasion, a plan for every man, woman, and child in the country to commit suicide.

The Japanese film director Akira Kurosawa wrote in his autobiography that on August 15, 1945, as he gathered with his coworkers in front of a radio (many Japanese didn't own radios in those days, so they had to share) to hear an announcement from the emperor, he fully expected instructions to kill himself—and that he and everyone he knew would "probably" do it. Some neighbors brought their samurai swords to the occasion. Instead, the radio came on and Emperor Hirohito instructed everyone not to commit suicide; rather, he said that Japan was surrendering for the first time in its history. But if Soviet tanks are rolling in from the north, while US troops are landing now in the south, the options for Japan are a lot starker. Hirohito may have given a different speech.

Presumably even with imperial instructions for mass suicide, not everyone in Japan follows through with the plan. Even if one hundred million do not go through with it (Japan's population was probably closer to seventy-two million), even if only 1% of the people die by their own hand—that's still three quarters of a million deaths. And if Kurosawa is to be believed, a lot more than 1% would have done it.

This, then, is Japan's dire end under a Wallace presidency. An idealist who only wanted to do what was right, who only wanted peace, Henry Wallace finds himself with the southern half of a divided Japan, invaded on two fronts, rapidly starving to death, and further ravaged by the sudden suicide of a significant percentage of its population. We were trying to do math here, but there's a lot of guesswork in adding the total casualties for the continued bombing, the famine, the American invasion, the Soviet invasion, and the suicides: A good estimate would be something around five to fifteen million Japanese dead.

And then, just as the Soviets built a north-south wall running across Berlin, now they build an east-west wall running across Tokyo. Just as an Iron Curtain falls across Europe, so an Iron Curtain falls across Japan.

(On the other hand, alleviating famines is pretty much Wallace's specialty, so he should be able to help Japan there.)

IV.

After the war, after the Axis had been defeated, there was the thorny question of the USSR.

Plenty of Americans have been enamored with Joseph Stalin, but few infatuations have survived much contact with him. Eleanor Roosevelt thought of the Soviet Union as a benign, progressive ally until she had to serve alongside it on the United Nations Commission on Human Rights. In the 1931 edition of his mammoth *Outline of History*, H. G. Wells praised Stalin as a "determined and uncompromising Communist" obsessed with stamping out "inequality"; the worst adjective Wells could muster against Stalin was "dour-spirited." By the 1961 edition of this work, Wells's friend, the journalist and former communist Raymond Postgate, charged with updating the history after Wells's death, gave Stalin many more pages and painted a *much less flattering* picture. The previous thirty years forced him to admit that the Soviets had set their eyes on conquest, the conquest of Europe.

It's hard to imagine Henry Wallace's rosy view of the Soviets lasting very long, but it wouldn't evaporate immediately. He was still grateful to Stalin for his help fighting the Germans. Socialite Evalyn Walsh McLean, owner of the Hope Diamond, said to him, "Now, Mr. Vice President, suppose you were in a barroom brawl and got rescued by a barroom bum. He might have saved your life. But would you take him home and let him share your house with your daughter and wife?"; the question was hypothetical, but Wallace was the sort who might have. What could Stalin get away with while he and Wallace were still on their honeymoon?

The first, but least important, postwar difference lies in the sharing of nuclear secrets. In our history Wallace was accused of lobbying to share nuclear weapons with the Soviets. He may not have—he denied it—but he was certainly looking to be more open with the scientific background, if not the technical specs, of the Bomb. Whatever extra information Wallace would have shared with Stalin is actually obviated by what Soviet spies were able to wrangle. Stalin may get a little head start in his nuclear program from Wallace, but only a little head start, and it doesn't change much.

Bomb or no bomb, though, Stalin has what may be the world's largest postwar army, and he's looking to make it work for him. While Truman began angling against Stalin almost right away, proposing the Truman Doctrine of pledging US assistance for countries fighting communist takeovers, Wallace tries talking things over with Stalin. Take some time to reason with Uncle Joe! Even Truman couldn't keep Poland and the rest of Eastern Europe from falling under Soviet puppet governments. Under Wallace, Greece becomes a Soviet satellite as well. Stalin quickly cements his hold on Austria before Wallace can muster an objection.

With Japan defeated, Japanese troops in China are easily routed, and the USSR is in a prime position to move in. It shares a very long border with China, and furthermore northern China is controlled by a Soviet ally, Mao Zedong. Under Truman, Mao took over China in 1949; Wallace would "lose China" (as they used to say) even earlier. Since Mao's repressive policies and foolish agricultural programs cause the deaths of thirty-four million Chinese, this sounds bad for China, but a faster end to civil war may actually end up saving lives, so call it even.

Truman went to war to keep the southern half of Korea from falling into communist hands. Wallace lets it go without a fight. A North Korea that controls the whole peninsula may be slightly less paranoid than one that looks across the DMZ at its opponent, but North Korea is still, for the second half of the twentieth century, one of the two or three worst places in the world to live. This is a terrible fate for the South Koreans.

For Western Europe, as well, things look rotten. Germany had pushed west twice in the century, and now Stalin and his enormous army control half of Germany, and (assuming China is for the moment still a client state) one fifth of the land on earth, and they're hungry for more.

Wallace has often been called an idealist and a dreamer, but he was not a fool. In 1944 he went on a diplomatic mission to Siberia and was duped into believing a Soviet slave labor camp was a pleasant village filled with pioneering volunteers. In 1948, while running as a fourth-party candidate for president, Wallace tried to orchestrate a meeting with Stalin to talk out an end to the Cold War. Okay, in 1944 and 1948 he was a fool—

—but by 1950 he had realized that Stalin did not want peace, did not want, as Wells claimed, "equality." Stalin wanted power, and Wallace eventually came to grips with this fact. In 1952 he wrote an extraordinary essay for *The Week* magazine, titled "Where I Was Wrong," explaining how he came to learn the shocking truth about the USSR.

Had he become president instead of Truman, Wallace would deal with the Soviets much more frequently, and he would wise up earlier. If he wises up soon enough, he may be able to organize an alliance similar to Truman's North Atlantic Treaty Organization (NATO), with the UK, France, West Germany, several other European countries, and Canada pledging with the US to join forces to deflect aggression—theoretically anyone's, but practically, in 1949, when it was founded, the Soviets'.

Wallace had always been a globalist, seeking to bring nations together in the spirit of fellowship: "Globaloney," Congresswoman Clare Boothe Luce called his more naive beliefs in this sphere. A sadder, wiser Wallace would see at last his dream of a peaceful unified world falling into the same armed camps he had sought to avoid. A powerful Soviet bloc that includes half of a crippled Japan and all of Korea (China asserts its independence soon enough, too large to fall under Soviet control) faces off against the attenuated and demoralized Western powers. Stalin and Mao, who each killed more people than Hitler did, have more time and room to play in. And the Cold War freezes on.

V.

This is a grim timeline, grimmer than our own, and all because Robert Hannegan was a minute slow to dismiss a political convention. The carnage wrought at Hiroshima and Nagasaki was so appalling that it may seem perverse to assert that Japan would have been better off after two atomic bombs than after none. The terrible accounts from the ground of physical agony—melted eyeballs, sloughed-off skin—are matched only by the traumatic experience of surviving in a city where there are not enough living to bury the dead, so that children (this is from the testimony of the Nagasaki resident Matsu Moriuchi) regard human corpses as no more important than dead ants. When the sick and wounded dragged, after the explosion at Nagasaki, their dying bodies into a bomb shelter (this is from the testimony of Sadako Moriyama) they no longer appeared to be human, and were mistaken for giant lizards.

So it is certainly perverse that Japan would thrive more in a world with the atomic bomb than a world without, but this is a genus of perversity common in history. In 1346, early in the Hundred Years' War, Edward III of England defeated a much larger French army at Crécy. It was a glorious victory, and celebrated in England—except his victory ensured that the Hundred Years' War, which England would lose in the end, lasted another *one hundred and seven years*. For over a century (with some brief armistices excepted), Englishmen battled and perished, only to lose everything they had fought so long for. Had Edward III retreated at the Battle of Crécy, it would have been the final battle in what we would call the Nine Years' War. Edward III is an English hero—no less than Arthur "Sherlock Holmes" Conan Doyle called his reign "the greatest epoch in English History," and the movie *Braveheart* goes so far as to imply that he is the son of Mel Gibson's character William Wallace—but England would have been better off without him.

And the same holds for many great battles. The winning side celebrates the victory, but if the battle makes the war last longer, it just adds up to more deaths. Phormio's naval victories over the Spartans in 429 BC allowed Athens to stay in the Peloponnesian War, and in his honor they dedicated a statue in the Acropolis; his victory ensured that the war would last three decades instead of three years; Athens lost anyway. Stonewall Jackson is a hero of the American South, but if he'd lost the Battle of Bull Run/Manassas right at the start of the war, three hundred thousand Southerners might not have died. As early as 1866, Southern historians recognized (perhaps for different reasons) that "the victory of Manassas proved the greatest misfortune that could have befallen the Confederacy."

The truth is that, for almost any war you're going to lose, you're better off losing it quickly. Even though it was on the winning side in World War I, France would have probably been better off losing the Battle of the Marne, and therefore the war, in 1914. The Germans had beaten them forty-three years before in the Franco-Prussian War, and nothing the French suffered in defeat in 1871 was as bad as four long years of trench warfare, let alone the sequel. France couldn't have *known* that, of course; they had no reason to surrender at the Marne. But it's hard to conclude otherwise in retrospect.

Japan would have been *best off* if the war had spontaneously ended without the Bomb, but there was no chance of that. The idea that Truman's decision to drop the bombs actually saved Japanese lives might have seemed a tough pill to swallow at the time. But it's hard to conclude otherwise (as they say) in retrospect.

And, of course, as bad as Hiroshima and Nagasaki were, we have seen that they were matched, for sheer awfulness and for scale, by numerous battles, sieges, and massacres in history. The Battle of Stalingrad, the siege of Leningrad, and the Soviet conquest of Berlin, just to choose three events close in time to 1945, all had much higher casualty rates, by a factor of ten, than Hiroshima or Nagasaki—many of the casualties, civilians. The bombings at Hiroshima and Nagasaki happened much more quickly than previous blood-soaked nightmares such as the Mongol conquests, the Taiping Rebellion, or Napoleon's adventures in Spain, but that's the twentieth century for you: Even though it was often no better than previous centuries, it was usually more efficient.

John Foster Dulles blamed the Soviets, but more likely we tell ourselves that the suffering of these two Japanese cities was unique in order to protect ourselves from the truth: that conventional war is also horrible, that noncombatants get shot and raped and starved to death constantly, that even the combatants are often just poor saps coerced into a war they would have rather avoided. Even the good wars are bad, even the just wars are unjust, even the necessary wars, if necessary, still tragedies.

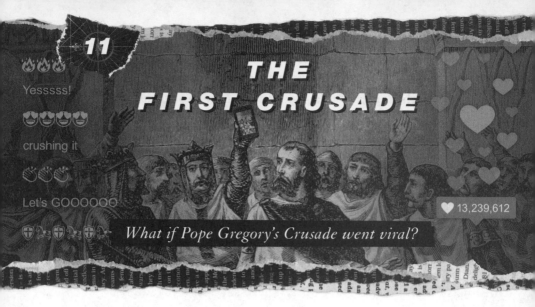

11

THE
FIRST CRUSADE

What if Pope Gregory's Crusade went viral?

Yesssss!

crushing it

Let's GOOOOOO

♥ 13,239,612

ROME, 1074

I.

The Crusades get a bad reputation. In a 1990 *Simpsons* episode, a TV producer, looking to cite an example of violence from the days "before cartoons were invented," presents as his only evidence the "tremendous violence" of the Crusades; and there are few people who would seek to contradict him. As far back as 1754, philosopher David Hume called the Crusades "the most signal and most durable monument of human folly, that has yet appeared in any age or nation." Charles Mackay, in his 1841 volume *Memoirs of Extraordinary Popular Delusions and the Madness of Crowds*, devoted over a hundred pages to the "folly" and "madness" of the Crusades. But the First Crusade did not begin as a random occurrence, an example of unprovoked imperialism, or even as a monument to folly. That's not to say that the First Crusade was good. The First Crusade was bad; but everything that happened in the eleventh century was also bad. Compared to the Paris Peace Accords or the invention of anesthesia, the Crusade was bad. Compared to the rest of AD 1095, the Crusade was neutral.

Specifically, the First Crusade was a response to three events that happened during the course of the eleventh century. It may not have been the *best* response, but it was a reasonable response. If it appears unreasonable, that's because the eleventh century was unreasonable.

The first event in question is the reign of Hakim the Mad. In the eleventh century, the Muslim world was divided up into various rival caliphates, each ruled by a *caliph*, a word that just means "successor," the successors of Muhammad. The Fatimid Caliphate controlled much of North Africa, including their home base of Egypt, as well as the Levant; most importantly, it controlled Jerusalem. Since different caliphs from one place or another had controlled Jerusalem since the year 637, this was just business as usual—until Hakim came to power. Hakim earned the title the Mad Caliph the hard way: He outlawed growing certain vegetables and the making of women's shoes, and he ordered every dog in Egypt killed. More significantly for our purposes, he first persecuted and then exiled Jews and Christians living in his realms, forcing conversions and destroying synagogues and churches, including the then seven-hundred-year-old Church of the Holy Sepulchre in Jerusalem. Jerusalem in general, and the Church of the Holy Sepulchre in particular, was a popular destination for pilgrims from Europe, who, for the first time in centuries, found themselves excluded from their most holy city. And then Hakim went ahead and declared himself to be God.

Or did he? Most of our information about Hakim comes from people who didn't like him, and medieval Islamic sources have a tendency to accuse splinter groups and heretical figures of impious acts. Hakim also executed the prophet ad-Darazi of the Druze, the only person who we know for certain went around claiming that Hakim was an incarnation of God, which is perhaps a sign that the caliph did not agree with his assessment. Hakim may have been less crazy than sources say. It's important to remember that if we only had medieval Christian sources to go by, we'd believe that Muslims worshipped an idol made of stone (*The Song of Roland*) and Jews ritually murdered Christian children (Chaucer's "The Prioress's Tale").

But even if he didn't kill dogs and usurp the title of Allah, Hakim certainly persecuted different religious minorities: Jews, Christians, and Sunni Muslims. The Mad Caliph himself disappeared mysteriously one night in 1021. A few years later the Christian Byzantine emperor in Constantinople paid to rebuild the Church of the Holy Sepulchre, with the permission of the post-Hakim Fatimids. But the reign of the Mad Caliph had already exposed some unpleasant truths that Europeans had spent centuries trying to deny.

Although religious persecution was more or less the norm throughout the Middle Ages, Hakim had taken the radical step of bringing religious persecution to a city that had generally enjoyed a precarious tolerance. Christianity in the Holy Land, it was now clear to Europeans, endured based on the whims of the infidel. Furthermore, pilgrimage to Jerusalem was a privilege, not a right.

And things got worse for the holy city. In 1073—the second of our three events—Turks conquered Jerusalem. After an unsuccessful revolt in 1077, the Turkish emir launched a general massacre of the population. Once again, the Christians of the Holy Land were in trouble; once again, pilgrimages were halted.

The Turkish conquest of Jerusalem was part of a larger Turkish expansion. The Turks had come all the way from the steppes north of China to carve out regions of influence in traditionally Muslim lands, picking up the religion of Islam along the way, and eventually pressing on into the Christian territories of the Byzantine Empire. In 1071, Turkish forces under Sultan Alp Arslan destroyed the Byzantine army at the Battle of Manzikert, taking Emperor Romanos IV prisoner. Byzantium never really recovered its former military might after the debacle. It also never recovered economically from losing so much of its heartland, as Turks took advantage of the aftermath of the battle to conquer and settle the place that we now, in their honor, call "Turkey."

Also never recovering was Emperor Romanos. He was ransomed and freed, but when he returned to Constantinople he found that there'd been a coup in his absence, and the new emperor's uncle put his eyes out and sent him to a monastery, where his infected eye sockets soon killed him.

But in 1095, another Byzantine emperor, Alexios, asked Pope Urban II in Rome for help reconquering Turkey from the Turks. He called for solidarity among Christians in the face of an expanding Muslim sphere. He pled for the fates of all the Christians who were now under the sovereignty of the Turks. The majority of the people of both Asia Minor and possibly Egypt, as well as a sizable minority of the Middle East, were still Christian at this point, despite their Muslim rulers. Emperor Alexis's request was the third event that brought about the Crusade, but he didn't quite get what he wanted. He had hoped that he could use foreign soldiers to win back the territory his Byzantine predecessors had lost two decades before. The Crusaders instead decided to conquer Jerusalem, which had not been part of the Byzantine Empire for over three centuries.

II.

No one knows quite what Pope Urban called for the Crusaders to do. Several mutually incompatible versions of his speech were passed down by medieval historians. Fulcher of Chartres, a Crusader himself who later wrote a history of the Crusade, claims that Urban specifically asked for a reconquest of the Byzantine lands of Asia Minor. On the other hand, Robert of Rheims, who did not go on the Crusade, wrote that Urban had called for the liberation of Jerusalem. Whatever Urban's intention, it was the march to Jerusalem that caught the fancy of the knights of Europe.

"Caught the fancy" is putting it too lightly. Every once in a while, an idea catches fire and sweeps over a country or a continent. In the Netherlands in the 1630s, tulips were rare imports from the Ottoman Empire, but such a passion sprang up for these rarities that *one bulb* was sold for forty-six hundred florins (enough to purchase thirty-eight hundred pounds of cheese) plus a new carriage and two horses with trappings. The price of tulip bulbs kept rocketing up, making fortunes as the Dutch neglected other industries to focus on purchasing tulip roots and planting tulip beds—until everyone lost interest, and those left holding tulips were left holding the bag. In later years we got a passion for hula hooping or Beatlemania.

The eleventh century had no radios, so the mania they got was a mania for "liberating" Jerusalem. You can see why it might have seemed like an exciting idea. Most Christians dreamed of making a pilgrimage to Jerusalem, if they could only afford it, which most couldn't. The Crusade was to be nothing less than the world's largest pilgrimage. The pope offered the additional inducement of a special dispensation—anyone who died along the way would be absolved of all sin.

Furthermore, all the Crusaders, or at least the educated leadership, knew that for three hundred years Christians had been on the defensive. In addition to the Middle East and North Africa, Muslims had conquered Spain and many Mediterranean islands. Only four years ago had Muslim rule in Sicily ended. In *The Crusades Through Arab Eyes*, Amin Maalouf cites the First Crusade as "the starting point of the millennial hostility between Islam and the West," but eleventh-century Christians would have cited as the starting point the last three centuries of Muslim expansion. Now at last was an opportunity to strike back.

The plan, make no mistake, was pretty foolish. If the Christian West wanted to fight Muslims, there were more sensible places to do it. Jerusalem was of limited strategic importance. A Crusade in Asia Minor, the way Emperor Alexios wanted, actually made more sense, since a strong Byzantine Empire would serve as a buffer state between Western Europe and Muslim incursion from the east. Or a Crusade in Spain could reconquer Islam's foothold in Europe. Or a Crusade in Egypt, an exceedingly wealthy and fairly Christian land, could have offered an excellent staging area for further conquest. (Several later Crusades actually tried this one.) Any of these plans would have had better long-term prospects than an attack on Jerusalem. But Jerusalem was where Europe's eyes turned, and no matter what Alexios, or the pope, or the Turks and caliphs wanted, Jerusalem would be where they marched to.

The fact that Jerusalem was not the best target was one argument against the Crusade. The desire not to add another war to a bloody century right at the beginning of history's bloodiest millennium would be another one. But the best argument against the Crusade—the argument any thinking person in 1095 should have made—was that it was almost certain to fail. There was simply no way several groups of knights with no recognized leader were going to be able to travel three thousand miles, largely through hostile territory, and outfight the hitherto pretty-much invincible armies of Islam. Everyone on this Crusade is going to die!

Except they didn't. Instead they conquered Jerusalem, established a kingdom called Outremer, which covered land that is now the countries of Israel and Lebanon, plus parts of Syria, Jordan, Turkey, and a sliver of Egypt—and ruled it for almost a century, with individual parts remaining in Crusader hands for 193 years. Nobody saw that coming. The Turks didn't see that coming.

III.

The success of the Crusaders can in part be chalked up to lucky timing. The Muslims in the Holy Land had been busy squabbling among themselves, first because of Turkish conquest and then because the Turkish leader Malik-Shah (son of Alp Arslan, who'd captured the emperor Romanos at Manzikert) got poisoned and died, and no one could agree on how to divide up his possessions. While the Turks fought against the Turks, the Fatimid Caliphate, which had helped start this whole trouble and which had lost Jerusalem in 1073, also fought against the Turks. The Fatimids managed to reconquer Jerusalem in 1098—after the Crusaders had started distracting Turkish forces northward—despite a succession crisis and ongoing civil war in Egypt. (This ongoing civil war is still more or less ongoing, by the way, *today*—in the form of a permanent schism in Islam between the Nizari and other Shi'ites.) While the Crusaders had no single leader, they were nevertheless unified in purpose; the Muslims they were fighting, on the other hand, couldn't stop fighting other Muslims.

Also important was the prevalence of the crossbow among the Crusaders. The Turks had had splendid successes in previous conflicts with a tactic that the Mongols later made great use of: They rode into battle lightly armored on fast horses and shot their opponents with short, recurved bows, keeping out of melee range for as long as possible. It's hard for an infantry, however puissant, to win a battle against a foe that will not close. The European crossbow, however, had an effective range comparable to the Turks' bows, preventing the Turkish forces from winning battles by attrition. The Turks could ride in a circle around the Crusaders' forces, firing in, but the Crusaders were at the same time firing out; and the Crusaders had better armor.

The crossbow had existed in Europe for centuries, but only in the decades leading up to the Crusades had its use become widespread. Crossbows are slow to reload, and less accurate than the English longbow that proved so deadly in the fourteenth century. But the crossbow has one advantage that neither English longbows nor Turkish shortbows could ever have: You can learn to shoot a crossbow in twenty minutes. In a couple of days, you're an expert. Archery had previously been a lifetime's learning; Turks trained from childhood to master their trick of firing while mounted; Edward III said: "If you want to train a longbowman, start with his grandfather." Crossbows could turn peasants into a viable fighting force rapidly. An apocryphal nineteenth-century advertising slogan for Colt revolvers ran: "Abe Lincoln may have freed all men, but Sam Colt made them equal." Before Sam Colt, crossbows made men equal, because for the first time, common folk had a weapon that could hurt a mounted, armored elite.

Unity and crossbows helped, but the Crusaders would have gotten nowhere without their other secret weapon: Crusader zeal. They had the luck to win their first battle with their Turkish antagonists, and the faith to interpret that victory as a divine mandate. They pressed on in situations where armies with lower morale would have turned back. At Dorylaeum, when one column was caught in an ambush, it held its ranks, fighting and dying but never surrendering against hopeless odds, until reinforcements, like a miracle, arrived. At Marra, when supplies failed them, the Crusaders ate human flesh from the slain. They persevered, even when things looked hopeless, because of their faith in the inevitable success of their cause.

The crisis point came at Antioch, a large city near what is now the southernmost extreme of Turkey. The Crusaders besieged Antioch for over seven months, failing to breach its ancient, impregnable walls, but sealing in its armies (which were led by Alp Arslan's grandson, Yaghi Siyan) in an attempt to starve the city into submission. The siege was going well enough, with the Crusaders driving off two potential relief forces. If the Crusaders were low on supplies, they could at least range over the countryside to forage, while the stores of Antioch must have been close to exhausted. In June, though, the Crusaders learned that they would not be able to wait any longer. The largest relief force yet was on its way, an alliance between rival, warring Turkish cities bringing the unified forces of Mosul, Aleppo, and Damascus marching to Antioch. The Crusaders were caught in a trap, with the hostile Antiochenes on one side, and a fresh, better-equipped, and better-provisioned army that also outnumbered them, on the other.

Realizing that they only had a couple of days to take the city or be crushed between two armies, the Crusader Bohemund of Taranto managed to bribe a disgruntled guardsman to let his Norman knights in, whereupon they opened the city gates to the Crusaders' main army. Local legend held that Antioch could never be taken by might, but only by cunning, and here the Crusaders proved cunning enough. Although Muslims still held the citadel, the Crusaders were safe behind the impregnable walls of Antioch, even as the great Turkish force rode into sight. Breathe a sigh of relief. The Christian army was safe! Ah, but everyone had forgotten that Antioch, before falling, had been on the brink of starvation. The Crusaders were indeed secure behind strong walls, but they were also trapped without supplies.

At that moment a lowly and hitherto anonymous Crusader, one Peter Bartholomew, stepped forward to inform the papal legate, Bishop Adhemar, that St. Andrew had appeared to him in a vision, informing him that the lance that had pierced Christ's side when he was on the cross (John 19:34) was buried here in Antioch, under St. Peter's Cathedral. A quick dig, and lo, the sacred relic was there.

Even medieval knights who believed in innumerable doubtful relics thought the miracle was a little too convenient. There was no reason for the lance to be in Antioch, no tradition linking Longinus (as later legend dubbed the Roman soldier whose lance it was) with the city. There was also no tradition linking the St. Andrew from Peter's vision with Antioch, or with the lance. Another version of this very same lance was already a famous relic in the reliquaries of Constantinople. But here was a lance, as St. Andrew and Peter Bartholomew had prophesied. And the Crusaders were in need of a miracle.

So, Bishop Adhemar had the lance bound to his standard, and rode out with the other Crusaders against the Turkish allied forces. The Crusaders were malnourished, exhausted, and outnumbered, but they had faith in the power of the lance. Perhaps the alliances between Turkish rivals was simply not strong enough. After a hard battle, their armies turned and ran, leaving behind supplies like manna to the starving Crusaders. So often in battle it is the morale of an army that wins the day, and the Crusaders had morale. From there they fought their way straight on to Jerusalem.

Pope Gregory calls a big Crusade years early → Man, does that Crusade fail → **COLUMBUS NEVER SAILS** → North America colonized first → United States of Hudsonia

I.

THE TURKISH VICTORY AT MANZIKERT WAS IN 1071. WHY DID it take the Byzantine emperor almost twenty-five years to call for help?

It didn't of course. The emperor turned to the West for help soon after the scope of the Manzikert disaster was clear. Although the western (Catholic) and eastern (Orthodox) Christians were not always friends or allies, the Turks were enough of a common threat that the pope at the time, Gregory VII, called for a Crusade on one glorious day in 1074.

Peace activists in the 1960s used to say, "What if they gave a war and no one came?" That's what happened in 1074. No one came. The pope's call for help fell on deaf ears. His plan didn't go, in a word, viral.

But what would a world where the Crusades were called a mere two decades earlier look like? It turns out it would be a completely different world.

First things first: If the Crusaders had left in 1074, the Crusades would fail. The Crusaders may have started with the same fiery zeal, but they would have been marching, in 1074, into a very different Middle East from the Middle East of 1095. In 1074 Malik was still sultan over all the Turks in the area. Malik was not as strong a figure as his father Alp Arslan, and the Turks may not have always obeyed him, but in the face of foreign invasion he made an excellent rallying point. At the very least, in 1074 the Turkish Empire was not in chaos, as it was after 1092.

You know what empire was in chaos in 1074? The Byzantine Empire, which was still staggering from the worst military disaster in its history and torn between rival claimants for the throne. In 1095 the Byzantines needed help reconquering lost territory; in 1074, the Byzantines just needed help. This would be a problem for the Crusade because the Crusaders in 1095 had relied on the Byzantines for their logistics—both food and transport from Europe to Asia. If crusading armies enter Byzantine lands still riven with political strife, there's every chance they'll get sucked into local politics, and never make it to Asia Minor in the first place. We know this could happen because it happened on a smaller scale several times: After the First Crusade, the Crusader Prince Bohemund decided to stop fighting Muslims and tried to besiege Constantinople instead; on his way to the Third Crusade, Richard the Lionheart stopped to fight a renegade Byzantine prince in Cyprus; most significantly, the soldiers of the Fourth Crusade, as part of a plan to get to Jerusalem, actually *conquered Constantinople and ruled it for fifty years.*

And if the Crusades had failed before they even got started? How would the world be different then? The historian Jacques Le Goff once joked that the most important result of the Crusades was that Europeans began eating apricots. Certainly, the territorial gains were short-lived.

Crusaders held the city of Jerusalem for less than a century, and maintained a significant presence in the Holy Land for less than two. Five cities (the so-called pentarchy) housed the original bishops of the Christian Church—Alexandria, Antioch, Constantinople, Jerusalem, and Rome—and in 1097 two of the five were held by Christians; by 1099, it was four out of five; by 1268, it was back to two out of five (and by 1453, as today, it's just one out of five—Rome).

Nevertheless, the impact of the Crusades on Europe was immense. They brought to this relatively insular continent an increased interest in and knowledge of Africa and Asia. Among other things (apricots, etc.), this knowledge encouraged European unity. An external enemy may not be a *sufficient* cause to get people to unify against it, but it may well be *necessary*. As Eric Hoffer has pointed out, you can have a mass movement without belief in a god, but you cannot have a mass movement without belief in a devil.

The expense of the Crusades forced the creation of a rudimentary financial system. In fact, the Crusading knights known as Knights of the Temple, or Templars, operated as something similar to Europe's first bank—until the French king Philip IV, who owed them money, decided to default in a novel way and accused the Templars of heresy in 1307. He arrested all members of the order; our old friend Jacques de Molay, last grand master of the Templars, he had burned at the stake with his lieutenants. Legend has it that when Louis XVI was beheaded by revolutionaries in 1793, a man on the scaffold held his head up to the crowd and shouted, "Jacques de Molay, thou art avenged!" But by that point, banking was well developed in Europe.

The Fifth Crusade, the one against the Byzantines, fatally weakened the empire, leading directly to its conquest by the Turks in 1453. As we have seen, Crusaders made walrus ivory fall from fashion, dooming the Greenlanders.

Timothy Dwight, eighth president of Yale, adds that "the Crusades had a favorable influence on taste" because "those who engaged in them had opportunities to see the remains of Grecian architecture, and carried home with them the feelings which they produce," so there is *that*.

But these are pretty vague effects, and difficult to measure. More direct and clear in its consequence is the fact that for centuries after the First Crusade, Christians were obsessed with reconquering (or re-reconquering) Jerusalem. And the Christian with the deepest reconquest obsession—well, it's probably hard to pick a winner, but one of the finalists would be Christopher Columbus.

II.

No one knows exactly where Columbus got the idea to sail across the Atlantic to reach Asia. (No one's certain where Columbus was born either; there's a lot we don't know about this guy.) Despite the enduring rumors, Columbus was definitely not trying to prove the earth was round. In the fifteenth century, being educated was synonymous with knowing the classics, and anyone who knew the classics would know, as the Greeks had deduced a millennium and a half earlier, that we stand our entire lives upon a ball.

As far as we can determine anyone's motivations from five hundred years ago, we can say that Columbus was motivated by a desire for gold; but he didn't want gold just for the sake of having it. Time and again in his life he pledged to devote all the wealth he gained to funding the reconquest of Jerusalem, even leaving a provision in his will to accomplish after death what he was never able to do in life. In the same way that Columbus proposed to reach Japan by sailing away from it, his every movement away from Jerusalem was designed to bring him closer to the holy city.

Columbus wasn't alone in this desire. One of his "rehearsal" voyages for his transatlantic trip was a southern jaunt to the Portuguese colony in Guinea, on the so-called Gold Coast of Africa. The wealth of the Gold Coast proved to be mostly illusory, but Portugal's expressed intent for colonizing the place was to use its riches to pay for another Crusade. In fact, Pope Eugene IV offered to those who fought to conquer Guinea the same dispensation (guaranteed salvation if you die!) that Urban II had offered to the Crusaders.

Without the siren song of Jerusalem to lead him, it's extremely unlikely that Columbus would have ever developed his own pet project. A world without the Crusades is a world without both apricots and without Columbus's discovery of the Americas.

Would that make a difference?

III.

In 1899, James D. Gillis, sometimes called the worst prose writer in Canadian history, wrote, "It may not be irrelevant here to remark what incalculable gratitude the greater part of the civilized world owes Spain. Were it not for Spain, America might not have been discovered." Gillis being Gillis, the remark was *completely irrelevant* to the rest of his book, but more importantly, it's wrong. Columbus could have stayed home in Genoa, and contact between Europe and the Americas would still have been made eventually. But—and this is the important part—it would not have been made in the fifteenth century, or even soon thereafter. It was going to take a while for someone else to stumble across the New World. Basically, if sailing to the New World and back was so easy, someone else would have done it already. In 1487, João Afonso do Estreito and Ferdinand Van Olmen made plans to co-captain a Portuguese voyage westward into the Atlantic. They never actually set sail.

Martín Alonzo Pinzón, who voyaged with Columbus as captain of the *Pinta*, alleged that he had been planning to zip across the Atlantic anyway when Columbus came along and swiped his idea. His heirs sued in sixteenth-century Spanish court (Pinzón himself had died in 1493, probably from syphilis), claiming the route taken was Pinzón's own discovery, one he had come across in an old book describing the westward route the biblical Queen of Sheba (!) took to reach Japan. Needless to say, no such manuscript is known to exist; and since the Queen of Sheba, ancestress of the Ethiopian (Axumite) emperors, lived ca. the tenth century BC, had she visited the islands of Japan she would have found them populated by hunter-gatherers who were not even Japanese. The Pinzón family's case was thrown out of court anyway.

Although not every "I would've done it even if Columbus hadn't" claim is necessarily as absurd as Pinzón's (it's only fair to note that it would have appeared less absurd in 1493 than it does now; Columbus himself wrote to the King and Queen of Spain that he had found, in the New World, the routes both to the mines of King Solomon and to the Garden of Eden), they all represent the surety of the proverbial Monday-morning quarterback. Sailing across the Atlantic looks easy once someone's done it. It sure didn't look easy before that. We don't know why Estreito and Van Olmen never made the voyage they planned, but a good guess is that they concluded it was suicidal to try.

Although some fifteenth-century technological innovations, such as square rigging, helped Columbus in his voyage, they were scarcely necessary for crossing the ocean—just ask Erik the Red! What was necessary was the will to try, mixed with the luck (or skill) of riding the right currents and winds. Also, money.

Columbus did not have an easy time getting backing for his voyage. Over the course of a long, frustrating decade, he was turned down by Spain, Portugal, France, and England before the Spanish monarchy reconsidered. Anyone else pitching a journey deep into the Atlantic would have had to overcome the same stumbling blocks that Columbus overcame. Few people in history have been as single-minded as Columbus, who kept hammering on his mad plan in court after court until he succeeded.

Furthermore, Columbus's entire journey was founded on an error: He thought the globe was smaller than it was, which is why he believed he could reach Japan in the first place. Most navigators knew the approximate size of the earth, and would not have been willing to venture the vast distance between Europe and Asia. There were certainly other people in Europe bad enough at geography to make the same blunder Columbus did, but none of them were simultaneously bad at geography and skilled at sailing and navigation. Columbus had a unique skill set in that he was above average in half the mariner's science and below average in the other half.

Without Columbus the Americas would have still been discovered eventually, but they may well have been discovered *in a different way*. English or Dutch ships would have taken a more northerly route, and started settling what is now Virginia or New York instead of what turned out to be the early centers of Spanish (and, starting in 1500, Portuguese) exploration. This is significant because the primary military threats to European conquest—the Aztec and Inca Empires—were in the south, where the Spanish started fighting them early in the process of New World colonization, in 1519 and 1532, respectively. The British colony of Jamestown, in contrast, was not founded until 1607. If the order of contact had been reversed, if the Aztecs had had another century to prepare for war with the Spanish, the results would have been different, and Pizarro would have failed had he faced an Inca Empire not torn by civil war. Half the advantage the Europeans had over formidable foes like the Aztecs and Incas was the advantage of surprise; they appeared from nowhere, and the native empires did not know what to make of them. Information may not have passed so well from North to South America—geography was against it—but word of strange new conquerors with strange new weapons is the kind of news that gets around, given a century.

North America also has a lot less gold in it than the Aztec and Inca Empires did. If Henry Hudson was the one to discover America, if he had landed in Canada in 1607, his report back to King James of a land of snow and trees would scarcely have galvanized the rush to conquer that Columbus's promises of gold did. The lower the impetus to conquer, the slower Europeans are to fight Aztecs and Incas, and the better chance these New World empires have against the Old.

The result is a North America colonized by the Dutch or English, while to the south the existing Aztec and Inca spheres of influence remain. Even if Europeans had managed to conquer these New World empires, the empires would have been stronger, more established foes. In our world, the people of the Americas, like those of Australia, largely lost their religion, their language, their culture, and their identity, but there are plenty of examples, such as French Indochina or British India, in which a European hegemony was grafted onto an existing power structure. A 1950s field survey, seeking to discover how many rural Indians knew that the British had left India the decade before, found instead that most *didn't know the British had ever ruled India in the first place.*

One tragedy of history that would not have been avoided without Columbus: The pandemic of European diseases that swept the Americas, brought by Columbus's sailors. European science would not learn of the transmission of germs for centuries after any plausible timeline for discovery, and the difficulty that governments even today have in containing epidemics—COVID-19 is just one example—is indicative of how quickly strange diseases can spread among a population with no native immunity. There was never a way to prevent a disaster that outstripped any war and even the bubonic plague—the greatest mass death in human history. With or without Columbus, geography dictated that contact between the two hemispheres would be marked by tragedy.

The Americas had the disadvantage of a relatively small population, and that disadvantage would have been exacerbated by the population's fall during the pandemic. But the Aztec and Inca Empires were at least more densely populated than the rest of the Americas, and although disease would severely reduce their numbers, those numbers would be on the upswing by the time Europeans began working their way to the south.

It goes without saying that the later that Europeans invade the American empires, the less likely they are to try eradicating the empires' cultures. The British in India worked hard eliminating some Indian customs—*sati*, or the act of burning widows, most notably—but the vast majority they recorded, studied, and even encouraged. Many British officers and representatives—most famously Major General Charles "Hindoo" Stuart—participated in native Hindu rituals and festivals. We know about these cases because the pastor Alexander Thompson wrote a book complaining about all these Christians backsliding into idolatry!

The difference between 1562, when conquistador/bishop Diego de

Landa burned all the Mayan books he could find, and 1784, when British philologist William Jones founded the Asiatick Society in Calcutta to study the languages and cultures of the subcontinent, is a difference in European thinking. The further away from 1562 that history pushes the conquest of South and Central America, the more likely it is that a Jones and not a de Landa will control the Mayan libraries.

Imagine a United States of Hudsonia, stretching, manifest destiny–style, to the Pacific; a somewhat older country than the 1776 one we know, and perhaps united with Canada. To its south lies the vast Aztec Empire, formerly a crown colony of Spain but now independent, ruled by a descendent of Montezuma. It includes the remaining Mayan cities, as well as surrounding lands in what we know as Mexico and Central America. On the Aztecs' border is the larger Inca Empire, which controls the west coast of South America, pressing halfway into Brazil. The east coast is a series of independent Portuguese and Spanish colonies (established later than they were in our history).

Despite a large missionary presence, the majority of the people south of Hudsonia still follow their native religious practices. They imitate western dress on both informal and business occasions, but weddings preserve local custom.

Among the fruits grown on the sunny west coast of the US of Hudsonia are grapes, oranges, strawberries—and no apricots.

12

ROMANTICISM

What if Samuel Taylor Coleridge started a commune in America?

CAMBRIDGE, 1794

I.

The first goal of art—and there may be many, but this is always the first—is to persuade people to notice it. This isn't always easy. If you just want to look at something beautiful, there are many competing beautiful things around. Trees are beautiful. Sunsets are beautiful. Cloud formations are beautiful. The moon is beautiful. Even if you live in some blighted wasteland devoid of natural beauty, you can probably look at the moon.

Nothing is valued unless it is rare. Sunsets happen literally every day, and the moon only takes a couple of nights off a month. Goethe says that nobody looks at a rainbow after it's been in the sky fifteen minutes. The thirteenth-century Persian poet Saadi points out that the sun is only appreciated in winter, when it rarely appears. Art, to be valued above any number of other lovely things, has to be *made rare*. Art is rare because it's hard to do. "The lyf so short, the craft so long to lerne," as Chaucer puts it.

Sonnets have rules, and the average person is not equipped to write a sonnet: Not a good sonnet, necessarily; I mean that the average person could not produce fourteen lines of rhyming iambic pentameter. It takes practice, and few of us have practiced. Playing a song on a piano takes practice. Producing a painting that looks like a person, a landscape, or a bowl of fruit takes practice. Therefore, there has generally been a limited number of such paintings available. It takes skill to produce a portrait, or a song, or a sonnet, and as there's only so much skill doled out to humanity, there's only so much art. Art is rare, which is how you know it's art. Sunsets aren't art, because they require literally no skill.

That's the history of art in a nutshell: From cave paintings through the late nineteenth century, a span of some forty thousand years, artists sought to hone their *skill*; they sought *technical mastery*. Then, in the second half of the nineteenth century, they achieved it. And everyone panicked.

The composer Richard Strauss (*Also sprach Zarathustra*, 1896) demonstrated an unmatched technique, making music perform, in Barbara Tuchman's phrase, "like a trained seal." In art, John Singer Sargent (*Fumée d'ambre gris*, 1880) managed to make watercolors look like oil paints; no artist before him had been able to make the brush behave so precisely. Lord Tennyson ("Crossing the Bar," 1889), meanwhile, by common consensus, possessed the "best ear" of any English poet; every line of his lyrics was exactly as sonorous and euphonious as he wished it to be. Technically, no one had ever been as good as Strauss, Sargent, or Tennyson. And yet.

And yet it was hard to shake the feeling that Strauss's compositions weren't as good as Beethoven's or Mozart's; that Sargent's paintings weren't as good as Leonardo's or Rembrandt's; that Tennyson's poems frankly couldn't hold a candle to Milton's or Shakespeare's. Technically, Strauss was the best, but he did not produce the best work. This was a crisis point: for art, but also for humanity. Literally for forty millennia we as a species had striven for a goal, and it turned out the goal was the wrong one.

So, artists declared that technical mastery was a mirage. Skill was a mere party trick. They called it, with a sneer, "talent" or "craft." Today only actors say *talent* or *craft* in a non-pejorative context. Art was from now on to be the province not of craftsmen but of *genius*.

Discarding skill, though, has a problem. Anyone can claim to be a genius. Under the old model, the proof was in the pudding: An incompetent painting had been easy to detect; it didn't look like something! Now that skill was a back number, the floodgates were open for anything to be art. And this surfeit of art would then have no value; it would not be art. Quick! Quick! Something had to be found to make art rare in the absence of skill.

That something was *audacity*. Audacity was the calling card of Modernism.

It would be thoroughly unfair to allege that Modernists lack skill. Not even James Joyce's harshest critics have dared to call him untalented. Although some Modernists attempted to dispense with skill altogether, demanding that art be composed at random by mechanized chance, most kept some vestige (Paul Klee) or a great deal (T. S. Eliot) of traditional "skill." And all had audacity. Audacity may not have been a sufficient trait to be a Modernist, but it was a necessary one.

It took audacity for Marcel Duchamp to enter a urinal in an art show as "sculpture." It took audacity for cubists to display their "ugly," "primitive" work next to traditional landscapes and rubicund nudes. Artists always have to be ready to endure criticism, but the lambasting Modernists received was unprecedented. Modern artists were a punch-line for decades: See any issue of the *New Yorker*, especially from the 1950s. A man mistakes a modern sculpture for a hat rack; cracks in the museum wall are mistaken for artwork; a dropped fern is mistaken for ("Masterful!" "Superb!" "Divine") a masterpiece; etc. A 1916 editorial in *Art World* confidently proclaimed, "We see therefore that Modernism is a spiritual disease." Painter Georges Braque (not even a philistine!) told Picasso in 1907, "You paint as if you wanted us to eat rope-ends or to drink petrol."

The 1913 ballet *Rite of Spring* was so audacious, the audience at its Paris premiere rioted. As far as riots go, it was fairly peaceful—seems like no one was hurt, although accounts vary. That same year, the rioting at a concert in Vienna was worse—at least in Paris they got to finish *Rite of Spring*, while in Vienna, Alban Berg's atonal *Altenberg Lieder* were cut off in the middle by the erupting violence. The work would not be performed in full for another thirty-nine years.

At a 1930 screening of the surrealist film *L'Âge d'or*, scandalized viewers threw ink at the screen, set off smoke bombs, and generally vandalized the theater and assaulted the audience. After Margaret Anderson and Jane Heap were convicted in 1921 (on obscenity charges) for publishing extracts from James Joyce's novel *Ulysses* in America, the *New York Times* crowed that the offending passages were "incomprehensible and therefore dull," only of interest to "psychopathologists." A judge on the case called *Ulysses* "the ravings of a disordered mind." No American or British publisher would touch *Ulysses* after that; it was eventually published in France.

De l'audace! But a problem eventually surfaced, which was that although first-generation Modernists required audacity to create their works, later generations would not. Nothing, nowadays, is safer than an abstract painting; the painting may be good and it may be bad, but it is always safe. Nobody's going to riot at your discordant compositions or your free verse chapbooks. Desperately, artists court any degree of controversy. By 1971, Chris Burden arranged to be shot in the arm as part of a performance art piece. By 1987, less imaginatively, Andres Serrano photographed a crucifix immersed in urine. How much audacity this took is questionable. Serrano slumbered the sleep of the just while unheard philistines vainly registered their complaints. Audacity is a dead letter, so we're due for another crisis soon.

But this is not the story of the future. This is the story of the past. Yes, yes, ca. 1900 people decided to replace skill with audacious genius, but they didn't come up with this idea out of the blue. They came up with this idea because of Romanticism.

II.

In 1794, two young friends in England made plans to travel to the wilds of America and start a utopian commune. By the nineteenth century, utopias would be an American staple—in 1840 Ralph Waldo Emerson would write that every literate man in America has "a draft of a new community in his waistcoat pocket"—but this would be one of the first, a radically egalitarian utopia "where," as one of the planners phrased it,

Virtue calm with careless step may stray,
And dancing to the moonlight roundelay,
The wizard Passions weave an holy spell.

Unfortunately for the wizard Passions, the two friends wrangled neither the funding nor sufficient willing participants, and eventually they quarreled and the whole scheme collapsed. One of these friends was Robert Southey, who would grow up to write "[Goldilocks and] the Three Bears" and become poet laureate of England. The other was Samuel Taylor Coleridge.

Coleridge later fell in with William Wordsworth, a promising young poet too diffident to publish his own work. Coleridge proclaimed him "the greatest poet since Milton," which might not have been strictly true, but was at least not far off. They became best friends, with Wordsworth's sister, Dorothy, forming the third leg of their tripod. They revised each other's poetry, they swapped stanzas, they plotted out works for the other to execute. Above all, they spoke, during endless rambling walks through the countryside, of the nature of poetry, or rather, what that nature should be. In 1798 Wordsworth and Coleridge published a joint book of poetry, *Lyrical Ballads.* Even though the two friends were undoubtedly two of the three greatest living poets in English, the book was alternately ignored and excoriated by the traditional press—but it inspired a rising genera- tion of poets. They would be the vanguard of one of the most influential artistic movements in history. They would be the Romantics.

"What is this Romanticism anyway?" you may want to ask, but that's the wrong question. You should never ask what an artistic movement is; you should instead ask what texts you should read to understand what an artistic movement is, because any attempt to summarize a movement is bound to be embarrassingly reductive. For example, Franz Kafka was a Modernist, but 0% of Kafka critics would identify *audacity* as a key component of his personality, despite anything I may have said in the preceding pages. Broadly speaking, if you must know, Romanticism rests on the four pillars of *1.* the triumph of the imagination, *2.* the splendors of nature, *3.* wouldn't it be interesting to be a shepherd? and *4.* vengeful ghosts. You'll find all four in Wordsworth and Coleridge's *Lyrical Ballads*. If you want to understand Romanticism, just read their book. All the Romantics did.

Coleridge founds a utopian society in the wilderness → And dies immediately → Romanticism is strangled in the cradle → NO ONE IS COOL

I.

OF COURSE, IF COLERIDGE HAD GONE OFF TO FOUND A UTOPIA in the American wilderness, there would have been no *Lyrical Ballads* in the first place. There would have been no school of British Romanticism. *Lyrical Ballads* was one of those works that "starts something"—such as Filippo Brunelleschi's 1415 painting of the Florence Baptistery. Brunelleschi's was the first to use modern perspective; after 1415, perspective *caught on*.

But perspective in 1415 was "in the air," as they say. If Brunelleschi hadn't figured it out, some other Italian artist would have soon after. More daring was the innovation Ludovico Ariosto made in his sixteenth-century epic *Orlando Furioso*. Ariosto invented the cliffhanger: Many cantos of his poem end with the hero in peril, and then the following canto takes up a separate plot thread, with a different hero (the *Furioso* has a large cast of characters). Contemporary critics hated this innovation, demanding to know why any sane reader would want to stop reading just as the interest was highest—why any sane reader would want to be left *in suspense*. Future bookworms would (of course) be kinder to Ariosto's invention, although the technique was associated enough with him that over a century later Walter Scott could half apologize for switching between characters by affirming in *Ivanhoe*, "Like old Ariosto, we do not pique ourselves upon continuing uniformly to keep company with any one personage of our drama." In 1791 the English translator John Hoole issued an improved edition of *Orlando Furioso* with "the narrative connected and the stories disposed in a regular series" so as not to frustrate the reader. And yet suspense endured, even flourished.

At the end of the eighteenth century, Romanticism was all the rage, but it was more like perspective than it was like cliffhangers. Romanticism was in the air. Wordsworth and Coleridge did not invent it on their rambles.

Indeed, it was a crisis of sorts that gave birth to Romanticism. The previous age—starting in the mid-seventeenth century—had been an age of classicism. John Dryden, and after him Alexander Pope, hammered out (in fancied imitation of the aesthetic of the ancients) precise, regular, rhymed couplets; the method had caught on, and poetry in their wake became a matter of "rule and compass"; it was, in a word, boring. After Pope died (in 1744), there was no shortage of poetry in English, but there were no longer any poets. Lord Macaulay calls the middle portion of the eighteenth century "the most deplorable part of our [i.e., English] literary history," which is harsh, and only true if we *1.* limit things to poetry and *2.* forget about the fallow fifteenth century.

The artistic bankruptcy of classical verse encouraged people to experiment with . . . anything else. Adumbrations of Romanticism keep cropping up in English poetry throughout the eighteenth century: in the nature imagery of Thomas Gray's "Elegy Written in a Country Churchyard" (1751), in the haunting melancholy of Oliver Goldsmith's (otherwise classical) "The Deserted Village" (1770), and especially in the works of William Cowper, who made a cottage industry of poems about nature ("Thou knowest my praise of nature most sincere") and rustics ("Oh, happy peasant! Oh, unhappy bard!"). Cowper was extremely popular "before the English world stopped reading him" (as Agnes Repplier put it in her cutting way), and his poetry helped change the public taste. By the time Robert Burns—an honest-to-God peasant who writes poems!—appeared on the scene in the mid-1780s, everyone was primed and ready for his rustic airs. Meanwhile, the new gothic novel (starting with *The Castle of Otranto*, 1764) brought the supernatural and the medieval into vogue.

Edmund Burke had distinguished, in 1757, between the aesthetics of *the beautiful* and the aesthetics of *the sublime*: Gardens and rolling hills are beautiful; jagged volcanic crags struck by lightning are sublime. Burke tended to draw, for his sublime quotations, on the works of John Milton, but only because he was writing before Romanticism took over. Had he written a century later, any number of passages from Coleridge or Byron could have filled in. If there's one thing the Romantics were, it is sublime.

After Burke, the world was ready for sublimity. It was ready for Romanticism. William Blake, toiling in obscurity, had already started his very, very sublime prophetic books in the 1780s. What with Cowper, Burns, Blake, and the gothic fad, you may wonder why the efforts of Wordsworth and Coleridge are even necessary at all.

They might not have been, except for the French Revolution.

Alan Ryan points out that France, over the span of some fifteen years, recapitulated the *entire history of ancient Rome*: from monarchy to republic to dictatorship to an empire that conquers Europe—and then the fall. Karl Marx would later claim that the tragedy of the French Revolution repeated itself as farce, but of course the revolution was already history repeating; all of France, compared to Rome, was a farce.

In England—which had had its own revolutions in 1688 (glorious!) and 1649 (less glorious)—the French Revolution was terrifying. France had long been England's chief rival, but it had always been, at the very least, a civilized nation. Now, not only were Frenchmen indulging in mass decapitations, impiety, incessant ("the revolution, like Saturn, devours its children") purges, and regicide—but England's own young radicals were sympathizing with the enemy! The revolution was romantic as all get-out. Years later, after another romantic revolution, Krupskaya—Lenin's wife—would say that "those who have not lived through the revolution cannot imagine its grand, solemn beauty," but in truth the revolution is never beautiful; the revolution is always sublime.

Eventually the course of the French Revolution would betray the sympathetic young radicals of England. "*Liberté, égalité, fraternité!*" was the revolutionary cry; the novelist team Robert Shea and Robert Anton Wilson would later claim that if you achieve *égalité* and *fraternité* you can have no *liberté*, which may or may not be true, but certainly the Terror, so-called, and the subsequent imperial conquests of Napoleon Bonaparte left the revolutionaries with no moral leg to stand on. One by one, everyone of sense (except the German author Johann Peter Hebel—never stop believing, Johann!) turned against the warmongering regime. But by this point, fairly or unfairly, nascent Romanticism had already been tarred with the revolutionary brush. A series of British government crackdowns on "sedition," backed in 1795 by the passing of the Treasonable Practices bill and the Seditious Meetings bill—which were just as repressive as they sound—sought to crush dangerous new ways of thought. They weren't necessarily designed to crush the burgeoning Romantic spirit, but they had that effect.

Coleridge, better known as a radical pamphleteer than a poet in his early years, was accused constantly, although never formally charged, with sedition, and he learned to be cautious in what he published. Wordsworth just kept his mouth shut. People might still read novels of supernatural terror; people might still speak warmly of the pastoral life; but Romanticism as a philosophical/aesthetic/political package looked to be in danger of guttering out, snuffed by the discrediting one-two punch of backing a revolution that was *1.* terrifying to the overwhelming power of the British authorities and *2.* terrifying to *everyone. Lyrical Ballads,* along with the other, often unpublished poems of Wordsworth and Coleridge that circulated in manuscript copies, were all that managed to keep English Romanticism afloat during this difficult era. The introduction (penned by Wordsworth) to *Lyrical Ballads* presented Romanticism, for the first time, as a system; while the poems themselves laid out a blueprint for future poets to imitate or rebel against.

II.

Had Coleridge and his chum Southey gone to America to live on a utopian commune, both would have died almost immediately. Neither was in the slightest bit prepared for life in the wilderness. Coleridge couldn't even handle the relatively stress-free life of being a poet with wealthy patrons: He got hooked on opium, squandered his talents, never finished anything, and started plagiarizing German writers. Without Coleridge's encouragement and example, Wordsworth would have lived and died happily walking with his sister among the natural splendor of England. He would have written little and published much less.

The fad of Romanticism in England would have died out before the nineteenth century even dawned.

But notice that that's in England. Romanticism outside of England could still flourish. There was a Romantic movement in France as well; Victor Hugo is only its most obvious practitioner. Among those most influenced by the French tradition of Romantic poetry is, of all people, the Cambodian dictator and Romantics fan Pol Pot. You might have thought that the failure of the French Revolution would have discredited Romanticism in France as it did in England, but the French took the novel approach of *romanticizing their revolutions*. See, again, Hugo and his *Les Misérables*.

But it's in Germany that Romanticism had its greatest impact, and neither Wordsworth nor the Germanophile Coleridge would have much of an influence on it. Twenty years before the English poet John Keats died of tuberculosis at the age of twenty-five, the German poet Novalis died of tuberculosis at the age of twenty-eight: Priority to Germany (although the younger Keats is three years more Romantic). Romanticism would remain a driving force in Germany up through the Second World War. National Socialism was nothing more than Romanticism + Nationalism + Evil. Hitler himself once proclaimed, "To understand Nazism one must first know [Romantic composer Richard] Wagner." The poet W. H. Auden used to teach a class titled "Romantic Writers from Wordsworth to Hitler."

With Coleridge dead in the woods, Romanticism survives on the Continent, but not in England.

III.

And here in the English-speaking world, the death of Romanticism has its own far-reaching effects . . .

In the short term, no Romanticism simply means a very different canon of English literature. The early 1800s belong to Romantics, both in poetry (Keats, Byron, P. Shelley) and the novel (Scott, the Brontës, M. Shelley). Romanticism had also given us that idea of art produced by a lone tortured genius. Coleridge and Wordsworth had imagined such a genius, and the second generation of Romantics were to live the dream. The genius of Lord Byron (like that of Shelley) was so misunderstood that he had to flee England for the Continent. Keats was so misunderstood that a bad notice in the *Quarterly Review* (according to legend; not really) made him sicken and die. Byron wrote:

> *Who kill'd John Keats?*
> *"I," says the* Quarterly,
> *So savage and Tartarly;*
> *"'Twas one of my feats."*

When the Romantics weren't wallowing in their own genius, they were composing hymns to England's youngest misunderstood genius, the proto-Romantic and pseudo-medievalist literary forger Thomas Chatterton, dead by his own hand at age seventeen, "the sleepless soul that perished in its pride" (Wordsworth), whose "solemn agony had not / Yet faded from him" (Shelley). Keats dedicated *Endymion* to Chatterton.

You'll notice that such a lone genius is precisely what Modernism fastened on to as a requirement for art. So that's one difference in a world without Romanticism: Lacking its example, Modernism will need something else to latch on to.

Here's another difference: Mark Twain—a dedicated anti-Romantic, as shown in the whole Grangerford sequence in *Huckleberry Finn*, for example—blamed the Civil War on Romanticism, more specifically on the novels of Walter Scott, which were so popular in the American South that Southerners sought to live the life of one of Scott's romantic knights by fighting a glorious "lost cause" against the stronger North. Twain's suggestion may sound excessive, but there are hints he's right in the specific, from which we might want to induce the general: Admiral Raphael Semmes, CSN, stated that he joined the Confederacy because of Scott's poem *The Lay of the Last Minstrel*. So, without Romanticism: no Civil War.

A third difference: Scotsmen in kilts. Historically, Scots wore the kilt only briefly, from the late 1720s, when it was invented, to 1746, when it was outlawed after rebels wore it during the Jacobite uprising. The prohibition ended in 1782, at which point Romantic Scotsmen (Walter Scott, again, at the forefront) latched on to the Romantic virtues (forbidden! rebellious!) of the kilt and decided to make it *1*. the national Scottish costume for Highland Games, etc., in perpetuity and *2*. the imagined garb of medieval Scotsmen, à la *Braveheart, Brave,* etc.

Kilts and the Civil War are weak sauce, though. The greatest influence of Romanticism on the contemporary English-speaking world, by far, is through the concept of *cool*.

Jazz saxophonist Lester Young came up with the word *cool* in the 1930s, and it filtered down, as so much contemporary slang did, from the jazz world to the beatniks to white mainstream teenagers to everyone. Jazz musicians are responsible for a lot of what we now think of as cool— sunglasses, lack of affect, heroin addiction; but the *cool* that came from jazz to mainstream America was not simply jazz cool. Rather, jazz gave white America a word for a concept it already vaguely knew existed, a concept that an earlier age would have called Romantic.

In 1959, Norman Mailer produced "the list" of what is hip and what is square. Crooks are hip and cops are square. Sex is hip and religion is square. But most importantly: Romantic is hip; classic is square. If *hip* and *cool* were not quite synonyms in 1959, they soon would be.

Coleridge and Shelley got their licks in, but Byron is the chief architect of cool. He slept with his sister (a rumor!); he swam the Dardanelles (perilous!); he died trying to become king of Greece (Greece must be free!); he was, in the words of his paramour Lady Caroline Lamb, "mad, bad, and dangerous to know." The tall dark stranger with a past—the Byronic hero so-called—persisted into the twentieth and twenty-first centuries as (among a thousand others) Clint Eastwood's Man with No Name or vampire Edward from *Twilight*: Nobody likes both of these characters, because each appeals to a different target demographic, but each is designed to tap into the notion of cool. Each is specifically cool to its audience. Each is also, perhaps without being aware of it, Byronic and Romantic. James Dean with his rebel sneer; Miles Davis turning his back to the audience; Grace Jones and Debbie Harry and the Fonz: Nothing is as ephemeral as cool, but the essential part of cool that remains is inexorably bound up with Romanticism. Cool is Romanticism modernized, and made palatable to a mass audience. I guarantee you: If Byron could walk in slow motion with a trench coat billowing around him, he absolutely would.

You can argue that Modernism could have pulled its lone genius idea from Germanic Romanticism (Beethoven the ideal). You can argue that Mark Twain is full of baloncy on the Civil War, and that kilts would have come back anyway, Romanticism or no. But this much seems clear: that without Romanticism to make the jazz concept of cool palatable and comprehensible to white America, cool would have remained an African American term.

Losing *cool* would torpedo the essential element of postwar pop culture—the fusion of African American and white American art styles into (for example) rock and roll. Insofar as Hollywood exported American cool around the world (to be reimported from Europe by Nico's heroin chic or from Asia by Chow Yun-Fat's two-gun style), *Lyrical Ballads* has indirectly had a global impact. What would we do if we didn't try to be cool?

Of any counterfactual world, this Unromantic world is the strangest and most terrifying. It would be a very square world.

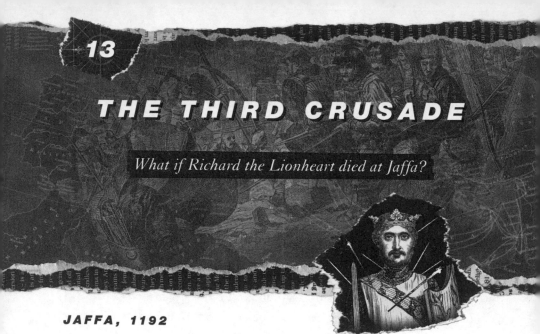

13

THE THIRD CRUSADE

What if Richard the Lionheart died at Jaffa?

JAFFA, 1192

I.

Eleanor of Aquitaine is the only human to have been queen of both France (1137–1152) and England (1154–1189). Her first marriage, to King Louis VII of France, was annulled by the pope, ostensibly because Eleanor and Louis had turned out to be distantly related but really because Eleanor wanted out and Louis was annoyed that his queen had only given birth to daughters. Eleanor then married Henry Curtmantle, soon to become Henry II of England, her third cousin and therefore technically a closer relative than Louis had been. Presumably no one told the pope.

Before she was a queen, Eleanor had been duchess of Aquitaine, a large and wealthy territory in southwestern France, and it is Aquitaine that made her an appealing wife to two powerful kings—and to everyone else in Western Europe! In the short eight weeks between the end of her first marriage and the start of the next, Eleanor had to baffle two kidnapping attempts—by Count Geoffrey VI of Nantes and Count Theobald V of Blois—who wanted to wed Eleanor for her duchy. (Count Theobald is remembered as "Theobald the Good," somewhat improbably for a would-be kidnapper and rapist; he also is credited with executing all the Jews in Blois after accusing them of ritually murdering a Christian baby. He later married Eleanor's daughter, of all people; he died on Crusade.)

King Henry II, when he married Eleanor, had become duke of Aquitaine, a title he would pass on to his son. This led to the awkward situation in which Aquitaine was ruled both by the King of England as a duke and the King of France as a king. The situation wasn't unique, as ever since the Norman invasion of 1066 the King of England had also been duke of Normandy (another French duchy), but with the addition of the duchy of Aquitaine, England now controlled more than half the land in France. The English king, whose native language had since 1066 always been French, ruled over as much land on the continent as he did in Great Britain. A scenario where one king is also vassal to another king is not going to play out smoothly, and it ultimately led to the Hundred Years' War, a 116-year struggle between England and France to determine who would be in charge of the continent's Atlantic coast. If England had won the war, then either the two countries would be one country today, or half of what we think of as France would be part of England (and I'd probably be writing this in French, as English would have become a provincial language, like Welsh). England didn't, so they aren't and it isn't (and I'm not), but for 116 years England tried, and life was miserable for pretty much everyone in Western Europe, or even more miserable than usual, considering that the Hundred Years' War came at the same time as the Black Plague.

Had Eleanor merely (*merely!*) been the cause of the Hundred Years War, she would be remembered as one of the most significant women of the Middle Ages. She also went on two Crusades, fomented rebellion against her second husband, and helped inspire the fad of "courtly love" that was immortalized in Sir Lancelot and Queen Guinevere's relationship in the Arthurian legends, holding (according to her contemporary Andreas Capellanus, who wrote the fad's bible, *The Art of Courtly Love*) a mock court for dissatisfied lovers where she offered judgments on their plights. The first book to mention King Arthur's Round Table and sword Excalibur was dedicated to Eleanor, as patroness of the arts; the queen loved stories of King Arthur. That's all good stuff, and certainly important, but she also had a son named Richard, and she did something even more important—she made him into a hero.

II.

What kind of hero Richard was is subject to debate, but he was really good at swinging a sword and leading armies in battle, which is what passed for heroism in the twelfth century. He was the perfect knight, brave and honorable, as skilled at tournament jousting as he was at war, a character out of one of the chivalrous romances Eleanor favored— except that he wasn't much on the love stuff. He even named his sword Excalibur! He failed in almost everything he tried, but quite by accident, centuries after his death, he saved Europe from foreign invaders. History knows him as King Richard the Lionheart, the only Crusader who is still a household name.

Richard was the younger son of Henry and Eleanor and grew up assuming he would never be king. Eleanor, quite against her husband's wishes, made Richard, who appears to have been a special favorite of hers, the official heir to her holdings in France, so Richard would have been at the very least duke of Aquitaine, even if king of Nothing. But Henry's children were truculent and ambitious, and Richard wasn't the only one more loyal to his mother than to his father; Eleanor encouraged her sons to rise up in armed rebellion against King Henry, and during the second such rebellion, Richard's older brother (named Henry after his father) died of dysentery. (Until the twentieth century, wars always killed more soldiers through disease than through violence.) Richard was now heir not only to Aquitaine but also to the English throne.

Gerald of Wales was a medieval geographer who once wrote a book about Ireland that correctly stated *no dragons lived there* and incorrectly stated a lot of other marvelous things; he was also an adviser to King Henry, and he asserted that Eleanor's rebellious perfidy was simply what you get, your majesty, when you call down the wrath of God by marrying your cousin. Henry himself also assumed it was divine punishment, but punishment rather for the death of Thomas à Becket, the archbishop of Canterbury whom four knights slew, perhaps on royal orders, in 1170. Archbishop Thomas was later sainted, and though the king paid for the crime with a large indemnity supporting the Crusader states in the Holy Land, the wrath of God did not leave Henry. In 1189, his son Richard rebelled for a third time, seizing the throne by force from his dying father. Richard didn't stay around to enjoy his new kingdom, though. He was a knight, and he wanted to go on a Crusade.

III.

Despite Henry's generous donation, things had gone poorly for Outremer—"overseas," or the general name for the land the Crusaders had conquered a century earlier during the First Crusade. That endeavor had succeeded in part because the Islamic power of the Near East had been divided between competing Muslim sects and peoples, while the Christians had fought with a unified purpose. That unity hadn't lasted, and the history of Outremer is a history of Christian bickering and infighting.

Even worse was the hostility between Crusaders and Byzantines. The antipathy had started during the First Crusade—the Crusaders thought the Byzantine emperor hadn't really helped them in their battles with the Turks and had instead spent his time selfishly gobbling up land the Crusaders had fought for (this is more or less true). By the 1150s, Prince Reynald of Antioch's pirate fleet had sacked the Byzantine island of Cyprus, and in retaliation the Byzantine emperor Manuel I led an army against the Crusader city of Antioch. Only last-minute diplomacy prevented all-out war, but now the Crusaders were no longer allies with the most powerful nearby Christian state. It's emblematic of the hostility between these powers that when Richard had a portable tower built for siege work against the Turks, he named it "death to the Greeks." The difference between Greek and Muslim had collapsed in the West's eyes as much as the difference between Turk and Arab.

The Muslims in the area, meanwhile, had unified under the Turk Nur al-Din, who by a combination of diplomacy and force built a Syrian state out of the disparate Turkish holdings south of Asia Minor. The local Crusaders had been warring with a weakened Fatimid Caliphate in Egypt, and the Fatimid Egyptians begged Nur al-Din to come help. Nur al-Din sent his general Shirkuh, who drove the Crusaders out of Egypt; and then he stayed, executing the Egyptian grand vizier Shawar, who had been the real ruler, and keeping the caliph al-Adid as a puppet in Cairo. The vizier and real power in Egypt was now Shirkuh's rebellious nephew Salah al-Din, or Saladin. When Nur al-Din died of a fever in 1174, Saladin married his widow and took over the whole operation. This was not very easy, in part because Saladin was not a Turk but a Kurd, a people completely unrelated to either Turks or Arabs. But Saladin had courage and cunning; he also had the wealth of Egypt and a plan to unify Islam by declaring a common enemy. That enemy, an enemy that seems obvious in retrospect but that had gone a century without being exploited for this purpose, was Outremer.

The Muslim world only a few years before had three caliphs—one in Baghdad, one in Cairo, and one in Seville in Spain, which was akin to the Christian world having three popes. Saladin couldn't get to Spain, but he had the Fatimid caliph al-Adid in his power, and when al-Adid died a natural death in 1171, Saladin just refused to allow a successor. Now all of Islam east of Morocco was to be united under the suzerainty of Baghdad's Abbasid caliph (who was himself a ruler with little power, controlled by Turks).

So ended the Fatimid Caliphate, a once-powerful state that had in past centuries conquered Sicily and invaded Italy. With a shrug, its loyalty was now to Baghdad, its subjects were now subjects of Saladin.

Saladin is one the few people, and perhaps the only major ruler, during the Middle Ages who appears to have genuinely tried to be a good person. He was so generous to petitioners that his treasurers learned to conceal any cash reserves from him, lest he distribute them all to the poor. He was notoriously merciful to prisoners of war, permitting the

Christians from practically all the cities he conquered to leave peacefully and regroup in Tyre. He was also good at fighting. At the Battle of Hattin, his unified state of Syria and Egypt routed the Crusader armies and captured the king of Jerusalem. There was no one left to stop him from seizing the bulk of the defenseless Crusader kingdom, including, after a short siege, Jerusalem itself.

Because Saladin was such a nice guy, people have tended to romanticize his character. Christian legend held that he was literally a knight, dubbed in Alexandria by the Templar Sir Humphrey of Toron in 1174; that he had spent his youth wandering around Europe in disguise, having sundry adventures; that he was part French; or that he was secretly a Christian, an assertion that doesn't really make sense, but such are legends.

We shouldn't confuse Saladin the decent human by twelfth century standards with any kind of contemporary standard of saintliness. It's not like Saladin never massacred prisoners, it's just that he rarely massacred prisoners. His conquests were not bloodless—war is never bloodless. When he conquered Jerusalem, he arranged for all the prisoners to be sold into slavery, but he also allowed them to be ransomed at well below market rate. If that doesn't sound wonderful to you, remember that when the Crusaders had taken Jerusalem, they just killed everyone they saw. The medieval standard for saintliness was odd; even Francis of Assisi went along on the Fifth Crusade.

So, while Nur al-Din was collecting scalps from Crusaders massacred at Antioch for display purposes, Saladin was releasing widows unransomed because their tears broke his heart. Saladin was a conqueror, make no mistake, but he brought a degree of chivalry and mercy to his conquests that has sadly been nearly as rare in modern times as it was in the twelfth century.

When Saladin had surrounded Jerusalem for a siege, a Christian knight, Balian d'Ibelin, requested permission for safe passage through the lines to enter the city and bring his wife out. Saladin granted permission with the proviso that Balian would go in unarmed, spend only one night in the holy city, and not fight the Muslim forces; and so Balian vowed. Once Balian entered, though, and found the city completely undefended—its entire army had been captured or killed at Hattin—with the walls manned by a bunch of noncombatants, largely women, children, and priests, plus a grand total of *one knight*, all pleading with him to stay and help them . . . he sent word to Saladin requesting to be freed from his oath. In a magnificent gesture, Saladin consented. Balian organized and led the ultimately doomed defense of Jerusalem, fighting off Saladin's armies for eight days and negotiating the eventual surrender. Saladin, meanwhile, sent an escort to lead Balian's wife to the safety of the Christian city of Tyre.

This was the man who took Jerusalem. And Richard the Lionheart had pledged to take it back from him.

IV.

Richard was hardly alone. He left England in the trust of his brother John and went on the Third Crusade (the Second Crusade had accomplished nothing and is always passed over with little comment) alongside King Philip II of France (Richard's mother's ex-husband's son) and Frederick Barbarossa, king of Germany and Burgundy and Holy Roman Emperor. Three of the most powerful monarchs in Europe, fighting together with the blessing of the pope—it sounds like an unbeatable dream team. But an aged Frederick died on his way to the Holy Land—legend would maintain that he was only sleeping, and would return, like King Arthur or Olaf Tryggvason, in an hour of need, to lead his people to glory—and soon enough Philip II would be returning to France to focus on invading English territory. This would leave Richard in command of a heterogeneous group of European knights and second- or third-generation Crusaders born in the hundred-year-old land of Outremer.

Ultimately, the Crusaders sought to reconquer Jerusalem, but most of the other nearby Crusader cities had also fallen to Saladin, and these were closer to the coast than inland Jerusalem was. First among them was Acre, the Crusaders' largest port. Crusaders had been besieging Acre for a year before Richard even left England, and the story of why it was under siege is emblematic of the Christian infighting that cost them Jerusalem.

It happened like this: King Guy of Jerusalem had been captured at Hattin and then, in a typical magnanimous gesture of Saladin's, set free once he promised never to take up arms again. Ah, but King Guy had lied (like many Crusaders, he conveniently decided that oaths to an infidel "don't count"), and once at liberty he headed for Tyre, the only nearby city that had held out against Saladin's sweeping victories. Tyre has always been notoriously hard to besiege; it took Alexander the Great seven months to conquer, and it never took Alexander seven months to do *anything else*. Other cities still in Crusader hands, such as Tripoli and Antioch, were much farther to the north, so Tyre was the sole foothold in the southern half of the Holy Land. It owed its continued independence to one Conrad of Montferrat, an Italian nobleman who was both the brother-in-law of the Byzantine emperor and cousin of the Holy Roman Emperor.

Conrad had been sailing up to the city of Acre when his sailors noticed that no church bells were ringing; this was because Acre had just fallen to Saladin, and, so warned, Conrad quickly sailed on to Tyre, a coastal city that was also under siege—but only on land, leaving the harbor clear for Conrad's ship. Once in the city, Conrad inspired the flagging defenders to resist. He proved his own determination when Saladin produced Conrad's father, a prisoner of war from Hattin, and offered to release the hostage if Conrad would surrender Tyre. Conrad fired a crossbow at the old man from the battlements, proclaiming that Tyre would never surrender and that his father had lived long enough anyway. (To be fair, Conrad missed, possibly intentionally.) Conrad and the forces of Tyre went on to fight off Muslim attacks by land and sea, finally breaking the siege. The remaining Crusader knights in the area flocked to the city, and Conrad asked only that they swear allegiance to him. For a little over a year, while King Guy was Saladin's prisoner, Conrad was the leader of the defense in the Holy Land.

(Later Saladin freed Conrad's father, no strings attached, just because Saladin was Saladin.)

So, when Guy showed up at the doorstep of Tyre assuming that the leadership role would be handed over to him, Conrad scoffed. Guy, Conrad claimed, had given up his kingship when he lost Jerusalem; Conrad was holding Tyre for the real kings, who were coming from across the sea from Europe.

So Guy was a king without a kingdom; rebuffed from Tyre, he was a king without even a city. All he had was the power of his title, and who knew how long that title would last? Guy needed a city, and if he couldn't take Tyre from Conrad, he'd have to take one from Saladin. People would still follow the nominal king of Jerusalem, and with whatever forces he could scrounge, Guy marched to Acre.

That should have been the end of Guy. Foolhardy courage is what had brought Guy to disaster at the Battle of Hattin; but he had learned nothing from his mistake. He set his armies to besiege Acre, a well-fortified city that was garrisoned by a force much larger than his own. Acre had access to the sea, and could not be starved out. And Saladin's main force could come up behind Guy at any moment, pinning him between two enemies.

But against all odds Guy's besiegers held out, and by the time Saladin got there, Guy had been reinforced by troops from all over Europe. They managed to blockade the harbor, so that Acre was properly under siege on all sides, and built sufficient defenses for their camp so that Saladin could not attack the besieging armies in their rear. The best Saladin could do was settle down nearby with his armies and wait. But because Guy's forces controlled the harbor, the Crusaders could continue to bring in reinforcements, both from other Crusader cities such as Tyre (Conrad of Montferrat joined the siege under the condition that he never serve directly under Guy) and, as word of this Third Crusade spread, from Europe.

Indeed, reinforcements under Richard and Philip were on their way to Acre by ship—the kings had to leave Europe together because neither trusted his rival not to invade the other's kingdom in his absence. Richard got blown off course and took a moment to capture a bandit king, the self-styled "Emperor of Cyprus," Isaac Comnenus, who briefly attempted the kidnapping and ransom of Richard's sister and fiancée. Isaac, pressed by a vengeful Richard, finally offered to surrender, with the sole condition that, as befitted an emperor, he not be put in irons. Richard had manacles of silver made, and Isaac found himself in the world's most expensive chains; technically, he was not "in irons." During the short time Richard was conquering Cyprus, Philip arrived at Acre and was persuaded that Conrad of Montferrat, lord of Tyre, should be the next king of Jerusalem. When Richard arrived, he, of course, was all for King Guy.

There were four kings besieging Acre then: the kings of England and France, and the two rival kings of Jerusalem, neither of whom had a kingdom.

V.

Often our ideas of history are shaped by later texts. For example, almost everything we think of when we think of pirates—buried treasure, peg legs, parrots on the shoulder, skull and crossbones—is derived from the book *Treasure Island* (1883) and the paintings of N. C. Wyeth (1911, etc.). Well, our ideas of the Middle Ages are all filtered through popular nineteenth-century books about the Middle Ages, especially the novels of Walter Scott. Walter Scott was the bestselling writer of his day, a darling of both critics and the public—a typical effusion from an 1885 magazine article in *The Overland Monthly* places Scott ahead of both Dickens and Shakespeare for English letters and calls him "the highest type of novelist the world has yet produced"—and Walter Scott thought the Crusades were *terribly romantic*! If people have ever thought of the Third Crusade as a chivalrous duel between two master warriors, Richard the Lionheart and Saladin, it is because Walter Scott wrote it into his novel *The Talisman*

(King Richard also makes a cameo in Scott's *Ivanhoe*, in disguise as the Black Knight).

Historians disagree on how effective a leader King Richard was. Harold Lamb wrote that Richard had no strategy, and could win battles but never follow up the victory with something productive of later aims; he just blundered around the Holy Land for a year fighting things. Rival historian David Miller, on the other hand, asserts that Richard was a master strategist, and that his understanding of logistics (rare in the Middle Ages) guided his actions; if it looks like he didn't accomplish much, this is precisely because the logistics as the Crusaders moved inland were untenable, and his perspicacity prevented him from losing his armies in unwinnable battles.

But no one has ever thought Richard couldn't lead men into battle. Even if he was just blundering around fighting things, he was fighting things *really well*.

The arrival of Richard and his armies at Acre gave the Crusaders renewed hope and a competent leader. A little more than a month after Richard's arrival, the walls were breached, and the city surrendered. Saladin's mighty army was right outside the Crusaders' siege lines, but was unable to succor the city. Its populace was taken prisoner (and mostly massacred later, when their ransom didn't arrive in time).

During the occupation, an event took place that appeared minor at the time, but that would change the course of Richard's life and, ultimately, European history. Richard and Philip set their respective banners up on the ramparts; Duke Leopold of Austria, leader and highest-ranking member of the German army—remember, the Third Crusade was supposed to have three monarchs, and only the German king Frederick's untimely death kept him from Acre—placed his banner next to Richard's. Richard, not about to stand on equal footing with a mere duke, had Leopold's banner cast to the ground. It was a small thing, but Leopold remembered it. He immediately left in a huff for Austria, and remembered it all the way home.

Philip was preparing to leave as well. The conquest of Acre seemed enough for one Crusade; also, he was ill—the climate of the Holy Land wreaked havoc on Crusaders' constitutions, but Philip had it worse than most, and his fingernails all fell out—and, what was more dire, the Count of Flanders had died during the siege, and without an heir. Flanders was an important county in France, and King Philip wanted to make sure that the succession went smoothly. Since he and Richard had agreed at the outset to share all land gained on the Crusade, he asked for half of Cyprus. Richard in turn asked for half of Flanders. They parted on bad terms, disagreeing still about who should be king of Jerusalem. Philip returned to France to look into ways of undermining Richard's kingdom. That left Richard—alongside either Guy or Conrad—in charge of the Crusader armies. They still had a job to do. They wanted Jerusalem.

To get closer to Jerusalem, Richard marched down the coast to Jaffa, fighting along the way many skirmishes against small harrying forces and defeating Saladin's massed troops at the Battle of Arsuf. Jaffa had been dismantled by Saladin to prevent the Crusaders from using it as a base, but Richard had it rebuilt. Jaffa lay only some thirty miles from Jerusalem, but when the Crusaders marched inland toward the Holy City they found their supply line too precarious to maintain, and they were forced to return to the safety of the coast.

In this way the armies established what was to be the pattern of the Third Crusade. Richard would win some battles and conquer cities along the coast. Saladin would dismantle and destroy what ports he didn't think he could defend. And although they advanced to within a few miles of Jerusalem, the Crusaders, no matter their victories, would never reach the city. Richard intentionally shielded his eyes from Jerusalem, vowing that he would not look upon it until he was ready to conquer it. But he was never ready.

Part of his problem was that he knew, even if he managed to take the city, he would not be able to hold it. The Crusaders had made a vow to conquer Jerusalem, not stay in it. As soon as the city fell, they would return to their old lives in Europe, having done their duty, and Jerusalem would be defenseless again.

Richard was dashing and brave, but numbers played against him; Saladin could afford to lose battles and cities, while the Crusaders needed to keep winning to keep their foothold. Another Hattin would doom them.

Probably Richard was hoping for a victory so overwhelming that Saladin's sultanate would dissolve. It may have been a desperate hope, but you don't get Walter Scott writing romantic novels about you if you don't fight for a desperate hope. Richard stayed in the Holy Land for over a year, fighting continually and securing the coast. A lot of people died, and Jerusalem stayed Muslim.

Richard tried diplomacy when simple warfare didn't work, at one point proposing that his sister be married to Saladin's brother, with the two of them ruling jointly over a cosmopolitan kingdom of Jerusalem. Saladin treated it as a jest and Richard's sister balked at the suggestion, which probably was unworkable in the first place, but Richard's willingness to entertain the idea indicates both the extent he would go to take Jerusalem and the high regard in which he held Saladin.

Of course, Richard also proved how badly he wanted Jerusalem by constantly risking his life in battle. Even among knights who valorized foolhardy courage, Richard was known for the brazenness with which he threw himself into danger. His derring-do became legend.

Legend has focused even more on the friendship between Richard and Saladin. The two men never met, despite Richard's entreaties, as Saladin said kings should only meet when hostilities ended. But through the intermediary of Saladin's brother al-Adil (known to the Crusaders as Saphadin), they exchanged courtesies, as chivalric tradition would dictate. When Richard fell ill, Saladin sent him sherbet to quell his fever. After Saladin captured, and refused to ransom, Philip's prized falcon, Richard sent two of his own falcons to Saladin as a gift. When Richard's horse was slain from under him at Jaffa, Saladin ordered two replacement horses to be led through the battle, so Richard could mount again.

They were, of course, still enemies. The whole reason Richard's horse had been slain was that Saladin was trying to kill him. Saladin had besieged the newly rebuilt Crusader city of Jaffa in Richard's absence, and broken through the walls. His troops had managed to occupy most of the city, and Saladin was bargaining with the citadel over terms of surrender when Richard and a small force arrived by ship, storming the docks by surprise. Although the Crusaders were vastly outnumbered—their modest army of bowmen and sailors only had eighty knights in it, with only three horses among them—their strength was hard to judge as they charged down the city streets, and the speed and ferocity of their attack routed the Muslim forces; Richard then fought off the counterattack until reinforcements arrived. It was another brilliant victory that kept the coast Christian, and did little else.

Saladin's best strategy, really, was just to wait Richard out. Richard wanted to return to Europe to fight his real enemy: France. Without their best field commander, the Crusaders would be torn between the two rival kings of Jerusalem, Guy (backed by Richard) and Conrad (backed by everyone else, because no one liked Guy).

Indeed, the situation of the rival kings was so clearly intolerable that Richard finally backed down. Guy sailed off to rule Richard's conquest of Cyprus. Conrad was hailed by all as the rightful king of Jerusalem, a kingdom he would rule from Tyre. A week later, though, he was assassinated.

VI.

Conrad was assassinated by Assassins, which only *sounds* redundant; the Assassins, or Hashashuns, were Muslims of the heretical Nizari sect. Hasan I-Sabbah, "the Old Man of the Mountain," gathered some of the Nizari faithful into his impregnable mountain fortress of Alamut, where, at least according to Marco Polo, he had built a pleasure garden that resembled paradise, with ingenious pumps producing streams of wine, honey, and milk. There, beautiful women danced and played musical instruments. The Old Man of the Mountain would drug one of his followers with hashish (hence the name *hashashun*), and spirit him to the garden, where the follower would get to dally for a while, before getting drugged again and brought back to the normal world. The Old Man of the Mountain would then tell his young disciple that he had had the barest taste of heaven, and would be permitted to return—but only in exchange for murder. The result was that Hasan I-Sabbah, who never left Alamut, had an army of fanatical assassins perfectly willing to die on a mission. After all, death would only lead them back to the literal streams of milk and honey, to the music of the dancing girls.

This story sounds rather far-fetched, and it may be false—all surviving writing about the Assassins comes from their enemies, and they had plenty of enemies. But certainly, fearless Nizari murderers operated in the region, killing both for the glory of their sect and occasionally at the will of the highest bidder, and if you can come up with a better explanation for their fearlessness than drugs + amusement park, you have done more than the historians since Marco Polo have.

Saladin tried to lead his armies against Alamut; the Assassins were Nizari heretics, after all, and Saladin, as a good Muslim, sought to stamp out heresy. He turned back, though, supposedly when a warning dagger appeared on his pillow mysteriously while he slept. Often the Crusaders and the Assassins had a common enemy (orthodox Islam) so they left each other alone. And yet King Conrad of Jerusalem had been slain, and no one knew why.

Perhaps some local Muslim potentate had contracted the killing, afraid to face a kingdom ruled by the sort of man who would shoot at his own father; perhaps it was a rival Crusader, or a partisan of a rival; perhaps the Assassins, who gained their power by fear, simply wanted to flex their muscles and show what they could accomplish. No one knew, and no one knows, but the Crusaders had to blame someone, so they blamed King Richard. Richard had never supported Conrad, after all.

Richard's enemies believed the charge and his allies disputed it, but it was of little importance to him. He was leaving anyway, despite having failed to conquer Jerusalem. He had earlier vowed to stay in the Holy

Land fighting until the Easter season, and if he had, he would have been there to see his arch-rival Saladin die of a fever in March of 1193. But it was not to happen; Richard had had enough. He and Saladin worked out a treaty that left the coast Christian and the Holy City Muslim, but with free passage for pilgrims. Many of the Crusaders made a visit to Jerusalem before they left, but Richard refused; if he could not enter Jerusalem in triumph, he would not enter it as a pilgrim.

When Richard sailed back to Europe that should have been the end of it. But along the way he blew off course (again), his ship grounding near what is now the Italian-Slovenian border. By great ill luck, this was part of the Holy Roman Empire, and the Holy Roman Emperor was sympathetic to Conrad, whom Richard was accused of murdering. Richard tried sneaking overland disguised as a Templar, but near Vienna he was recognized and brought to the duke of Austria. Here Richard's luck was worse, for not only was the duke of Austria Conrad's first cousin, he was that very Leopold whom Richard had insulted at the siege of Acre. Leopold wanted revenge.

In the Holy Land, Richard had courted every danger, only to escape unscathed—and be taken captive in the heart of Europe. A delighted Leopold passed Richard on to the Holy Roman Emperor, Henry VI, who kept him prisoner, ostensibly on the charge of murder.

According to legend, Richard's location remained unknown until an English minstrel, passing through Germany, heard someone singing English lute songs from a lone tower, and recognized the voice of the king. This is scarcely to be credited, but certainly Richard remained prisoner for a year, and was only released after the payment of a literal king's ransom, thirty tons of silver. He went on to spend the rest of his life fighting the French until he died gloriously in combat.

Duke Leopold, for his part in capturing the noble Crusader Richard, was excommunicated by Pope Celestine III; but on the upside, the Holy Roman Emperor granted him a third of Richard's ransom. Leopold used the money to build walls around Vienna.

The Crusader kingdoms would gradually weaken and be conquered by Muslims. Acre falls in 1291, Tyre shortly after. The walls of Vienna remain until 1857. They were finally torn down to make room for the grand boulevard known as the Ringstrasse.

*Richard dies at Jaffa → Vienna gets no walls → **THE OTTOMAN EMPIRE ROLLS OVER AUSTRIA → Germany is like the Balkans and it's war forever***

I.

NOW WHAT IF RICHARD HAD DIED ON THE CRUSADE? It could have happened—the king was an inveterate risk taker. At Cyprus he was the first off the boat, running ahead of his men onto a beach defended by Isaac's troops. Later, riding outside the Crusader city of Ramla, Richard spied a Turkish patrol and charged them alone. (The Turks scattered.) Let's say that at Jaffa Richard's horse is not shot out from underneath him; let's say that Richard is shot off his horse. The Lionheart dies, AD 1192.

The battle for Jaffa was already won by that point, and all the gains Richard made on his Crusade were already shored up. The borders of Outremer and the Sultanate will stay the same.

If Richard had contracted the death of Conrad, then a dead Richard would mean a live Conrad; but probably he had not, so Conrad dies anyway.

Richard's body is now buried in the Holy Land—possibly, with the kind permission of Saladin, in Jerusalem. At the very least his heart is buried there, even if his bones are shipped back to England. On the Italian-Slovenian border, a ship runs aground, but no one really cares. Richard's brother John becomes king, and ineffectually fights the French. Perhaps the Magna Carta is signed a few years earlier; perhaps nothing different happens at all. Dead-Richard history looks very like our own. And then . . .

In our world, three hundred years after Vienna got its walls, the

Ottomans, under their greatest sultan, Suleyman the Magnificent, decided to knock them down.

II.

In history as we know it, Suleyman ruled, in the sixteenth century, a realm vaster than the eastern Roman Empire. Sprawling across three continents, it stretched from Algiers to the Persian Gulf, from the Red Sea to the Caspian Sea. In Europe, Suleyman's land included the entire Balkan peninsula and spilled north and east into what is now Ukraine and Russia. Although he had not yet annexed Hungary (he would later), Suleyman shattered its strength at the battle of Mohacs, killing its king. He torched the great Corvina Library in Buda to eliminate any record of Hungarian culture; Hungary was practically if not officially under Ottoman suzerainty, and although Duke Ferdinand of Austria claimed right (by marriage) to the empty Hungarian throne, Suleyman managed to get his own candidate, John Zapolya of Transylvania, elected as king. The Ottomans were contemptuous of Duke Ferdinand, referring to him as "the little man of Vienna." In 1529 Vienna was the only thing standing between the Ottomans and Austria.

The Ottomans had started their empire as masters of war, bringing to the west mobile horse-archer tactics perfected on the Asian steppes. They expanded their empire as masters of diplomacy, exploiting the political divisions between continental powers. The Habsburg family (which controlled Austria) was forever at war with the French; the Lutherans (a new element in 1529) were jockeying for power in the Holy Roman Empire against the Catholics. Although Christian Europe would in theory want to unite against a foreign Muslim invader, in actuality they were usually more afraid of other Christian powers, and the Ottomans took full advantage of this disunity.

Before besieging a city, the Ottomans would offer the inhabitants a traditional set of options: They could *1.* convert to Islam and live in peace under the sultan; *2. not* convert to Islam, but surrender their city, and still live in peace under the sultan; *3.* gather their goods together and leave the city, living wherever they wished; or *4.* fight and be anni-hilated. To make the fourth option even less attractive, the Ottomans were as implacable against those who resisted as they were generous to those who submitted. The example of Famagusta, a port city on Cyprus, is particularly grisly. In 1571, after four months of siege, Famagusta finally capitulated to the Ottomans. Although they were at first offered safe passage to Crete, the Famagustans had, by fighting for four months, given up their chance for the Ottomans' clemency. The leading citizens of Famagusta were beheaded; the populace at large enslaved; the governor, Marco Antonio Bragadin, had his ears and nose removed. Wearing a mule's halter, whipped like a beast of burden, Bragadin bore stones on his back to help repair damage to the Ottoman camp. He was forced to literally eat the dirt before the tent of Lala Mustafa, the Ottoman commander. Then he was flayed alive, starting with the feet, dying only when the skin was halfway off. This skin was stuffed with straw, and the Ottomans mounted Bragadin's mannequin on his own horse and paraded it through town. Later his skin became a flag for the Ottoman navy. No wonder so many of the Ottomans' opponents decided it was a better idea just to capitulate.

Emperor Zahiruddin Muhammad Babur, founder of the Mughal dynasty in India, recorded in 1500 a "Turkish proverb" that ran: "Trust not your friend: he will stuff your hide with straw." Bragadin had obvi-ously never had a chance to read the writings of Babur.

Justly or unjustly, Christian Europe believed the Ottomans to be espe-cially cruel to their captives. Pierre de Bourdeille, seigneur de Brantôme, the sixteenth century's leading authority on French upper-class gossip, records the bawdy story of a court lady who "was questioning a poor slave escaped from the Turks as to the tortures and sufferings these did inflict on him and other unhappy Christian captives, who did tell her enough and to spare of cruelties so inflicted of every sort and kind. Presently she did ask him what they did to women. 'Alas and alas! Madam,' said he, 'they do it to them, and go on doing it, till they die.'—'Well! I would to God,' she cried, 'I might die so, a martyr to the faith.'"

When the Ottomans sent their four traditional options to the little man of Vienna in 1529, he made the surprising decision to fight. Actually, the little man of Vienna retreated, for safety's sake, to Bohemia, but he ordered the Viennese to get fighting. Three hundred years after the Lionheart's ransom, Vienna's walls were Austria's only defense.

A naysayer may point out Vienna could have gotten walls anyway in the three centuries since the Third Crusade. But they could also have modernized their walls—*and they didn't.* The Ottomans were facing antiquated and thin city walls—*thin* in this context meaning only six feet thick, which may have been cutting edge in the 1190s, but was woefully inadequate for the sixteenth century. There had been a time when city walls could stay "up to date" for centuries: The land walls of Constantinople remained unbreached for over a thousand years before improved cannon technology brought the Ottomans through and changed the city's name to Istanbul. By the sixteenth century, defensive walls were being built with cannon in mind: They were lower, and sloped, so that cannonballs would deflect off them harmlessly; they were also built much, much thicker. The modern walls of the fortress of the Knights of St. John, in Rhodes, were forty feet thick, over twice as thick as the great walls of Constantinople and *five times* as thick as Vienna's puny six-footers. And Suleyman's forces had conquered Rhodes in 1522 regardless!

But even if the walls of Vienna were outmoded against modern cannon, this was only a danger if Suleyman could bring his modern cannon to bear. Rhodes is an island, and the Ottomans could just sail their largest guns up to their siege camp. To get to Vienna, however, the Turkish forces had to drag their guns all the way across the plains of Hungary. Unusually heavy rains that year meant the great guns would be stuck in the mud, so the besiegers arrived at Vienna without them. And the rains continued, which obviously was more of a nuisance to the besiegers, in their campaign tents, than to the besieged, who were in their homes. The battle moved underground, as the Ottomans, unable to knock even these ancient walls down, tried digging underneath them, setting mines to blow them up, while the Austrians dug their own tunnels to intercept the Ottoman miners. Steady rain does not make for the best digging, though. And then, unseasonably, it began to snow. Thwarted as much by the weather as by anything else, the Ottomans broke the siege and returned home.

III.

This check of Ottoman power at the walls of Vienna marked the turning point in Turkish fortunes in Europe. Suleyman launched another assault against Austria three years later, but it never even reached Vienna. Ferdinand, the little man in Vienna, became Holy Roman Emperor in 1558. In 1571 Ottoman control over the Mediterranean was broken at the sea battle of Lepanto. Although the Ottomans besieged Vienna again in 1683, they were by this point no longer the invincible empire they had been. Nevertheless, the siege of 1683 was deadlier to Vienna than the siege of 1558 had been. The Viennese had in the intervening years strengthened and modernized their walls, with moats and extra defenses around the main city walls, and it's a good thing for them that they did, because the Ottomans drove through all of them during two months of siege, and were threatening to breach the city walls proper, King Richard's walls, when the Austrians finally managed to assemble a relief force from their allies in Poland and the German lands. The Ottoman army had suffered somewhat from supply problems, because its Magyar and Tatar allies, irregular forces under no central control, had so effectively plundered the nearby environs that there was little forage for the besiegers; in addition, the Ottomans, assuming the siege would be short, had not effectively defended their camp from outside attack. When the multinational relief force attacked, the Ottomans found themselves trapped against the unbreached city walls.

The resulting battle was a disaster for the Ottoman Empire. Its army was cut to ribbons. Kara Mustafa, the grand vizier in charge of the Ottoman forces, was punished for his role in the debacle with a garrote (the Turks avoided shedding noble blood). There are some battles that a state simply cannot recover from: Manzikert for the Byzantines or Mohacs for the Hungarians. The Ottoman navy never recovered from Lepanto, and their army never recovered from the second siege of Vienna. The Ottomans would not threaten central Europe again, although they would hold most of their European possessions for centuries.

IV.

Without Richard's captivity, though, without Vienna's walls, things would have gone very differently. Central Europe becomes another *eyalet* (province) in the Ottoman Empire.

We know that the Ottomans were skilled at exploiting disunity in their opponents: For example, the timing for the second siege of Vienna was occasioned in part because Austria's armies were tied up on its western frontier—Austria was ruled (until World War I!) by the powerful Habsburg family, and France was *always* at war with the Habsburgs. If lack of walls had rendered the first siege of Vienna less a siege and more of Ottomans rolling over Austria, the rich Holy Roman Empire would have lain before them. And few states in history have lived and breathed disunity as the Holy Roman Empire did. A confused patchwork of hundreds of semi-independent kingdoms, principalities, and city-states that sometimes warred against one another, the empire was, in 1558, trembling on the brink of disaster. In our history, disaster did not come until 1618, when all of central Europe fought among itself for thirty extremely arduous and bloody years (hence the term Thirty Years' War). But the seeds of this conflict—seeds watered by the rivalry between Protestant and Catholic regions of the empire, as well as between those portions of Europe under French suzerainty and those controlled by the Habsburgs—were present in the mid-sixteenth century, and the Ottomans knew of them. Only in 1555 had civil war between Lutherans and Catholics ended, and now the Turks arrive a mere three years later.

The Ottoman Empire permitted more leeway in its subjects' religious choices than most European states of the time. Traditionally,

Islam has been tolerant of Christians and Jews—"people of the book," who trace their religious tradition to the patriarch Abraham, just as Muslims do. Furthermore, the doctrinal differences between various Christian denominations—including Catholics, Lutherans, Calvinists, and Eastern Orthodox—were mostly ignored by the Ottomans, just as Christians of the time rarely grasped the differences between Sunni and Shi'ite Muslims. Therefore, some Orthodox Christians and Calvinists in Hungary and Romania willingly fought for the Ottomans against the Holy Roman Empire, believing that they were better off with Muslim than Catholic overlords. Since Calvinists in the Holy Roman Empire had no legal standing (*even after* Lutheran Protestants were recognized), they probably would have served Ottomans there, too.

One complaint Protestants had against Catholicism was that Catholics venerated statues of saints—which violated, Protestants said, the commandment against graven images. Statues so offended Protestant theologians that in England Puritans even destroyed crosses, calling them idols. It turns out that this is *exactly the same complaint* that Islam has traditionally filed against Christianity. Lutheranism is still young in 1558, but there are far more Lutherans than Calvinists in the Holy Roman Empire, and if they can find common cause against the Catholic emperor and his statuary, as the Calvinists had in Hungary, the Ottomans will make themselves a powerful group of allies. Since the Lutheran powers are centered farther north in the empire, while the Ottomans are entering through Austria in the south (the name *Austria* looks like it means "southern land," the way *Australia* does, but it's actually an Anglicization of the German *Österreich*, or "eastern kingdom"—not "south" but "east," although it lies both south and east of Germany), the Lutherans won't even see the Ottomans as a threat at first, just the enemy of their enemy. The Catholics, after all, are between them!

The Ottoman invasion is a catastrophe for the Germans. Being conquered is generally a catastrophe for any people, but the inevitable German civil war means that the carnage of the Thirty Years War—the bloodiest religious war in European history—arrives half a century early, and the extra carnage the Turkish conquest brings is simply added to that. Furthermore, the Holy Roman Emperor will find that his people are fighting a three-front war. Not only are the Ottomans attacking, not only are they torn by internal strife, but their greatest enemy, France, will hardly stand idly by when there are gains to be made in the territories of the Habsburg dynasty. Naturally, the French are invading from the west.

It may seem strange for the Christian nation of France to join with the Turkish infidels against their fellow Christians, but it is precisely what really happened. France and the Ottomans had been firm allies since 1536, and in our history would continue to be until the days of Napoleon. In 1543 the French and Ottoman forces actually teamed up to besiege and plunder Nice, a city that at the time was not French, but part of the independent duchy of Savoy. In 1544 France permitted the Ottoman navy to use its port city of Toulon as a base to attack Spain and Italy.

This alliance was *very controversial* in Christian Europe. Popes condemned it. The Spanish wrote satirical tracts accusing the French of being "half-Turkish." Religious men across Europe lamented that the country that had led so many of the Crusades should turn its back on Christendom like this. The French just denied that they were allied with the Turks at all, and then, when the denials became too implausible to maintain—after the sack of Nice, for example—they asserted that the alliance was for the good of Christians already under Ottoman control. The French, by dint of their agreement with the Ottomans, were able to serve as the protectors of Christians in the East. This was sophistry; but politics, as they say, makes strange bedfellows, and it would hardly be the last time France would forge alliances across religious lines: In 1629 Cardinal Richelieu allied France with Protestant Sweden against the Catholic Habsburgs. Any excuse to fight the Habsburgs!

And so, somewhere in central Germany, the Turkish and French forces meet and establish a boundary between their two empires. A few German principalities manage to maintain independence, but they are small, and politically unimportant. The power of the Habsburg family is now centered in Spain and parts of Italy, but it is a shadow of its former glory.

The allies, the French and Ottomans, quickly learn that it is easier to be allied with someone half a continent away (and at war with your common enemy) than it is to be allied with a neighbor. The two states squabble over the exact dividing line of their spheres of influence, and central Europe becomes a perpetual battlefield.

In the long run, it is unlikely that the Ottomans can continue to maintain an empire throughout Europe. The Ottoman economic system was simply not set up for the kind of modern financing that helped propel Europe to riches, and, more importantly, the Ottoman political system ensured that its economic system was too inflexible to evolve into something that could accommodate modern finance. Economic influence rested with the religious authorities, and the Ottoman religious authorities were conservative, in the literal sense that they resisted change. An overextended Ottoman Empire decays and crumbles, just as it did in our history—only faster, because it's more overextended. While Western Europe is busy developing markets in and plundering gold from the New World, the Ottomans slowly withdraw to Constantinople, leaving a benighted central Europe to blink in the sun.

What would that central Europe look like?

A quick answer is that it might look like the Balkan Peninsula—that roughly defined southeastern part of Europe that contains Greece, Albania, Bulgaria, Romania, Serbia, and other states—which the Ottomans had ruled since the fourteenth century (and would continue to rule, in most places, until the nineteenth).

The legacy of Ottoman rule is not a happy one, and by most metrics the Balkans do not do well. Balkan countries consistently have lower standards of living than the rest of Europe. It's likely that some of this is due to the legacy of the Soviet bloc—former Soviet bloc nations tend to linger behind capitalist nations—but there are plenty of former communist countries in Europe, such as the Czech Republic, or the eastern half of Germany, that are on par with Western Europe. The conventional wisdom is that the Balkans have been a poor corner of Europe even before Stalin's mid-twentieth-century takeover, which makes intuitive sense:

The Balkans have seen centuries of internecine warfare, as various local warlords have tried to throw off the Turkish yoke, while simultaneously keeping hostile neighbors at bay. It's not the most conducive atmosphere to developing a healthy economy. When Dame Rebecca West toured Montenegro in the 1930s she came across a World War I monument that listed the dates of the war not as 1914–1918 but rather as 1912–1921—that was life in Montenegro. Until very recently, the only major military engagements in Europe proper since the end of World War II had been in the Balkans.

And so, if central Europe is in some sense like the Balkans, it is, as opposed to the Germany we know, poor; also not unified, but rather divided up into small warring states, more belligerent toward one another than they were under the Holy Roman Empire. (The word *balkanization*, its etymology obvious, means the fragmentation of a region into small, hostile states.) Balkanized Germany is too busy scraping a living together to produce a writer as influential in western Europe as Johann Wolfgang von Goethe. In fact, a lot of Germans' influence on Europe would be suppressed. It would be a Europe with a lot less classical music, for example, and a lot less philosophy: no Bach, Mozart, Beethoven, Brahms, Handel, Wagner, Mendelssohn, or Mahler; no Kant, Hegel, Schlegel, Nietzsche, Schopenhauer, Schiller—or Karl Marx. In other words, try to name a classical composer or a non-Greek philosopher, and most likely you'll be naming a German or an Austrian. Although Balkan writers and artists in past centuries have doubtless been creating great works of art that deserve as much international attention as all those famous Germans', you'll notice that few or none of them has garnered any international attention. Mihai Eminescu is not a household name outside of Romania, nor Hristo Botev outside of Bulgaria. Who's the most famous Bosnian you can name? Beethoven is more famous than he is.

On the other hand, insofar as the story of the first half of the twentieth century in Europe was the story of expansionist German adventurism, an enervated Germany sounds like it might be good for the world. Without

Karl Marx, the rise of totalitarian dictatorships in Russia especially is less assured (ha ha! I mean the rise of a totalitarian dictatorship in Russia other than the Tsar, of course)—and without World War I, as we've seen, there would have been no Russian Revolution in the first place.

V.

But although World War I sounds unlikely without Germany, we must remember the true cause of World War I. The true cause was "some damn fool thing in the Balkans"—that's what Prussian chancellor Otto von Bismarck, as early as 1888, predicted would lead to war. To answer the question from the previous page, the most famous Bosnian you can name is probably Gavrilo Princip, the man who assassinated the Austrian archduke and started the whole disaster. Princip didn't precipitate the war alone, of course: The Balkans were a powder keg, and everyone was lighting matches. Bismarck actually predicted the explosion would come six years earlier than it did. It's true that Princip was trying to free Bosnia from the Austro-Hungarian, and not the Ottoman, Empire when he kicked the war off; but Austria-Hungary had only formally annexed Bosnia from the Ottomans some five years earlier, in 1909. It was the legacy of Ottoman rule, combined with Austro-Hungarian expansionism, that brought the world to crisis.

Now imagine all of Germany, Austria-Hungary, and even northern Italy (the Ottomans would have certainly extended their reach to Venice, their ancient rival) are the Balkans. Both France and Russia are hungry for land there, and neither the anemic Ottomans nor the tired Germans are able to resist. The German states have tied themselves in alliances with the other continental powers: Spain, England, perhaps Poland or Sweden. Some of these countries are Protestant, and some Catholic, just like the little German states, increasing the impetus for alliances. Our world knew the nineteenth century, at least after the Napoleonic wars, as a time when the continent was mostly at peace; if the Balkan powder keg blows up earlier, the nineteenth century will be a century of war. At first the war is conducted along traditional lines, with soldiers marching in formation and lining up to shoot one another—the same way Frederick the Great, or Napoleon, had fought. Quickly, though, the technological innovations that made World War I so unprecedented in its bloodshed begin to appear, starting with the Maxim gun in 1883—or earlier, as nations at war have greater incentive to invent new weapons. By the time the twentieth century rolls around, machine guns have been pinning weary soldiers down in trenches for years. The carnage that four years of World War I wrought continues decade after decade. Europe disappears into a maelstrom of its own endless violence. Perhaps England can retreat into isolationism or turn from the continent to focus on its overseas empire. Otherwise, whatever contributions Western civilization has to offer to the world will have to come from the Americas, Australia, or Iceland.

Vienna, instead of bringing to mind an elegant waltz, the early days of modern psychology, or the novels of Robert Musil, will be a nameless crater, filled with mud and the dead.

The city still has no walls. It also has no buildings. Nowhere in its ruins is there left a single wall.

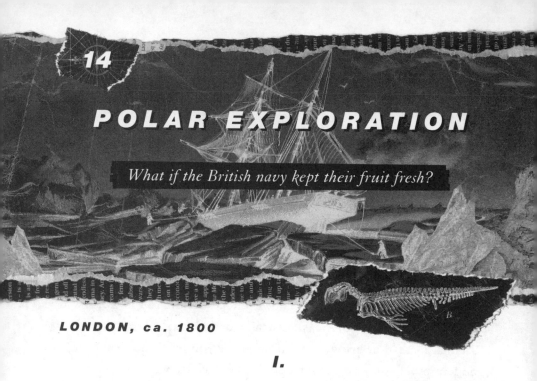

14

POLAR EXPLORATION

What if the British navy kept their fruit fresh?

LONDON, ca. 1800

I.

Here's a scary story for you. It's a true one, too, from the book John Franklin wrote about his 1819–22 voyage of exploration "to the shores of the polar sea."

Franklin had been sent by the British government with two dozen men, mostly locals, to chart the northern coast of what is now Canada. At first everything goes well; they travel farther and farther north by land, mapping as they go. In August of 1821, they find themselves far from civilization but low on supplies. Time to head back before winter hits.

Unfortunately, the area they've wound up in is so barren that even in August they have a hard time "living off the land." There are very few animals to hunt. When the party does manage to bag a partridge or something, there are no trees this far north, and therefore no fuel to cook it with. Soon, the men are subsisting mostly on berries. Then the berries give out and they subsist on lichen. Everyone is growing weak and sick. Some hunters on patrol manage to kill a deer, but they are so enervated that they can only carry a small portion of it back to camp. The men start dropping excess baggage they have become too weak to bear. The party reaches a river and decides to try ice fishing, but it turns out their fishing tackle was in one of the bags discarded along the way. There will be no fish today. They eat more lichen.

The weather is getting colder. Often they trudge through snow several feet deep; when they do not, they walk on sharp, ankle-twisting rocks. At night they sleep in their clothes, removing only their boots. To prevent the boots from freezing solid in the night, they sleep on top of them. For want of food, they eat the bones of a long-dead deer carcass they find. One day they manage to limp along eight miles. Another day it is only five and a half.

Finally, they find themselves only forty miles from a trading post, Fort Enterprise. All they have to do is cross the Copper-Mine River. Hilariously, though, among the excess baggage they'd discarded were their boats. Two attempts to build a raft are thwarted by want of sufficient trees. Dr. John Richardson, Franklin's second-in-command, attempts to swim the Copper-Mine with a towline, but he is too weak, the water too cold; he has to be towed back with his own line. Finally, after several days of dithering and starving, one of the men contrives to build a little canoe, and the whole party is ferried across the river. It's time for a sprint to Fort Enterprise now, but hunger and disease have taken their toll. The men have eaten their shoes; some of them simply cannot go on.

John Franklin decides to split the party. Dr. Richardson and Robert Hood stay behind with the very weakest men while Franklin and George Back take the rest of the company on a forced march to the fort, to assemble a relief party. Richardson and Hood keep the tent and the bulk of the supplies. Franklin will be marching light.

But before long, two of Franklin's men prove too weary to keep up with the party and get sent back to Richardson. No sooner are the pair out of sight when one, Michel Teroahauté, kills the other and starts to eat him. Another straggler, also sent back by Franklin, comes across this grisly scene, and Teroahauté kills him too. Teroahauté eats his fill, and then returns to Dr. Richardson's tent. He comes bearing meat, which he says comes from a partridge. Later he turns up more meat, which he claims he tore off a wolf carcass he found. Richardson and his camp-mates are glad to have even these scant provisions, and devour them. But Teroahauté has eaten much more than they have. He rests up. He has much work to do. He's a murderer, after all, and the truth is going to come out eventually. He decides to start *killing the party, secretly, one by one.*

Hood is the first to go. Teroahauté shoots him in the head and then claims that Hood's gun, lying nearby, discharged accidentally. But the story doesn't add up. Richardson begins to doubt that the wolf meat was wolf meat. Somehow Teroahauté ends up with a rifle and two pistols. He is by far the strongest man in camp, being the only one who has eaten several good meals recently. Richardson's only hope is that Franklin's relief party returns to them before Teroahauté kills again.

But Franklin and the four men remaining in his party, meanwhile, have forged on to Fort Enterprise. At the end of his strength, John Franklin staggers into the building only to find, to his horror, that it has been abandoned and stripped of all supplies. Despairing, Franklin's men dig through garbage in search of bones to gnaw on, and stay warm by burning, bit by bit, the wooden structure they are sheltered in. They collapse, and wait around to die, knowing that with their death, Richardson and his party will go too. They do not know, of course, that their friends are in more danger from the mad Michel Teroahauté than from starvation. It is the end of October. The cold is closing in.

The end.

II.

That's not really the end, of course. Obviously, Franklin has to survive to write a book about his journey. Richardson, it turns out, managed to sneak a pistol, and when Teroahauté advanced to finish him off, the good doctor felled him with one shot.

George Back, meanwhile, had made his way painfully from Fort Enterprise to some nearby friendly natives, the Yellowknives, who came and brought food and basically saved the day.

John Franklin made two more expeditions into the Arctic and this was not the worst one. The worst one was in 1845, when Franklin with two ships and all hands disappeared while vainly seeking the Northwest Passage. The ships, HMS *Terror* and HMS *Erebus*—Erebus in Greek mythology is darkness personified, the son of Chaos and the brother of Night, so you can see just how cheerful an enterprise this was—had previously taken James Ross safely around the ice-choked Antarctic Ross Sea; the north was less lucky for them. Their sunken wrecks were finally located in the twenty-first century, the only remains of the expedition outside of a few sailors' bodies, well preserved by the cold. Franklin, a century and a half later, is still missing (presumed dead).

If Franklin had found a northwest passage, which he didn't, all the suffering and death would have been worth it. In the nineteenth century, everyone was dreaming of a viable northern sea route connecting the Atlantic and Pacific Oceans. There was no Panama Canal in 1845, so the only way to get from one coast of America to the other by water was the long way down around South America: generally, either through the narrow, tricky Strait of Magellan or farther south, by the open ocean area between the southern tip of the Americas and Antarctica known as the Drake Passage.

Our idea of wind is a flawed idea. Almost always, the wind we encounter is blocked by buildings, trees, or hills. The air is much less still than we imagine, as you can perceive by flying a kite or looking at a flagpole. Similarly, our idea of waves is flawed, because just when waves start getting some speed, they tend to run into land. There is, in fact, only one place on earth where neither wind nor waves ever meet an obstacle. This is the Drake Passage, where wind and waves can fully circle the globe with nothing to slow them down; consequently, the passage is infamous for its incessant storms. So the Strait of Magellan and the Drake Passage are hardly the most commodious routes to travel, even if you forget that they are located south of the fifty-third parallel, and therefore conveniently situated to get from Argentina to Chile, but inconveniently situated for, say, Canadians. A passage in the north would be a great boon for British shipping. Unfortunately, it didn't exist in any practical form in that labyrinth of perpetual ice that comprises the northern islands of Nunavut. (It does now, thanks to global warming.)

The hypothetical northwest passage was a good reason to explore the polar north. There wasn't really a good reason to explore the polar south. That didn't stop people, of course. Antarctica was there, a whole continent that humans had never set foot on.

Antarctica is the only continent posited before it was ever seen. A classical desire for symmetry wanted an equal amount of land in the Southern Hemisphere to "balance out" the land in the Northern Hemisphere; there must therefore be some southern continents, as certainly there are an awful lot of northern continents. Dante, in the *Divine Comedy*, maintains the landmass balance by setting in the Southern Hemisphere *one gigantic mountain*: The mountain is Purgatory. But although the world's tallest mountain could plausibly shift the globe's center of gravity enough to serve as a counterbalance to all the Northern Hemisphere's land, most early cartographers chose instead to make the southern continent *really really big*. The 1570 Ortelius map, for example, features an enormous southern continent, reaching from the South Pole to the Tropic of Capricorn. Tierra del Fuego is a small peninsula of this huge landmass; there is no Drake Passage to be seen. Ortelius labels the continent *Terra Australis nondum cognita*—as yet unknown southern land.

No one had seen the *Terra Australis*, but everyone assumed it was there. In 1605 Philip III sent Pedro Fernandez de Quirós to conquer this antarctic continent in the name of Spain, and also convert all the natives. Quirós sailed south but only managed to reach one of the islands that is now part of the Melanesian nation of Vanuatu. He assumed the island was the tip of a huge antarctic continent (not even close) and declared all this hypothetical land, up to and including the South Pole, to belong to the Spanish Empire. Then he got lost and went home.

Over 150 years later, James Cook captained the first ship to sail south of the Antarctic Circle. It was not his worst voyage; south of the Antarctic Circle there were no natives to kill him.

Whalers set up bases among the outlying antarctic islands; seal hunters hunted seals there. Gradually people became aware that there really was a continent in the south and that it was relatively small, surrounded by ice, and completely inhospitable to humans. Quirós was not going to find anyone to convert here.

Naturally, people decided to head straight into the heart of this continent in quest for the South Pole. No one "searched" for the South Pole the way previous explorers had searched for the source of the Nile, say. Everyone already knew where the South Pole was. They just wanted to stand on it.

Specifically, they wanted to be *the first to stand on it*. The only previous claimant had been Captain Nemo, who in Jules Verne's *Twenty Thousand Leagues Under the Sea* (1870) reached the South Pole by submarine, an impressive if implausible feat; being fictional, he didn't count. The race for the pole was on. It would be dangerous, but as Arctic explorer George Melville put it, "If men must die, why not in the honorable pursuit of knowledge? Woe, woe, to America when the young blood of our nation has no sacrifice to make for science." But it wasn't Americans going for the pole. The first couple of attempts were British, and they were both failures: Robert Falcon Scott in 1901–4 and Ernest Shackleton (who had accompanied Scott on his earlier effort) in 1907–9 pressed ever deeper into Antarctica, without quite reaching the pole before turning back. In 1910, though, Scott and the Norwegian Roald Amundsen launched simultaneous and rival expeditions for the pole. It was an actual race!

Both parties sailed into the Ross Sea with plans to set out across the Ross Ice Shelf, which spans the great divot in Antarctica. Amundsen had sledges pulled by dogs; Scott, who'd had bad experiences with dogs on his last attempt, relied more on sledges pulled by ponies. Each group made preliminary sorties in order to lay caches of stores for the return journey, and then wintered in Antarctica—Scott in Cape Evans, Amundsen at the Bay of Whales—waiting for summer, when they could set out. Scott began to cross the ice shelf on November 1; Amundsen, October 19.

The men were taking different routes, and communication in 1911 was not about to let them keep tabs on each other. Neither Scott nor Amundsen knew at any moment who was ahead. They could receive no news from the outside world at all. The only thing they knew was their own progress, carefully ascertained and noted.

Part of the problem with dogs in the Antarctic is that as your supplies get lighter—because you've cached them or because you've eaten them— some of the dogs you brought become superfluous. You can't exactly let them go; dogs can't live in Antarctica. Basically, you have to kill the dogs. By the end of November, Amundsen had killed over half of the fifty-two dogs he'd set out with. Scott's soft heart was one reason he'd decided against bringing dogs. His ponies died, one by one, anyway. His men pulled the sleds. As the men cached their supplies—well, it would hardly do to kill the men, so they simply turned back. Scott's party got smaller and smaller. For the final burst to the pole—170 miles or so—Scott had only four men with him. They traveled light, and they traveled fast. On January 17, 1912, Scott and his men achieved their goal; they had found the South Pole, which looked like any other frozen place; except this one had a Norwegian flag flying, and a letter from Roald Amundsen, who had arrived and departed a month before.

The letter did not say, "Better luck next time, loser." These were gentlemen, and this was before World War I. It was an age of gentlemen. The letter was actually from Amundsen to the Norwegian king, with the request that Scott deliver it personally. It was a gentlemanly gesture of faith that Scott would make the pole, too, and make it back. Amundsen's party had also left a small cache of supplies for Scott's use. They would not be enough.

Scott's long slog back home from his silver-medal finish was one long disaster. The men were weak. They were low on food and, especially, fuel. Frostbite was setting in. On February 17 one man, Edgar Evans, just lay down and died. Another man, Lawrence Oates, had frostbitten feet and an old war wound on his leg that was reopening; he was slowing the party down. He staggered out of the tent after camp was set on March 16, and slipped off into the Antarctic wastes to die alone, in the hopes that his sacrifice might save his friends. It was a beau geste, but it came too late. Whatever hopes the rest of the party had were dashed by a blizzard. Eleven miles from a supply dump that would have saved them, Scott and his two remaining companions wrote their last letters and died in their tent. "For God's sake, look after our people," was the last thing Scott wrote.

Amundsen, who all his life had been obsessed with the far north and didn't really give a rat's ass about the South Pole, went on to fly over the North Pole in 1926. Since all previous claims to the North Pole—Cook's and Peary's by land, Byrd's by air—were probably either erroneous or fraudulent, Amundsen was the first to reach both the South and the North. He was also, in 1906, the first man to lead a ship through the Northwest Passage. It was an utterly impractical route and took over three years; but it's not a bad record. He eventually died in the Arctic he loved, while on a rescue mission to succor other explorers.

The absolutely arbitrary goal of standing on the South Pole having been accomplished, people needed to construct other arbitrary goals. In 1914, Ernest Shackleton decided he would take a party all the way across Antarctica, *through* the South Pole and out the other side. He didn't do it. In one of the great nightmare tales of Antarctic adventure, his ship was caught and then crushed in the ice. His crew of twenty-six men and one hapless stowaway had to tow three small lifeboats across the frozen sea, camping on ice floes that at times cracked in half beneath them—cracked right beneath their tents, dropping men still tangled in their sleeping bags into the ice-cold sea. When they could, they rowed their overcrowded boats through open water, working for days on end without sleep. Finally, after 497 days on water and ice, they struggled onto solid land—desolate Elephant Island, named for the elephant seals that are its only visitors. Relatively safe (seals offered both fresh meat and oil for burning; the eternal snow offered drinking water) but facing the prospect of living the rest of their miserable lives on a wind-battered, barren rock that had never been visited by humans, they decided to gamble on an impossible eight-hundred-mile journey across the Drake

Passage—remember, the stormiest region of the globe—to a whaling port on mountainous South Georgia Island.

Most of the party stayed on Elephant Island while Shackleton and five picked men—crew members Shackleton worried couldn't handle the boredom and isolation of the months-long wait—took the most seaworthy of the three boats and set off. With only the crudest of navigational instruments they traveled the storm-tossed Antarctic sea for sixteen days before reaching the south shore of South Georgia. The whalers they'd hoped to reach were on the north shore, but everyone in Shackleton's party was so frostbitten and faint that they decided to pull the boat up onto one of South Georgia's few "beaches"; time enough to circle the island tomorrow. Unfortunately, in making a beachhead the lifeboat's rudder broke off. The men were now marooned on an island larger but only slightly less desolate than the one they'd set out from.

Most of South Georgia's coast is made up of sheer cliff faces; there was no way to walk the perimeter of the island. Two members of the party could no longer walk anyway. Shackleton left them with the rest of their supplies and with his other two companions set out to perform another impossible task: He would climb the ridge that ran down the island's center, something no man had done before. They had one pickax and fifty feet of rope. With no charts or maps, still weary and ill, and not yet dry, they made their way up the frozen cliff, the lead man cutting handholds with the pickax. It took them two days, with no tent or sleeping bag; when they said they were traveling light, they were traveling *the lightest*. Once over the summit, on the way down, night fell while they were still cutting footholds in the cliff's sheer surface, and, aware that they could never actually climb down in the dark, they just let go and slid, blindly down the icy rock face. By miracle they rode the slope down and coasted to a gentle stop. When they walked into the whaling camp on the north shore, they had been missing for a year and a half. They were unrecognizable, their frames emaciated, their skin chalk-white from constant exposure to sea salt, their faces black from huddling around an oil stove, their hair and beards wild. The first man they introduced themselves to began to weep.

Shackleton's adventure has a happy ending. No one even dies. (Except the sled dogs; the sled dogs all die.) The stowaway loses some toes. No one manages to cross Antarctica until 1955, and by then it had lost some of the romance. What was even the name of the captain who succeeded? I'm sure you could look it up somewhere?

III.

The North Pole had experienced its share of fantasies and delusions. A 1606 Mercator/Hondius map shows the pole surrounded by four large islands, one of them labeled with the warning: *"pygmei hic habitant 4 ad summum pedes longi"*—pygmies live here, at most four feet tall; the pole itself is depicted as a "rock black and high," apparently magnetic. King Arthur once sought to conquer the North Pole, but some of his ships were destroyed by magnetic rocks; others were sucked into the "indrawing seas" that surround the pole—apparently some kind of maelstrom.

Maelstroms do exist in the northern seas, but they are not really reckoned one of the great dangers of polar exploration. Cold is much worse. Antarctica can reach 120 degrees below zero, the Arctic 90 below, which is why polar explorers try to venture out only in the summer. (Also: Winter means eternal night.) Storms spring up, and storms at these latitudes are blizzards of unprecedented ferocity. Icy seas are especially treacherous and unpredictable: The physics of how ice flows—breaking up and re-forming chunks of ice, crashing together in endless currents— is simply something no ship's captain has a lot of experience with. Ice can freeze ships in place, and frozen ships can be slowly crushed by ice pressure à la Shackleton's.

The cold makes your eyes water, and the tears drip down to the tip of the nose to freeze there, in an ever-lengthening icicle. When the icicle breaks off, it takes a bit of skin with it. The first time this happens it's not so bad, but that sore never heals. The icicle is always forming and always breaking off, always breaking off on an open wound.

Food is scarce. There is little or no flora or fauna around the poles, so all you can eat is what you bring in. Adolphus Greely—to take just one example from the innumerable possibilities of polar exploration—wintering off Ellesmere Island in 1883–84, lost almost three quarters of his men to starvation when supply ships failed to reach them. And what little fauna the polar regions offer can be hostile. In 1896 a rampaging walrus damaged explorer Fridtjof Nansen's kayak off Franz Josef Land. In 1919 a polar bear clawed a chunk out of Roald Amundsen's buttocks. Two members of Ernest Shackleton's party were attacked (or so they claimed) by a sea leopard. And then there are the mosquitoes. John Franklin rarely complains about his hardships, but he really harps on the mosquitoes. He takes the time in his memoirs to mention that the bites of mosquitoes he encountered in Canada are "infinitely more painful" than the bites he knew in the Old World. He goes on: "Cold, famine, and every other concomitant of an inhospitable climate must yield the pre-eminence to" the mosquito. "It chases the buffalo to the plains, irritating him to madness; and the reindeer to the seashore, from which they do not return till the scourge has ceased."

Less melodramatically, the Danish explorer Peter Freuchen specifically mentions that the reason summers are so nice in Greenland is that that's when there are no mosquitoes. Freuchen's experiences highlight another, novel trouble that can plague explorers: While trekking across Greenland he became imprisoned in a cave of ice that formed around him as he took shelter from a blizzard. Unable to free himself with his bare hands, he *froze his own dung into a chisel*, and chipped through the ice with this improvised tool.

And then there's disease . . .

Disease was always a problem for tropical explorers. As John Speke drew near Lake Tanganyika while searching for the source of the Nile, a beetle bored into his ear, rendering him mostly deaf, and an unrelated ailment left him temporarily blind, so he was obliged to lament that "the lovely Tanganyika Lake could be seen in all its glory by everybody but myself." His adventuring companion Richard Francis Burton, meanwhile, was too ill even to walk. But there's very little *nature* around the poles, in contrast, so there are very few germs. The polar regions are nearly anti-septic, so even if you leave your food lying out in the open, it will never spoil. Even the mosquitoes stop when you get far enough north. But the disease that took out polar explorers wasn't malaria or yellow fever. Their nemesis was transmitted by no insect and caused by no pathogen. Their nemesis was scurvy.

Scurvy isn't a disease you can catch; it's just a vitamin deficiency. It's a name for what happens to you when you don't get enough vitamin C in your diet. The symptoms—which include loosening teeth; a reopening of old wounds; painful, swollen, blackening limbs; lethargy, incapacitation, and death—sure look like a disease, but a little vitamin C will fix you right up. Since for most of history vitamin C was in just about everything people thought to eat, no one had scurvy. Preserved foods, though, are often preserved in ways that leach out the vitamin C. Eat too much of this preserved food—meaning, really, not enough fresh food—and you'll start exhibiting vitamin C deficiency.

As long as there was no good reason to eat all your food out of cans while letting the fresh food around you rot on the vine, everyone got enough vitamin C. But sailors on long voyages relied on food that had been packed up and stored for their trip. Sailors got scurvy. This is why pirates called one another "scurvy dogs." They were speaking the truth!

No one understood this at the time, of course. In the seventeenth century no one knew what a vitamin was—the word didn't even exist until 1912, when it was spelled *vitamine*. You can hear in old movies people using the pronunciation *vita-meen*. The word was supposed to be a com-bination of *vita* (the root word for *vital*) and *amine* (a chemical term for certain derivatives of ammonia); when it became clear that not all vita-mins were in fact amines, people dropped the terminal *e*. But try telling all that to a seventeenth-century scientist. Back then, people thought you got sick only from what entered your body, not from what *failed* to enter your body.

Even if scientists didn't understand the cause of scurvy, they had stumbled across the cure: lemon juice, which is chock-full of vitamin C. Naval surgeon James Lind first proposed the treatment in 1747, and fifty years later the British navy became the first to formally require all sailors to take a daily ration of lemon juice. Since the words *lemon* and *lime* were used interchangeably at the time, British sailors got called *limeys*. And they didn't get scurvy. The British sailed the world around, staying at sea for months on end, and they didn't get scurvy. They established blockades during the Napoleonic wars, sitting watchfully on their ships without setting foot on land, and they didn't get scurvy. Gradually, other navies, noting how well things worked for the British, started establishing similar practices. Scurvy, like measles in America, was on the way out.

But scurvy, like measles in America, could not be held down for long.

As the years passed, the daily ounce of lemon juice morphed into a daily ounce of lime juice. For the British, at least, this change made economic sense, since limes were grown in their colonies in the West Indies, while lemons they had to import from foreign Sicily. As the terms *lemon* and *lime*, which ultimately derive from the same Arabic word, were so often confused, officials may not have even noticed the difference. The sailors, presumably, could taste it, but no one asks sailors. Unfortunately, limes are much lower in vitamin C and therefore only about one fourth as good at staving off scurvy as lemons.

But that was not the real problem. Recall that preserving food is what kills its vitamin C content. British sailors were not sucking on fresh limes. They were kicking back lime juice that had been stored in vats and pumped out through copper tubes; and contact with copper absolutely destroys vitamin C. The juice they were drinking, in other words, was pretty much worthless.

Nobody noticed, though. Nobody noticed, and everyone kept drinking their juice and assuming it was working. How would they know? They weren't getting scurvy anyway.

Because by the latter half of the nineteenth century, ships had become fast enough, and the general nutrition of the populace had improved enough, that no one spent sufficient time without vitamin C to notice a problem. Scurvy had been conquered by drinking juice, but scurvy remained conquered for other reasons. People kept drinking juice more or less as a superstition. Why would they stop when it seemed to be working?

There was a problem, though. Although sailors sped between ports fast enough to get their vitamin C, polar explorers absolutely did not. When you explored Africa, you had plenty of fresh food all around you, but the first rule of a polar expedition is that you only get to eat what you take in with you. What you take in with you is preserved. What you take in with you has no vitamin C . . .

Suddenly scurvy had returned. George Nares had his 1875 attempt to reach the North Pole aborted by an outbreak of scurvy among the crew. They were drinking their juice! It wasn't fair! No one had an explanation but everyone began to worry. The talisman had failed.

You can't read an account of polar explorers without coming across scurvy. As early as 1853, Elisha Kane had struggled with widespread scurvy during his arctic voyage in search of John Franklin's remains. The first ship to winter in the Antarctic ice—the *Belgica* in 1898, with a young Roald Amundsen serving as first mate—was beset by scurvy until the crew began eating penguin meat, which, being fresh, had the vitamin C they needed. On Scott's 1901 race for the South Pole everyone—especially Shackleton, but also everyone—got scurvy. Edgar Evans, who lay down and died on Scott's final mission? You guessed it. Scurvy. And he couldn't have been the only one. Scurvy makes old wounds reopen, and Lawrence Oates had his war wound . . .

Just as an example of how little people understood the disease, look at Fridtjof Nansen's account of his 1893 shot for the North Pole, in which he worries about bringing "germs of scurvy" on his ship. Scurvy's not a contamination; you can't bring it anywhere, and it doesn't have germs. But Nansen didn't know.

It didn't have to be this way, of course. It's easier said than done, but the facts were there for someone to put together. Unlike cures for bacterial infection ("something involving mold?") or prevention of polio ("just get a vaccine, I guess?"), the cure for and prevention of scurvy is simple enough that any one of us, if sent back in time, could pass the details along to concerned sailors in a few minutes. Citrus. Fresh food. It's the easiest cure! Even a few crates of lemons—too heavy to carry into the interior, of course, but easy enough to bring by boat to the winter camp, where they could be sucked on during the long winter nights—would have given Scott's men the vitamin C they needed for their polar dash.

Amundsen, who never forgot the scurvy outbreak on the *Belgica*, also never forgot that fresh meat ended it. He brought live animals to his Antarctic winter base and killed them there; his men ate their dogs after killing them. And, of course, he won the pole.

Scurvy is cured for real → Polar exploration is easier → Amphibian fossils found earlier → **YOUR FAVORITE DINO IS A SALAMANDER**

I.

BUT WHAT IF SOME ENTERPRISING SCIENTIST FIGURED OUT the cause of, and cure for, scurvy a few decades earlier? There'd be no more scurvy, in that case. But scurvy is hardly the bubonic plague, killing one third of Europe and sweeping away the medieval world. What difference would a lack of scurvy make?

In a world without scurvy . . . polar exploration would be a lot easier, for one thing. Still not simple, of course—the cold is the cold, and all sorts of malnutrition threaten explorers of the frozen wastes. Food historian Diana Noyce notes that the presence of sodium bicarbonate in Scott's team's biscuit rations may have destroyed all the thiamine therein, leading to beriberi, a disease whose symptoms resemble scurvy. Even if you get enough vitamin C, there are plenty of other vitamins to worry about.

But scurvy had been the particular bugbear of explorers for so long that even if other vitamin deficiencies skulked around the borders, a little vitamin C would still go a long way. Without scurvy, Scott's team would have made it back to civilization with their second place. Actually, without scurvy, Scott may well have made it to the pole on his first attempt way back in 1901. Without scurvy, someone else may have made a serious effort even earlier.

In 1923 John Buchan, most famous now for his novel *The Thirty-Nine Steps* (1915), tried to name a positive result of polar exploration. He hemmed and hawed a bit, and the best he was able to come up with was that arctic exploration creates heroes. This statement may have sounded less ridiculous in 1923 than it does today; nevertheless, it does not make polar exploration sound like a fruitful area of historical inquiry. If the only result of exploration at the poles is hero generation, then it's not like we're going to get more heroes by making things *easier*. Would anything actually change if people had "conquered" (as we used to say) the continent by the late nineteenth century?

II.

Here's an interesting fact: When Scott and company's frozen bodies were eventually discovered, eleven miles from shelter (and twenty-four miles past where they had originally planned on laying that shelter—oops!), one thing that was found among the corpses and the tear-jerking diaries were forty pounds of fossilized plants. Forty pounds is a lot for a dying man to carry. These were among the first fossils ever discovered in Antarctica, and they offered evidence that this barren continent had once been covered in forests. It would be fifty years before anyone dug up an Antarctic fossil of an animal. It was an amphibian's jaw.

Most of the fossil digs in Antarctica have been on surrounding islands—by necessity, because most of Antarctica proper has a permanent ice cover you'd need to dig through before reaching a fossil bed. There's really no telling what kind of fossil finds some digs in the interior would yield; but where we do not know, we are welcome to guess.

"No ancient legend of fabled monsters," the folklorist Donald A. Mackenzie wrote in 1917, "surpasses the modern scientist's account of extinct gigantic fauna." Dinosaurs, every red-blooded American child knows, used to rule the earth. But before dinosaurs ruled the earth, crocodilians ruled the earth; and before crocodilians ruled the earth synapsids—such as dimetrodons and moschopses—ruled the earth. I don't know who ruled before them—scorpions maybe? But somewhere mixed in there you'll find giant amphibians, too.

Giant amphibians thrived on the earth for a long time (250 million years or so) but by the Cretaceous period they were on the wane. The Cretaceous is pretty much the golden age of dinosaurs—most of the dinosaurs in *Jurassic Park* were from the Cretaceous period, not the Jurassic, title notwithstanding—but it was competition from crocodiles that spelled the doom of these giant amphibians. Crocodiles in the Cretaceous could reach thirty-five feet in length (*Deinosuchus*), and you could see how they'd be tough competition. But crocodiles don't like the cold, so giant amphibians survived in the antarctic regions longer than anywhere else.

The earth was warmer then, and none of the continents were in the right place. Antarctica did not girdle the South Pole. Thanks to continental drift, Australia was just as far south as Antarctica, the two of them half in, half out of the Antarctic Circle; much of what we now guess about prehistoric life in Antarctica is based on what we know about prehistoric life in Australia, just because Australia is a much easier place to dig fossils nowadays. The earth was warmer, but life below the Antarctic Circle was still cold, cold enough that huge amphibians such as *Koolasuchus* could thrive with no crocodilian interference.

Koolasuchus was some fifteen feet long, looking like an oversize salamander with a large, flat head. Fifiteen feet is pretty good, but amphibians could get much larger—270 million years ago, long before *Koolasuchus*, *Prionosuchus* was thirty feet long. If there are other, larger amphibians waiting to be discovered in Antarctica—well, it's certainly a possibility.

There's a biological "law," proposed in 1847 by Carl Bergmann, that maintains that colder climates promote larger specimens of animals than warmer climates. This law may be spurious—broadly stated, nineteenth-century laws have a tendency to get debunked—but everyone knows that grizzly bears and polar bears are much larger than the brown bear or the Southeast Asian sun bear; as far as deer go, moose are much larger than pudú (13" tall, S. Am.) or muntjac (15" tall, S. Asia). Elephants are big, but mammoths were bigger. I'm not saying Bergmann is correct, and I'm not saying he even intended his law to apply to amphibians, but "there are strange things done in the midnight sun," and no reason not to believe Antarctica could once have bred much larger amphibians, extinct now and buried in the cold, cold ground.

III.

Why am I telling you this?

Much like art or morals, animals have a faddishness. This was more pronounced in the nineteenth century, when Victorian England would be swept by the mania for a certain species simply because one, for the first time, was being brought to the London Zoo. The craze for hippopotamus kitsch—breast pins, knickknacks, "The Hippopotamus Polka"—that swept London in 1850 after Obaysch the hippo was installed in the zoo can only be compared to the furor Paris experienced in 1827 over a newly arrived giraffe that brought about giraffe-inspired hairstyles, clothing colors, collar buttons, etc. Later in London there would come a madness for elephants in 1865 with the arrival of Jumbo (not the first elephant in England, but the first of genus *Loxodonta*, and therefore the largest; his name has become a byword for size). And Paul Du Chaillu's account of his explorations in Africa, published in 1861, made the gorilla the fad of the day—even though people still weren't 100% sure the gorilla was not a myth; R. M. Ballantyne's contemporary boy's adventure book *The Gorilla Hunters* features three friends on a trip to Africa to prove that *gorillas are real*. No live gorilla would be seen in England until 1887. His name, when he arrived, was Mumbo.

Zoological gardens were new ca. the nineteenth century. Eccentric rich people had long held private menageries, but it was between the 1790s and the 1820s that the first public zoos opened. The animals that seized the public consciousness in the following decades would remain default zoo animals . . . forever. A hippo, a giraffe, an elephant, and a gorilla make a pretty good generic drawing of a zoo—for example, three quarters of these animals appear in the zoo in the children's book *Curious George Takes a Job* (1947), and if there's no gorilla, that's probably because George himself is too ambiguous in his species to allow other primates for contrast. The only zoo animals more comfortably canonical would be the lion, the tiger, and maybe the zebra.

Sometimes popular culture decides to freeze in a certain time period. All of your favorite superheroes were created either around the threshold of the 1940s (Superman, Batman and Robin, Wonder Woman, Captain America) or the threshold of the 1960s (Spider-man, Hulk, Iron Man, Thor, Supergirl). Sixteen of the twenty most played Christmas songs on the radio ("Rudolph," "White Christmas," etc.) are from the 1940s or '50s: Christmas is stuck in the mid-twentieth century. Zoos are stuck in the nineteenth century; only the giant panda has managed to make it into the pantheon as a twentieth-century zoo animal—and the latter part of the twentieth century at that. As late as 1946, an account of the travels of the hunter Dean Sage Jr. calls the panda a "monstrous raging beast"; only a lucky shot saves Sage from a panda attack. That's how little the West knew about pandas in 1946.

How about dinosaurs?

Brontosaurus: discovered 1879. *Stegosaurus*: discovered 1887. *Triceratops*, 1889. *Tyrannosaurus*, 1905. *Ankylosaurus*, 1908. A quarter century for all your favorite dinosaurs. (*Velociraptor* is the outlier here, and that's obviously because of *Jurassic Park*.)

The importance of this pantheon of dinosaurs for popular culture can hardly be overstated. But if obscure dinosaur specimens *Deinocheirus* (1970), *Suchomimus* (1998), or *Aquilops* (2014) had been discovered earlier, you'd know what they were. Similarly, if *Koolasuchus* had been discovered earlier, you'd've known what that was before anyone said the words *fifteen-foot-long extinct amphibian.*

The golden age of dinosaur discovery falls right before the golden age of antarctic exploration—unless a lack of scurvy makes Antarctica less forbidding. Unless lack of scurvy moves everything up a few decades.

Imagine hardy adventurers digging unafraid through the antarctic strata. Edward A. Wilson (Scott's naturalist—the guy who found the plant fossils) stumbles upon a cache of giant amphibian fossils. They are just as strange and diverse in their body types as the dinosaurs we know and love are. Bring them to light at the right time and it's a hypothetical prehistoric amphibian that gets famous, not ankylosaurus. Bring enough of them to light and ancient amphibians would have their own cachet, the way non-dinosaur prehistoric reptiles like plesiosaurs or pterodactyls do. They might not fully replace dinosaurs on lunchboxes and T-shirts—there are a lot more dinosaur fossils for people to find—but people's imaginations are strange and fickle, and if these amphibians strike the right chord, if they're large enough and exotic-looking enough, they just might.

(Fossils of the amphibian *Diplocaulus* were actually discovered in Illinois in 1877, but *Diplocaulus* is only three feet long, and no one was certain it was an amphibian at first anyway.)

So now Raquel Welch, in the movie *One Million Years B.C.* (1966), encounters crazy amphibians instead of a triceratops and a brontosaurus. King Kong (1933) fights amphibians, not a tyrannosaur. *The Land Before Time* (1988) features the adventures of five little amphibians. Baby Bop is a tadpole.

It would require some astonishing finds and some good luck on the part of paleontologists—but stranger things have happened. People cured and then accidentally gave themselves scurvy.

IV.

The first mass-market dinosaur toys were metal figurines from France, but the ones everyone remembers come from an American company, the greatest and most successful dinosaur toy manufacturer of them all:

Marx, 1955–79. Marx's dinosaur sets included synapsids ("mammal-like reptiles" they were once called) such as *Sphenacodon* and *Dimetrodon* and non-dinosaur prehistoric reptiles from the very beginning, and later added mammals to the mix. Small, plastic, monochromatic, and covering a wide range of extinct species, Marx figures are beloved by collectors, in part for their high production values.

Those high production values meant that when there was one error in a batch, Marx might well throw the whole batch out. Prototypes, sometimes cast in different colors, got tossed as well. Overprints: tossed. Marx had its own landfill in West Virginia, and all its trash was buried there.

When Marx went out of business in 1979, that landfill became public land. Anyone can go there. The lots surrounding it are still private property, so it's hard to gain access—supposedly you have to pay a toll to some gun-toting local on perpetual watch—but once you get to the landfill you can do what you want. And what people want to do is to dig.

This is all true. Twenty miles outside Moundsville, West Virginia, toy collectors, in a curious mimesis of paleontology, dig deep into the toy-filled strata. They have to dig past weathered, formless toys, past uninteresting toys—trains and cars and a plastic Alamo (Marx molded a lot more than just dinosaurs in its day)—to find those rarest of fossils: an unreleased prototype, or a bag of mint-condition figures untouched by human hands.

If grown adults sifting through the sands of time to find some pseudo-paleontological relic of a lost childhood melts your icy heart—and it works on mine—try imagining something more. Imagine a slightly different world, a scurvy-less world. Imagine that a paleontologist in West Virginia blows the dirt from, and holds up to the sun, a tiny plastic *Diplocaulus*.

Diplocaulus wasn't as large as a *T. rex*, say, but its gigantic arrow-shaped head makes a distinctive little toy.

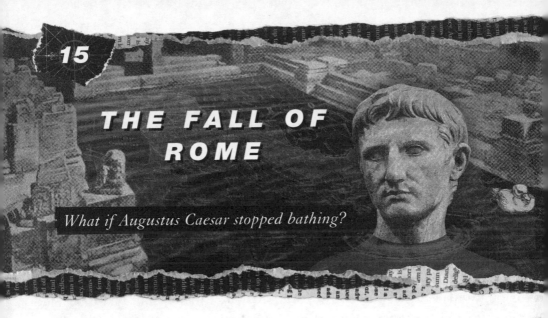

15

THE FALL OF ROME

What if Augustus Caesar stopped bathing?

ROME, AD 9

I.

The three most important things to understand about Rome are that it was really powerful, it wasn't so bad, and it was full of people who really liked baths.

For most of its history, Rome had no genuine rival. The great empires of India and China, or even Ethiopia, were too far away to have any direct contact, and even if they'd heard of Rome (they'd probably *heard* of Rome; Roman coins have been found all over the place, including Vietnam and Madagascar) there could never be any real conflict between them. Roman territory included all of Europe south and west of Germany, most of Britain, North Africa, Asia Minor, and the Near East. Every inch of land that bordered the Mediterranean Sea was Roman, a feat no other empire or state has managed. Nowhere was there a threat to imperial stability. On Rome's borders were loose confederations of nomads—barbarians, as the Romans thought of them—plus small kingdoms like Armenia and the vast empire of Persia, which may have considered itself Rome's equal, but which almost always lost when the two empires fought. Rome sacked the Persian capital several times, while Persia never marched far into Roman territory, restricting itself to border raids. Although Persia killed or captured a couple of Roman emperors, this was only possible because those emperors had pushed too deep into Persia. Only after Rome fell was Persia something of an even match for the Roman remnant, the Byzantine Empire. Rome, at its height, stood alone.

It's surprising to us today, but people liked being part of the Roman Empire. They wanted to be Romans! We think of empires as exploiters whose people yearn to be free, but for most of its history this empire was populated by people who were happier inside its borders than out.

Before Rome was an empire it was a republic—the largest and most successful democratic state of the ancient world. Attalus III, king of Pergamon, took the extraordinary step of *leaving his country* to the Roman Republic *in his will*. And even after the republic had fallen, the empire was attractive enough that barbarians petitioned for the right to move into Roman territory and become Roman subjects. When generals in Britain or Gaul rebelled against Rome, they didn't declare themselves independent, for no one wanted to be independent of Rome. They instead claimed to be the true leaders of the empire and fought until they either ruled Rome or died. It may seem strange to us, but even rebellious splinter groups didn't want to be separate from the empire; they just wanted to be in charge.

True, the empire's leadership does not have the best reputation to modern eyes. In the novel *Jane Eyre*, when young Jane wants to insult her cousin (whom she has already called a "murderer" and "slave-driver") she brings out the big guns and says he is "like the Roman emperors." There's a 1963 Superboy story in which the Boy of Steel must face the three most evil men in history, and one of them is the emperor Nero (the other two are Adolf Hitler and John Dillinger, which isn't really fair to Dillinger). Leopold von Sacher-Masoch—the word *masochism* comes from his name—fantasized in 1870 that the cruel woman he would like to have torture him might have the "soul of Nero." Certainly, some emperors are watchwords for cruelty and capricious tyranny. Dorian Gray (in Oscar Wilde's *The Picture of . . .*) becomes corrupted by a book detailing the vices of five of them: Tiberius, Caligula, Nero, Domitian, and Elagabalus.

Roman emperors persecuted Christians, and most later historians who studied Rome were Christian and therefore partisan; Roman emperors also frequently murdered their own family members and plenty of their fellow Romans, not to mention whoever else they could get their hands on. To return to Nero, no one's favorite human being: He tried to poison his mother so often that she began to take antidotes regularly *just in case*; he built a trap ceiling in her bedroom to crush her while she slept (unsuccessfully); he finally managed to coax her onto a trick boat that sank with her on board, and when she swam to shore he just had one of his guards finish her off. This was his mother, remember. John Dillinger wouldn't have done any of that to his mother.

So there were some bad emperors. But the Roman Empire was huge and most of its subjects would never have even seen the emperor, let alone have been in a position to be murdered by him. Even in times when the emperor was completely insane, as some were, or evil, as some were, bandits, barbarians, and invaders were more of a threat to the average person than the emperor was. And Rome's borders were designed to keep out bandits, barbarians, and invaders.

Inside the borders, everyone was taking a bath. Not just any bath: a super-hot, sauna-like bath.

The Romans learned about bathing from the Campanians, a people of southern Italy. The Campanians *voluntarily offered to be subjects of the Roman Republic* in order to gain the protection of a small but rising power (everybody wanted to be Roman), and along with the fertile Campanian land, the Romans picked up the local bathing culture. Since Romans never did anything by halves, bathing became a Roman obsession. Over time, Romans began bathing every day in large public bathhouses, popular places to gather and exchange gossip or transact business. Even the poor went to the baths, but the idle rich could obviously spend more leisure time bathing, and emperors were the richest of all. Commodus, to give one example, reportedly took seven or eight hot baths every day.

As Roman civilization spread, the bath spread with it. Bathhouses in Rome became larger and more ornate—the Baths of Caracalla, built in the third century to fit sixteen hundred bathers, have served more recently as an opera house and the racetrack of the Rome Grand Prix—but even the humblest and most distant reaches of the empire featured bathing facilities. The city of Bath in England is named for the Roman bath complex built there in the first and second centuries. The historian Tacitus said that the Britons became so addicted to baths that it made them decadent and weak.

But the baths may have had another inimical effect on the Romans throughout the empire. Hot baths have been shown to reduce sperm counts.

II.

Roman baths continued to be used after the fall of Rome. We tend to think of the Middle Ages as a filthy time, but Paris in the thirteenth century had twenty-six bathhouses offering hot baths to the public; many medieval medical books—such as the *Trotula* anthology (ca. 1150), Felix Hemmerli's *Treatise on Natural Baths* (ca. 1450), or Peter of Eboli's only semi-medical *On the Baths of Puteoli* (ca. 1220)—advise bathing, including Roman-style hot baths, for good health.

Certainly, though, medieval baths could not have been as popular as they were in Roman times. People in the Middle Ages had *children*.

People in Rome, not so much. As early as AD 9, Augustus Caesar was so concerned about the dwindling population of Rome that he passed laws giving special rights and privileges to the parents of large families, while forbidding the unmarried from inheriting property or attending gladiatorial matches. Laws of this nature are not uncommon among nomadic tribes living in inhospitable areas where an entire people risks death if its numbers are not kept up. The ancient Hebrews match this description, which may be why the Bible requires a man to marry his brother's widow (Deuteronomy 25:5–6) and forbids non-procreative sex (Genesis 38:9–10) and homosexuality (Leviticus 18:22). Such strictures are usually less pressing among large bodies of settled people like the Romans; and yet, here Augustus was.

Augustus's laws didn't work, of course. Augustus couldn't have known that hot baths lead to infertility, so he didn't do the only thing that could have helped: He didn't ban hot baths. The population kept declining.

When the barbarians started pressing at the borders of the empire, many writers stressed the large numbers of their tribes. Ammianus Marcellinus compares the onrushing of the Gothic armies at the Battle of Adrianople to a lava flow. Modern historians are unanimous in their judgment that the barbarians' numbers were exaggerated, possibly to make losing to them less embarrassing for the Romans and possibly because Romans from underpopulated regions were just not used to seeing large groups of people outside cities.

But, really, a decline in Roman population hardly sounds like a big deal. After all, *everyone wanted to be a Roman*. Rome kept conquering new lands and incorporating more people. The Roman Empire could keep its total numbers up through immigration.

This is true, but upper-class Romans spent a disproportionate amount of time in the baths, and Roman emperors spent the most time of all. This is what ends up being a big deal.

III.

Augustus was the first emperor of Rome, but he didn't start off calling himself emperor. The Latin word *imperator* just means something close to "general," and is merely one of several titles that got applied to Augustus over the years. Over time it became synonymous with (and is indeed the source of our word) *emperor*. After Augustus's death, the title *imperator*—and therefore rulership of the Roman Empire—passed to his stepson Tiberius. Follow me here: At Tiberius's death, his grandnephew and adopted son Caligula assumed the purple but was such a horrible person that he was assassinated to popular acclaim, and his uncle Claudius took over; Claudius was succeeded by his grandnephew and adopted son Nero.

You may be wondering what this has to do with bathing. But look at this quick roster of the early emperors: Not one of them managed to produce an heir. Augustus tried desperately, with three successive wives, but his only child was a daughter. (The Romans were not about to let a woman lead their empire.) Tiberius had only one son, who drank himself to death long before Tiberius died. Caligula had a daughter (assassinated in infancy). Claudius had two sons, neither of whom lived to adulthood, and two daughters—points for effort. Nero had a daughter who died in infancy and was immediately declared to be a goddess. As a consequence, each emperor had to adopt an heir, or (in Caligula's case) have one selected from his nearby family. Even Augustus, the heir of Julius Caesar, was just Caesar's grandnephew. By the time Nero was condemned to death, for—well, for being Nero—he'd killed so many members of his extended family that there were no good candidates left to take over. Nero was the last of the so-called Julian dynasty.

IV.

For several centuries, the Roman Empire was the most powerful game in town, and everyone in its borders was really happy about it. In AD 117 these borders stretched from Scotland to the Persian Gulf. In AD 395 it still stretched from Scotland to the Red Sea. By 410 barbarians were looting the city of Rome and by 476 the empire was no more. How could that have happened?

Ultimately, it happened because of all the baths. But you can say it in another way: *Rome fell because it became the custom to try to make it fall.* The barbarians tried to conquer Rome because *everyone* was always trying to conquer Rome, and they succeeded because plenty of people succeeded.

Long before the empire fell, the Roman *Republic* had fallen for the very same reason—it had become the custom for the Roman Republic to fall. Starting in 88 BC, strongman general after strongman general took over the republic and ruled as dictator, generals such as Sulla, Marius, Cinna, Pompey, and most famously, Julius Caesar. Then, after Caesar, Mark Antony made a bid to follow in his footsteps. The politician Catiline tried hard to join the ranks of dictators, but Cicero thwarted him through the power of his oratory; Cicero next spoke out against Mark Antony, who cut off the great orator's head and hands and displayed them in the Senate as a warning. Real strongmen were not afraid of mere words.

A democracy can get taken over by a dictator and recover, but after fifty-plus years of various dictators fighting it out, it becomes clear that that democracy no longer stands. By the time Julius Caesar's adopted son, Octavian, took over in 27 BC, it was too late for him to reign as just another senator or as a consul (the traditional elected head of the republic); there was no republic left for him to lead. So, Octavian took the name Augustus ("respected") and the title Princeps ("first citizen") and allowed some appearance of democracy to continue. Augustus was indeed elected consul, but he was elected consul *every year* for the rest of his life. Some Romans were scandalized, but many more were relieved; if everyone had stopped wishing for the return of the republic fifty years earlier, they could have avoided a half century of violence!

That was the republic. In the same vein, the Roman Empire fell because the Roman Empire kept falling. Long before barbarians were a threat to Rome, Romans were a threat to Rome.

So what happened after Nero died? It was called the year of four emperors—AD 69—because one general after another rose up to become emperor, only to be killed by his successor (or in one case by the Praetorian Guard—ostensibly his bodyguards). The fourth emperor, Vespasian, proved hardy enough that no one even tried to kill him. He died a natural death ten years later and passed the emperorship on to his natural-born son—*the first Roman Emperor ever to do so.*

Vespasian's son died a natural death, and the Senate then elected his younger son, who proved tyrannical and got assassinated. Even though Vespasian set a precedent by keeping the imperial title "in the family," there wasn't actually a rule that his sons would inherit—it's just that each son seemed an obvious choice, and no one had a more persuasive suggestion.

Vespasian had no more family members, so the Senate put an aged senator, Nerva, on the throne. Nerva had no children, and he was sixty-five when he became emperor, so he knew there was a very real danger that when he died there would be civil war again.

Nerva decided to select a successful general, Trajan, to be his heir, and indeed Trajan took over when Nerva died of old age. Trajan also had no sons, but he chose Hadrian to succeed him. Hadrian also had no sons, but he chose Antoninus Pius to succeed him. Antoninus Pius had no sons, but he named Lucius Verus and Marcus Aurelius to reign together after he died.

And after them it was all downhill. Things would never go this smoothly again. These emperors, sometimes called the Five Good Emperors, saw Rome at its height. The historian Edward Gibbon once wrote that the happiest a people has ever been—the happiest anyone has ever been in all of history anywhere in the world—was in the Roman Empire during the eighty-four years of the reign of Nerva and his adoptive heirs. Edward Gibbon lived in the late eighteenth century, so there was a lot of our history he hadn't seen, but his declaration of Roman happiness is still a bold statement, especially when you consider that Gibbon wore spectacles and would have had a hard time reading his Latin in the second century.

It's easy to say that Rome was happy, Gibbon-happy, under the good emperors precisely because the emperors were good. Certainly, that didn't hurt. The empire was flourishing. It had expanded its borders to their greatest extent. Persia had been humbled in a couple of wars. Everything was swell.

But there was still the problem of inheritance. Each of the good emperors got around the problem by selecting an heir ahead of time, and they chose wisely. But anyone could be chosen! Rome had a rigid class system, and the emperor always chose his successor from the upper class—the senatorial class, they called it—but that still left a large number of potential heirs.

We've already seen that Antoninus Pius had two emperors rule after him, a strange setup. Rome had never had two emperors ruling side by side as equals before; but there were no rules against it. There were no real rules for the emperor at all. You may expect two emperors to squabble between them, but Lucius Verus and Marcus Aurelius seemed to get along, and Lucius Verus died young, of natural causes (he had no surviving children), leaving Marcus Aurelius to rule alone. Marcus Aurelius, the last of the good emperors.

Marcus Aurelius was the wisest of emperors. He studied philosophy, specifically the school of Stoicism, and his book of philosophical notes, usually called the *Meditations*, is in print today in several popular translations, and is full of good advice.

He was successful in war; he was just and temperate in his judgments. Marcus Aurelius only made two big mistakes in his life: He had a son, and he left that son the empire.

The son in question, Commodus, does not get counted among the good emperors (Lucius Verus doesn't get counted either, but that's just because he was overshadowed by his co-ruler). You may remember Commodus as the heavy from the movie *Gladiator*, but before he was the villain in a Russell Crowe film he was a villain in history. Maybe it was having a father famed for his Stoicism—Stoics are not known for "having a good time"—but Commodus rejected philosophy in favor of frivolity, becoming obsessed with the Romans' favorite non-bathing pastime: gladiatorial games. He also tried to rename Rome, the months of the year, several legions, and the branches of government after himself. He executed plenty of his fellow Romans without trial, as bad emperors tend to, but he may really have been assassinated because the Romans were afraid they'd spend the rest of their lives living in the city of Commodiana.

Whatever the reason, Commodus was strangled in his bath in 192 and then Rome was in a pickle. It had been nearly a century since they'd had to worry about how to find a new emperor. The Senate had the responsibility to pick someone, but they had no experience in picking someone qualified. So they chose a senator named Pertinax.

In the past, starting in the reign of Claudius, emperors had paid the Praetorian Guard—the elite army unit that guarded them and policed the city of Rome—a bonus upon their accession. Pertinax promised the

Praetorians a similar bonus and then only paid part of it, so the Praetorians killed him. Then the guard did something unprecedented: They put the empire up for auction—highest bidder gets to be emperor. The Praetorians had no authority to do this, technically, but as the emperor's bodyguard they had a strong say in whether the emperor was murdered or not, so they got away with it.

The senator Julianus got in the winning bid, promising twenty-five thousand sesterces per soldier—not a bad sum, considering it would take a common foot soldier over a decade to earn that much. The Praetorian Guard declared Julianus to be emperor, and they were frightening enough that the Senate ratified their decision. But the rest of the empire was scandalized that a rich man had purchased the throne; and many soldiers must have thought that if the Praetorian Guard could choose an emperor, why couldn't they?

Enter the anarchy. For four years four men, including Julianus, would fight over the right to rule Rome. Three died, and the general Septimius Severus was proclaimed emperor, ruling by right of the sword.

Septimius Severus was a good fighter and not so bad as far as emperors go. He even had two sons, and the two of them jointly took over after he died. One son then murdered the other, and the survivor, after a reign of six years, was murdered by a disgruntled ex-Praetorian. The new emperor, Macrinus, a Praetorian guardsman himself, who may have arranged the assassination, lost a civil war and was killed. A pattern is emerging, but we'll keep going down the roll, line by line.

The new emperor after Macrinus, a scandalous lad known as Elagabalus, was killed by Praetorians. His successor, Severus Alexander, won one civil war and lost a second one, so he was killed. Maximinus Thrax, the winner of that second civil war and therefore the new emperor, defeated four other claimants for the throne before being murdered by his own men. And it goes on like that. Septimius Severus had died in the year 211 and it's not *until 297* that an emperor managed to restore order. Almost everyone else in between is overthrown, assassinated, or killed in battle—or, in the case of Valerian, captured alive by the Persians and used as a human footstool for the rest of his life. It's hard to count the number of emperors declared between 211 and 297, because so many usurpers and would-be usurpers controlled only parts of the empire—but it's over fifty. At least two of these emperors were members of the Praetorians, bodyguards that had an increasing tendency to murder the body they should have been guarding.

These emperors' reigns tended to be both bloody—and short. Long reigns are not a sure sign of stability, of course. Between 1643 and 1792—a century and a half—France had only three monarchs; in 1792 the third one was deposed, and his head was chopped off a year later. *Vive la révolution!* But shorter reigns do mean more successions, which means more succession problems. If the only way an emperor can avoid being murdered is if he quickly dies of disease, as was the case in third-century Rome, you're going to have a lot of succession problems.

Finally, in 297 order was restored under what was called the "tetrarchy"—two senior emperors assisted by two junior emperors, working in concert. No one had ever set the empire's rulership up in quite this fashion, but remember: There were no rules about the emperorship. The tetrarchy sure sounds like a recipe for disaster, but it functioned smoothly as long as the strongest emperor (Diocletian: remember that name) kept his hand on the reins. After he retired, there were two decades of civil war. And it goes on like that.

The empire saw periods of peace, but these periods were less common than periods of anarchy, civil war, multiple simultaneous usurpations, and assassinations. Around the year 260 *nine different generals* declared themselves sole emperor and fell to fighting one another. In ten years' time they were all dead. Barbarians and Persians fought the Romans, too, during this time, but the damage they did to the empire is tiny compared to the damage the empire did to the empire. Every successful usurpation encouraged other usurpations; every unsuccessful rebellion led to massacres and reprisals, generating enough ill will to bring about another rebellion.

Previously, all emperors had come from the upper class, the so-called senatorial class. These were the "finest families" of Rome, something akin to the British peerage. Starting with Macrinus, the Praetorian guardsman-turned-emperor mentioned above, the so-called equites, or knights—a kind of Roman middle class—started assuming imperial power. Once there was precedent for middle-class emperors, there was no turning back. And this was important because there were *a lot more equites than senators*. Emperors like Nero might fear a usurper, but they only had to keep their eyes on a relatively small number of blue bloods, families they had known all their lives. No emperor could keep an eye on all the equites; the next emperor could come from *anywhere*.

Historians call the time we just covered "the Crisis of the Third Century," which seems to imply that the fourth century was better. It was a little better. There were still lots of civil wars, usurpations, and rebellious provinces, but with less frequency. Perhaps the equites took fewer baths, and so had more children than the old senators. Really, though, the damage of the third century had already been done. Every successful Roman general now knew he might be the next emperor. In fact, every successful Roman general knew that the custom was to try to become the next emperor.

It's conventional wisdom that the once-mighty French stopped being able to win wars after the Age of Napoleon because every French officer remembered the way the "little corporal" struck out on his own and rose to stardom (and an imperial throne) through the force of his genius and will. Essentially it became the custom among French officers to disobey orders for their own aggrandizement. Whether this is true or not—conventional wisdom is often wrong, especially when it's about another country—it *sounds* true. Certainly the career of François Darlan (the WWII French admiral who collaborated with both the Nazis and the Allies in order to secure his own, independent fleet) is easier to understand if we assume Darlan was working toward the goal of seizing power; he certainly couldn't have been working for the good of France; "Let us all be thankful we have never had to face the trials under which he broke," Churchill said at his death. But if French officers only *sometimes* tried to grab the reins of state, Roman officers did it constantly.

And while fighting foreign wars can make a country rich—so much gold poured into Spain after its conquests of the Aztec and Inca Empires that it underwent *two centuries* of massive inflation—civil wars are always a zero-sum game. Every civil war weakened Rome—imagine the effect of a hundred civil wars!

Sure, Rome at its height could afford to engage in a civil war or two. But a hundred civil wars is a death of a hundred cuts. As Rome grew weaker, it could less well suffer the attrition of manpower and resources. There were barbarians massing on Rome's borders in the fourth and fifth centuries, but barbarians had *always* been massing on Rome's borders— Gauls sacked Rome in 390 BC, back before the city was an empire, or even a very powerful city. The barbarians were always there, but now Rome had a harder time doing anything about it because they were too busy fighting among themselves.

And remember Diocletian? In addition to restoring order, he had done something else that had long-term effects. He divided the empire in half. He had ruled as part of a tetrarchy, so Rome had four rulers. Diocletian assigned two to the western empire and two to the eastern empire. Diocletian meant for the empire to remain unified, with these divisions serving a primarily administrative purpose, but within one generation the empire split, with two rival emperors sitting on two rival thrones, glaring at each other across the divide. Constantine reunited the empire, but it would not stay united for long. Soon there were two empires instead of one, and although the two emperors were sometimes allies, they were often at war with each other—and sometimes both situations happened simultaneously: When Magnus Maximus usurped the western throne, the eastern emperor Theodosius invaded the west to depose him and restore his friend, the former western emperor.

The eastern empire fared better than the western one, for two reasons. The most important was that it was richer. The eastern empire could trade with Persia, with Armenia, with the Arab states, and by long trade routes with Abyssinia, India, Central Asia, and China. The western empire could trade with a bunch of barbarians and not much else; its border was mostly just the Atlantic Ocean—the end of the world. The Romans grew their grain on the fertile fields along the coast of North Africa, but it was the eastern empire that possessed Egypt, the most fertile region of all (Egypt alone generated about three times as much wealth as all the rest of Roman Africa). Later on, a group of Germanic barbarians, the Vandals, traveled through Spain and conquered the western half of North Africa, cutting the western empire off from its food supply. For a decaying empire already suffering from financial troubles, this was a terrible blow.

As the empire became poorer, tax collectors had to get more aggressive just to keep things running. Although tax collectors are never popular (as early as the first century AD, Philo of Alexandria wrote that people in arrears on their taxes would commit suicide in order to avoid being tortured by tax collectors), writers in the later empire bring despair in the face of taxes to a pitch that Benjamin Franklin could only dream of. Salvian the Presbyter wrote in 440 that Romans in Gaul prayed that their land would be conquered by barbarians just to free them from the Roman tax burden. It's hard to keep an empire from falling when the taxpayers inside it are all hoping it will fall.

The second advantage the eastern empire had was its capital. Byzantium—renamed Constantinople by the emperor Constantine, à la Commodus—was located on a peninsula near a heavily traveled waterway, the strait leading into the Black Sea. Constantinople was therefore wealthy, because so much trade had to go right past it, and also easy to defend: two of the city's three sides faced water. It had been selected as the capital of the eastern empire specifically for its wonderful location. Rome, in contrast, was ancient, sprawling, hard to defend, marshy and unhealthy, far from the sea, and far from the wealthiest provinces of the empire. Nobody *chose* to make Rome the capital of the empire; nobody *selected* its location—rather, they were stuck with it.

The Gothic king Alaric contemplated attacking Constantinople and decided it was too hard to conquer; he sacked Rome in 410, the first time foreign armies had entered Rome in eight hundred years! The western Roman Empire didn't fall that day, although Rome fell; but it was a demoralizing blow. St. Jerome called it the end of the humanity. The message was clear: Rome couldn't keep barbarians out, while Constantinople could. It would not be the last time barbarians sacked the great city. In 476, the barbarian king Odoacer deposed the last Roman emperor of the West. Odoacer didn't even bother to kill him, he just kicked him out; that's how little a threat the emperor was. The former western empire was divided up between squabbling barbarians. Odoacer would be killed by another barbarian invasion; soon everyone would be getting killed by barbarian invasions.

Constantinople, meanwhile, was the center of the eastern empire for another thousand years. We now call this eastern empire the Byzantine Empire, but its inhabitants called themselves Romans. They spoke Greek and lived eight hundred miles from Rome, but they called themselves Romans. When Seljuk Turks conquered central Asia Minor in the eleventh century they named their state the Sultanate of Rûm, or Rome—because it was land they'd taken from the Romans. Constantinople traditionally refused to acknowledge the German Holy Roman Empire because they said there was already an emperor of Rome, and there could scarcely by two; the real emperor of Rome, they said, was the emperor who lived in Constantinople.

The eastern empire's wealthy provinces could rest easy against barbarian attacks, because, for example, if barbarians were going to overrun Egypt, they would have done it ten thousand years earlier. The cities of the eastern empire were old and were used to defending themselves against attack. When parts of the eastern empire fell, it tended to be to completely new and unprecedented forces: first, Arabs inspired by a new religion, Islam; and later by Turks who had come all the way from the longitude of China. No one could have expected Islam or Turks.

Augustus could not have expected Islam or Turks, but he couldn't have expected Goths either. He just wanted people to have more children!

Augustus outlaws bathing → Really so many Romans → Emperor succeeds emperor in orderly succession → ROME NEVER FALLS → J. P. Marat saves la révolution

I.

AUGUSTUS NEVER FIGURED OUT A WAY TO MAKE ROMANS reproduce, and it's unlikely he ever would have guessed that baths were to blame. But he could have outlawed baths for other reasons, such as Tacitus's theory that they made the strong weak. Preserving Roman simplicity and vigor is the kind of thing Augustus would have striven for.

And forbidding baths because they make Romans weak would have had the unintended effect of making Romans fertile. For infertility is what ended the Roman Empire.

If Augustus had had a son, the empire would have passed to him. Augustus could have insisted the empire pass to him. All you need is sons. Of course, the Romans could have adjusted their culture to allow female emperors (it happened eventually, under the Byzantines), in which case Augustus, at least, would have had a direct heir. It would have doubled the chances of inheritance. But they didn't, and without a way of permitting inheritance, every emperor risked assassination and every imperial death invited funeral games.

Nero didn't fiddle while Rome burned—that's a myth—but many a Roman emperor lolled in his bath while Rome fell all around him.

II.

During the French Revolution, not long after Louis XVI had been made nine inches shorter, the revolutionary leader Jean-Paul Marat took a bath.

This was July of 1793, which was right around the start of what is now called the Reign of Terror. The revolution had been getting bloodier and bloodier, and it was about to step over a cliff and become an orgy of death. Marat was treating his skin condition with a dip in the tub when a woman named Charlotte Corday came to see him, allegedly with information about political traitors in the city of Caen. The actual political traitor was Corday, though, who represented a rival revolutionary faction. While the two were talking, she pulled a knife, and that was the end of the naked, defenseless Jean-Paul Marat.

Would a live Marat have been able to curb the worst excesses of the revolution? His sister sure thought so, and went on record with a list of revolutionary leaders who would never have been guillotined "had my brother lived." They were guillotined, of course, and their deaths only led to more deaths, reprisals, and counter-reprisals. The historian Thomas Carlyle, hardly a Marat fan, nevertheless blamed the murder for "whetting old animosities tenfold."

On the other hand, Charlotte Corday testified, "I killed one man to save a hundred thousand." They beheaded her, and soon they were beheading everyone.

Of course, if Augustus had outlawed baths, things would have been different. Marat would scarcely have been lolling in his bath in contravention of eighteen hundred years of custom. Eighteenth-century clothing was heavier than what we're used to in July, and Charlotte Corday, who went for the heart, would have had to stab Marat through his coat—a much more difficult feat. Marat survives, and the whole history of the French Revolution is changed.

Oh, yeah, and also the French Revolution is the Gaulish Revolution, because Marat is just a provincial leader in the immortal, unceasing Roman Empire.

ALASKA

What if Lewis Powell stabbed Secretary of State Seward in the eye?

WASHINGTON, DC, 1865

I.

Even people who have never heard of William Henry Seward have heard of Seward's Folly. It's not Alaska's official nickname—that would be (don't tell *space*) "The Last Frontier"—but Seward's Folly is more famous than many an official state nickname. No one knows that Arkansas is "The Natural State"; no one believes that New Jersey is "The Garden State"; everyone knows Alaska is Seward's Folly.

It didn't start out as Seward's Folly, of course. It started as Seward's Good Idea. Secretary of State Seward's 1867 purchase of Alaska from imperial Russia had to be ratified by Congress, and if purchasing Alaska had been unpopular from the get-go, it never would have happened.

Unfortunately, William H. Seward was a bit of a pompous jerk and no one liked him. In 1867 Congress was gearing up to impeach President Andrew Johnson, and Seward stood by the president—not a popular stance. Also, Seward wanted to purchase not only Alaska but all sorts of other territory, too—the Danish West Indies, British Columbia, Baja California, Hawaii, the Isthmus of Panama, Greenland, Iceland, Puerto Rico—and people thought he was going overboard. Land crazy. The *Sacramento Daily Union* accused him of going after Madagascar and Fiji, too, but it may have been joking.

Seward managed to purchase none of these, although later, after Seward's death, the US did acquire Hawaii of course (1898), Puerto Rico (also 1898), the Danish West Indies (rechristened the US Virgin Islands, 1917), and (by lease) part of Panama (1903), just as the secretary had planned. The only other territory the US did annex under Seward was uninhabited Midway Island (which would become famous in 1942, as the site of the decisive WWII battle). But Alaska was the big one.

By any standard, Alaska is always the big one.

II.

The Russians were in Alaska in the first place partly because of the fur trade and partly because Tsar Peter the Great was ambitious and indefatigable. Everyone else was colonizing America (was Peter the Great's basic idea), so why can't we? And unlike the rest of Europe, Russia could come through the back door.

> *Russian Columbuses, despising gloomy fate,*
> *shall open a new path mid ice floes to the east*
> *and to America our empire shall extend*

. . . rhymed Mikhail Vasilyevich Lomonosov in 1760 (in Russian, it rhymes) in his poem *Peter the Great*.

Great Peter died before his vision was achieved, but he had already set things in motion. The Russian Mikhail Gvozdev became the first European to sight mainland Alaska, in 1732. Not long after, Vitus Bering, a Dane sailing for the tsar, led an expedition that mapped the east coast of Siberia and the west coast of Alaska. Bering gave his name to the Bering Strait, the Bering Sea, and Bering Island, where he died (as was the custom) of scurvy in 1741. He was so cold at the end that he requested to be buried alive, to grant him some degree of precious warmth, and was covered with dirt up to the waist. After he died, his men had to dig him up again, to make the grave a regulation depth.

The Russians were in Siberia partly for fur and partly for ivory;

the Russians extracted somewhere in the ballpark of *six thousand tons* of ivory from Siberia over the course of three centuries, all of it from exhumed mammoth carcasses. But mostly for fur, and over the years, as the fur-bearing mammals of Russia—especially the sable, an exquisitely glossy black weasel—became skinned into scarcity, Russian trappers had simply moved farther and farther east, into virgin territory. The Pacific Ocean stopped them briefly; but then there was Alaska. Mimicking the original route by which people reached the Americas, fur traders crossed the narrows. No sable here, but: seal, otter, fox. Traders enslaved the natives, and massacred those who resisted slavery. The preceding sentence is more or less the summary of all colonial exploits, but those who compare these things say that the Russian fur traders were worse than most.

If the Russians had figured out a way to make fur a renewable resource, they never even would have reached Alaska. In the mid-nineteenth century, the Russian government needed money (the Russian government usually needed money), and with Alaska's fur supply dwindling, their original reason for crossing the Bering Strait was drying up. Selling Alaska to Seward may have simply made economic sense.

But Russia may have divested themselves of Alaska not because they didn't want it, but because they feared they couldn't keep it. Earlier in the nineteenth century, American settlers had pushed into Spanish territory in Texas and more or less taken over gradually before *1.* declaring independence and *2.* merging with the US. The story of Americans in California had been eerily similar. Alaska was much closer to American centers of civilization (say, San Francisco) than Russian centers of civilization (say, Moscow). Alaska—Russian America, it was called at the time—had relatively few Russians in it. There was nothing to stop Americans from pushing into Russian territory gradually and just shouldering the Russians out, "pulling a Texas."

Well, there was one thing to stop them. There was British Columbia, conveniently located in the way.

III.

Seward didn't want Alaska, really. That's not to say there was no reason why he should have wanted Alaska: American whalers wanted Alaska, and whaling was important not only for America's economy but also for America's prestige as a naval power. The American whaling fleet had been crippled during the Civil War by the predations of the CSS *Shenandoah*—in fact the last shot of the war had been the *Shenandoah* firing at, and then capturing and destroying, a whaling ship in the Bering Sea—so securing the Alaska coast for the US whaling industry would not only have helped out struggling whalers but also made official a fait accompli: American whalers had moved into Russian territorial waters. But still, Alaska wasn't what Seward wanted. Seward wanted British Columbia.

This is less crazy than it sounds. British Columbia was at the time a sparsely populated, unincorporated British colony. It wasn't part of Canada; it wasn't part of anything, other than the sprawling British Empire. The locals claimed it was poorly run, and they resented the colonial overseers and the distant London government. In the 1860s, most British Columbians (nine out of ten, a contemporary newspaper claimed) wanted to join the United States.

And the British owed the Americans. During the Civil War Britain had supplied the Confederacy with ships—not for free, but still perhaps in violation of Britain's alleged neutrality; America wanted compensation, and Britain was embarrassed enough about the incident that it was willing to pay. Seward wanted territory in lieu of cash. He wanted British Columbia.

It's likely that Seward arranged for the purchase of Alaska just because it would flank B.C. and encourage the British to hand it over. With Alaska American territory, and Washington State American territory, British Columbia looks like it ought to be American territory. It would (as one might say) "look good on a map." Looking good on a map may sound like a silly reason to claim territory, but (one might say) it's most of the reason the Republic of Ireland claims Ulster or Argentina claims the Falkland Islands. Looking good on a map is very persuasive to a lot of people. Seward's plan might have worked.

But as it was, Canada itself began the process of absorbing British Columbia, agreeing to build a railroad linking the future province to the east coast. Whatever agitation there had been to join America faded. British Columbia became Canadian, stranding the already purchased Alaska as a strange, noncontiguous outpost.

The ambiguous status of British Columbia doubtless not only fueled Seward's desire to buy Alaska; it also fueled Russia's eagerness to make the sale. Russia may have feared Americans gradually muscling into Alaska, but Russians *really feared* Canadians muscling into Alaska. Canadians were Englishmen, and Russia and England had only a decade earlier fought each other in the Crimea. At least America was an *ally*. Just as Great Britain had offered material help to the Confederacy during the Civil War, Russia had sent ships to support the Union. Russia and America were friends. Russia and Britain were mortal enemies. Russia never would have stood for a hostile British/Canadian presence in Alaska, only fifty miles from its shore. That is what will prove important.

IV.

In 1862, Seward wrote that "assassination is not an American practice or habit, and one so vicious and so desperate cannot be engrafted into our political system." Unfortunately, he was proved wrong three years later.

The day Lincoln was shot by the handsomest man in America, Seward was stabbed in the face. It was part of an intended "decapitation attack," aiming to take out President Lincoln, Vice President Johnson, and Secretary of State Seward, thereby leaving the country with no leadership and plunging the Union into chaos. But Johnson's would-be assassin chickened out and Seward's was unlucky. Lewis Powell, the unlucky assassin, knew that Seward was confined to bed after a carriage accident (broken arm, broken jaw), and bluffed his way into the house by pretending to be a physician's assistant. Frederick W. Seward, William Seward's son and future biographer, tried to question him, so Powell decided to gun him down, but the pistol misfired, after which he beat Frederick almost to death with the pistol butt. So far so good.

Powell charged into Seward's bedroom and started stabbing Seward in the face and throat. Seward, however, had a metal brace on his neck and face, immobilizing his broken jaw; all that stabbing sliced his face, but could not hit anything vital. Face wounds bleed a lot. Face wounds always *look* bad. Powell assumed his target was dead. On his way out of the house, he stabbed (not fatally) three more people. Three days later he was captured; later, hanged.

Seward survived to purchase Alaska two years later.

Seward stabbed in the eye → *Nobody buys Alaska* →
Soviets roll their nukes into North America →
NUCLEAR ARMAGEDDON

I.

A SEWARD WITH NO BRACE ON COULD HAVE DIED IN 1865.
A more cunning assassin could have fatally wounded even a man with a brace. (The historian Walter Stahr morbidly suggests Powell should have gone for the eyes, or for an infection-prone stab to the belly.) That could have been the end of William Seward.

In many ways, a dead Seward alters little. The attack would still not have been a decapitation attack (because Johnson lived). Politically, Seward was on the side of the angels, or more precisely the side of history, favoring both civil rights for emancipated Blacks and "malice toward none" repatriation for Confederate soldiers, but his death probably would not have changed the course of Reconstruction, which could scarcely have gone worse. But it would have kept Alaska out of the Union. He wasn't the only one who wanted it, but he was the only one who pushed for it. No Seward, no Alaska.

II.

The term "Seward's Folly" does not appear in print until 1880, eight years after Seward's death. By 1891, Seward's son and biographer (that would be pistol-whipped Frederick W.; he survived) was immortalizing the myth that Seward's purchase was considered a gigantic joke. Frederick W. Seward depicts his father laughing with friends over his so-called folly and reading aloud clippings "from old newspaper files" criticizing Jefferson's then-current "purchase of the 'desert waste' of Louisiana, and the treaty for the 'noxious swamps' of 'snake-infested Florida.'" Ha ha ha. But by 1891, Frederick Seward could employ the term *folly* with irony. Because a decade before Fredrick was writing, prospectors Joe Juneau (yes, *that* Juneau) and Richard Harris struck gold near the coast. Alaska, it turned out, was rich in gold. People knew it in 1891, though the real bonanza for Alaskan gold did not hit until 1899. By that point, the concept "Seward's Folly" was itself regarded as folly. Alaska was rich. Alaska paid for itself.

Gold is nothing. Gold is passé. What *The Beverly Hillbillies* called "black gold"—oil—became an Alaskan export in 1957. Ten years later, in fact, Alaskans struck America's largest oil field in Prudhoe Bay. Nobody would be laughing at Seward now.

There was something else, though . . .

III.

Back in 1867 the *National Republican* mused, "If this country ever had a national friend it has been Russia," which is cute. Britain and the US, meanwhile, were a little wary of each other in 1867. The English were still miffed about the loss of their colonies; and the War of 1812, when the British, you know, *torched Washington, DC*, was still in living memory. The American Civil War was divisive in Britain because while the traditionally abolitionist British people favored the Union—including Karl Marx, who wrote a series of newspaper columns (many by Friedrich Engels, ghostwriting under Marx's byline) praising Lincoln—the realpolitik British government saw the advantage of a Confederate victory and a weakened US. That's why they gave ships to the CSA and why they let Confederate privateers resupply in their ports.

The US and Canada—or the British colonies that would one day make up Canada—had had border squabbles before. In 1837, Canadian forces invaded New York waters in the Niagara River, seizing an American boat (the good ship *Caroline*) and killing an American sailor. The boat was set on fire and sent over Niagara Falls. An international incident ensued; the British had a pretty good reason for burning the *Caroline* (it was transporting arms to Canadian insurgents) but perhaps a less than good reason for doing it off the coast of New York. New York authorities arrested Alexander McLeod, a British subject suspected of being responsible; the British government demanded his release, and events spiraled toward war.

But there was no war. Secretary of State Daniel Webster got the then governor of New York—William Seward, as it turned out—to promise to pardon McLeod if he was convicted; and then he was found not guilty after all. The crisis was averted.

In 1844, James K. Polk was elected to the presidency under the slogan "Fifty-Four Forty or Fight!" He meant that the contested northern border of the US along the Pacific would be 54°40' latitude—or else! Britain, of course, favored a latitude more like 42°. No less a figure than Senator Henry Clay thought that Polk's obdurate stance would cause Britain to join forces with Mexico and invade the US from two sides simultaneously.

Well, the US-Canadian border isn't 54°40', and yet we didn't fight. Polk and the British compromised on 49° latitude, and so it remains. It's easy to see why everyone would agree on the 49th parallel—it looks good on a map. Have a gander: It lines up perfectly with the border of Montana and North Dakota.

There are still a few places along the border where the US and Canada have never come to agreement—for example, two desolate islands between Maine and New Brunswick: Machias Seal Island and (barely an island at all) North Rock. This is the crucible of distrust that saw Britain electing to build a transcontinental railroad rather than sell a neglected territory to Washington.

Needless to say, America's relationship with Britain, or with Canada, would not remain as chilly as it was in the years after the Civil War. And its relationship with "national friend" Russia had nowhere to go but down.

Maybe the latter friendship never ended, exactly. Maybe America's friendship with tsarist Russia remained intact. Till death do us part! But tsarist Russia died with the 1917 abdication of the tsar, or else it died with the tsar and his wife and five children before a Bolshevik firing squad in 1918. With the Soviet Russia that followed (the Soviets did not technically get their union until 1922), the US had a dicier relationship.

In fact, in 1918, the US *invaded* Soviet Russia.

IV.

Back in 1848 and 1849, revolutions were surging across Europe: in Italy, in France, in Denmark, in the Netherlands . . . and in the German state of Saxony, where the frustrated Russian anarchist Mikhail Bakunin got swept up in the uprising. The uprising failed, and Bakunin went to jail for eight years in three different countries (he'd been causing trouble all over Europe, so everyone wanted a piece of him). He was sentenced to death twice—commuted both times—and finally found himself imprisoned back in his native Russia, where after years of suffering and the loss of his teeth, his family's petitions finally got him freed from prison—and sentenced instead to perpetual exile in Siberia.

Once in Siberia, Bakunin found himself with very few things to set on fire, so, desperate to return to Europe and foment more revolutions, he formed a plan. Heading west back through Russia would only lead to his rearrest. So Bakunin figured *the only way out is through*: He traveled east, ever deeper into the frigid Siberian wastes, until he was able to ride the Amur River into what was then Manchuria. From there he caught a boat to Japan, where an American ship brought him to San Francisco. Bumming money as he went, he managed to sail to Panama, catch a railroad car across the isthmus, and then make his way up to New York, where he wired friends in London for a ticket across the Atlantic. He was back, baby!

I tell this story because the idea of crossing Siberia to get to Europe sounds incredible, but Bakunin did it. And in 1918, sixty thousand other people did it: the fabled Czech Legion.

The Czech Legion had assembled during World War I to fight for an independent Czech homeland. The Czechs lived under the dominion of the Austro-Hungarian Empire, so Austria-Hungary was the enemy they wanted to fight; since officially Czechs were fighting *for* Austria-Hungary, Czech nationalists had to find another country to fight for, and proximity made Russia the obvious choice. A gradually swelling legion of Czech soldiers was incorporated into the Russian army. The Czechs got to shoot Austrians; the Russians got to bolster their troop count. Everyone was happy.

But in 1917, the Russian Revolution overthrew the tsar, and the new revolutionary government made peace with the Central Powers and withdrew from World War I. From the point of view of the other Allies, such as the UK and France, this move was illegal: Russia was not allowed, by treaty, to make a separate peace; they were also stealing all the war supplies that had been sent to them in good faith. From the point of view of revolutionary Russia, the tsarist government's dimwitted moves, like getting caught up in this endless war, were exactly why a revolution was needed, and rejoining the war would just be throwing good money after bad. The Russian army was perfectly happy to stop fighting.

From the point of view of the Czech Legion, though . . . they were only in Russia to fight Austrians. Why were they even in Russia if there wasn't going to be any fighting? The Czechs wanted to switch to France, to fight on the Western Front—but of course, the Central Powers weren't about to let them just cross over their territory, and the Russians didn't want to violate the peace treaty by loosing sixty thousand soldiers on their new German friends. The Czechs were just going to have to cool their heels in Russia for the duration.

Except the Czechs decided to pull a Bakunin. Unable to reach the

Western Front by heading west, they decided to travel across Siberia, and the rest of the world, in search of Austrians to fight.

This would have been difficult enough in the best of circumstances. But the Russians, at German prompting, declared all-out war on the legion. The Czechs had to fight their way across the entire continent.

And that's when America invaded.

It wasn't just America; the Allies sent a multinational force into Siberia, which sounds like an odd decision. But tsarist Russia had been an ally, and it had been overthrown. The enemy of my friend is my enemy. Furthermore, all those American armaments and supplies sent to Russia when it was on "our side" were in danger of being passed along to Germany. And then there was the Czech Legion. The Czech fighters were still Allies. They had fought hard for the Allied cause, and wanted to keep fighting. They were stranded in Russia. Someone had to go rescue them. As to how much the Siberian Expeditionary Force was supposed to interfere in the ongoing Russian civil war and how committed to fighting the Bolsheviks the Allied troops were supposed to be—these were issues the American government and the rest of the Allies never quite agreed on. The Siberian Expeditionary Force did manage to hook up with the Czech Legion, but by the time the Czechs were in a position to be evacuated to the Western Front, there was no Western Front. The war was over.

The civil war in Russia wasn't quite over, though. The Czechs did some fighting in Siberia, as did the erstwhile Allies, facing off against the victorious Bolsheviks. Seventeen months after the end of World War I, Allied troops finally left Russia. By that point the US and the new Soviet power had gotten off on the wrong foot. The US would not recognize the legitimacy of the Soviet Union until 1933.

And it didn't really get better from there. Despite the brief thaw during World War II, relations between the two countries after the war could hardly have been worse. I'm an American, so I blame the Soviet Union for this, but even if I'm biased, how can you not be biased against Stalin? Probably history's worst mass murderer, clinically paranoid (the only person Stalin ever trusted was Adolf Hitler, and look how well that ended

up), and, what is more, so rude that Lenin wanted him fired as general secretary of the Communist Party . . . just for rudeness. That last part doesn't
sound so bad, but Soviet leaders were always consistently and flagrantly
rude. When Richard Nixon took Nikita Khrushchev on a tour of a model
American home in 1959, Khrushchev pointed at a kitchen appliance and
announced, "This is probably always out of order." Lenin himself was
never the most diplomatic of men (his older sister characterized him as
"exceedingly presumptuous and rude"). Stalin must have taken rudeness
to a whole new level to be called out for it among Soviet leadership.

Oh, right, and also, he murdered twenty million people. He arrested
so many of his own citizens that in 1938 Leningrad puppeteer Lyubov
Vasilievna Shaporina wrote in her diary, "At this rate they may as well
arrest the table or sofa."

So, everyone looks good after Stalin. Even Stalin's successor, Nikita
Khrushchev, looks good after Stalin. By no other metric does the mass
murderer Khrushchev look good. If you went back in time to 1938 and
asked the 102 members of 1937's Ukrainian Central Committee what
they thought of Khrushchev—99 would be unable to answer, because
Khrushchev had already executed them. But Khrushchev looked good
compared to Stalin. Stalin was the one who sent Khrushchev to Ukraine
in the first place.

Khrushchev was willing to risk nuclear war in order to put missiles in
Cuba, some one hundred miles from US territory.

Alaska is about five hundred miles from Washington State.

V.

Russia had been afraid that Canadians or Americans would come hus-
tling into Alaska on the QT. We have to imagine that the Russians, if they
do not sell Alaska to dead Seward, take steps in the nineteenth century to
stop these hustlers.

Tsarist Russia being tsarist Russia (Stalin had to learn it somewhere!),
these steps may take the form of massacres. Or the Russians can send col-
onizers ("volunteers"—ha ha!) to Alaska. They can set up a bureaucracy

to permit American or Canadian prospectors to enter in return for a cut of their findings. They can threaten and bluster in a way that a small country like Mexico could not have when it saw its territories of Texas and California slip away. By the 1880s they certainly have a motive to keep Alaska Russian—the best motive, gold!

Perhaps after the Russian Revolution, tsarist loyalists could hold Alaska as a kind of Russian Taiwan, but this is unlikely. The death of the Russian royal family left no rallying point for the loyalists, and the tsarist generals tended to be too corrupt or bloodthirsty (the Bolsheviks had to learn it somewhere) to hold on to much of anything. One, Baron von Ungern-Sternberg, conquered Mongolia in 1921, hoping to lead a Mongol army back into Russia to overthrow Lenin's regime. Even he was beaten by the Red Army, and the Mongols can conquer almost *anything*.

So Alaska becomes Soviet. And now the Russians' patience pays off.

We think of the Cold War as being tense for the US, with backyard fallout shelters, classroom "duck and cover" drills, and a general anxiety that nuclear attack could come at any time. But this Cold War tension was in one way asymmetrical: The US had nuclear missiles a lot closer to the USSR's major population centers than the USSR did. The US had missiles in West Germany, in Turkey, and all around Europe. This was why the Russians were trying to sneak missiles into Cuba in 1962: They wanted parity with the US. In fact, withdrawal of US missiles from European bases was one of the Soviet demands at the time.

Shortly before his assassination by a Rosicrucian, Robert F. Kennedy wrote a memoir of his experiences during the Cuban Missile Crisis. Two things stand out in his account: *1.* how many advisers and politicians wanted President Kennedy to make a "strong" response to the Soviet encroachment on Cuba, regardless of whether such a response would spiral the world into war; and *2.* how the luxury of several days of debate in the White House allowed an initial violent impulse to mellow into an embargo against Cuba. RFK speculated that if they'd only had twenty-four hours to make a decision, that decision would have been more hawkish—with the implication that it would have led to nuclear war.

Well, the presence of Soviets in Alaska means that as soon as Soviet science develops an atomic bomb (1949), that bomb can be rolled over the Bering Strait to North America. The Russians had been hard at work adapting and improving the German V-2 rocket; maybe they would slap an atomic warhead onto one of their own rocket designs. Maybe they'd just fly a plane down the coast. Even if they don't do it immediately, they could do it at any time. No chance for an embargo. No time for the American president to debate a response. No moral leg to stand on, even. How can the US ask Russia not to build a military base on its own soil?

Not to mention the fact that the earth's largest land army can now reach US soil . . . by land. The United States trembles on high alert. The man in charge of deciding whether to start rolling troops and launching bombs? History's second-worst human, Joseph Stalin.

Compared to this nightmare, the missiles in Cuba seem like a minor diplomatic kerfuffle. The Cuban Missile Crisis, JFK later estimated, had had at least a one-in-three chance of ending in nuclear armageddon; and it was only thirteen days long! How many days could the US and Russia stare at each other across British Columbia?

In 1946, the peacenik Bertrand Russell briefly panicked and advocated preemptively attacking the USSR before it could develop the bomb. He spent the rest of his life backpedaling from that one hasty statement, and it's not our goal to hold him to it. But the point is: Even a great mind like Russell's could panic. Would the US, faced with the prospect of Russian bombs at its doorstep, start a preemptive war? The Soviets developed the bomb faster than anyone thought they would. A war between these two powers would start as a conventional war and end as a nuclear one.

This is what we get without Seward. We get nuclear war. We get folly.

ETHIOPIA AND YEMEN

What if Abraha and his elephants had conquered Mecca?

MECCA, 552

I.

Fifteen hundred years ago, an African emperor conquered the southern part of the Arabian peninsula. This hardly seems remarkable, as history is more or less nonstop conquest, and everybody invading everybody, but this one was unusual. Although sub-Saharan Africa has invaded northern Africa (Egyptian dynasty XXV, 760 BC) and sub-Saharan Africa has invaded southern Africa (Bantu expansion, ca. AD 300), only once in all of history has sub-Saharan Africa left its continent and invaded somewhere else. This was 523, when Yemen was invaded by Ethiopia.

By *Ethiopia*, I mean Axum. You may never have heard of Axum, but you're not a medieval African. In the sixth century Axum was the most powerful state in Africa. The Axumite Empire (Axum, like Rome, was the capital and eponymous source of the empire) covered northern Ethiopia and what is now Eritrea—Abyssinia, people used to call the region. The empire lasted nearly a thousand years, and for most of that time it was a Christian state. In fact, it may have been the first Christian state in the world. Armenia usually gets precedence, and historians can fight over who's right, but if Axum isn't the first Christian state, it's the second.

It started in the fourth century, when a shipwrecked Syrian Christian named Frumentius became a slave in the Axumite royal court. After working his way up through the jobs of royal secretary, treasurer, and adviser to the young emperor Ezana, Frumentius was freed and sent back to Syria, where he suggested a bishop should be sent to Axum to shepherd the few Christians who lived there. In a surprise twist, Frumentius got the job himself.

Frumentius, bishop of Ethiopia, returning in glory to the city he had lived in so long, persuaded his old charge, Emperor Ezana, to embrace the faith. As went the emperor, so went the empire.

It didn't hurt, of course, that Ezana was a successful ruler. Meroe, the kingdom north of Axum, was in a state of decline, and could not protect the overland trade routes to Egypt. Trade was Axum's lifeblood, and raids on trade routes by nomadic bandits were a real threat. From the purely altruistic motive of bringing peace and stability, and protecting people from bandits, Ezana marched his forces northwest up the Nile basin. Near the modern city of Atbara in what is now Sudan he raised a stele thanking the Christian God for his victories. Protecting trade routes would prove to be the special concern of Ethiopian emperors in the centuries to come, just as erecting steles had been the special concern of Ethiopian emperors in centuries previous.

Soon (around 330) Axum was Christian—not just overwhelmingly Christian, as Syria probably was at the time, but officially Christian, as Syria (part of the Roman Empire) certainly was not. The emperor Constantine wouldn't be baptized on his deathbed until 337.

Before it was Christian, it may have been Jewish. According to the early Jewish historian Artapanus, Moses, in his youth, leads an Egyptian army into Ethiopia. He then teaches the Ethiopians the practice of circumcision, which is odd, because he had neglected to circumcise his own son (Exodus 4:24–25). The slightly later Jewish historian Josephus gives Moses a romance with an Ethiopian princess named Tharbis; the pair marries after she betrays her country and delivers the capital city of Saba up to him. Josephus is probably trying to explain a stray biblical passage, Numbers 12:1, which asserts in contradiction to Exodus 2 that Moses had married an Ethiopian. In Exodus, Moses's wife is from Midian.

Many years after the Exodus—476 years, according to one Old Testament chronology—Ethiopians encountered Judaism again, when the Queen of Sheba visited King Solomon. Both Solomon and the queen were renowned for their wisdom, so they spent their time asking each other riddles. The queen made Solomon promise not to hit on her; Solomon made the queen promise not to take anything of his without asking. But at dinner he fed her spicy meat, and in the middle of the night she awoke to find a bowl of water by her bed; which, being very thirsty on account of the dinner, she drank without asking. All promises now void. When she left for Ethiopia, the Queen was pregnant.

Later her son returned to Israel to meet his father and absorb wisdom. By stealth and magic he took with him, when he left, the Ark of the Covenant, which people have vainly sought in Mount Nebo or the city of Tanis. It really rests in Ethiopia.

Before the Queen of Sheba's visit, Ethiopians worshipped the sun; afterward, they worshipped the creator of the sun, the Jewish God. Solomon immortalized the queen in his Song of Songs: "I am black, but comely, O ye daughters of Jerusalem" (1:5a).

Now, there are several problems with these stories. There's no evidence for any of them outside of oral tradition, not recorded until a millennium or so after the fact. They all take place long before Axum or its empire existed. It's not even clear they're about Ethiopia at all. *Ethiopia* is a country and therefore a precise term in our day, but was vague to the Greeks and Romans, who could call any land south of Egypt *Ethiopia* (this is what happens in Acts 8:27), and who consistently confused Abyssinia and India—a practice perpetuated as late as 1789 in Samuel Johnson's translation of *A Voyage to Abyssinia by Father Jerome Lobo a Portuguese Missionary*. Who's to say that Sheba is even in Ethiopia, and that its anonymous queen was Ethiopian? Olaudah Equiano, in his 1789 autobiography, suggests that his people had customs eerily similar to the Jews'—and his people were in what is now Nigeria, all the way across the continent from Ethiopia.

A literalist may argue that Sheba was *really* the land of the Sabaeans in southern Arabia, but it's not clear what *really* means in this context. The riddling, midnight-thirsty queen is unlikely to have *really* been anyone. It's like when people say "the real King Arthur" was a Roman general named Lucius Artorius Castus. The real King Arthur is a collection of heroic folklore motifs; Lucius Artorius Castus is meanwhile not British, not a king, and not named Arthur; he never even owned a magic sword. As Richard Adams once asked, "Of what value is the grain of sand at the heart of a pearl?"

One place where they're pretty certain the Queen of Sheba came from Ethiopia . . . is Ethiopia. The *Kebra Nagast*—the "Glory of Kings," a medieval Ethiopian historical and religious text—is the source for several of our tales above. The text of the *Kebra Nagast* postdates the rise of Axum, but it presumably rests on older traditions. Whether or not Emperor Ezana was Jewish before Frumentius converted him, he was probably circumcised. The Ethiopian Orthodox Church still conducts infant circumcisions today.

II.

Two hundred years after Ezana, the emperor Kaleb ruled a cosmopolitan Axumite Empire. Greek was the language of the court, in much the same way as French would later be the language of choice among Russian and Prussian nobility. The people were heretics by the standards of the European church due to semantic differences in describing Christ, but from a modern standpoint indistinguishable from any other Christian sect.

Axum was an empire of traders, sailing between Egypt (in the Byzantine Empire) or Arabia and India. Ethiopia had its own resources to export, most prominently elephant ivory, but more than a source of product itself, Axum served as a middleman, shuttling Byzantine goods to India, and Indian goods back again.

One of its trading partners was Yemen. And Yemen was disrupting trade.

It wasn't called Yemen back then, or at least *Yemen* referred to a region, and not a state. Yemen was the region the Romans called Arabia Felix—roughly, the "good Arabia," the Arabia "full of gardens and vineyards and olive trees," as opposed to Arabia Deserta. Yes, this is the story of Ethiopia and Yemen, but really, it's the story of Axum and Himyar. The state in Yemen that was causing trouble for Axum was called Himyar.

The Himyarites had ruled the area for hundreds of years, and in the fourth century they had converted to Judaism. The conversion was probably pragmatic: Christian Rome and Zoroastrian Persia were flexing their muscles to the north, and if the Himyarites chose one of these religions or the other, it would mean getting bound in an alliance with a state so much larger that little Himyar would inevitably be a client or puppet kingdom. Judaism had the unique attraction of being a religion with no state connected to it: The Himyarites were hardly going to become puppets to the Jews of the diaspora. Even if they'd initially embraced the Jewish faith more or less for convenience, in time the Himyarites became true believers. They were aware that their coreligionists were scattered across the globe and everywhere persecuted. The Jewish scriptures counsel against revenge (Leviticus 19:18), but they do not exactly *consistently counsel* against revenge (Judges 16:28): The Himyarite Jews decided that while they had the opportunity, they would get back at the world. Under their king, Yusuf As'ar Yath'ar—called Dhu Nuwas, or "long haired"—they began persecuting the Christian population that lived within their borders, climaxing in a general massacre in 523 in the city of Najran.

Was revenge truly Yusuf's motivation? Was he just a proselytist? The surviving contemporary sources are pretty sparse, and not necessarily reconcilable, and later writers have seen fit to speculate, and I'm not always sure where the facts end and their fancy begins. The massacre is probably not made up out of whole cloth. Himyar Christians appealed to the most powerful Christian state extant, the Roman or Byzantine Empire, for assistance. The emperor Justinian was not about to send forces so far from his home territory, so close to his mortal enemy Persia, so he turned to the Axumite emperor Kaleb, and requested ("ordered," some older books say, although Justinian was in no position to order Axum to do anything) that his fellow Christian emperor help out the believers who were so close to his shores.

How close? A narrow strait some sixteen miles wide separates modern Yemen from Africa: That's narrower than the English Channel. Ethiopia has always shared a lot with the Arabian peninsula. Edward Gibbon assumed the Ethiopians were Arab colonists, which is the kind of thing someone would assume in the eighteenth century. Linguistically, at least, they're close: Amharic, the national language of Ethiopia, and Tigrinya, the most widely spoken language in Eritrea, are the second and third largest Semitic languages—after Arabic and ahead of Hebrew.

Around 523, Kaleb's forces sailed to Himyar and drove its king, Yusuf Dhu Nuwas, from his throne.

It took two invasions—after the first, a down-but-not-out Dhu Nuwas just started a guerrilla war against the Axumite garrisons—but finally, Axum trapped the Himyarite army with their backs to the sea. As the Axumite forces advanced, Yusuf turned his horse and rode into the waves, never to be seen again. Yemen was now part of the intercontinental Axumite Empire. Only briefly, though; a native Himyarite Christian served as viceroy at first, but the Axumite Christians who stayed in Himyar declined to be ruled by a Yemeni. They overthrew the viceroy and installed, in his place, an Axumite general named Abraha, who declared the kingdom independent.

Kaleb made two attempts to reconquer his erstwhile colony, failed, and eventually retired to a monastery. From now on, Axum's adventures would be confined to the African continent. Abraha was under no such strictures, though. He had a wealthy and powerful kingdom, he had a history of military successes, and he had lots of war elephants.

Abraha's first move would not be war, though. His first move would be trade. Around 547 Abraha called an international conference in the city of Marib, ostensibly to celebrate repairs on a dam there, but probably to cement trading partnerships with the powers in the area. The Byzantine and Persian Empires, eternally warring, also competed in influencing smaller states in the area. Abraha's Christian Himyar was a natural ally for the Byzantines, who tended to support Christian communities in the Middle East, but Abraha invited Persian ambassadors as well, to make sure the rich trade routes to the east would face no interference. He even invited ambassadors from Axum, his erstwhile ally and enemy; no need for old hostility to interfere with a lucrative partnership.

Peace secured, Abraha started rebuilding the old churches that Dhu Nuwas had torn down during the persecutions. He encouraged pilgrims to come to Yemen, to visit, especially, the great church at San'a. He . . .

Well, we're in the realm of folklore here. This is going to start out plausible, and grow increasingly sketchy.

Abraha's greatest building project was the ornate church at San'a, a church remembered by Arab historians under the name al-Qalis. Al-Qalis was designed to be an ecumenical attraction for both Christian and pagan pilgrims from all over the Arab world. And yet, beautiful as the building was, the pagan Arabs preferred to make pilgrimages to Mecca, site of the ancient Kaaba.

The Kaaba—the name means simply "cube," referring to the shape of the building—housed at the time not only a large number of idols but also the Black Stone, an artifact that has been sacred to Arabs since time immemorial. The Kaaba was built by Abraham, Islamic tradition claims. The pure white stone was brought to him by an angel; the sins of the earth turned it black. Insofar as anything has "always been there," the Black Stone has always been there, and pilgrims have been visiting it. This irked Abraha, who decided that if his namesake could build the Kaaba, he could destroy it. With no Kaaba, people would have no choice but to travel five hundred miles to the south to see al-Qalis instead.

This was a bad plan.

III.

We know this was a bad plan because something even more audacious was tried 360 years later, when a heretical Islamic sect, the Qarmatians, sacked Mecca, stole the Black Stone, and set it up in a rival shrine in

Bahrain. The Qarmatians, thinking like supervillains, believed that by controlling the Black Stone they could control all of Islam.

It's easy to see the Qarmatians as supervillains because everything we know about them is filtered through the writings of people who hate them. Of course, one reason these writers hated the Qarmatians was that the Qarmatians had plundered Mecca, killing thirty thousand unarmed pilgrims and desecrating the holiest places in Islam. The Qarmatians presumably thought they were the good guys who embraced true doctrine and built a utopian community along the shores of the Persian Gulf from Iraq to Bahrain, which they controlled for a century. Devoted egalitarians, they owned property in common. They were primarily vegetarians, earning the nickname "Greengrocers." They were also a latter-day mystery religion: Openly, they announced that there were esoteric teachings hidden in the Quran, which could be revealed to those initiates who would swear allegiance; the rest of their teachings were therefore secret, a series of revelations that built upon one another as the initiated progressed through the ranks. By the fifth degree, the initiate was taught that Muhammad was a liar; by the sixth, he was drinking wine and trampling on the Quran. Further revelation, and mandatory incestuous (!) orgies followed. Or so say the orthodox historians.

There's no way that's true, of course. Even if there were Qarmatian orgies (a frequent slander against new religions, including, in the early days, Christians), the idea that they were by necessity incestuous is one step too far for reality. The secret teachings of the Qarmatians remain secret, replaced by slanderous fantasies.

But there may be a grain of truth there. The Qarmatians appear to have believed that certain aspects of Islamic tradition were in danger of becoming, in a loose sense, "idols." Qarmatians saw the pilgrimage to Mecca as the survival of a pagan rite, and therefore pagan. They saw the holy sites of Islam as distractions from the word of Allah. It's very possible they also saw traditional Islamic attachment to Muhammad or the Quran as a form of idolatry as well. Killing thirty thousand idolators sounds terrible to us, but it wouldn't have sounded so bad to Oliver Cromwell, and it may have looked to the Qarmatians like a sacred duty. The pilgrims deserved it, for treating the Black Stone of the Kaaba as an idol.

But, of course, to the Qarmatians the Black Stone of the Kaaba was not only an idol, it was also an opportunity.

The capital of Qarmatian activity was Hajr, in Bahrain, and it was to there that Abu Tahir, leader of the Qarmatians, brought his prize. All subsequent pilgrimages, the Qarmatians insisted, would have to come to Qarmatian-controlled Bahrain. A beautiful island! The ancient Sumerians called it Dilmun, the site of the original earthly paradise: "In Dilmun the raven shrieked not. The kite shrieked not kitelike. The lion slew not. The wolf plundered not the lambs." Also: It's where the Black Stone is! What choice do you have? Pilgrims, flock to Bahrain!

This gambit may sound hypocritical for a group of iconoclasts; it was also thoroughly cynical. Essentially, the Qarmatians were banking on the fact that all other followers of Islam really did see the Black Stone as an idol. Unfortunately for the Qarmatians' plans of world domination, no one came to their tourist attraction. Everyone kept going to Mecca, Muhammad's hometown and the site of Islam's founding, Black Rock or no Black Rock. The power of the Qarmatians waned. Abu Tahir caught gangrene, and worms ate away his flesh until he died horribly, as was inevitable. Eventually, after twenty-three years of fruitless possession, the Qarmatians returned the Black Stone, broken, perhaps symbolically, into seven pieces (one for each imam recognized by Qarmatian theology) to Mecca. Between 978 and 988, the Qarmatians suffered a series of disastrous military defeats. By 1077, their last stronghold had fallen. They are now an extinct embarrassment, remembered, fairly or not, only for their atrocities and their addiction to incest.

So we know, with the benefit of hindsight, that Abraha's plan was not going to work. Abraha couldn't have known that, though.

IV.

We left Abraha plotting to destroy the Kaaba. He set out with his elephants and his invincible army; perhaps he took the pilgrim roads. He let it be known that the people of Mecca need not fear him. He did not want to hurt them; he came only to demolish one building. Of course, if anyone stood in his way his invincible army was ready to clear a path. No one in the environs of Mecca had seen an elephant before. It must have been terrifying.

Abdul-Muttalib, a leader in the community (and who would later be Muhammad's grandfather), reasoned that the Kaaba was God's house. If God wanted to save it, he could; if he didn't, then no earthly arms would help. Some 850 years earlier, when marauding Gauls threatened Delphi, the holiest place in Greece, the Delphic Oracle told people not to worry: Apollo would take care of everything. According to Pausanias, earthquakes, lightning, avalanches, and blizzards killed twenty thousand Gauls. Thanks, Apollo! If Apollo could protect his home, then surely Allah could protect his.

Years later, Muhammad would prophesy that the Kaaba would someday be destroyed by an Ethiopian known as Old Thin Legs (Dhul-Suwayqatayn). Perhaps Abraha's legs were too fat. As he entered Mecca, unopposed, suddenly the sky darkened with birds, each holding two stones in its claws and one in its beak. They dropped these stones on Abraha's army, annihilating it. A grievously wounded Abraha fled, to die in the desert.

The Arabs named it the Year of the Elephant, elephants being the most amazing thing they saw in that year of miraculous birds. And that's the year Muhammad was born. (Actually, it was several years before Muhammad was born, but tradition fudged the dates.)

This will never do for the literal minded. Deadly birds do not bomb armies. The birds do appear in the Quran (sura 105), but later apologists have sought alternative explanations, as later apologists always do. In Plutarch, for example, young Theseus fights not a half-man, half-bull monster but a Cretan wrestler whose name happens to be Taurus.

Or: In 2010, scientists discovered a way in which strong steady winds could hypothetically create a mud-flat passage across the Red Sea; they called their article "Dynamics of Wind Setdown at Suez and the Eastern

Nile Delta," and innumerable popular articles seized on the most tit-illating aspect of it and titled their reports something like "Exodus Explained!" Salivating reporters crowed: "It all makes sense now! Moses used the wind!"

Needless to say, none of that makes the least bit of sense. Fleeing Israelites blundering into a once-in-a-lifetime freak meteorological occurrence during the four hours it lasts, in the one place on earth it can happen, is scarcely less of a miracle than the seas up and parting for them. A hashem with the power to lead Moses to this one place and time could also have the power to part the seas with sheer divine might; since he had a long-standing grudge against the sea (see Psalm 29; Psalm 74:13–14; Psalm 77:16–20; Psalm 104:6–9; etc.), you'd expect him to take the second path.

Perhaps the ten plagues Moses visits on the Egyptians were natural events, caused by climate change and volcanic eruption, which is the argument of the National Geographic two-part special *The Ten Plagues of the Bible* (2010); there are endless similar theories. It's a weird hobby, making up explanations like this; it's like affirming that all the events in a novel are true, while simultaneously denying the existence of its central character.

But something must be done about those birds! Maybe Abraha's army merely fell victim to a plague, perhaps smallpox. This sounds rational, and furthermore it echoes the biblical fate of the Assyrian army when it marched on Jerusalem: 2 Kings 19:35 ascribes it to an angel, but all later commentators have assumed an epidemic wiped out 185,000 Assyrian soldiers.

> *And the might of the Gentile, unsmote by the sword,*
> *Hath melted like snow in the glance of the Lord!*

. . . is Byron's apt summary.

The eighteenth-century German botanist Kurt Sprengel theorized that the smallpox epidemic that swept southern Europe in the 780s, killing two Merovingian princes and one Merovingian queen, *inter al.*, might have been carried to Europe by Byzantine troops in Abraha's employ. It all seems to fit! So, call smallpox the deliverer of Mecca and be happy?

But Sayyid Saeed Akhtar Rizvi, in his *Life of Muhammad the Prophet*, points out, correctly, that smallpox makes hardly more sense than birds. How did smallpox break out only among the army, without spreading to *the city they were currently in?* How did it work so abruptly and so fast? And so thoroughly? You might as well believe that birds drop rocks!

The actual truth about Abraha is probably more boring than birds and plagues. The grain of sand in the heart of this pearl may be a short and abortive invasion, at the instigation of the Byzantine emperor Justinian, into Persia's sphere of influence—in this case, toward Mecca. According to Procopius, writing soon after the fact, Abraha "began the journey and then straightaway turned back." Perhaps it was a feint; perhaps Abraha was just irresolute.

Abraha did not die on that expedition, but somewhat later, and probably at home. The Christian Axumite state in Himyar did not long outlive him: Abraha was succeeded by his sons, but they had to deal with Sayf Ben Dhi Yazan, a resurgent Arab, probably Jewish, who sought to return Himyar to native rule. Exactly what happened to the sons is also a mystery, but around 570, Sayf Ben Dhi Yazan managed, with Persian assistance, to take the throne of Himyar from them. Although he was later assassinated by disgruntled Axumites, whereupon Persia took direct control of the area, Sayf Ben Dhi Yazan remained a Yemeni folk hero. In the fifteenth century the local legends about him were assembled into an epic, the *Sirat Sayf Ben Dhi Yazan*, in which he encounters many genies, has many magical adventures, and, in one disturbing scene, encounters a tree on which sexy ladies grow. It turns out the ladies are fruit, and Sayf Ben Dhi Yazan plucks and peels one. Her insides look like an orange, and when he eats her flesh, he says it tastes "like the taste of tender walnut, and sweeter than honey, finer than all other foods."

Mecca would remain out of Christian hands.

Abraha conquers Mecca → Muhammad looks toward Ethiopia for the expansion of Islam → Persia remains Zoroastrian →
PEACE IN THE MIDDLE EAST

I.

ABRAHA, DESPITE WHAT FOLKLORE TELLS US, PROBABLY DID not want to enter Mecca, smash stuff, and leave. In Himyar, Abraha had proven himself to have stickier fingers than that. If he had gotten into Mecca—past the smallpox and the deadly birds—he would have kept Mecca. The Axumo-Himyarite Empire would have absorbed the city, and probably some of the neighboring cities as well. This is the real question: What would have happened then?

The answer will take us from the rise of the Himyarites through the Byzantine Empire's second darkest hour and the rise of Islam to land us in the twenty-first-century Middle East, a peaceful and tranquil place.

II.

Empires can fall if they get too large; everyone knows that. Decline, says Gibbon, is the "inevitable effect of immoderate greatness." But empires also fall if they don't get large enough: Little Himyar was too small to have a chance against anyone backed by the might of Persia, as Sayf Ben Dhi Yazin had been. Perhaps if Abraha had never rebelled against Axum, the combined might of Ethiopia and Yemen could have held the Persians off; but Himyar alone never had a chance. A hypothetical Himyar that expands, though, is another story. A Himyar that manages to incorporate several powerful or rich cities into its borders . . . may be unstable and self-destruct, but may find a balance that can keep the Persians at bay. The Persians have enough to worry about with the Byzantines on their frontier; they don't want to have to be distracted by an unnecessary fight with a powerful state. So Himyar conquers Mecca in 552 and stays independent. Mecca is now part of an officially Christian nation, one that is culturally Ethiopian and that has strong diplomatic ties with the Byzantine Empire.

About sixty years later, one of the most important events in history happens. It happens in Mecca, where Muhammad is called to preach a new religion. This is our real question: How would Muhammad's mission have been different if he had been born a Himyarite subject?

III.

In 621 Muhammad made his famous Night Journey to Jerusalem on the back of a winged horse with a human face. Along the way (so says tradition) he was hailed by three voices, begging him to "tarry a moment"— voices that he ignored. Later, Muhammad learned that had he heeded the first voice, his people would have converted to Judaism; had he heeded the second, his people would have converted to Christianity; and had he heeded the third, his people would have been damned. But he remained faithful to his goal, and his people converted to Islam.

This tale may betray an anxiety that Muhammad's mission could have been diverted to one of the other Abrahamic faiths. Muhammad grew up primarily among pagans, but in a community that knew Christians and Jews well. Nevertheless, the only voice he heeded was the voice of Allah, and it was Islam that he was prophet of. There's no reason, really, to assume that Himyarite suzerainty would make a difference here. Simply having more Christians around him—presumably, under the Christian Himyarites most city officials would be Christian—would hardly change his thought or teaching.

You might imagine that heresy-hunting Christians would stop Muhammad from preaching from the get-go. But the truth is that Christian Mecca could hardly have been less receptive to Muhammad's message than pagan Mecca was. In our timeline, the people of Mecca were so hostile to Muhammad that first some of his followers fled for safety (to Ethiopia of all places), and later, in 622, Muhammad himself, to avoid assassination, slipped out of Mecca at night for the more tolerant streets of Medina. Muslims date their calendars from this flight, the Hegira; AD 622 is year 1 in the Islamic world.

The Christian rulers of the Axumo-Himyarite Empire might actually welcome a monotheist denouncing idolatry to the pagan population of Mecca, at least at first. If Muhammad and his followers grow too numerous and powerful, and if they refuse to embrace Christianity—which we have to assume is what will happen—orders may come from San'a demanding that authorities crack down on the new heresy. Muhammad may have to slip away sooner or later; but it's also possible that with so many non-Christians in its borders, the Axumo-Himyarite Empire would avoid persecuting anyone until they had a broader power base. Either in Mecca or nearby, Islam would have a chance to grow and thrive.

To see what would happen next, we need to pause and look at our world. It's not necessarily a great idea to extrapolate a pattern from so few data points, but we can only work with what we've got. Look at this. This is non-hypothetical history:

Christianity arose in and around Jerusalem, part of the Roman Empire. Christianity radiated out from Jerusalem in every direction, but made its most significant and lasting inroads in the Roman lands. Rome itself remained the first city of Christianity—in prestige, if not always in power—for over a millennium, and is still the seat of the pope.

Islam arose in and around Mecca, within the sphere of influence of the Persian Empire. Islam radiated out from Mecca in every direction, but made its most significant and lasting inroads in the Persian lands—first in other Persian client states throughout Arabia, and later in Persia itself. Baghdad, only twenty-two miles from the Persian capital of Ctesiphon, remained the most powerful city in Islam for centuries.

These statements are true, but they're not exhaustively true. Christianity obviously reached Ethiopia, which Rome never did. But we can still make the generalization that early Christians looked to the Roman Empire as their field to sow, and early Muslims looked to the Persian Empire. It's probably significant that the first Roman regions Muslims conquered—the Levant and Egypt—had been under Persian dominion for much of

Muhammad's adult life. The Persians ruled Jerusalem for only fifteen years, but those fifteen years were 614–629. Muhammad's public ministry extended from 613 to 632. When Muhammad rode that winged horse to Jerusalem, it was Persian Jerusalem he visited.

If a religion founded among Romans turned toward Rome, and a religion founded among Persians turned toward Persia, wouldn't a religion founded among Ethiopian Himyarites look toward . . . first Himyar and then Ethiopia?

The first wave of Islamic expansion was pretty much unstoppable, and we can safely imagine that wherever it turned, it would take. If it turned south, it would quickly absorb Yemen; and it's only sixteen miles from there to Africa, remember. By the mid-seventh century, Ethiopia is Muslim. The caliph sits in Axum.

The early Muslim conquests in our history built a vast empire that reached from Spain to Pakistan, but it was only a Muslim empire in the sense that the ruler was Muslim. Most of the subjects were Christian or Zoroastrian or whatever they had been before they were conquered, and only over the centuries did their descendants gradually convert. We can imagine that Muslim Axum kept a large Christian population, and probably a large pagan population as well. Our knowledge of medieval African states is not the best, but certainly the Muslims would have moved northwest, into the Christian Nubian kingdoms of Alodia, Makuria, and Nobatia. The geography of Africa is famously difficult to navigate, but in its first century Islam accomplished plenty of impossible things. Who am I to say it could not have pushed its borders south to Lake Victoria, or onward into the veldt?

Our history's unified Islamic Empire splintered apart in the mid-eighth century, and there's no reason that a caliphate primarily in Africa wouldn't undergo the same process. But it's clear from our history that this splintering did not prevent individual Muslim states—Ottomans, Timurids, Mughals—from continuing to conquer. The first burst of Islamic expansion should hardly be the last. We can certainly expect our Axumite Caliphate to keep extending its borders, and we must assume that the riches of Byzantium and Persia would lure it back into Asia or North Africa. In our history Islam conquered Persia and Egypt in the seventh century. Why couldn't Axumite Islam conquer Persia in the eighth? Well, they probably couldn't, and the answer is, as always, timing.

IV.

We've seen that Rome and Persia were often at war, and that Persia tended to get the short end of the stick. In the seventh century, though, things turned around. For once, Persia was winning.

In 602 an army revolt over vacation time (!) had brought civil war to the Byzantine Empire, and a rebellious general had captured the emperor Maurice and tortured him to death. Unfortunately, Maurice's son-in-law was the current Persian emperor, Khosrow II, and he invaded to avenge his father-in-law's death. The Byzantine Empire was in chaos. By the time a new general managed to seize the throne, execute the rebels, and restore order as Emperor Heraclius, Khosrow had already captured Syria and Egypt, the first time a Persian had ruled Egypt in almost a millennium. Persian allies—barbarians from the north—were harrying the Byzantines' European territory. Soon, the Persians had advanced across Asia Minor and were camped directly across the Bosporus from Constantinople, preparing for a siege.

At that moment—or sometime near that moment—Khosrow received a letter "from an obscure citizen of Mecca" inviting him to convert from Zoroastrianism to Islam. Khosrow tore up the letter. Muhammad predicted that Allah would likewise tear up the Persian Empire.

And so it was to be. The new Byzantine emperor, Heraclius, slipped out of his besieged city, assembled an army, and attacked the Persian homeland—far from the great Persian army, which was at the walls of Constantinople. Soon the Persians were losing; then they were consumed by civil war. Khosrow was deposed by his son, who promptly died of plague. The war with Byzantium was over, but it had lasted a quarter century, and Persia was still in utter disarray. When Muslim forces invaded in 633, Persia had suffered through ten rulers in the last two years, every one of whom had been assassinated. The decisive battle was in 636. It took another fifteen years of continued losses before the Persian Empire was no more.

In 637, the Arabs took Jerusalem. It had been back in Byzantine hands for only eight years. Egypt went next. At the death of Heraclius, the Byzantine Empire had lost its wealthiest provinces permanently.

V.

In 636 the Persians couldn't even stop other Persians from overthrowing their empire. They certainly weren't going to stop the caliphate. But if the Muslim Arabs move on Himyar and Axum first, if Persia has even a decade to recover, the caliphate will have a harder time of it. And so, the Persian client states get incorporated into the Islamic Empire, but Persia itself stands strong. Byzantium, given a chance to recover from the war, is similarly in a position to keep the Levant and Egypt—its breadbasket.

This means the map of the seventh-century Near East is very different. Instead of two powers facing off against each other, we have three: the Byzantine Empire to the west, the Persian Empire to the east, and to the south, the Axumite Caliphate—comprising Arabia and a land empire extending from Ethiopia. This is obviously a very inadequate map: The Byzantines have on their borders plenty of "lesser" nations, such as the kingdoms of the Lombards or the Visigoths. The Merovingians had united France, and their efforts will pave the way in another century and a half for the kingdom of Charlemagne and the Holy Roman Empire. Persia, of course, has an eastern border, abutting several Indian states as well as the shifting kingdoms of Central Asia; in our history, in the next century, the Muslim rulers of Persia would battle China along that border. But let's worry about one theater at a time. Let's worry about the three great powers in the Middle East in the mid-seventh century. Their borders are unstable, but let's say that all three powers meet at the city of Circesium on the river Euphrates.

These three powers have very different cultures: one is Hellenized Roman, and Christian; one is Sassanian Persian, and Zoroastrian; one is a blend of Ethiopian and Arab, and Muslim. By the standards of our day, all three are ruled and populated by religious fanatics. They probably all hate one another, but note one thing: The Persians and the Byzantines hate each other more than either cares about the upstart caliphate. They've hated each other for six hundred years. But the caliphate is aggressive, and so both Byzantines and Persians know that if either is weakened, their mutual enemy will fall upon them.

There follows a war of diplomacy, in which the goal of both Persia and Byzantium is to persuade the caliphate to invade and weaken Byzantium or Persia. The Byzantines became known, at least in western Europe after the Crusades, for their honeyed, empty words and their perfidy. The Persians were known, at least to the ancient Greeks, for the very same thing; Xenophon's memoir *The Anabasis* (370 BC) is a record of the calamity that befalls Xenophon and his friends because, for one moment, they trusted the word of a Persian (Alcibiades's buddy Tissaphernes, as it turns out). You have, therefore, two of the most canonically cunning and duplicitous empires in history trying to bamboozle the new adherents of a creed that demands from its followers simple straightforwardness. Probably, they cancel each other out.

This delicate balance remains, with intermittent but inconsequential wars on different sides. The standoff cannot last forever, though. In the Zoroastrian scriptures, the god Ahura Mazda explains that he made all peoples love their native land, even if that land was wretched, because if people looked around at other countries dispassionately, "the whole living world would have invaded Airyana Vaêgô," i.e., the Persian homeland. Someone's going to invade Persia eventually. Even if the Muslims don't, sooner or later Mongols are going to swoop unstoppably down from the east, driving Turkic peoples before them and bringing Turkic peoples with them. And one thing about the Turco-Mongol conquerors: Although they started out as worshippers of the sky god Tengri, they tended to switch over to the religion of the people they conquered. In our history, Mongols in China became Buddhist while Mongols in western

Asia became Muslim. If they invade a Zoroastrian Persia, they will doubtless become Zoroastrians.

There's a chance that Persia would not remain Zoroastrian long enough for the Turks and Mongols to arrive. Not that it would embrace Islam or Christianity, of course—to do so would be to spoil the three-way standoff along the Euphrates. But Zoroastrianism had a rival in Persia; like Zoroastrianism, it taught that there were two powers in the world, one good and one evil, but unlike Zoroastrianism it syncretically incorporated aspects and iconography from Christianity and Buddhism. This was Manichaeism, the religion of the prophet Mani. It's perhaps best remembered today as the religion that St. Augustine converted to (briefly), but in its day it was a rival to Christianity and Zoroastrianism. St. Cyril memorably called it "the garbage bin of all heresies." In our history it finally died out in Persia after the Muslim conquest—there are no Manichaeans anymore—but Zoroastrians clearly had a harder time squelching it than the monotheistic religions did. It's much closer to Zoroastrianism, after all, with the two rival gods. It would be tempting to Persians who found themselves flanked by Christians and Muslims, because it offered a backdoor way to stop being the odd man out—Manichaeism, like Christianity or Islam (or Judaism), is an Abrahamic faith.

So, when the Mongols arrive, they conquer and convert to Manichaeism. They are pretty much unstoppable, of course, being Mongols, so they flow into Palestine. They may leave, and then return, and in the ebb and flow, Manichaean Persia, part Turkish now, will doubtless end up holding on to the conquered land. The Levant had been Christian for a thousand years, but its proximity to other religions and its long history of flirting with heterodoxies make it easy for the Manichaeans to stay; there's little holy fury to drive them out, even if Constantinople tries to whip some up. This is the great shift of borders on the map. There may be Crusades and there may be other incursions, but they're temporary. As the modern era rolls around, the Manichaeans control the Holy Land and half of Egypt up to the east bank of the Nile; the west bank of the Nile is Byzantine; Upper Egypt (as the southern part is called) has fallen to Muslim conquest traveling downriver from Nubia.

To an Ethiopian or an Iraqi this redrawn map would mean a very different life; to Americans, as to Western Europeans, it makes almost no difference at all. Regardless of the religions of the Middle East, most of European history will chug on the way it was going to anyway. Roman Catholic and Eastern Orthodox Churches will still split. Protestant sects will still split again. The wars of religion that ravage Germany, that seesaw through the Tudors in England, will not involve Zoroastrians. The Spanish and Portuguese will conquer South and Central America, just as the British and French will conquer North America. Life for most Westerners is probably the same.

But consider one place where life is very different. Consider Jerusalem.

Jerusalem is one of the obvious flashpoint spots in the world today precisely because three religions want it. It's the holiest place in Judaism; it's the holiest place in Christianity; it's the third holiest place in Islam. After trading hands a couple of times, it had been ruled by Muslims until World War I, when the British conquered and held it until handing it over, under extremely complicated and violent circumstances, to a nascent Jewish state. Everyone knows this, and everyone has very strong emotions about who belongs in Jerusalem and why. I'm not really interested in throwing my hat into this ring; my hat would be torn to shreds. You're probably already getting mad because I brought the place up, even though I'm trying not to express an opinion about it. That's what I mean by a flashpoint. If there's going to be another world war, Jerusalem might be the place to start it, because everyone's interested in Jerusalem.

Zoroastrians have precisely zero interest in Jerusalem.

Manichaeans might have *some* interest in Jerusalem; they were interested in Jesus after all, and the story of Jesus is difficult to imagine without Jerusalem. But Manichaean dogma (which is only partially understood, as it's impossible to ask an extinct religion for clarification on the difficult points; Mani was a good artist, so he was able to attract illiterate followers by painting pictures explicating his doctrines, but none of those pictures survive) seems to have stressed the spiritual aspect of Jesus over the bodily, suffering-and-dying aspect of Jesus. I'd wager that there are plenty of places in Persia that are holier to Manichaeans than a city that the prophet Mani never even visited. Certainly, Manichaeans have less interest in Jerusalem than Muslims do.

If, after World War I, a Christian country (the UK) took over Jerusalem and if, after World War II, the climax of a long influx of Jewish immigration leads to a Jewish state around Jerusalem, the Manichaeans who lost their land would not be happy about losing their land. But cities get conquered all the time, and yet most conquered cities do not become international flashpoints.

To the Muslims in Arabia and Ethiopia, foreign control of Jerusalem is a foregone conclusion; Jerusalem had always been ruled by an infidel. They wouldn't care. To the international Manichaean community, the loss of Jerusalem would be no different from the loss of Cyprus (if there were Manichaeans in Cyprus) or any other area that traded hands after the world wars.

It's a very different Middle East, primarily Manichaean with a Muslim Arabia and a Jewish enclave in Israel. Aside from the usual squabbles and border disputes, it's a region at peace.

If tomorrow our world explodes in nuclear fire, you'll know to blame it on Abraha's irresolution.

AARON BURR

What if Harriet Beecher Stowe turned the other cheek?

I.

Hating politicians is nothing new. John Quincy Adams's 1828 campaign song threatened

> *Slavery's comin', knavery's comin'* . . .
> *Plague and pestilence is comin',*
> *Hatin's comin', Satan's comin',*
> *If John Quincy not be comin'!*

Satan, in this case, would be Andrew Jackson (who beat Adams, by the way).

An anonymous 1864 pamphlet suggested that Satan (the other one) arranged for Abraham Lincoln to be made president for life in exchange for "something like a million of victims" dead in the war. (If true, then the devil, as is his wont, obeyed the letter of the bargain but still cheated.) Lincoln, of course, received an unprecedented burden of hate; and then they shot him. In a 1999 *New York Post* poll, Bill Clinton was designated the second most evil human of the last millennium (behind Hitler, but ahead of Stalin), with Hillary at number six. This data supersedes Mme. Tussaud's annual poll of the most hated people in history, which Hitler topped every year except 1972 and '73, when the winner was Nixon.

And then there was Aaron Burr: senator, vice president, arch-villain. To be fair, Burr did some things to earn this hatred: He killed Alexander Hamilton in a duel; he tried to found his own empire in the west; he wanted to abolish slavery. Unpopular actions all around.

Burr was a New Yorker who ran for president, which doesn't sound so crazy, but in the republic's first century, it was hardly a path to popularity. Northerners did not do well in the electoral college. Of the first eight US presidents, five were from the South and three from the North, which is nearly balanced. But *every Southerner among them served two terms, and every Northerner served but one.* Northerners would persist in being lame ducks throughout the first half of the nineteenth century. The first Northerner who looked like he might serve two terms was Lincoln, and we all know how that turned out. No Northerner completed two full terms until 1877, when General Ulysses S. Grant *literally had to win a war* against the South to be allowed to serve his time.

But more than his Northern abolitionism makes Aaron Burr a hated man. Burr had the triple threat of his duel, his adventurism, and Harriet Beecher Stowe.

II.

Harriet Beecher Stowe needs no introduction. She wrote America's all-time bestseller (proportional to population), that deathless classic *Uncle Tom's Cabin* (1852). If I say that the deathless classic is also unendurable, with trite characters chewing the scenery of melodramatic set pieces, and the whole thing washed in pious clichés—well, surely this is jealousy speaking. As hard as I have tried, I have never written a book that changed American history. *Uncle Tom*'s influence on the abolition movement, and the subsequent conflagration, can hardly be overstated. Abraham Lincoln called Stowe "the little lady who made this big war," and who am I to question Lincoln?

The "young and flippant critic" Agnes Repplier wrote in 1891 that the problem with *Uncle Tom's Cabin* was that it implied "that the thirteenth amendment was a ghastly error, and that the war had been fought in vain" because any system that could produce an angelic and saintly character like Tom must be an ennobling system. Therefore, slavery is moral, QED.

Repplier may be flippant, but she is always perceptive; here she has zeroed in on Stowe's weakness as a writer more than her weakness as a logician, and surely Repplier's interpretation has remained a minority one. Even after the war, *Uncle Tom* maintained its grip on the public imagination, morphing into a popular stage play and later into (of all things) a minstrel show, with the titular Tom singing and shucking and jiving, between his Christlike sufferings. The book would be parodied in any number of animated cartoons—"Uncle Tom's Crabbin" (Felix the Cat, 1927), "Uncle Tom's Bungalow" (Merrie Melodies, 1937), Mighty Mouse in "Eliza on Ice" (Terrytoons, 1944), "Uncle Tom's Cabana" (MGM, 1947)—that are no longer shown on television, and in a 1920 comic strip that cast Olive Oyl (Popeye's girlfriend) in the role of Eliza—despite the fact that Olive Oyl is white. By 1900, two characters from the book, Topsy (she's like nine years old!) and Tom, would each namesake a brand of tobacco. There would also be Uncle Tom–branded root beer, cereal, peanuts, sugar, card games, and brooms.

Before Tom was a marketing phenomenon, Stowe was a marketing phenomenon: The success of her first novel made Stowe a reliable best-seller. In 1859 she cranked out *The Minister's Wooing*, a who's-going-to-marry-the-heroine melodrama (and altogether better-written book than *Uncle Tom's Cabin*), costarring none other than Aaron Burr. Aaron Burr doesn't get to marry the heroine; he's too busy being a cad and a rake. An excerpt: "Burr was one of those men, willing to play with any charming woman the game of those navigators who give to simple natives glass beads and feathers in return for gold and diamonds; to accept from a woman her heart's blood in return for such odds, ends, and clippings as he could afford her from the serious ambitions of life."

Aaron Burr is worse (Stowe goes on) than someone who poisons the eucharist (!). He lies so habitually that his atrophied "vital nerves of truth" can no longer distinguish fact from fiction. He was "a man of gallantry: this, then, is the descriptive name which polite society has invented for the man who does this thing!"

"This thing" is Harriet Beecher Stowe attempting to talk about sex.

III.

Stowe would not be the first to try to assassinate Burr's character. As Whig writer Joseph B. Cobb succinctly put it in 1850, "Burr's path to renown was crossed by his evil genius," and that "evil genius was Thomas Jefferson." Jefferson called Burr a traitor and drove him into exile. Hamilton called him a libertine and goaded him into that fatal duel. Unlike the self-justifying Jefferson and Hamilton, who always wrote with one eye on posterity, Burr never bothered to present an apologia for his life and conduct. Burr's first biographer, Matthew Livingston Davis, took Burr's surviving letters, burned them, and then proceeded to assert, now that the evidence was gone, that they revealed a debased and profligate character. "No terms of condemnation," Davis asserts, "would be too strong," so you see with what moderation he comported himself in destroying the only evidence.

Remarkably, though, Burr's reputation survived this "deliberate stab" (as a president of the American Historical Association would write). He was a genuine Revolutionary War hero, and what was more, one of his finest moments was both inspirational and visually compelling: At the Battle of Quebec, "with wonderful strength" he bore away the body of his commanding officer, the dying General Montgomery, on his back, through heavy musket fire and heavy snow. John Trumbull produced a famous painting of Montgomery falling dead into Burr's arms, and knockoff engravings of the picture proliferated throughout the nineteenth century. Even more melodramatic prints, of Burr bent underneath Montgomery as at a station of the cross, were once common classroom decorations.

In 1847 popular historian George Lippard called Burr "the Enigma of our history"; and perhaps this is the fairest description of him. But after 1859, the enigma was over. In 1859, as biographer Roger G. Kennedy would later put it, "Mrs. Stowe finished the job."

The question, though, is why she bothered. *Uncle Tom's Cabin* she wrote to tar slavery, which makes sense. Why bother tarring Burr?

IV.

Calvin Stowe, Harriet's husband, was a noted biblical scholar, an early advocate of the public school system, and himself a bestselling author (nonfiction). But Calvin Stowe was no Beecher.

Harriet's family was an eminent one; her father, Lyman Beecher, was a famous Presbyterian clergyman and abolitionist, and a founder of the temperance movement. Her brother Henry Ward Beecher was an *even more famous* Presbyterian clergyman and abolitionist; he was hailed by none other than Abraham Lincoln as the greatest living American—and who am I to etc.? He was celebrity enough to star in a surprisingly clean limerick:

> *There once was an eloquent preacher,*
> *Who said to a hen, "You dear creature!"*
> *When she, just for that,*
> *Laid three eggs in his hat.*
> *And thus did the Henry Ward Beecher.*

. . . as well as other limericks, less suitable for polite company.

Abolitionism and temperance were both progressive, even radical causes, and Lyman and Henry's devotion to them brought the two into conflict with the Presbyterian old guard. Henry was refused ordination for a time, while in 1835 Lyman was tried for heresy, which apparently is the kind of thing that could still happen to Presbyterians in the nineteenth century. The humiliations that the Beecher family suffered eventually split the church.

Gradually, the traditional Calvinist pieties became controversial in the Beecher household. Harriet's older sister Catharine demolished several Calvinist doctrines in a series of books and articles. One German theology professor, upon learning that the dogma of predestination had been refuted by a woman from New England, cried out, "God forgive Christopher Columbus for discovering America!" Harriet remained a more pious Presbyterian (Presbyterians are just Scottish Calvinists) than her sister, but in 1857 she had her own crisis of faith. In 1857, her son Henry, while away at college, drowned.

Basic Calvinist doctrine separates people into the elect (who are saved) and the preterite (who are damned), and Henry Stowe's worldly and frivolous life had given few "signs of election." Henry Stowe was probably doomed to Presbyterian hell, and his mother found this conclusion unbearable. The year after her son's death, Stowe began work on *The Minister's Wooing.*

No New England Presbyterian could struggle against doctrine without struggling against the writings of Jonathan Edwards, the great American theologian most famous for proclaiming all people "sinners in the hands of an angry God." Edwards had died a half century before Harriet Beecher Stowe was born, but his legacy was the legacy of American Calvinism, and it was Edwards that sister Catharine always specifically took pains to refute. Harriet spoke more kindly of Edwards's legacy—"Some of his sermons are more terrible than Dante's 'Inferno,'" she wrote in a letter, but she meant it as a compliment—and yet she could never reconcile Edwards's teaching with Henry's fate. Several of HBS's books record her attempts to come to grips with the pernicious effect Edwards and Calvinism had on the human conscience.

Guess who Edwards's grandson is. Edwards's grandson is Aaron Burr.

Was Burr's ancestry important to Stowe? The first thing Stowe mentions about Burr in *The Minister's Wooing* is that he is popular; the second thing, literally sentence two, is that his grandfather is Jonathan Edwards. "You are the son of a holy ancestry," the heroine tells Burr, with some degree of irony.

Go back to the *Wooing* passages above. Burr is never an individual in these descriptions of him. He's always a type. He's "a man of gallantry"; he's "one of those men." Here's another one (there are many others), still from *Wooing*, Stowe on Burr: "He was one of those persons who systematically managed and played upon himself and others, as a skillful musician on an instrument."

Critic James Wood once accused Tom Wolfe of calling all his characters "the kind of man who"; and perhaps Wood's keen eye can help us see the same situation developing in Stowe's prose. Burr is hardly a character in *Wooing*; he's not even a bad character: He's the kind of character who would be bad. He represents the bad thing.

You don't need to dig too deep into Stowe's psyche to see what bad thing Burr represents. She might as well have titled the novel *This Is What Calvinism Does to You.*

"Mrs. Stowe finished the job." After this book, Burr's good name would be a bad name. Or as Stowe put it: "It is well known that for many years after Burr's death the odium that covered his name was so great that no monument was erected, lest it should become a mark for popular violence."

But what if she hadn't nursed such a grudge against Jonathan Edwards and his seed? Perhaps her son drowns after a conversion experience, and therefore goes straight to heaven; perhaps her father and brother are welcomed into the bosom of the Calvinist diehards; perhaps her sister is a less skilled disputant. Maybe she simply refuses to attack a man for the sins of his grandfather. So, she never writes a bestseller about how Aaron Burr is literally worse than a church poisoner; the enigmatic Aaron Burr is remembered as the hero of Quebec, the third US VP, the committed abolitionist. What would happen then?

Harriet Beecher Stowe decides the sins of Jonathan Edwards do not pass on to his descendants → *She picks a new villain* → *YOUR FAVORITE CD IS RUINED!!!*

THE BROADWAY HIT OF 2015 IS CALLED BURR. BURR'S FACE is on the ten-dollar bill. That's it.

VIETNAM

What if French cartographers kept the name Cochinchina?

PLAN
DE LA VILLE
DE
SAIGON
(COCHINCHINE)
1878

GENEVA, 1954

I.

Every once in a while a counterfactual alternative history will pop up with the Confederate States winning the Civil War: *Bring the Jubilee* (1953); *Captain Confederacy* #1 (1986); *C.S.A.* (2004); come the predictable naysayers, with charts and graphs, pointing out that the South could never, ever have won the Civil War.

And whenever this happens, I think: "I bet that's exactly what Robert S. McNamara said to LBJ."

McNamara's charts and graphs promised a US victory in Vietnam; but no US victory was to come. Nixon blamed the loss on the peace movement. Nixon blamed an awful lot of things on the peace movement, including the lack of a peace treaty in 1969 ("Irony," said Nixon) and the potential coming end of Western civilization, but he's probably right that the peace movement eventually persuaded Americans to turn against the war. Every war has peace protesters (the Mexican War: Henry David Thoreau; WWI: Bertrand Russell; WWII: Oswald Mosley; etc.), so the question is: Why was this peace movement so effective? There are three answers, two of which are quickly taken care of.

One is simply demographics. The foot soldiers drafted for Vietnam tended to be Baby Boomers, and there were a lot of Baby Boomers; it's how they got the name. If your plan is to send representatives of a small demographic into danger, you'll probably get away with it, but the plan to send representatives of a large demographic into danger is, to put it lightly, riskier. Peace is an attractive alternative to danger, not only for the teeming hordes of Boomers but also for the large numbers of their worried parents, sweethearts, advertisers who need teeming hordes of Boomers to market to, etc.

Another is color photography. You can see this for yourself: Flip through a book of photographs from the Vietnam War and a book of photographs from World War II, and the first thing you'll notice is that in Vietnam, for the first time, war is really bloody. Obviously, war is always bloody, but when blood is the same color as mud and shadow, you can kind of fudge things in your mind. The garish red of '60s film stock makes the blood really pop. One theory on the fall of the British Empire maintains that, to hold on to an empire, you periodically have to shoot the locals to keep them cowed; and once communications became good enough that the British back home learned about all the shooting, they no longer supported the empire. Well, the American people were certainly happier to support wars that were abstracted, or that had the anodyne black-and-white look of a Hollywood war movie. It was harder to support an endeavor that spilled all that bright red blood.

The third is words on a map. This is where it gets interesting.

II.

How do you get rid of a planet?

You could disintegrate it, I suppose, with "a beam of pure antimatter" (as mentioned in *The Rocky Horror Picture Show*). You could use an "etheric ray" to modify the spin of the planet, causing it to careen off into space (as in Edmond Hamilton's 1928 short story "Crashing Suns"). You could shatter it with a "superlaser" (as in *Star Wars* episode IV), presumably sending an entire planet's mass worth of rubble into escape velocity simultaneously somehow.

Actually, these all sound really difficult. Getting rid of a planet sounds really difficult. But someone must have done *something*, because when I was born there were nine planets and now there are only eight.

You see the trick there. But this is the most powerful weapon we have, the power of making definitions. By changing definitions, we literally change the world. We can change the number of oceans there are—there used to be five, but in 1953 the International Hydrographic Organization, in the third edition of its publication *Limits of Oceans and Seas*, decided there was no Southern Ocean around Antarctica; with the stroke of a pen it got rid of an ocean. If we wanted to, we could agree that Eurasia should be a continent, and thereby reduce the number of continents to six. All we need to do is decide.

This is the power of words. "A road is made by people walking on it," the philosopher Zhuang Zhou said twenty-five hundred years ago; "things are so because they are called so." Until the sixteenth century, the word *turtle* referred only to birds (such as what we'd call a turtledove); it was only around midcentury that the reptile got pegged with that name—which means that until the sixteenth century turtles could fly. By definition.

The map says North Vietnam and South Vietnam. And that made all the difference.

III.

The US fought the Vietnamese for the first time in 1861. The SS *Saginaw*, while on a diplomatic mission and under a white flag, was fired on by a Vietnamese fort in Qui Nhon Bay. The *Saginaw* returned fire, reducing the fort. Determining that "after such a reception, there was little use communicating with the officials on shore," the *Saginaw* left. There were no American casualties.

"That went well," Americans may have thought of this first conflict. The Americans probably had no idea why the Vietnamese would fire on a peaceful Western ship, but we can guess. In 1861, Vietnam was in the process of being invaded by France. In the upcoming years, France would take over all of Vietnam, partitioning it into three colonies (technically one colony and two "protectorates"). South Vietnam was Cochinchina, North Vietnam was Tonkin, and in between was Annam.

This wouldn't be the first time North and South Vietnam would be separated. In the thousand-year history of Vietnam leading up to the Vietnam War—from 939 to the early 1960s—the northern and southern parts of the country had been united for under 150 years. This statistic is not quite fair, because for the first five hundred years of this time, what we consider to be southern Vietnam would have been the independent (and not at all Vietnamese) kingdom of Champa, with parts belonging to the Khmer (i.e., Cambodian) Empire. But even if you start around 1475, when people from Hanoi successfully pushed south far enough that you could conceivably call part of the country "north" and part "south," you're still left with the same fact: During half a millennium, north and south were one country for less than a century and a half.

For contrast, during this same five-hundred-year span, Norway and Denmark were one country for over four hundred years.

This doesn't mean that Norway and Denmark "should" be one country, any more than it means that North and South Vietnam "should" be two. I'm not in charge of dividing up countries! It just means that if you looked at a map of Southeast Asia from a random date, you'd have a pretty good chance of walking away assuming that Hanoi and Ho Chi Minh City (formerly Saigon; before that, Prey Kor) belonged in different countries.

The southern Vietnamese were influenced by the peoples they absorbed—the Chams and the Khmer—who were in turn influenced by India. It's sometimes said that the border of Cambodia and Vietnam marks the dividing line between Indian and Chinese spheres of cultural impact, but the two mingled in South Vietnam. It's probably impossible for foreigners to understand how culturally distinct two peoples they've never met are, and I wouldn't want someone to complain that the obvious cultural disparities between New York, Los Angeles, and New Orleans imply any fatal disunity in the US. But North and South Vietnamese, even decades after unification, still see a difference between the two populations. The North views the South as cosmopolitan; the South sees the

North as diligent. In the same way that upscale clothing shops in the US might call themselves after a European capital to add a touch of class, clothing shops in Hanoi invoke the exotic name "Saigon." Each half of the country has a distinct cuisine.

The French started meddling in Vietnam in the late eighteenth century, at a time when the country had been divided between north and south for over a hundred years. With French help, a man named Nguyen Anh unified the country under his own rule in 1802. But this was the Age of Imperialism, and few European powers could resist demanding a price for such assistance. In this case the price meant French hegemony—delayed because of events back home (defeat of Napoleon; revolutions in 1830, 1832, 1848; stuff like that) but irresistible. Nguyen Anh's unified Vietnam lasted less than sixty years; by 1859 the French owned Saigon, and their territory only grew.

As part of the French overseas empire, Vietnam got lumped together with Cambodia and Laos under the rubric French Indochina. This was the largest state in the Indochinese peninsula since the height of the Khmer Empire, nearly a millennium before.

Turn your gaze some two thousand miles to the west for a moment, to India. After World War II, Britain's plan was for India to become independent as one state—which is a little weird because India had never been one state in its three thousand–plus years of existence. Chandragupta almost unified it (ca. 295 BC); the Mughals (Turco-Mongol invaders) almost unified it (ca. 1700); usually it was a patchwork of small kingdoms and slightly larger empires. The British came in and conquered all of it and called it "India," and in 1947 a lot of people acted under the belief that India was naturally one country, even though a unified India was a British fiction. It's not that there was nothing culturally or historically binding India together; there's plenty culturally and historically binding Europe together too, yet the fact that the Romans or Napoleon conquered a lot of Europe doesn't mean that Europe is one country. But Gandhi died campaigning for a unified India. It didn't quite work; British India is now four countries. But even the country that is now India is a larger state than the usual spate of kingdoms that checkered India for most of its pre-Mughal history.

The British created India *by calling it India*. The French created something called Indochina, but this fiction fell apart, too. Probably Laos, Cambodia, and the three sections of Vietnam didn't have enough in common to ever want to be one state. Vietnam, however, had been one country before, however briefly. The Japanese invaded Indochina during World War II and created a series of puppet governments—the independent "Empire of Vietnam," as it was known, was just as much a Japanese client state as French Indochina had been a French client state, but it was Cochinchina plus Tonkin plus Annam—what we would now call Vietnam.

The decline of imperialism and the worldwide push for colonial independence would have spelled the end of French Indochina anyway, but the events of World War II—the enervated French state, the Japanese rhetoric of a Vietnam unshackled from European control—hastened it. And the focus of the Vietnamese independence movement was a certain Ho Chi Minh.

Ho was calling for a unified Vietnamese state (under his control, of course), so in order to counter his propaganda the French proclaimed their own unified state of Vietnam. This unified state was hypothetical, in the sense that Ho's Viet Minh troops controlled part of the alleged unified territory. But it was a rallying point. It was a goal. After a decade of war that went poorly for the French (as wars will), the 1954 Geneva Conference divided what had been the three French sections of Vietnam into two countries: the Democratic Republic of Vietnam and the State of Vietnam. But everyone just called them North Vietnam and South Vietnam.

IV.

America went to Vietnam because of the Russians. Also the Chinese, but the Chinese were a worry because of the Russians. The Soviet Union had spent the immediate aftermath of World War II gobbling up what parts of Europe it could reach. This was, you may recall, exactly what Hitler had done to start the war in the first place. Hitler's invasion of Poland had been the proximate cause of World War II, and the Soviets moved into Poland in Hitler's wake and never really moved out. There was no second war for Poland. Hitler's seizure of Czechoslovakia *would have been* the proximate cause of World War II if British prime minister Neville Chamberlain hadn't decided to let it slide; *appeasement* was still a dirty word in 1948, but that's the year the Soviets seized Czechoslovakia, and they were appeased. Tsarina Catherine the Great's dictum had been "That which stops growing begins to rot," and Stalin took it to heart. The Soviets were collecting puppet states, virtually unopposed, until eventually the US under Harry S Truman started supplying arms to the potential puppets—which kept the Soviets out of Greece. But the Soviets still had a good collection going.

Then in 1949, Mao Zedong—with significant help from the Soviet Union—seized control of China from Chiang Kai-shek (who was, to be clear, receiving significant help from the US). Communist China and the communist Soviet Union became fast friends. For a decade, the world's largest country (by area) and the world's largest country (by population) were working in concert. Together they waged war against the US (and most of the rest of the United Nations) in Korea. Together they were a juggernaut.

China, however, had no interest in being a puppet state of anyone. China should be the one collecting puppet states! *Differing interpretations of Marxism* is cited as the reason for the eventual Sino-Soviet split, but it's more likely the disagreement was simply over who was to be in charge. China got sick of referring to the Soviet Union as "elder brother." Each country went its separate way, in search of territory to grab.

You know what country had been an on-again, off-again puppet state of China over the last millennium? You guessed it: Vietnam. But if Vietnam was currently part of France, well, neither China nor the USSR wanted a war with France, and therefore with NATO—of which France was an on-again, off-again member.

While each communist country was, at times, perfectly willing to impose its will on another state by driving tanks over its border (Tibet, 1950; Hungary, 1956), each had another arrow in its quiver. That arrow: to back communist insurgents inside a state's borders. Communist insurgents were already in Vietnam, and both China and the Soviet Union vied with each other in seeing who could funnel the most arms to them. The idea was that the greater benefactor would gain the loyalty of the eventual communist state. It was touch-and-go for a while, but in the end, the Russians won that contest. The communists in Vietnam would front a Stalinist, not a Maoist, insurgency. The head of the communists was Ho Chi Minh.

Ho Chi Minh, like Mao or Che Guevara, eventually became a romantic figure in the US; and it can be difficult to ferret out the truth about romantic figures. Certainly, Ho was interested in Vietnamese independence before he was interested in Stalinism. In 1919 he showed up at Versailles in the wake of World War I to try to extract a concession of Indochinese freedom from the triumphant allies. No one would meet with him; frankly, there was 0% chance that the French, who were busy greedily snatching land and colonies from defeated Germany, were going to give up one inch of their empire in 1919. So, Ho looked for more receptive allies, which is how he became a communist.

Compared to certain other Indochinese communist leaders of the time, Ho looks good. While a young Pol Pot (eventual leader of communist Cambodia) was making brass knuckles in shop class (!) or slipping into King Monivong's harem for illicit trysts with his wives (!!), young Ho was studying the Confucian classics and working menial jobs as he traveled around the world, learning about the plight of the working class throughout the US and Europe. Some of this may be romantic nonsense. No one knows much for sure about Ho, including his birthdate. "I like to hold on to my little mysteries," said Ho—but it's still more respectable than brass knuckles.

Ho's nationalist struggle was not necessarily frowned upon by the American government. The US actually lobbied for Indochinese independence during World War II. One of Franklin Roosevelt's avowed war goals was dismantling European colonial empires. After the war, though, the ascendency and rapaciousness of Stalin's Soviet empire changed priorities. A strong France was required to help defend Western Europe from Soviet aggression. And not just a strong France but also a happy France; France wanted to keep its overseas empire, and if the Western powers had insisted France give them up, France would have gladly withdrawn its support (as it did, in fact, in a fit of pique in 1959). So, in what would be a continuing trend, hope of Vietnamese independence evaporated in the face of larger strategic concerns.

This could have simply set up the story of Vietnamese rebels fighting French overlords. But then the Vietnamese rebels would have lost. The Viet Minh survived and prospered because of a constant flow—first from China and later from the Soviet Union—of arms, money, advisers . . . and combat troops. Although their presence was downplayed or suppressed at the time, 320,000 Chinese soldiers served in the North Vietnamese army through the course of the war, while Soviet pilots flew combat missions for the North Vietnamese Air Force.

And this, from the Americans' point of view was the problem. An independent Vietnam was a great idea! Vietnam as a colony of France was endurable. Vietnam as a puppet state of either China or the USSR was another thing entirely, and after the mid '60s it was the Soviets who had Ho's heart. North Vietnam was a Soviet puppet, and in the Soviet manner, it was looking to expand. That's what the US sought to prevent. Not so much because Vietnam itself was of great strategic importance, but because, as Zhuang Zhou (again) says, "If you give in at the beginning, there is no place to stop." The Soviets had orchestrated the fall of nationalist China; the Soviets had invaded Hungary; the Soviets had formed a puppet state in Cuba; the Soviets' Korean adventure had ended in a draw, but they were otherwise doing pretty well. Indochina was just supposed to be another notch in the belt.

Meanwhile, Maoist-backed communists in Indonesia were invading

Malaysia and threatening to press on and pincer attack Vietnam from the south.

A specter was haunting Asia. A specter was haunting the world. The United States' goal in the Vietnam War was to exorcise that specter. It didn't go well.

V.

After a decade of escalating involvement—of dwindling popularity for the conflict, and, not coincidentally, a rising death toll of US servicemen— the US reached a point where it could claim a stalemate, draw up a peace treaty, and leave, having "technically" accomplished its goal of preserving South Vietnamese independence from the North. That's just what Nixon did in 1973.

Of course, the North Vietnamese broke the treaty, invaded, and by 1975 had conquered South Vietnam, uniting the country, while the US, sick of fighting and still reeling from the Watergate scandal, did nothing. Nobody wanted to return to Vietnam, to a war seen alternately as a quagmire or the equivalent of Athens's Sicilian expedition.

Perhaps a different US strategy could have achieved a different ending, but I'm going to argue that a different ending would have been very difficult to achieve, regardless of how the war was fought. By the time the US was in Indochina, it was already too late to win the war. The map, you see, had already been drawn.

At the time there was what was called the domino theory: the theory that if Vietnam became communist, Cambodia would become communist, and then Laos would become communist, and then the rest of Asia would become communist, each state falling like dominoes. Cambodia fell to the communists the same month Vietnam did, and Laos followed four months later. Although "the rest of Asia" stayed stable, the fall of Vietnam was followed quickly by Soviet-backed communist puppet governments in Angola, Cape Verde, Mozambique, Madagascar, Afghanistan, Grenada, and Nicaragua. This list skips around too much for *dominoes* to be a good metaphor, but I'll tell you what dominoes is a good metaphor for: The moment people started using the terms *North Vietnam* and *South Vietnam*, the dominoes started falling; the last domino was the fall of Saigon.

During the Vietnam War era, there existed the two neighboring countries of West Germany and East Germany. Germany had only been a unified state for about seventy-five years out of the last two thousand, but everyone assumed these two halves "belonged" together. If they weren't destined to be reunited, no one would've named them West Germany and East Germany. Indeed, all it took was the weakening of the Soviet Union—the active force keeping the two apart—and they snapped back into their "natural state." Austria, which had been part of Germany when the country was originally partitioned in 1945, did not reunite with Germany in 1990. After all, it had a different name.

Korea remains two states, North and South, but the official rhetoric is that there is actually only one Korea, and the two governments are some sort of temporary aberration. The two countries competed as one in the 2018 Olympics. Everyone talks as though reunification is just around the corner. Only two things are keeping the two apart: The constant US garrison presence, and the absolute ape-nuts madness of the North Korean regime, which could not successfully reunify with anything. Even with these two factors, Koreans speak of one Korea, as though it were already accomplished.

With China and Taiwan, the official rhetoric is also that there is only one China. Taiwan isn't even a member of the United Nations! But, although the "real names" of the two states are similar—People's Republic of China vs. Republic of China—everyone calls them China and Taiwan. Reunification here is a pipe dream. If Taiwan had been dubbed East China, it would have been conquered by West China long ago.

The Vietnam War was "sold" to the American public in different ways. It was a war to keep South Vietnam free and democratic (not so very free or democratic, considering the corrupt warlords who ruled it, but nevertheless *relatively* free and democratic compared to their northern neighbors). It was a war to defend US allies. It was a war to hinder the spread of communism. But always there was the assumption that it was a civil war, which the US was stepping into. This assumption wasn't completely false; especially during the earlier years, the South Vietnamese government was fighting homegrown communist insurgents from right there in South Vietnam, the Viet Cong. But the Viet Cong were funded by, and answered to, North Vietnam. If North and South Vietnam are one country, then even North Vietnam's interference is just part of a civil war. But if Tonkin is fomenting rebellion in the sovereign state of Cochinchina, then you are talking an invasion.

Everyone agrees that going around invading sovereign states is bad! Imagine the headline: "Denmark Invades Norway!" Who would oppose helping defend the Norwegian borders? But no one ever successfully sold the American people on the idea that the Vietnam War was about preventing one state from invading another. How could they? The names on the map told a different story.

VI.

Sorry, Nixon, but the peace movement did not turn people into pacifists (alternately: Marxists) who therefore wanted to withdraw from Vietnam. The peace movement was never all that popular in the 1960s. The Students for a Democratic Society were viewed much more unfavorably, according to a 1970 Gallup poll, than the South Vietnamese (42% unfavorable vs. 13% unfavorable)—while still being more popular than the Viet Cong at least (69% unfavorable).

In 1966 the "Ballad of the Green Berets," a jingoistic tale of "America's best" sung by the Purple Heart vet who composed it over a military drumroll and featuring a trumpet fanfare at the climax, hit number one on the Billboard charts. That's three months after the Byrds' "Turn, Turn, Turn" held the top spot, five months after the Beatles' "Yesterday," six months after Barry McGuire's nihilistic protest anthem "Eve of Destruction." The truth is, most Americans supported the troops and distrusted the protesters.

And yet by 1968 most (meaning a Gallup poll majority) Americans thought the war was a mistake.

Essentially, the peace movement was a commercial. Nobody likes commercials, but they work anyway. The peace movement was a commercial the American people saw on their TVs every night, a commercial for the message *the war isn't worth it*. The government had its own commercial, but as the war went on, and the American death toll crept up, the peaceniks' commercial became more and more persuasive; the government commercial sank into what people at the time called the "credibility gap." The map, remember, the map said the government was not credible. As the influence of the peace movement waxed, so waxed the boldness of the North Vietnamese. No one's going to talk peace with an enemy who's obviously wavering.

Nixon never had a chance, as no force on earth is stronger than commercials.

France calls South Vietnam Cochinchina → **THE VIETNAM WAR ENDS IN 1968** → *Hippies are nowhere, man* → *Drugs are uncool, just like Nancy Reagan said*

I.

AT FIRST, IN 1954, THE FRENCH CALLED THE STATE OF VIETNAM *Cochinchina*, but they didn't stick with it. They could have. They could have called the Democratic Republic of Vietnam *Tonkin*. Ho was going to call it the Democratic Republic of Vietnam even though it was (like most democratic republics) neither democratic nor a republic, but the French could have called it Tonkin. They call Deutschland *Allemagne*, regardless of what the Germans say (we call Deutschland *Germany* regardless of what the Germans say). France could have insisted, not officially but in the anarchy of everyday usage, on Cochinchina and Tonkin—but they didn't.

A French exit from Indochina was inevitable; but the rest could have gone differently if France had chosen its words differently post-Geneva. Because if American maps showed Tonkin invading Cochinchina, the peace movement starts from a far less credible position. Ho Chi Minh starts from a far less credible position. It's possible that world opinion would have kept Mao from even funneling arms through Hanoi to the Viet Cong; but that's probably too optimistic. Imagine instead that the war wraps up in a stalemate in 1968. The Viet Cong have been sufficiently injured to prevent Tonkin from keeping the insurrection going inside Cochinchina (this is indeed what happened in our history). But Tonkin cannot risk the international opprobrium that a direct invasion like the Tet Offensive would incur. Peace in 1968. Lyndon Johnson, hailed as a hero, runs for another term.

Would history have been very different if the Vietnam War (called the Tonkin War, probably) had ended, with two states firmly in place, in 1968? Well, obviously, history would have been very different for the Vietnamese. Also for the Cambodians and Laotians whose own governments got dominoed into communism. Although in our history the North Vietnamese takeover was not followed by as many massacres and atrocities as some people had feared (it was not comparable to the number of massacres and atrocities performed by the Communist Viet Minh in the 1950s, for example), it was nevertheless followed by a number of massacres and atrocities. About two million South Vietnamese risked their lives to flee the triumphant North Vietnamese regime, taking to the open sea in small boats or dodging government patrols to sneak into neighboring countries, living witness to the nature of the workers' paradise Vietnam had become.

Meanwhile, in Cambodia, the massacres and atrocities were *far worse than anyone had dared to imagine*. Pol Pot's Khmer Rouge regime set new gold standards for communist tyranny. During their four-year tenure, the Khmer Rouge achieved a world record for murdering the largest percentage of their own population for any state in recorded history. To the brutality, the paranoia, the genocides against ethnic and religious minorities, the tortures, the tendency to invite foreign journalists to visit and then murder them, and the occasional medical experiments, add that other problem endemic to communist regimes: the fact that mismanagement of agriculture led to terrible famines. Laurence Picq, a French woman who worked as a translator for the Khmer Rouge, records that upon leaving the bunker she'd been isolated in, she noticed with surprise that the fields she passed were fallow and overgrown; she'd been translating propaganda claiming that an agricultural miracle had brought *all this land* under cultivation. Needless to say, there was no agricultural miracle, and the nightmare of the Khmer Rouge's reign only ended when they started a war with their larger, richer, more successful neighbor, the victorious and unified Vietnam. The Khmer strategy was, quite literally, to have each Khmer solider kill thirty Vietnamese soldiers. Had they been able to achieve it, the strategy would have worked. Instead, Cambodia became a Vietnamese puppet state; a Soviet grandpuppet.

So we know, in our counterfactual history, that life would have been very different for the people of Cochinchina, as well as the people of Cambodia and Laos—the last of which is generally neglected because of the comparable lack of massacres; nevertheless, a whopping 10% of the Laotian population fled the country in the wake of communist takeover. But Americans—how to put this delicately?—have traditionally been more concerned with their own welfare than the welfare of the Indochinese. In 1965, one of Johnson's advisers said the Vietnam War was 70% about preserving the United States' larger strategic position in the Cold War and only 10% about helping the Vietnamese. (The other 20% was about foiling world communism.) Have a look at the history section of any bookstore or library and see how many books there are about the Vietnam War compared to books about the history of Vietnam in general. At my local library, the ratio (I counted) is 44:1. Americans care about the decade-long American experience in Vietnam forty-four times more than the other thousand years of Vietnamese history. The odds are that Americans reading this book are wondering how history would have been different for America.

Fortunately, the answer is easy. It would have changed the '60s youth movement. Rather, it would have changed how we remember the '60s youth movement. And therefore, it would have changed how we remember the '60s.

II.

The youth movement of the 1960s had two defining characteristics. It was on the one hand outrageously silly—the giddiness of Twiggy stating in an interview that her salary was "a skillion dollars," or the "nutty world of semi-existentialism, of cuckoo-clocks and antique lampshades, of beat-up old cars and Indian boots" (that daffy list is from the liner notes to the Mamas and the Papas' first album). It was on the other hand deadly serious. It was about changing the world. Say what you will about Charles Manson, but he was deadly serious about changing the world (by starting a Beatles-themed race war through murder—I didn't say it was a good plan). No other serial killer has been this serious.

Sometimes the two characteristics are just supposed to be the Early '60s (silly) and the Late '60s (serious), which makes a kind of sense: The Monkees had started out silly but by 1968 even they released an art film *that incorporated actual atrocity footage*. But the single silliest action of the entire 1960s took place in 1967, when the Beatles, the four most famous humans on earth, tried to drive across England in a psychedelic-branded bus having adventures (they failed). The constant mixture of the silly and the serious was what made the '60s the '60s. Pop art and domestic terrorists. Batman and Ravi Shankar. In 1967 protesters surrounded the Pentagon, with the intent of levitating it through chants and Mayan magic; this was silly; they were doing it to end the Vietnam War.

For better or for worse, the youth culture of the Baby Boomers set the standard for the rest of the twentieth century. The enshrining of rebellion as a touchstone of youth, the spread of the sexual revolution, the permanence of the generation gap—Boomers had their own reasons for embracing these cultural touchstones (cough, Freud, cough), but unlike most youth cultures, this one lingered. Sure, it lingered in part because there were so many Boomers. But it lingered mainly because unlike every youth culture that succeeded it, '60s youth culture had gravitas; '60s youth culture was about something; '60s youth culture had the Vietnam War.

There have been some attempts in later years to graft onto the '60s events that happened before or after it. The civil rights movement started and flourished when Boomers were still in short pants; women's liberation was primarily a '70s phenomenon. But of course, sure, civil rights and women's lib existed in the 1960s too. The '60s would not have been *all silly* without Vietnam. But every generation gets tangled up in social issues; social issues would hardly have made the 1960s unique. What made the 1960s unique was the presence of a large youth culture that was the cynosure of media attention, combined with the possibility that representatives of that youth culture may be sent off to die—while still too young to vote, as Barry McGuire points out in song.

During World War II, war took over pop culture, and there were war movies (Abbott and Costello in *Buck Privates*), and war songs ("Little Bo Peep Has Lost Her Jeep"), and war comic strips (*Sad Sack*); none of these examples, you will notice, are particularly intent on conveying gravitas. Everyone assumed that World War II was serious, so people could joke about it. The pop culture of the '60s was haunted by war, too, but it was insistent that its war *1.* was serious, *2.* was a tragedy, and *3.* affected everyone. In Peter, Paul, and Mary's "The Great Mandella" (1967), a war protester is nagged by his hawkish father, is arrested for draft dodging, and starves himself to death in a hunger strike, whereupon the narrator explains that his struggle was in vain because mankind is irredeemably bellicose. It was released as a B side of a single that peaked at number nine.

The number of 1960s war songs, which, "Green Berets" aside, are overwhelmingly anti-war songs, is staggering. Peter, Paul, and Mary's "Where Have All the Flowers Gone?" (1962), Phil Ochs's "I Ain't Marching Anymore" and "Draft Dodger Rag" (1965), Barry McGuire's aforementioned "Eve of Destruction" (1965), Country Joe and the Fish's "I-Feel-Like-I'm-Fixin'-to-Die Rag" (1965), Pete Seeger's "Waist Deep in the Big Muddy" (1967), Arlo Guthrie's "Alice's Restaurant Massacree" (1967),

Eric Burdon and the Animals' "Sky Pilot" (1968), Creedence Clearwater Revival's "Fortunate Son" (1969), the Monkees' "Mommy and Daddy" (1969), Plastic Ono Band's "Give Peace a Chance" (1969), etc. Not all of these were hits (Phil Ochs literally couldn't have recorded a hit to save his life), but none of them are obscure. In 1970, Three Dog Night's "Joy to the World" and Edwin Starr's "War (What Is It Good For?)" would be released; both hit the top of the charts. The war, of course, would not end for a few more years, so the songs would keep coming.

Some of these songs are satirical, or plain goofy, but even the goofy ones are serious. The Smothers Brothers joked about the Vietnam War on television, but their jokes were serious. They weren't joking the way Abbott and Costello were joking. Their seriousness made the 1960s irresistible for the next forty years or so. Irresistible for Boomers themselves as a nostalgic go-to—in a 1987 sitcom episode, Susan St. James's character would still be bragging that her generation had stopped the war, and that bragging will never stop as long as Boomers live—but also as a template for youth culture, and therefore pop culture in general.

What would the musical *Hair* be without the Vietnam War? If no one gets drafted, the worst thing the protagonists could look forward to would be having to get a haircut and a square job. Every other generation feared a haircut and a square job, and therefore their time was a farce. The Boomers feared being sent to their deaths, and therefore their time was a tragedy. Everyone else has been jealous.

Remove the Vietnam War *as tragedy* and you remove the 1960s' gravitas; remove that gravitas and future generations need not hold on to rock as the primary musical idiom.

Without the example of the 1960s, pop culture would not need to be synonymous with youth. Movies would be about grown-ups (as opposed to about *1.* teenagers or *2.* teenage power fantasies). Easy-listening music would be the trendsetter.

Furthermore, there would be no Twenty-Sixth Amendment to the Constitution permitting eighteen-year-olds to vote, and so every election since 1971 would be different. (Just kidding! Eighteen-year-olds don't vote!)

The greatest cultural legacy of the 1960s was not rock music or institutionalized rebellion or teenagers as a marketing category or the Carter presidency, though. The greatest cultural legacy of the 1960s is the mainstreaming of drug use. It sounded like a great idea at the time, as things do. Marijuana and LSD are the signature drugs of the 1960s. "That went well," people thought, as they experimented.

Then, suddenly, it did not go well.

The degree to which drugs pervaded American culture—it's easy to forget that by the 1970s, the word *cool* was literally synonymous with "habitually using drugs," as in "are you cool?" = "do you partake?"—and the speed at which it became clear, even in the most progressive circles, that drug culture could easily become dangerous, are hard to overstate. In 1968, Steppenwolf's single "The Pusher" contrasted the gentle, benign pot dealer with the "monster" that was the drug "pusher." This warning would not be heeded.

In 1967 (just to take one isolated statistic; but all statistics from this time show the same trend; the trend is *more* and *worse*) there were 142 known cases of drugs being smuggled in hollow recesses into America; in 1971 there were 3,848. It's possible that a 1968 end to the Vietnam War would be too late, that drug use would have already reached a tipping point. But if the 1960s lose their gravitas, drug addiction could stay an anachronistic fad, like coonskin caps. The history of the 1970s and 1980s would be different without rock and roll, but it would be *very different* without the various drug epidemics and the concomitant spike in crime.

This is the legacy of the Vietnam War that would disappear if the French had chosen their nomenclature more carefully: America's War on Drugs.

Not to forget the fate of the millions of residents of Indochina.

20

GLOBAL THERMONUCLEAR WAR

What if Jimmy Carter had a bad day?

WASHINGTON, DC, 1979

I.

Here's a fun party game: Name the most important person in history. No fair naming your mom; you're supposed to figure out who's impacted the most lives.

Jesus, or Paul, or Muhammad, or Gautama Buddha is a popular pick. You might instead go for Isaac Newton or Johannes Gutenberg.

These are all terrible choices, though, because they're wrong. The actual answer is Jimmy Carter. This is a book about Alexander the Great, Saladin, and Adolf Hitler, and none of them are as important as Jimmy Carter. Because Jimmy Carter had the opportunity to blow up the world and chose not to do it.

There was no reason for him to do it, of course. He never came close. He was probably never tempted to do it. In a famous *Playboy* interview, Carter admitted to being tempted by women, but he never added, "Also tempting: nuclear apocalypse." But he could have done it. He easily could have started a nuclear war with the Soviet Union. He could even have ordered nuclear strikes on all major American cities. Someone probably would have tried to stop him if he'd made a go at that, but maybe not; it depends on how willing people were to take unquestioned orders from Jimmy Carter. It might have been easier, if Carter wanted to blow up

New York, for him just to shoot some missiles at Moscow and wait for the Russians to order their own nuclear counterstrike. It would look less suspicious that way.

Truman established the precedent that the president alone decides when nukes get deployed. At least since Eisenhower it's been recognized that in a pinch the president would need the ability to give launch orders immediately. The whole point of the nuclear weapons program is deterrence, which means that the president has to be able to launch a nuclear strike without wading through congressional debate and approval (the traditional method of starting a war). At the president's sole discretion, nuclear missiles can launch from *1.* land-based silos, *2.* submarines hidden somewhere in the oceans, and *3.* jets that are either *a.* warily circling US airspace or *b.* on the ground ready to circle warily at a moment's notice. (It used to be always the former; now it's generally the latter.) These are the three legs of the so-called nuclear triad. What happens after they launch depends on where the missiles are headed, but there'll probably be a counterattack, and a counter-counterattack. It would be a bad day.

This state of affairs was hardly inevitable: not the nuclear standoff, but the fact that the nuclear standoff can be broken by one guy. As Richard Nixon once told some congressmen, "I could leave this room and in 25 minutes 70 million people would be dead." He probably didn't mean it as a threat, he probably meant it as an example of the weighty responsibility of the presidency; but *still*. It's weird we ended up here. Nuclear weapons policy was a series of ad hoc decisions made by leaders who were wrestling with a constantly changing geopolitical situation, and a constantly changing technology, and it would not have been easy to predict where any of this was going.

Nuclear fission was discovered right before World War II, and nuclear weapons were developed during the war, behind a veil of absolute secrecy. Without the impetus of military necessity, a working A-bomb may never have been developed at all. The R&D was expensive and time-consuming, and for a long time no one was sure the finished product would work. Manufacturing plutonium was so costly that (according to Art "Kids Say the Darndest Things" Linkletter, who swears he has an inside source) when a janitor accidentally dumped two vials down the drain, scientists tracked the material through the sewers with Geiger counters to get it back. And the finished product—in 1945, after *two billion dollars* and *five years* of labor by an all-star team of the world's greatest physicists, the United States' Manhattan Project had managed to build a grand total of three atom bombs: One was tested in the New Mexico desert; the other two were dropped on Japan. There were no more left; there wasn't even enough enriched uranium in America to make a fourth. Truman told the Japanese that more were coming if they didn't surrender, but this was pure bluff. It would have been months before another bomb could have been assembled. Nobody in Japan (and almost nobody in America) knew it was a bluff, though, because every aspect of the Manhattan Project was top secret.

So secret, that in 1944 the Army Counter Intelligence Corps visited the offices of the pulp magazine *Astounding Science Fiction* because its March issue had contained a story about a deadly bomb powered by the uranium 235 isotope—just like the Manhattan Project's nascent weapon. The eerie accuracy of the science in "Deadline" by Cleve Cartmill can be overstated, as Cartmill's pulpy prose leaves room for only vague descriptions of his U-235 bomb's operation (breathlessly delineated by an alien commando with a prehensile tail whose task is to destroy it), but it was sufficient for the CIC to suspect a leak. Turned out that an innocent Cartmill had simply extrapolated the Bomb from publicly available sources, and his editor, John W. Campbell, who had studied nuclear physics at MIT and Duke, had helped with the research. So no one got arrested.

Meanwhile, Alfred Hitchcock always maintained that his fortuitous inclusion of smuggled uranium as the MacGuffin in the film *Notorious*, which started preproduction in 1944, had attracted the suspicions of the FBI, who surveilled the director for three months. Ah, but Hitchcock was a most notorious teller of tales, and as a rule of thumb the more entertaining one of his stories, the less it is to be trusted. But Hitchcock is right about one thing: No one was supposed to know about how important uranium was in 1944.

In fact, Roosevelt had kept the Manhattan Project so secret that his vice president didn't even know about it. Harry S Truman first learned of the Bomb after FDR's death; it must have been an awkward conversation. Truman continued the tradition of nuclear secrecy, while establishing the tradition of presidential primacy. Only Truman (Truman insisted) could order a nuclear strike. Extrapolating from the specific to the general, only the president could order a nuclear strike. The so-called nuclear football, a satchel with launch codes and some way to implement them (this is still secret in its details) accompanies each US president wherever he goes.

The Soviets had a similar system, with three footballs, one each in the hands of the Soviet head, the defense minister, and the chief of the general staff, although it's still not clear, through the veil of an iron curtain, who exactly had what authority to launch when. Still, if you wanted to say Brezhnev instead of Carter when listing the most influential person, we wouldn't dock any points.

Also unclear: Who can launch American nuclear missiles? Not who *should be able to*—that's the president!—but who *can*. Because the president doesn't launch the missiles, he just gives permission to members of the armed forces. Someone else turns the key—two people, actually, because there are two keys, and they need to be turned simultaneously. In 1977, some of the crewmen who would do the actual launching revealed to reporter Ron Rosenbaum that they had worked out a way, with a spoon and string, to circumvent this failsafe and launch missiles solo. By 2011, Rosenbaum reports, the Spoon Loophole had been fixed, and two people were once again needed. But that's two people. That's only two people.

Trust is the paramount issue in any discussion of the nuclear launch system. If the order comes to launch, how do you know it's a real order? There are codes in the nuclear football, but what if the nuclear football falls into the wrong hands, perhaps during one of the president's innumerable state visits to foreign lands? Doubtless someone has thought these things through, but they won't necessarily tell us what safeguards have been put in place. In 1973, Air Force major Harold Hering, while training for the position of key-turner, asked how he would know, when the nuclear launch order came from the president, whether the president was sane or not. No one could think of an answer, so Harold Hering was fired.

One complicating factor with nuclear war is that whoever launches first has a distinct advantage. Whoever launches first can target the other side's nuclear missiles, reducing the ability to retaliate (that's why so many missiles are on submarines, their ever-shifting locations a secret). Whoever launches first can also target the other side's president. Who's going to issue the order to strike back if there's no president? There's a line of succession, of course, but a nuclear strike on Washington is going to strain it. Imagine standing before the nuclear keys and getting a call that runs something like: "This is the Secretary of Labor and technically I'm in charge right now; I need you to nuke Russia."

I'm not saying these questions don't have answers—even if no one could answer Harold Hering in 1973, we've had fifty years to meditate on a quality response—just that these questions are difficult. This is why a lot of nuclear thinking has been about a *credible second strike*. Everyone knows how to launch a first strike; it's striking back that's the challenge. Fear of a decapitation attack that eliminates the president and enough of the chain of command that no retaliation is possible, was plausible enough to encourage the planning of a so-called doomsday machine, a device capable of launching nuclear weapons automatically, without the messy nonsense of human intervention. This is both the plot to the movie *Dr. Strangelove* and a real thing the Russians may have built, according, at least, to military expert Bruce G. Blair. Exactly how automated the Russian Perimeter System (as it's called) is, is debatable, but the *possibility* of its being real is itself a deterrent, because it minimizes the possibility of a decapitating first strike, and maximizes the chance of striking back. And the entire point of nuclear deterrence is the ability to strike back.

Because the other entire point of nuclear deterrence is that nuclear weapons are too terrible to risk being struck back with.

II.

There's a long, tragic history of making weapons that are too terrible to use. When Hiram S. Maxim invented the machine gun, the March 28, 1897, *New York Times* proclaimed, "These are the instruments that have revolutionized the methods of warfare, and because of their devastating effects, have made nations and rulers give greater thought to the outcome of war before entering upon projects of conquest or battling over matters that can be settled by arbitration. They are peace-producing and peace-retaining terrors." The satirist Hilaire Belloc, on the other hand, that same year parodied British imperialism with the couplet:

> *Whatever happens we have got*
> *The Maxim Gun, and they have not.*

They were the exploited peoples of Africa, as Belloc makes clear, and his poem underscores the problem of deterrence, which is that if only one side has the terrible weapon, no one is deterred, and peace, regardless of the *Times*'s opinion, is neither produced nor retained. It is perhaps unnecessary to point out that the *Times* was completely wrong about the pacifying nature of that "pert little vigilant" machine gun, as the next few decades would prove.

Alfred Nobel, inventor of dynamite and contriver of the Nobel Prize, did not originally intend dynamite to be used in war, but, when it was, he positively crowed that his "factories will put an end to war sooner than your congresses," because the explosive power of dynamite was so great that "all civilised nations will surely recoil with horror and disband their troops." They did not.

The machine gun and dynamite are just two of the many weapons-to-end-war that the nineteenth century coughed up. The whole movement of seeking destruction so terrible that peace will follow as the night the day reached a vulgar apotheosis in an 1880 book by patent-medicine peddler and future US congressman James Henry McLean, titled on the cover *Dr. J. H. McLean's Peace-Makers* (and on the inside *Ukase: We Command*

All Nations to Keep the Peace). Although the book is credited to, and copyrighted by, Dr. McLean, it is written entirely in the third person, apparently by the journalist Myron Coloney; Coloney and McLean lay out their purpose at the beginning, and it should sound familiar:

> **Hearing of the killing and slaughter of the brave soldiers in Europe and Asia at the will of their rulers, he [Dr. McLean] resolved to develop such terribly destructive weapons of war, arms, torpedoes, and fortresses, and such perfect defenses, as would compel all nations to keep peace toward each other.**
>
> **"SAVE THE LIVES OF THE PEOPLE" IS HIS MOTTO.**

What follows are two hundred pages of advertisements for McLean's patented—literally patented—killing machines.

Some of McLean's inventions are clearly practical (breech-loading cannon), some clearly impractical (machine-gun pistols). His unsinkable battleship is suspiciously similar in design to the unsinkable *Titanic*. Harder to judge are items like the Ikea-style modular forts that are quick to assemble or disassemble. McLean has given his products names that range from the delightfully Tom Swiftian ("Dr. J. H. McLean's Wonderful Hydrophone") to the straight-up terrifying ("The Annihilator," "The Pulverizer," or "The Lady McLean" (which can, "like a giant's sabre, . . . cut down whole ranks at a sweep"—it is "named in honor of Dr. McLean's Wife"). There's very little discussion of peace, but there is a mailing address provided for "capitalists wishing further information" about inventions such as Dr. J. H. McLean's Incendiary Time Shells—which look harmless but explode later, when civilians have emerged from their bomb shelters, having assumed the danger was over.

McLean sent free copies of his book to the heads of state around the world in an attempt to drum up some interest, presumably without material result. Two years later he was sitting in Congress. His book's odd combination of idealism, greed, and inventive bloodthirstiness was perhaps unprecedented, but McLean's basic idea—that the only thing keeping war going was the problem that it was too pleasant—was all too common in his era. In his memoirs General William Tecumseh Sherman justified burning Atlanta by saying, "We cannot change the hearts of those people of the South, but we can make war so terrible [and] make them so sick of war that generations would pass away before they would again appeal to it." Thirty-four years after Atlanta burned, Southern troops served the US honorably in the Spanish-American War; in the years between, the American Armed Forces were filled with Southern men, sick of nothing.

And then there was the atomic bomb. No, forget the atomic bomb. Even the atomic bomb may not be dangerous enough. It sure sounds dangerous, but we rarely notice that right from the beginning everyone had an incentive to overstate the power of atomic weapons. The Americans, when they had a monopoly on the Bomb, wanted to stress how don't-tread-on-me puissant it was; the Japanese meanwhile wanted to emphasize how inevitable surrender was in the face of atomic fire. The rest of the world, having no firsthand experience, just had to take their combined word for it. And so everyone exaggerated. In 1946, Robert Oppenheimer opined that spies smuggling a couple of atomic bombs into New York could destroy the city, which, given, the power of the Bomb at the time, was a gross exaggeration. Ground-level detonations are much less destructive than airbursts, and a smuggled-in Hiroshima-style bomb would only destroy 1% of New York City. Far from optimal, but also hardly the end of the Big Apple. Oppenheimer had run the Manhattan Project, and certainly knew better, but he always liked to make dramatic statements; he famously claimed to have intoned spontaneously, at the first atomic test, the verse from the *Bhagavad-Gita*: "I am become Death, destroyer of worlds." This is very poetic, but it's also something Oppenheimer started claiming years after the test. On the day of the test, what he said was, "It worked."

So much for the atomic bomb. But the thermonuclear hydrogen bomb was something else. The H-bomb was so powerful that it required an A-bomb just to *trigger* it. New York City would not want to meet an

H-bomb. Truman feared, when he learned about the possibility of developing such a weapon, that creating one was immoral, and he collected a General Advisory Committee to help him decide on whether to pursue it. The committee voted 6–2 *against* ever building a weapon so deadly; the two dissenters, physicists Enrico Fermi and Isidor Isaac Rabi, actually wanted to avoid the H-bomb as well: They merely wanted to get the Soviets to promise to avoid such weapons, too, and considered nixing an American H-bomb contingent on that assurance. Truman listened to their advice and then decided to go ahead with the research anyway, as he was afraid of the Soviets managing to piece together one of these "super-weapons" in secret. In 1952 the US successfully tested a thermonuclear hydrogen bomb; in 1953 the Soviets followed suit. The 1952 H-Bomb was a thousand times more powerful than the atomic bomb dropped on Hiroshima. This is when things really started to get dangerous.

It was Oppenheimer himself who first recognized the way in which people could live peacefully with the Bomb over their heads. Although the doctrine of mutual assured destruction (or, hilariously, MAD), was not named until a decade later, as early as 1953 the Oppenheimer Panel (of which Oppenheimer was chair) noted that a nuclear world "may enjoy a strange stability arising from the general understanding that it would be suicidal to 'throw the switch.'" Because this is the problem with nuclear weapons, a problem that only became clear gradually throughout the 1950s and '60s, as the Soviets developed atomic and then thermonuclear capabilities, and as intercontinental ballistic missiles became capable of sending thermonuclear bombs anywhere on earth: If you can use them, the other side can use them. It's like the maxim gun; it's like dynamite; it's like Dr. J. H. McLean's Aerial Rocket Torpedo. The 1983 movie *WarGames* likens thermonuclear war to tic-tac-toe: It's always a draw, and "the only winning move is not to play."

And yet we remember the inveterate use of the Maxim gun, and we have always worried that someone would play. John Mueller, in his book *Atomic Obsession*, catalogs a series of dire pronouncements in the years since Hiroshima, experts confidently predicting atomic catastrophe:

C. P. Snow in 1960 declared that nuclear violence in the next decade was a "certainty"; John McPhee in 1974 prophesied we'd see a nuclear bombing "every 4 or 5 years"; Hans Morgenthau in 1979 noted that nothing could prevent a coming nuclear war; etc.

And yet . . . not only has there been no full-scale exchange of nuclear weapons, the world has not even seen any nuclear explosion in warfare since 1945. In the early days of nuclear weapons, it was assumed that small, tactical nukes would be a staple of upcoming wars. Eisenhower said in 1955 that the armed forces could use nukes "exactly as you would use a bullet": viz., to kill the enemy. But during the Vietnam War, General William Westmoreland wanted to look into using nuclear weapons to break the siege of Khe Sanh, and Lyndon Johnson refused to even consider it. Some two decades later, General Colin Powell, assigned to study the tactical use of nuclear bombs in the Gulf War, concluded that tactical nukes were simply not practical. The US probably didn't have many tactical nukes at its disposal in the early '90s anyway: Most of them had been scrapped when it became clear that they were not being used. If you see a chart of the number of nuclear weapons showing a huge increase in the 1950s that tapers off afterward, it's in part because of all the small weapons that were once in the nuclear stockpile, later discarded.

Winston Churchill famously claimed that nuclear weapons were the only thing that had prevented World War III. Soviet expansionism being what it was—remember, in the wake of World War II, Stalin seized control of Europe as far west as the Werra River in Germany, adding a half dozen nominally independent satellite states to the de facto Soviet Empire—it was only the West's possession of nuclear weapons that prevented further Stalinist adventurism: at least in Churchill's estimation. You can quibble with Churchill here, but he actually has the best record of sniffing out the schemes of expansionist dictators *of anyone in the twentieth century*. Historian Elspeth Rostow, similarly, once said that the Bomb should be awarded the Nobel Peace Prize. It's Alfred Nobel and his dynamite come full circle! Happy ending all around. Nothing could go wrong.

After the Cuban Missile Crisis, as we've seen, Kennedy said that he estimated there had been a one in three chance the crisis would have ended in nuclear war. This is a very poor estimate! It might have been a sober estimate *during* the crisis, but by the time the crisis was over, and Kennedy had a chance to consider the risks, it was clear that there was a 0% chance that anything else would have happened. Remember: You have a fifty-fifty chance of predicting a coin only before it's flipped. After it's flipped, you know perfectly well what had to happen. *Every counterfactual* has a 0% chance of having happened. (Or approaching 0%; we're rounding down. There's always the chance that this is all a dream.)

So, although there have been several so-called close shaves with nuclear war, in fact, we now know that none of them could possibly have gone other than they did, viz. swimmingly.

The most famous such shave, Cuba aside, was in September of 1983, during a time of high Cold War tension. The USSR had earlier that month killed a US congressman and 61 other Americans (also killed, incidentally: 207 foreigners) by shooting down a lost Korean passenger plane—oh, and the congressman just happened to be the president of the John Birch Society, the most prominent and most fanatical anti-Communist organization in America; so, you can see why tensions would be high. And then on September 26 a malfunctioning Soviet warning system indicated a sneak attack from the US: five incoming nuclear missiles. The Soviet officer on duty at the time, Lt. Col. Stanislav Petrov, correctly guessed that no sneak attack worth its salt would send only five missiles, and decided not to retaliate with his own strike. If he had decided differently (Petrov later said he was only 50% certain the system was in error), and had ordered a retaliatory strike, it would have been a very bad day. But we now know that there was a 100% chance the system was in error, and a 0% chance Petrov would have retaliated. (Could a lieutenant colonel really have launched the Soviet arsenal with no upper-level say-so? Hard to say; the Soviets played it close to the vest.)

Two months later, the Soviet Union had another scare when it misinterpreted NATO military exercises as buildup for another sneak attack, and a terminally ill Soviet leader, Yuri Andropov, prepared for war from his deathbed. Nothing happened.

Later, in January of *1995*—which is to say *after the Cold War had ended* and nuclear fears had nominally been allayed—Russian radar picked up an incoming high-altitude missile. It was no malfunction this time: There really was such a missile, but it was a harmless Norwegian research rocket. The Norwegians had notified Russia of its launch (as was the custom), but the notification had not been passed on, and the Russian president Boris Yeltsin prepared, but ultimately did not launch, a massive nuclear retaliation.

And that's it. I mean, there were other, similar situations, but they came to naught. The history of nuclear warfare, it turns out, was only three days long. It ended in 1945 (as, incidentally, did the history of the cavalry charge: Polish cavalry overran German troops at the Battle of Schoenfeld, March 1, 1945; last time that ever happened). A nuclear war would be too terrible, so no one ever started one. After Nagasaki, there's nothing more to say.

Until, you know, tomorrow.

Jimmy Carter has a bad day → **NUCLEAR ARMAGEDDON**
→ *All trust evaporates, nothing changes*

I.

BUT WHAT ABOUT TOMORROW? OR, SINCE THIS IS A HISTORY book, what about yesterday? What about the time Jimmy Carter surrenders to the desire to press what *Ren and Stimpy* once called "the beautiful, shiny button; the jolly, candy-like button"? What happens then?

It will be a bad day, but no one knows how bad. That's never stopped us before with this book—no one knows how any of this stuff that never happened would have happened if it had happened, which it couldn't, but we keep guessing anyway—but with nuclear war everyone *thinks they know* and *no one knows*. Remember that Richard Nixon guessed his nuclear launch would have killed 70 million people. Ron Rosenbaum finds an expert who'll estimate that a US first strike on Russia would kill 275 million Russians immediately, with the death toll creeping up to 325 million after six weeks, and reaching 600 million counting people in neighboring countries, who may avoid the initial blast—but this number doesn't include the "tens or hundreds of millions more" killed by firestorms, which are left out of most estimates. It also doesn't include the number of Americans killed in the inevitable reply. Nixon was several decades ago, but these figures still disagree by an order or magnitude.

Rosenbaum is nothing if not a nuclear alarmist of the Oppenheimer school (he would probably say there's good reason to be alarmed, which is a fair point), so I have no way of knowing how seriously to take his numbers. In 1982 Brian Martin estimated a total of 200 million dead from a full nuclear exchange, which sounds closer to my ear. Estimates for casualties in a nuclear war are always all over the place, at least in part because no one knows the particulars of a hypothetical war that has not been fought. Approximately zero people on earth could have correctly guessed in 1914 the total number of WWI casualties—everyone (with the unique exception of Lord Kitchener, whose mustachioed face you know from the "Your Country Needs YOU" posters) thought it would last only a few months. Kitchener said three years. History says four and a third, by which point Kitchener and twenty million others had been killed. Nobody in the casualties pool had bet on twenty million and one.

A freak rainstorm can almost completely end the danger from fallout. Some scientists (such as the late Carl Sagan) have warned that nuclear explosions could cast a canopy of soot over the earth, blocking out the sun and leading to nuclear winter; on the other hand, Carl Sagan *also* predicted a similar effect from the 1991 Kuwaiti oil field fires, and that was a bust.

Also unclear is the exact extent of weaponry at play here. Many features of the US nuclear arsenal are classified, and other countries are not exactly transparent either. The total megatonnage of US nuclear weapons peaked sometime in the 1960s. Megatonnage may not be the best way of quantifying destructive power, though, as an increase in accuracy (and technological advances have certainly given us an increase in accuracy) can make a huge difference. Even as treaties have limited the number of missiles a country can have, innovations in weaseling have placed more warheads on each missile. We may have weaseled our way back to where we started.

Would Carter's missile attack on the Soviet Union trigger an all-out response? Once the missiles start flying, would both sides keep retaliating until there are no more nuclear reserves? The only actual test case of nuclear war that we have was 1. limited (in the sense that it only involved two bombs on two cities) but also 2. total (in the sense that it involved committing the entire US arsenal; the definition of ambiguous.

The prevailing assumption, at least among laymen, is that no one would ever half-ass a nuclear war. As Macbeth said:

> *I am in blood*
> *Stepp'd in so far that, should I wade no more,*
> *Returning were as tedious as go o'er.*

That's the layman's nuclear strategy in a nutshell: *In for a penny, in for a pound.* And this is the layman's assumption: that any nuclear war would end in the extermination of humanity. You'll note, for example, that this was the assumption the chapter started with (*Jimmy Carter had the opportunity to* blow up the world, *and chose not to do it*) and you probably didn't blink an eye. Robert F. Kennedy's book on the Cuban Missile Crisis trots out the possible "end of mankind" in its second paragraph. Wars, though, are no longer fought by laymen. Although the effects of nuclear war are difficult to predict beyond *really bad*, it's extremely unlikely that one would end in human extinction. First of all, the goal of nuclear war is not extinction; the goal is winning the war, which means an emphasis on military, not civilian targets. Even a war that kills two billion people—greater than Rosenbaum's estimate—still leaves five and a half billion people alive. In the number of the dead this would be much greater, but by percentage of the world population this would be about the same as were killed by the Black Death in the fourteenth century. Humans survived that one.

Aerospace engineer John Schilling once compared one particularly grim model of nuclear war to "arguing that Napoleon Bonaparte was an existential threat to humanity because all the magazines of the French Empire and its allies held enough black powder for a billion or so musket shot and there were only a billion people alive at the day."

II.

There are several obvious scenarios for a nuclear war that does not escalate into the US and Russia (or China) trying to obliterate each other. The US and Russia could fight a proxy war (as they have tended to do) blowing up each other's allies, such as Syria or Israel, without opening the can of worms that is a direct attack. A smaller nuclear power, such as India or France, could get into a conflict that larger powers wash their hands of. North Korea could bomb Los Angeles, or even Seoul; that might be the end of North Korea, but most of the world would be all right.

National Security Adviser McGeorge Bundy, fearing a spiraling escalation of retaliatory strikes, suggested that a country sustaining nuclear fire might launch back only half the missiles it was hit with. There's always time to shoot the moon later. A "Bundy strike" would be retributive (and therefore a deterrent) while still diminishing the number of deaths with each iteration. It would still be a bad day.

We're already making Jimmy Carter—whose worst sin in our reality was releasing a book of earnest poems—launch a nuclear war; we may as well make him shoot the moon as well. In for a penny. Let's have him focus on civilian targets, allowing the Russians (heck, and the Chinese) he's attacking maximum motive for striking back at our own civilians and maximum firepower to take us out. Okay. So then, there's the bad day. You know: two, three billion.

What happens next?

Albert Einstein says, on bumper stickers across the nation, "I do not know how the Third World War will be fought, but I can tell you what they will use in the Fourth—rocks!"; Einstein is wrong. A lot of people have said that Einstein is wrong about a lot of things—George Francis Gillette once said, "As a theoretical physicist, Einstein is a fair violinist," which is pretty harsh—but Gillette (author of the "backscrewing theory of gravitation") was a crackpot, and for all I know Einstein was right most of the time. But he was wrong about the rocks.

There was a time in human history when fairly basic technological innovations could be forgotten: The Sumerians discovered how to build the arch, and then promptly forgot. For over a thousand years only intermittently would someone build an arch, and then finally the Romans started using arches for everything. Look at the famous examples of ancient Greek architecture: the roof is held up by hundreds of claustrophobic columns, and it's really cramped and they just didn't know any better. No arches. But no one's going to forget how to make an arch now. There are too many references to arches, too many books and too many drawings; there are probably too many arches. No matter how many books and drawings and structures the war takes out, there'll be more. People will remember arches.

And people will not fight with rocks, because people will remember spears, and bows, and atlatls. Everyone knows what swords are, and even though most people don't have the firmest grasp on how to make a sword, everyone knows the basic (you heat metal; it's got a pointy end) idea. The Turco-Mongol leader Kichik Khan said that the sword was the most trustworthy of weapons because axes and maces do their business with only one part of the weapons, while the sword "works from head to foot." Even if the words of Kichik Khan are forgotten, the idea of a weapon that works from head to foot will be too tempting to shift to using rocks.

The Swedish folklorist Viktor Rydberg wrote that the ancients "believed the sword to be a later invention than the other kinds of weapons, and that it was from the beginning under a curse"—you know, like nukes. So, disregard swords, then: Everyone knows the basic idea of gunpowder, so even if its precise formula is lost (which it won't be, because it's been written down too many places), enough people know to look for ways to make bat guano explode that the formula would be rediscovered.

The Jimmy Carter War will destroy infrastructure, so there may be no factories rolling large numbers of guns off conveyor belts. But some guns will survive the conflagration, and if there aren't enough guns to go around, people with spears will turn their attention to making guns. It will not be lost, the rough revolver blueprint that floats vaguely, Plato-style, in the back of the head of anyone who has watched a Western. And most importantly, people will remember what it took humans until the nineteenth century to learn: that it's easier to mass-produce weapons than to handcraft them. Handcrafting is a stopgap until the factories are back up and running. World War IV will take a while to fight, because a world war requires enough infrastructure to communicate with, let alone transport large numbers of people to, different parts of the globe. But the wars between WWIII and WWIV, which will be endemic as civilization crumbles, will be fought with modern weapons. People will be very busy rebuilding their stockpiles of modern weapons.

This may sound surprising. After all, the world *just* experienced its worst day since the death of the dinosaurs: surely people will turn away from weapons in disgust; they may even turn away from science in disgust! The Romanian philosopher Mircea Eliade proposes that people will be "allergic to science for at least a century or two" after the apocalypse, and any number of science fiction characters (*Canticle for Leibowitz,* etc.) have sworn off the scientific method after science betrays them.

Yet it is all but certain that this is not what will happen. People will not turn away from weapons because there is a lesson in the Carter War. The lesson is not "war is bad" or "science is dangerous." If you believe war is bad, you can decide not to arm; but this only works if you believe your neighbors are also failing to arm. If your neighbors are not failing to arm, they will come and run roughshod over your unarmed corpse. Because the lesson of the Carter War is this: You cannot trust your neighbor to do the thing that is to everyone's benefit. Nuclear deterrence depended on no one destroying the world, and then in the Carter War everyone destroyed the world. If you turn your back on weaponry, someone else will Jimmy Carter you; if you don't turn your back on weaponry, of course, someone else will still try to Jimmy Carter you. But maybe you can Jimmy Carter them first.

It's not easy to learn from history. World War I taught the Western world a series of lessons—that war can be avoided if we all just sit down and talk things over, for example—that World War II *proved were false*. If the Allies had been hotheads who declared war on Germany in 1938, the war would have lasted three weeks; they did not because World War I had "taught them a lesson."

But the lesson of the Carter War is inescapable. The world placed all its eggs in the basket of mutual trust, and Jimmy Carter kicked over that basket.

Civilizations have founding myths. You can say our current civilization's founding myth is the Garden of Eden (moral: do what you're told) or you can say our current civilization's founding myth is the American Revolution (moral: don't do what you're told). But the post-Carter civilization has only one founding myth, and only one moral. And after a long time, after the world gets back on its feet, and nation-states reassert themselves, this will be the moral people remember: Do not trust.

When you (in our world, today) hand a store clerk $2.00 for a $1.19 purchase, you wait for change, unafraid; because you know that only a crazy store would take the cash and refuse to give you anything back. It would be self-destructive. The profit would never justify the harm the store's reputation would suffer. We don't even need to run this mental calculation while shopping: We have a bond of confidence, however small, that lets us know that the clerk can be trusted, if only for the few seconds it takes to hand over our change.

In a post-Carter world, that level of trust is unavailable. You tell the clerk, "I have two dollars here." The clerk readies eighty-one cents. Simultaneously, and cautiously, like suspicious schoolchildren swapping toys on the count of three, you exchange the dollars for the change and a can of soda. Only when you have stepped away from the register can you begin to relax. Have a Coke and a smile.

So much of our daily lives depends on a small level of trust, a trust that other people will not do something willfully self-destructive for no reason. The New York City subways used to have seats made of rattan, and later a fake leather called velon. These seats were comfortable, but easy to destroy, and yet they lasted in the subways for decades, because vandalizing subway seats would be pointless and self-defeating. There was no need to guard against a crime that could have no motive!

By the mid-1960s, though, this was no longer true. A spate of velon seats sliced through, the padding scattered, led to the beginning of fiberglass seats, which could be scored but not destroyed by a pen knife. By the time Jimmy Carter took office, all seats were molded plastic, and the comfortable days of wicker and pleather a distant memory.

In other words, the post-Carter world would resemble our own post-Carter world.

But it would probably also be worse.

HOW CAN YOU MAKE THINGS THAT
DIDN'T HAPPEN HAPPEN?

A philosophical postlude

I.

Friedrich Nietzsche said that we should love the world just the way it is, no matter how it is. This is really hard to do, and Nietzsche died in the nuthatch. The rest of us, I assume, will want to change something.

Now that you've read this book and gotten some ideas about things that didn't happen, you'll probably want to travel back in time and make a few changes so that the things that didn't happen do. You could prevent World War I; you could keep Columbus out of America. This desire is only natural! I'm not here to tell you what to do.

But if you do decide to travel back in time and change history, there are two caveats. An infinite number of caveats, actually, because there are an infinite number of unintended consequences. Also, there's a good chance that you simply cannot change the past by traveling back in time, because if you travel back in time you'll simply be traveling back to a time that already happened. You were already back in time! It's been taken into account! That's why the philosopher Monte Cook suggests that you'll maximize your chances of success by traveling back to a time when the historical record indicates a strange visitor appeared. Maybe it was you!

But if it turns out that you can change the past . . . you may be worried about accidentally killing your parents, or accidentally preventing them from ever hooking up, Marty McFly–style. I am here to tell you (and this is the first caveat) that things are much more dangerous than that.

II.

If you travel back in time and meet someone, you have killed all his or her unborn children. I mean, those children will never be born. You don't have to alter anyone's romantic life; you don't even have to alter anyone's life in any way they're aware of. All you have to do is say *hi*. Or say *hi* to someone who will later say *hi* to that someone.

Saying *hi* to someone won't alter most parts of a life. If you say *hi* to a juvenile version of your father, he might say *hi* back, and walk away slightly puzzled. The rest of his day will go the same as before. Most things that happen to you don't alter your life. You can get hit in the face with a pie, and by the next day your life is probably back to normal. You'll slide out of bed on the same side; you'll put on the usual clothes; you'll take the same path to school or work. Every day is pretty much the same, and one pie or one *hi* won't change it.

Of course, every day is only *pretty much* the same. "The same" has a lot of wiggle room. You put your feet down on the carpet as you slide out of bed, but they do not hit the exact same spot every time. They may hit the same part of the carpet, but every day they are a millimeter left or millimeter right. Your two feet make a slightly different angle, even if it's only off by a degree. You take the same route to school, but your feet do not land in yesterday's footsteps exactly. The knot you make in your shoelaces is slightly different every day; every knot is a fingerprint, and every day that fingerprint is different.

If someone stops you and says *hi*, your day after that will be pretty much the same as before the *hi*. But it will, inevitably, be slightly different. Not so different that you'd notice, but all your actions will come a second later than they would have had you not wasted a second returning the greeting. Your footsteps will not land in the exact same place they would have; they'll land close, of course, because your day is going to be pretty much the same. But it's not the same; it's like a new day, and every footstep is a little off. When you get into bed at night, it will be a second later, and you'll toss and turn in a slightly different order. The pattern of wrinkles in your sheet will be slightly different, as it is every day.

And this is true for the rest of your life. Every day will be slightly different from the hypothetical way it would have been had no one said *hi*. There's no reset button that puts your life back to the previous stream.

Perhaps this tiny *hi* difference will matter in your life—*that time a car misses you by an inch*—but probably it won't. The classicist Arthur Platt once wrote that "nearly everybody was born in 1809"—Darwin, Dickens, Lincoln, Poe, Tennyson—but some people died in 1809 as well, of course, and one death is illustrative here. In 1809 Jean Lannes (the Napoleonic general) was sitting during a lull in battle with his legs crossed, dangling in a furrow. A stray cannonball happened to hit him right where his legs were crossed, breaking both legs at once. He lingered a week, and then died. If he'd only sat with his legs splayed, the cannonball would have missed him. Perhaps a small difference would have saved General Lannes. One year earlier, at the Battle of Oravais in Finland, Lieutenant-Colonel Johann Reinhold von Törne had stood with his legs apart while a bullet passed between his knees and destroyed his coattails. That could have been Lannes!

But that's the exception. If you walk into the big job interview a second earlier or later, it doesn't matter. The epoch-making catch that wins the game is unaffected. Your life is probably mostly the same, because almost everything either *a.* is equipped with enough wiggle room that the difference is immaterial, or *b.* gives you enough information that you can correct for the difference. The interview is case *a.* and the catch is case *b.* Most everything is covered by one or the other.

Except sex, when a hundred million sperm cells are all in a photo finish to fertilize that egg. The least difference in timing on the part of either partner will cause a different sperm to win. Essentially, you're guaranteed to have a different zygote.

So, if you go back in time and disrupt your parents' lives in the slightest way, or if you disrupt the lives of anyone who will ever meet them, or the lives of anyone who will meet anyone who will meet them—the eventual result will be a different zygote in your mother's womb, and a different zygote is not going to grow into you.

If you travel far enough back in time, you may end up causing pretty much everyone who would have been alive in the twenty-first century to be a different person, you included.

You will, essentially, have murdered an entire world.

III.

That's the least of your worries, though. The real problem is that no one knows how to travel through time. You'll never even have a chance to murder yourself before you're born!

Perhaps you are a clever fellow and plan to *invent* a method of time travel as a necessary first step. It's so crazy it just might work.

There's a difficulty, though. You'll notice that there is a distinct lack of time travelers from the forty-fifth century dropping in on the present, as you would expect them to if people ever invented time travel. Whether or not you can invent time travel right now, the evidence indicates that no one else in the future history of the world has ever been able to do it. Why might that be?

There are only two real possibilities. Either traveling backward in time is literally impossible, or it's possible but so complicated that humanity becomes extinct before anyone actually masters its techniques.

If the former, then of course you should not waste your time pursuing a quixotic impossibility! But if the latter, then most definitely you should not pursue time travel, because most likely the human race will become extinct before you succeed in your goal. The more progress you make toward traveling back in time, the closer the *terminus ad quem* of humanity gets! You are literally ushering in our extinction. You probably want to stop your research immediately!

But I'm not here to tell you what to do.

NOTES

Tip of the hat to Daniel Nayeri for coming up with this whole idea. **v** Francis Leo Golden, *Tales for Salesmen* (Pocket, 1954) 86. **xi** Lewis Carroll, *Complete Works* (Vintage, 1976) 617. **xii** Bede *Historia ecclesiastica gentis Anglorum et Historia abbatum, et Epistola ad Ecgberctum, cum Epistola Bonifacii ad Cudberthum* (Clarendon, 1881) 4.

0

1 Jane Austen, *Northanger Abbey* (Penguin, 2003) 97. **2** Paul Rée, "Determinism and the Illusion of Moral Responsibility" https://web.nmsu.edu/~jvessel/Ree-D&MR.pdf (thanks to Jeff Marques who left this essay, as photocopies of mysterious provenance, lying around his room) *passim*; A. B. Paine, *Mark Twain* (Harper & Bros., 1912) 397. **3** Imagine two animals: Arthur Schopenhauer, *Essays and Aphorisms* (Penguin, 2004) 42. **4** entire print run: *ib.* 27; still water: Schopenhauer, *On the Freedom of the Will* (Blackwell, 1985) 43. **6** Plutarch, *The Rise and Fall of Athens* (Penguin, 1984) 301. **7** Ashida Kim, *Secrets of the Ninja* (Citadel, 1981) 83.

1. WORLD WAR I

9 James Fiske, *Under Fire for Servia* (Saalfield, 1915) 87. **10** Clair W. Hayes, *The Boy Allies with the Cossacks* (Burt, 1916) 111. **11** John T. McCutcheon, *In Africa* (Bobbs-Merrill, 1910) 2; Mary Shelley, *Collected Supernatural and Weird Fiction* (Leotaur, 2010) vol. I, 276. **14** Jim Jones: Jeff Guinn, *The Road to Jonestown* (Simon & Schuster, 2017) 448; Barbara Tuchman, *The Proud Tower* (Macmillan, 1966) 147 (but the quote should probably be attributed not to Eliot but to his cousin Charles Eliot Norton; *v.* Richard Hershberger, *Baseball Research Journal* [Spring 2017], sabr.org/journal/article/with-a-deliberate-attempt-to-deceive-correcting-a-quotation-misattributed-to-charles-eliot-president-of-harvard/); H. Irving Hancock, *The High School Left End* (Altemus, 1910) 240–41. **15** W. B. Yeats, *The Tower* (Scribner, 2004) 38, 34. **16** "shrill, demented," etc.: *Poems of the Great War* (Penguin, 1998) 3, 125; "until peace": Charles H. Sorley, *Marlborough* (Cambridge UP, 1919) 73; Alexandre Dumas, *The Three Musketeers* (Little, Brown, 1900) 62; H. Irving Hancock, *Uncle Sam's Boys in the Ranks* (Altemus, 1910) 12, 18. **17** Owen: Jon Silkin, *Out of Battle* (Palgrave, 2001) 225; Edward Gibbon, *Decline and Fall of the Roman Empire* (Penguin, 1995) vol. II, 340; Oxford University: Daniel Grotta, *J.R.R. Tolkien* (Running Press, 1992) 60; André Varagnac: Tuchman, *The Guns of August* (Macmillan, 1962) 439. **18** "the flower of Scottish gentility": H. Johnson, *Immortal Lycanthropes* (Clarion, 2012) 124; "all was lost": Walter Scott, *Familiar Letters* (David Douglas, 1894) vol. I, 72; Clemenceau: Roger Parkinson, *Origins of*

World War One (Wayland, 1973) 72; political cartoon: Stephen Hess and Sandy Northrop, *Drawn and Quartered* (Elliott & Clark, 1996) 85; *Peter Pan*: Jackie Wullschläger, *Inventing Wonderland* (Free Press, 1995) 110; James Hilton, *Lost Horizon* (Washington Square, 1965) 181. **19** *Punch*: Constance Rover, *The Punch Book of Women's Rights* (A.S. Barnes, 1971) 112; few would vote: Robert Graves and Alan Hodge, *The Long Week-End* (Norton, 1963) 21. **20** Charles Sheldon, *In His Steps* (Advance, 1897) 106, 113, 114; John William Kirton, *The Water Drinkers of the Bible* (National Temperance Publication Depot, 1885) 141; Alexandre Dumas, *The Count of Monte Cristo* (Grosset & Dunlap, 1901) 26; F. E. Smith: Paul Fussell, *The Great War and Modern Memory* (Oxford UP, 2000) 66; Hardy: William Frederic Hoehn, *No-License in Quincy* (Eastern, 1899) 91; 1888 etiquette guide: *The Correct Thing in Good Society* (Dana Estes, 1888) 82; 1828 play: Douglas William Jerrold, *Fifteen Years in the Life of a Drunkard* (Samuel French, n.d.) 21. **21** "saloons deprived women": Mabel Willebrandt, *The Inside of Prohibition* (Bobbs-Merrill, 1929) 278; Emma Alton: *The Fountain and the Bottle* (Case, Tiffany, 1850) 48ff.; Anne Brontë, *The Tenant of Wildfell Hall* (North Books, 2003) 193, 353; Catt: Elizabeth Frost-Knappman and Kathryn Cullen-DuPont, *Women's Suffrage in America* (Facts on File, 2005) 351; "professional wets": Willebrandt 264. **22** Samuel Vanderlip Leech, *Three Inebriates* (Phillips & Hunt, 1886) 80; Willebrandt 150, 19, 30ff.; Edmund Pearson, *Queer Books* (Doubleday, Doran, 1928) 15. **23** Capone: Martin Short, *The Rise of the Mafia* (John Blake, 2009) 68; real estate: "Mob Rule in New York Construction Depicted," *NYT* 4/30/1988 nytimes.com/1988/04/30/nyregion/mob-role-in -new-york-construction-depicted.html and Robert O'Harrow Jr., "Trump Swam in Mob-Infested Waters in Early Years as an NYC Developer," *WP* 10/16/2015 washingtonpost.com /investigations/trump-swam-in-mob-infested-waters-in-early-years-as-an-nyc-developer /2015/10/16/3c75b918-60a3-11e5-b38e-06883aacba64_story.html.

2. VIKINGS IN NORTH AMERICA

25 *Greenlanders' Saga*: Magnus Magnusson and Hermann Pálsson, eds., *The Vinland Sagas* (Penguin, 1985) 50; Jordanes: Gwyn Jones, *History of the Vikings* (Oxford UP, 1969) 22. **26** arrows ambidextrously: Oddr Snorrason, *Saga of Olaf Tryggvason* (Cornell UP, 2003) 100. **27** Helge Ingstad, *Westward to Vinland* (Harper Colophon, 1972). **29** things were not going well: the following pages are indebted to chapters 6–8 of Jared Diamond's *Collapse* (Penguin, 2004). **30** Fimbulwinter: Lee M. Hollander, trans., *The Poetic Edda* (UTexasP, 1987) 8, and *v.* 50n. **33** Henry Rowe Schoolcraft, *Historical and Statistical Information* (Lippincott, Grambo, 1851) vol. I, 119. **34** David Hatcher Childress, *Technology of the Gods* (Adventures Unlimited, 2000) 165ff. **35** split in two: William H. Prescott, *The Conquest of Peru* (Heritage, 1957) 123; Bartolomé de las Casas, *A Short Account of the Destruction of the Indies* (Penguin, 1992) 21. **36** outbreak in Greenland: Donald R. Hopkins, *Princes and Peasants* (UChicagoP, 1983) 29. **39** Beothuk never adopted firearms: Ingeborg Marshall, *History and Ethnography of the Beothuk* (McGill-Queens UP, 1998) 421. **41** *viruela*: Although this word resembles a diminutive of *virus*, the words are etymologically distinct; *huey zahuatl*: Kim MacQuarrie, *Last Days of the Incas* (Simon & Schuster, 2007) 48; Sweden, possibly Germany: Hopkins 29.

3. ALEXANDER THE GREAT

43 Safder Ali Khan: Patrick French, *Younghusband* (HarperCollins, 1994) 79; Ethiopian manuscript: E. A. Wallis Budge, ed., *Life and Exploits of Alexander the Great* (Clay & Sons, 1896) 385; John Gower, *Confessio Amantis* (UTorontoP, 1986) 351 (VI.1799); D. T. Niane, ed., *Sundiata* (Longman, 2001) 52. **44** Hannibal: Adrian Goldsworthy, *Punic Wars* (Cassell, 2001) 328; some have alleged: Plutarch, *Age of Alexander* (Penguin, 1973) 333 and Paul Doherty, *The Death of Alexander the Great* (Carroll & Graf, 2004) *passim*; Saki: H. H. Munro, *Rise of the Russian Empire* (Grant Richards, 1900) 109. **45** Cassander: Waldemar Heckel, *Who's Who in the Age of Alexander the Great* (Blackwell, 2006) 79. **48** "pen and paper": Plutarch, penelope.uchicago.edu/Thayer/E/Roman/Texts/Plutarch /Lives/Eumenes*.html. **49** *Secret History*: R. P. Lister, *Genghis Khan* (Dorset, 1990) 26. **50** absent, or deaf, or uncaring: Peter Green, *Alexander to Actium* (UCaliforniaP, 1990) 55. **51** war elephants: Shubha Khandekar and Souren Ray, *Megasthenes* (India Book House, 2007) 4. **53** knock-kneed: W. W. Tarn, *Antigonus Gonatas* (Clarendon, 1913) 14; G. W. F. Hegel, *Philosophy of History* (Batoche, 2001) 289, 244 (*v.* Alan Ryan, *On Politics* [Norton, 2012] 668–9); Egyptian text: Budge 355; Baldesar Castiglione, *The Book of the Courtier* (Penguin, 1976) 312. **54** Syriac Christian: Emeri van Donzel and Andrea Schmidt, *Gog and Magog in Early Syriac and Islamic Sources* (Brill, 2009) 20; Jacob Abbott, *Alexander the Great* (Harper & Bros., 1848) 278; Arrian, *The Anabasis of Alexander* (Hodder & Stoughton, 1884) 369–70; Posidippos: Edward Storer, ed., *The Windflowers of Asklepia- des and the Poems of Poseidippos* (Egoist, 1920) 22. **55** Carthaginian territory: Diodorus Siculus, *Library of History*, penelope.uchicago.edu/Thayer/E/Roman/Texts/Diodorus _Siculus/20B*.html (XX.40§41); Livy, *Rome and Italy* (Penguin, 1982) 239. **57** John Mandeville, *Travels* (Penguin, 1983) 173–5. **58** H. G. Wells, *The World Set Free* (Dutton, 1914) 90; Apollonius: Kenneth Sylvan Guthrie, *The Gospel of Apollonius of Tyana* (Platonist, 1900) 8; G. R. S. Mead, *Apollonius of Tyana the Philosopher-Reformer of the First Century A.D.* (Theosophical, 1901) 75.

4. THE INCA EMPIRE

59 Robert Penn Warren, *Portrait of a Father* (UP of Kentucky, 1988) 58; Winston Churchill, *History of the English-Speaking Peoples* (Bantam, 1963) vol. I, 120; Jacob Abbott, *William the Conqueror* (Harper & Bros., 1854) 91; Prescott, *Conquest of Peru* 203; John S. C. Abbott, *Ferdinand De Soto* (Dodd, Mead, 1873) 73; Lawton B. Evans, *America First* (Milton Bradley, 1926) 10. **61** "birds in my dominions": Prescott 239 ("somewhat of a hyperbole" notes Prescott). **63** Bernal Díaz, *The Conquest of New Spain* (Penguin, 1963) 289. **64** Prescott 28; Kaïumarth: Sabine Baring-Gould, *Legends of the Patriarchs and Prophets* (William L. Allison, n.d.) 93. **65** Edward P. Lanning, *Peru before the Incas* (Prentice-Hall, 1967) 166. **67** Prescott 171. **68** Harvey Kurtzman, *Weird Science* #5 (Russ Cochran, Septem- ber 1993). **69** Ronald Reagan, speech at the UN, 9/21/1987, c-span.org/video/?57653-1/united -nations-speeches 1:06. **70** death toll: MacQuarrie, *Last Days of the Inca* 229. **71** one third the population of Bengal: Hopkins, *Princes and Peasants* 145. **72** Thomas Babington Macaulay,

History of England (Dent, 1953) vol. V, 170. **73** Doboyba and Zenu: Prescott 89. **74** "a more lamentable explosion": Macaulay, *History* vol. V, 163. **75** prophecy spread: Lillian Estelle Fisher, *The Last Inca Revolt* (UOklahomaP, 1966) 116.

5. FREEMASONRY

76 Thomas Paine, *On the Origin of Freemasonry* (Elliot & Crissy, 1810) 3. **77** "t t ot": *King Solomon and His Followers* (Allen, 1947) 184; Manly P. Hall, *The Secret Teachings of All Ages* (Philosophical Research Society, 1977) 176; less eccentric authors: Michael Baigent and Richard Leigh, *The Temple and the Lodge* (Arcade, 1993) 193ff. **78** Henry Adamson, *The Muses Threnodie* (George Johnston, 1774) 84; Aberdeen: Jasper Ridley, *The Freemasons* (Arcade, 2001) 23; "good character and reputation": nymasons.org/site/discover; Carl Glick, *A Treasury of Masonic Thought* (Thomas Y. Crowell, 1953) xi, 256. **79** John Coustos, *Unparalleled Sufferings of John Coustos, Who Nine Times Underwent the Most Cruel Tortures Ever Invented by Man, and Sentenced to the Galley Four Years, by Command of the Inquisitors at Lisbon, in Order to Extort from him the Secrets of Free-Masonry* (Sketchley, 1790) 26–7; "world is in pain": W. Chappell, *A Collection of National English Airs* (Chappell, 1840) 61. **80** martyrology: M. W. Redding, *The Scarlet Book of Free Masonry; Containing a Thrilling and Authentic Account of the Imprisonment, Torture, and Martyrdom of Free Masons and Knights Templars, for the Past Six Hundred Years* (Redding, 1885) 3. **81** 1830 Maine: Allen E. Roberts, *Freemasonry in American History* (Macoy, 1985) 237. **82** Cornwallis: Baigent and Leigh 214ff; even crazier sources: Neal Wilgus, *The Illuminoids* (Sun Books, 1981) 31. **83** P. Hal Sims, *Pinochle Pointers* (U.S. Playing Card, 1935) 7; Hunt: Edward Storer, ed., *Leigh Hunt* (Herbert & Daniel, n.d.) 38; 1895 collection: Grace Townsend, ed., *The Speaker's Companion* (Monarch, 1895) 9. **84** Horatio Alger, *Ragged Dick and Mark, the Match Boy* (Collier, 1962) 352; Edward S. Ellis, *High Twelve* (Macoy, 1912) 209. **85** M. Hall 140; Heroes of America, etc.: James M. McPherson, *Battle Cry of Freedom* (Ballantine, 1989) 695, 763–4, 783. **86** drunken jerks: Joseph Hayes, "The Mischievous 'Ghost Hoaxers' of 19th-Century Australia" atlasobscura.com/articles/ghost-hoaxing; "Beeta Lamda": William Moulton Marston and H. G. Peter, *Wonder Woman Archives* (DC, 1998) vol. I, 58. **87** Coustos 45. **88** Karl Popper, *Conjectures and Refutations* (Routledge, 2002) 165–6.

6. SIGMUND FREUD

90 Martin Amis, *The War against Cliché* (Hyperion, 2001) 282; "Viennese quack": Peter Quennell, ed., *Vladimir Nabokov: A Tribute* (Weidenfeld & Nicolson, 1979) 124. **91** faith healing: E. M. Cioran, *Anathemas and Admirations* (Arcade, 1987) 16; Louis Auchincloss, *Motiveless Malignity* (Houghton Mifflin, 1969) 154. **92** live rats: Sigmund Freud, *Three Case Histories* (Collier, 1993) 13; Claude Lévi-Strauss, *Structural Anthropology* (Basic Books, 1974) 217. **93** Mark Leyner, *My Cousin, My Gastroenterologist* (Harmony, 1990) 5; Westermarck: Steven Pinker, *How the Mind Works* (Norton, 1997) 460; "second mother": Frederick C. Crews, *Freud: The Making of an Illusion* (Metropolitan, 2017) 632. **94** Einstein: Alice Calaprice, ed., *The New Quotable Einstein* (Princeton UP, 2005) 261. **95** "primeval sexual cult": Crews 503; "fairy tale": *ib*. 498. **96** "not finished": *ib*. 494, 544; medallion inscribed: Eli Zaretsky, *Secrets of the Soul* (Knopf, 2004) 76; Brothers Grimm faked: John M. Ellis, *One Fairy Story Too Many* (UChicagoP, 1983); Augustine, *Confessions* (New City Press, 1997) 201. **97** Eric Hoffer, *The True Believer* (Harper Perennial, 1985) 110; René Girard, *"To Double Business Bound"* (Johns Hopkins, 1988) *passim*. **98** "In the mountains": Friedrich Nietzsche, *Thus Spake Zarathustra* (Modern Library, 1917) 39; evidence shows: A. H. Chapman and Miriam Chapman-Santana, "The Influence of Nietzsche on Freud's Ideas," *British Journal of Psychiatry* 166 (1995) 251–3; "'I have done that'": Nietzsche, *Beyond Good and Evil* (Penguin, 2003) 80. **99** Abigail Van Buren, *The Best of Dear Abby* (Andrews McMeel, 1989) 69; "inferiority complex": Edmond Hamilton and Curt Swan, *World's Finest Comics* #143; (DC, August 1964); Fredric Wertham, *Seduction of the Innocent* (Rinehart, 1954) 191; Ber gler: Karal Ann Marling, *As Seen on TV* (Harvard UP, 1996) 11; Spock: William McDonald, *The New York Times Book of the Dead* (Running Press, 2016) 271. **100** Erik Erikson, *Young Man Luther* (Norton, 1993) 19; Dear Abby clippings: Van Buren 44 (these are not literally clippings). **102** Samuel Taylor Coleridge, *Table Talk* (Routledge, 1884) 269; Sophocles, *Ajax* (J. Hall, 1906) 20; August Schlegel, *Course of Lectures on Dramatic Art and Literature* (AMS, 1965) 109. **103** *Trachiniae*: René Girard, *Violence and the Sacred* (Johns Hopkins, 1979) 190ff.; William Blake, *Marriage of Heaven and Hell* (Dover, 1994) 19. **104** Thomas Carlyle, *The French Revolution* (Thomas Nelson, 1902) 673; Martha Louise Rayne, *Gems of Deportment* (Tyler, 1881) 115, 119. **105** Helen Gurley Brown, *Sex and the Single Girl* (Pocket, 1964) 4, 7.

7. ATHENS AND SPARTA

107 Miguel de Cervantes, *Don Quixote* (Penguin, 2000) 143. **108** Gibbon vol. I, 313, Snorre Sturlason, *Heimskringla* (Dover, 1990) 644; Edmund Burke, *Reflections on the Revolution in France* (Penguin, 1984) 169; Everard Digby: John Heneage Jesse, *Memoirs of the Court of England During the Reign of the Stuarts* (Richard Bentley, 1855) vol. II, 191. **109** Lord Macaulay, *Works* (Longmans, Green, 1875) vol. VII, 702, 692; "Athenian War": Donald Kagan, *The Peloponnesian War* (Viking, 2003) 2n. **111** influenced Hitler: Yvonne Sherratt, *Hitler's Philosophers* (Yale UP, 2013) 58; "rough heroic valor": Ernst Haeckel, *History of Creation* (D. Appleton, 1880) 170–1. **112** "sack needs grain": Herodotus, *History* (UChicagoP, 1987) 231–2 (3.46); Plutarch, *Rise and Fall of Athens* 246; Bion: Diogenes Laertius, *Lives of Eminent Philosophers (Loeb)* (Harvard UP, 1925) vol. I, 427 (IV.49); Anaxarchus: James A. Froude, *Short Studies on Great Subjects* (Longmans, Green, 1886) vol. IV, 412. **115** "drew his sword": *Plutarch's Nicias and Alcibiades* (Scribner's, 1912) 63. **123** Plutarch: *Athens* 117. **124** Plato, *The Trial and Death of Socrates* (Hackett, 2000) 34ff. **125** Aelian, *Varia Historia (Loeb)* (Harvard UP, 1997) 199 (IV.16). **127** *Thucydides* (Clarendon, 1900) vol. I, 242–3. **128** *Thucydides* vol. II, 284, vol. I, 244; Ismenias: Aelian 45 (I.21). **129** fifth to the fourth century: Victor Hanson, *A War Like No Other* (Random House, 2005) 291. **130** Friedrich Nietzsche, *The Birth of Tragedy and The Case of Wagner* (Vintage, 1967) 96; Macaulay, *Critical and Historical Essays* (Longman, Brown, Green, and Longmans, 1852) vol. I, 382; Francis Bacon, *Philosophical Works* (Routledge, 1905) 885, etc.; Gregory Bar-Hebræus, *The Laughable Stories* (Luzac,

1897) 11–12 (I modernized the deliberate archaisms of this text; this story in older texts is told of Diogenes the Cynic: e.g., in Diogenes Laertius vol. II, 59 [VI.58]); Farid ud-Din Attar, *The Conference of the Birds* (Interlink, 2003) 57; *The Riverside Chaucer* (Houghton Mifflin, 1987) 735. **131** "violently ignorant onagers and asses": John Gower, *Complete Works* (Clarendon, 1902) vol. IV, 27 (*Vox Clamantis* I.191). **132** Stedinger: William Mackay, *Extraordinary Popular Delusions and the Madness of Crowds* (Harmony, 1980) 473–5; T. S. Eliot, *Murder in the Cathedral* (Harcourt, Brace & World, 1963) 12; Harrington: Ryan, *On Politics* 509; Algernon Sidney, *Discourses Concerning Government* (J. Darby, 1704) 123 (II.xvii). **133** Archestratus: Plutarch, *Athens* 165. **134** Henry Ward Beecher et al., *Universal Suffrage* (Rand & Avery, 1865) 5 (on p. 6 Beecher explicitly says: "On no ground, except that of crime, can you deny the elective franchise to any class," without for one moment meaning "*any* class"); Alice Duer Miller, *Are Women People?* (Doran, 1915) 92ff. **135** Aristotle, *Politics* (Penguin, 1992) 363 (VI.ii) (*cf.* 286 [IV.25]). **136** R. J. Rummel, "War Isn't This Century's Biggest Killer," *Wall Street Journal* 7/7/1986, hawaii.edu/powerkills/WSJ.ART.HTM; *id.*, *Statistics of Democide* (LIT Verlag, 1999), 1, hawaii.edu/powerkills/NOTE5.HTM; *id.*, *Death by Government* (Transaction, 1994, 6, hawaii.edu/powerkills/DBG.TAB1.2.GIF. **137** two witches per day: Mackay 463 (*cum grano salis*); *Holinshed's Chronicles* (J. Johnson, 1808) vol. V, 269; Snorra Sturlusonar, *Heimskringla Eda Sogur Noregs Konunga* (W. Schultz, 1870) 77; Snorre, *Heimskringla* 68.

8. WORLD WAR II

139 Sebastian Haffner, *The Meaning of Hitler* (Harvard UP, 1979) 49. **140** E. V. Lucas and George Morrow, *Swollen-Headed William* (Methuen, 1914) 4; Canetti: George Steiner, *In Bluebeard's Castle* (Yale UP, 1971) 61. **141** Hitler: William L. Shirer, *The Rise and Fall of the Third Reich* (Simon & Schuster, 1960) 119. **143** Baldwin: William Manchester, *The Last Lion: Winston Spencer Churchill,* vol. II: *Alone, 1932–1940* (Delta, 1989) 181; "The shame": *March of Time* 9/16/1938, otr.com/marchtime.htm. **144** Chamberlain: Manchester, *Last Lion* vol. II, 300; literally vomited: *ib.* 524. **146** Winston Churchill, *The Gathering Storm* (Houghton Mifflin, 1948) 337. **147** *Mein Kampf:* David Kahn, *Seizing the Enigma* (Houghton Mifflin, 1991) 67; George Orwell, *Collected Essays, Journalism, and Letters* (Harcourt Brace Jovanovich, 1968) vol. II, 401. **149** government memo: Shirer 833. **150** Reynaud: John Lukacs, *The Hitler of History* (Vintage, 1997) 77. **151** Roberts: Douglas Martin, "Lord Aberconway, 89, Met with Göring Secretly in '39," *NYT* 2/8/2003, nytimes.com/2003/02/08/world/lord-aberconway-89-met-with-goring-secretly-in-39 .html. **152** Truman: Paul Johnson, *A History of the American People* (HarperCollins, 1997) 804; G. K. Chesterton, *What's Wrong with the World* (Dodd, Mead, 1927) 32.

9. JULIAN THE APOSTATE

153 Bede, *Historia ecclesiastica* 18 (I.vi). **154** Trajan: Robert L. Wilken, *The Christians as the Romans Saw Them* (Yale UP, 1984) 28; 40% per decade: Rodney Stark, *The Rise of Christianity* (Princeton UP, 1996) 6; Ammianus Marcellinus, *The Later Roman Empire* (Penguin, 1986) 98; Commodus: David Magie, trans., *Historia Augusta (Loeb)* (Harvard UP, 1932) vol. I, 305; Plutarch, *The Dryden Plutarch* (E. P. Dutton, 1917) vol. III, 467. **156** Diogenes the Cynic: Diogenes Laertius 39 (VI.37); thirteenth-century German poet: Heinrich von dem Türlin, *The Crown* (UNevadaP, 1989) 36. **157** Plutarch: *Alexander* 266. **160** Julius Caesar himself: Gibbon vol. I, 719; Tacitus, *The Agricola and The Germania* (Penguin, 1971) 81. **162** newspaper syndicates: Martin Sheridan, *Comics and Their Creators* (Hyperion, 1977) 20; Harington: *Select Epigrams* (Sampson Low, 1797) vol. I, 1; Ammianus 239. **163** Marcus Minucius Felix: Alexander Roberts and James Donaldson, eds., *The Ante-Nicene Fathers* (Scribner's, 1904) vol. IV, 172ff. **165** "a barber that I want": Gibbon vol. I, 853. **166** the casualties: Ammianus 284. **169** Aldhelm, *Poetic Works* (Brewer, 1985) 124 (although this is my own translation, based on a Latin text file Neil Manterfield sent me—thanks, Neil!); Issac Newton, *Theological Manuscripts* (Liverpool UP, 1950) 61ff. **171** A. H. Armstrong, *Plotinus* (Collier, 1962) 45. **172** Gaetano Negri, *Julian the Apostate* (Scribner's, 1905) vol. I, 265; Henrik Ibsen, *Emperor and Galilean* (Heinemann, 1911) 359. **173** the Senate was still pagan: Gibbon vol. II, 74. **174** Theos Hypsistos: Polymnia Athanassiadi and Michael Frede, eds., *Pagan Monotheism in Late Antiquity* (Oxford UP, 1999) 81ff.; "Great Pan is dead!": Plutarch, *Moral Essays* (Penguin, 1971) 54 (for further explication, *v.* Giorgio de Santillana and Hertha von Dechend, *Hamlet's Mill* [Gambit, 1969] 276ff.). **175** Cicero, *Tusculan Disputations, Etc.* (Harper & Bros., 1899) 347, 340, 255–56; Gregory of Nazianzus: Athanassiadi and Frede 95. **177** Ernest Renan, *History of the Origins of Christianity* (Mathieson, 1875) vol. VII, 332; David Ulansey, *The Origins of the Mithraic Mysteries* (Oxford UP, 1991)—major spoiler. **178** every single Mandaean priest: Andrew Philip Smith, *John the Baptist and the Last Gnostics* (Watkins, 2016) 46. **179** Béroul, *The Romance of Tristan* (Penguin 1978) 101, 103.; Ælfric: Bruce Mitchell and Fred C. Robinson, *A Guide to Old English* (Blackwell, 1997) 191. **181** al-Biruni: *Alberuni's India* (Norton, 1971) 35, 36, 43, 65, 67, 105, etc. **182** flowers for heads: Finbarr Barry Flood, "Lost Histories of a Licit Figural Art," *International Journal of Middle East Studies* vol. 45, no. 3 (2013), jstor.org/stable/43303038.

10. VICE PRESIDENT HENRY WALLACE

187 "Pop has tried": John C. Culver and John Hyde, *American Dreamer: A Life of Henry Wallace* (Norton, 2000) 313; faster-growing crops: William L. Brown, "H. A. Wallace and the Development of Hybrid Corn," *The Annals of Iowa* vol. 47, no. 2 (1983) 179. **189** Gordon: Lytton Strachey, *Eminent Victorians* (Anodos, 2019) 123 (but *cf.* Demetrius C. Boulger, *The Life of Gordon, Major-General, R.E., C.B: Turkish Field-Marshal, Grand Cordon Medjidieh, and Pasha; Chinese Titu [Field-Marshal], Yellow Jacket Order* [Unwin, 1896] vol. II, 45ff); Norman Littell: Culver and Hyde 356; Dahl: Jennet Conant, *The Irregulars* (Simon & Schuster, 2008) 124. **191** Robert Hannegan: Culver and Hyde 191; "spirit of liberty": George S. Caldwell, ed., *The Wit and Wisdom of Harry S Truman* (Stein & Day, 1973) 71. **192** North Burma: Ruth Benedict, *The Chrysanthemum and the Sword* (Mariner, 2008) 38; "model prisoner": *ib.* 41. **194** over a million: William Manchester, *American Caesar* (Dell, 1979) 438; Japanese diplomats: Justin H. Libby, "The Search for a Negotiated Peace," *World Affairs* vol. 156, no. 1 (1993) 35–45, jstor.org/stable/20672371; unconditional surrender: Ronald Takaki, *Hiroshima* (Little, Brown, 1995) 34; Japanese demands: Herbert P. Bix, *Hirohito and the Making of Modern Japan* (Perennial, 2001) 512. **195** Woody Guthrie, "Sally,

Don't You Grieve," woodyguthrie.org/Lyrics/Sally_Dont_You_Grieve.htm; 1942 comic: Basil Wolverton, *Scoop Scuttle and His Pals* (Fantagraphics, 2021) 22; Dan Gilbert, *Emperor Hirohito of Japan: Satan's Man of Mystery Unveiled in the Light of Prophecy* (Zondervan, 1944) 26; Szyk: *Collier's* 2/14/1942; "Burma-Shave": Frank Rowsome Jr., *The Verse by the Side of the Road* (Stephen Greene, 1965) 96; Gallup poll: McGeorge Bundy, *Danger and Survival* (Random House, 1988) 83; Takaki 100ff. **196** Bundy 88; George Allen: Culver and Hyde 341. **197** Ichiro Hatano: Richard H. Minear and Leon E. Clark, *Through Japanese Eyes* (Center for International Training & Education, 1994) 135. **198** Atsugi: William Manchester, *The Glory and the Dream* (Little Brown, 1974) 473. **199** Shindo Renmei: Daniel M. Masterson and Sayaka Funada-Classen, *The Japanese in Latin America* (UIllinoisP, 2008) 137ff. **200** Iraq: Barbara Crosette, "Iraq Sanctions Kill Children, U.N. Reports," *NYT* 12/1/1995, nytimes.com/1995/12/01/world/iraq-sanctions-kill-children-un-reports.html; moved the date: Charles Stephenson, *Stalin's War on Japan* (Pen & Sword, 2021) 44. **201** Dulles: Bundy 241. **203** Akira Kurosawa, *Something Like an Autobiography* (Knopf, 1982) 145–6. **204** H. G. Wells, *Outline of History* (Garden City, 1931) 1136; H. G. Wells and Raymond Postgate, *Outline of History* (Garden City, 1961) 954, 959, etc.; McLean: Conant 111. **206** Clare Boothe Luce: *ib.* 117. **207** Moriuchi: Takashi Nagai, *We of Nagasaki* (Duell, Sloan, & Pearce, 1951) 123; Moriyama: *ib.* 136; Arthur Conan Doyle, *Memories and Adventures* (Cambridge, 2012) 80. **208** "victory of Manassas": Edward A. Pollard, *The Lost Cause* (E. B. Treat, 1866) 152.

11. THE FIRST CRUSADE

210 *Simpsons*: frinkiac.com/caption/S02E09/755138, frinkiac.com/caption/S02E09/758842; David Hume, *History of England* (United Co., 1775) vol. I, 255; Mackay, *Popular Delusions* 354. **211** *The Song of Roland* (Macmillan, 1960) 84; "The Prioress's Tale": *Riverside Chaucer* 210. **213** tulips: Mackay 91 (*cum grano salis*). **214** Amin Maalouf, *The Crusades through Arab Eyes* (Schocken, 1989) xvi. **216** "longbowman": Bret Devereaux, "Archery, Distance, and 'Kiting,'" 7/4/2019, acoup.blog/2019/07/04/collections-archery-distance-and-kiting. **217** Antioch: Harold Lamb, *The Crusades* (Doubleday, 1931) vol. I, 141. **219** Jacques Le Goff: Christopher Tyerman, *God's War* (Belknap, 2006) 912. **220** Eric Hoffer, *True Believer* 91; Theodore Dwight, *Decisions of Questions* (Johnathan Leavitt, 1833) 109 (*cf.* Mackay 460). **222** James D. Gillis, *The Cape Breton Giant* (Jonathan Lovell, 1899) 19. **225** 1950s field survey: William Manchester, *The Last Lion: Winston Spencer Churchill,* vol. I: *Visions of Glory, 1874–1932* (Little, Brown, 1983) 856n.; Alexander Thompson: William Dalrymple, *White Mughals* (Viking, 2002) 37.

12. ROMANTICISM

227 Johann Wolfgang von Goethe, *Maxims and Reflections* (Penguin, 1998) 161; Saadi, *The Rose Garden* (Octagon, 1974) 100; "The lyf": *Riverside Chaucer* 385. **228** "trained seal": Tuchman, *Proud Tower* 297; "best ear": T. S. Eliot, *Essays Ancient and Modern* (Harcourt, Brace, 1936) 186 (Auden, meanwhile, says "the finest ear, perhaps, of any English poet": W. H. Auden, ed., *A Selection from the Poems of Alfred, Lord Tennyson* [Doubleday Doran, 1944] ii). **229** sculpture for a hat rack: Peter Arno, *Hell of a Way to Run a Railroad* (Simon

& Schuster, 1956) 62; cracks in the museum wall: Ralph Stein, ed., *What's Funny About That?* (Dutton, 1954) 39; dropped fern: Ernie Bushmiller, *Artists and Con Artists* (Kitchen Sink, 1990) 12; *Art World* vol. 1, no. 2 (November 1919), 81 books.google.com/books?id =QeJMAQAAMAAJ; Braque: J. M. Nash, *Cubism, Futurism and Constructivism* (Barron's, 1978) 16; Paul Hammond, *L'Âge d'or* (BFI, 1997) 60. **230** *New York Times*: Edward de Grazia, *Girls Lean Back Everywhere: The Law of Obscenity and the Assault on Genius* (Random House, 1992) 14, 12; Emerson: James David Hart, *The Popular Book* (UCaliforniaP, 1963) 106. **231** "Virtue calm": "Pantisocracy," in *The Portable Coleridge* (Penguin, 1980) 63; "since Milton": Adam Sisman, *The Friendship* (Viking, 2006) 306. **232** left in suspense: Daniel Javitch, *Proclaiming a Classic* (Princeton UP, 1991) 91ff.; Walter Scott, *Ivanhoe* (Penguin, 2000) 152. **233** John Hoole, *The Orlando of Ariosto* (J. Dodsley, 1791) i; Lord Macaulay: *Critical and Historical Essays* 687, 147; *The Poems of William Cowper, Esq.* (Charles Wells, 1835) 169, 55; Agnes Repplier, *To Think of Tea!* (Houghton Mifflin, 1932) 115. **234** works of John Milton: *v.* esp. Edmund Burke, *On the Sublime and Beautiful* (John B. Alden, 1885) 53, 55; Ryan, *On Politics* 495; Krupskaya: Edmund Wilson, *To the Finland Station* (Farrar, Straus & Giroux, 1972) 471. **235** Robert Shea and Robert Anton Wilson, *Illuminatus!* (Dell, 1983) 199–200. **236** Philip Short, *Pol Pot* (John Macrae, 2005) 31; Hitler: Yvonne Sherratt, *Hitler's Philosophers* 30; Auden: Michael Dirda, *Classics for Pleasure* (Harcourt, 2007) 178. **237** Lord Byron, *The Complete Poetical Works* (Houghton Mifflin, 1905) 237; "the sleepless soul": William Wordsworth, *Poems* (Macmillan, 1897) 61; "solemn agony": *Shelley's Poetry and Prose* (Norton, 1977) 403; Mark Twain, *Life on the Mississippi* (Bantam, 1990) 219. **238** Semmes: Hart 69; kilts: Eric Hobsbawm and Terence Ranger, eds., *The Invention of Tradition* (Cambridge UP, 2003) 20ff.; Lester Young: Joel Dinerstein, *The Origins of Cool in Postwar America* (UChicagoP, 2017) 37; Mailer: *ib.* 229.

13. THE THIRD CRUSADE

241 Andreas Capellanus, *The Art of Courtly Love* (Columbia UP, 1990) 168–70. **242** Gerald of Wales, *History and Topography of Ireland* (Penguin, 1982) 50. **243** "death to the Greeks": David Miller, *Richard the Lionheart* (Phoenix Press, 2005) 54. **249** Joseph Le Conte, "The General Principles of Art and their Application to 'the Novel,'" *The Overland Monthly*, 2nd series, vol. V (April 1885) 346, books.google.com/books?id =ECVIAQAAMAAJ. **250** Harold Lamb, *Crusades* vol. II, 195ff.; D. Miller 169–70. **257** Corvina Library: Alberto Manguel, *The Library at Night* (Yale UP, 2008) 124; "little man of Vienna": Jason Goodwin, *Lords of the Horizons* (Henry Holt, 1999) 87; set of options: John Stoye, *The Siege of Vienna* (Pegasus, 2006) 95. **258** Famagusta: Andrew Wheatcroft, *Infidels* (Random House, 2005) 19–20; "trust not": *The Baburnama: Memoirs of Babur, Prince and Emperor* (Modern Library, 2002) 92; Pierre de Bourdeille, *Lives of Fair and Gallant Ladies* (Alexandrian, 1922) vol. II, 175. **263** "half-Turkish": Anthony Piccirillo, "'A Vile, Infamous, Diabolical Treaty': The Franco-Ottoman Alliance of Francis I and the Eclipse of the Christendom Ideal," Georgetown thesis, 2009, hdl.handle.net/10822/555505, 64. **265** Rebecca West, *Black Lamb and Grey Falcon* (Penguin, 2007) xxxvi.

14. POLAR EXPLORATION

268 This chapter leans heavily on Maciej Cegłowski, "Scott and Scurvy," *Idle Words*, 2010, idlewords.com/2010/03/scott_and_scurvy.htm, and, before that, John Franklin, *Narrative of a Journey to the Shores of the Polar Sea* (John Murray, 1824). **273** Jules Verne, *Twenty Thousand Leagues under the Sea* (Ward, Lock, n.d.) 252; Melville: Sandra Neil Wallace and Rich Wallace, *Bound by Ice* (Calkins Creek, 2017) 169. **275** His crew: Ernest Shackleton, *South* (Lyons, 1998) 76, and Alfred Lansing, *Endurance* (McGraw-Hill, 1959) viii. **277** "indrawing seas": Thomas Green, "John Dee, King Arthur, and the Conquest of the Arctic," *The Heroic Age* 15 (October 2012), heroicage.org/issues/15/green.php. **278** open wound: Lansing 112; Franklin 189; Peter Freuchen, *Arctic Adventures* (Halcyon, 1938) 314; *id.*, *Vagrant Viking* (J. Messner, 1953) 179; John Hanning Speke, *What Led to the Discovery of the Source of the Nile* (William Blackwood, 1864) 203. **281** Fridtjof Nansen, *Farthest North* (Macmillan, 1897) 509. **282** Diana Noyce, "Hoosh, Dogs, and Seal Meat," anmm.blog/wp-content/uploads/2011/08/amundsen-vs-scott-by-diana-noyce.pdf. **283** John Buchan, *The Last Secrets* (Thomas Nelson, 1923) 61; amphibian's jaw: "Antarctic Fossils," expeditions.fieldmuseum.org/antarctic-dinosaurs/antarctic-fossils. **284** Donald A. Mackenzie, *Crete and Pre-Hellenic Myths and Legends* (Senate, 1996) 9. **285** R. M. Ballantyne, *The Gorilla Hunters* (Thomas Nelson, 1861) 19. **286** Christmas songs: Randall Munroe, "Tradition," xkcd.com/988; Dean Sage Jr.: Harvey Fuller, "Facing Death in a Panda's Mouth," *Heroic Comics* #35 (Eastern Color, March 1946). **288** Moundsville: Joe Demarco, *Dinosauriana* compendium disc (Demarxo, 2013)—thanks to Fred M. Snyder for bringing this resource to my attention.

15. THE FALL OF ROME

290 Charlotte Brontë, *Jane Eyre* (Penguin, 2006) 17; Superboy: Edmond Hamilton and John Forte, "The Supervillains of All Ages!" *Adventure Comics* #314 (DC, November 1963); Leopold von Sacher-Masoch, *Venus in Furs* (B&N, 2004) 35; Oscar Wilde, *The Picture of Dorian Gray* (B&N, 2003) 148. **292** Tacitus: *Agricola and Germania* 73; reduce sperm counts: A. M. Devine, "The Low Birth-Rate in Ancient Rome: A Possible Contributing Factor," *Rheinisches Museum für Philologie* 128, no. 3/4 (1985) 313–17, jstor.org/stable/41233558; Paris in the thirteenth century: Barbara Tuchman, *A Distant Mirror* (Ballantine, 1987) 159. **293** Ammianus, *Later Roman Empire* 417. **296** Gibbon vol. I, 103. **299** number of emperors: These counts rely on Adrian Goldsworthy, *How Rome Fell* (Yale, 2009) 425ff. **300** Churchill: William Manchester and Paul Reid, *The Last Lion: Winston Spencer Churchill,* vol. III: *Defender of the Realm, 1940–1965* (Little, Brown 2012) 590. **302** Philo of Alexandria and Salvian the Presbyter: Donald Kagan, ed., *The End of the Roman Empire* (D. C. Heath, 1992) 59, 57. **303** St. Jerome: Augustine, *City of God* (Penguin, 1986) x. **305** "had my brother lived": P. A. Kropotkin, *The Great French Revolution* (Putnam's, 1909) 452; Thomas Carlyle 703; Corday: *ib.* 702.

16. ALASKA

306 *Sacramento Daily Union*: Walter Stahr, *Seward* (Simon & Schuster, 2012) 496. **307** Lomonosov: Vladimir Nabokov, *Verses and Versions* (Harcourt, 2008) 27. **308** ivory: Avram

Davidson, *Adventures in Unhistory* (Tor, 2006) 231. **309** contemporary newspaper: Stahr 497. **310** Seward: *ib.* 434. **311** for the eyes: *ib.* 436. **312** Frederick W. Seward, *Seward in Washington* (Derby & Miller, 1891) 368; *National Republican*: Stahr 488. **313** Robert V. Remini, *Henry Clay* (Norton, 1991) 677. **317** Lenin wanted him fired: Robert Conquest, *The Great Terror* (Macmillan, 1969) 537; Khrushchev: Karal Ann Marling, *As Seen on TV* 276; "presumptuous and rude": Bertram D. Wolfe, *Three Who Made a Revolution* (Beacon, 1959) 95; Shaporina: Martin Amis, *Koba the Dread* (Hyperion, 2002) 190; Ukrainian Central Committee: Conquest 256. **318** Robert F. Kennedy, *Thirteen Days* (Norton, 1969) 110. **319** JFK: *ib.* 102; Caroline Moorehead, *Bertrand Russell* (Viking, 1993) 469.

17. ETHIOPIA AND YEMEN

321 Artapanus: James H. Charlesworth, ed., *Old Testament Pseudepigrapha* (Hendrickson, 2010) 899; Josephus, *Antiquities*, sacred-texts.com/jud/josephus/ant-2.htm. **322** chronology: Matthew McGee, "Old Testament Timeline," matthewmcgee.org/ottimlin.html; Samuel Johnson: Jerome Lobo, *A Voyage to Abyssinia* (Elliot & Kay, 1789) 197; Olaudah Equiano, *The Interesting Narrative* (Penguin, 1995) 45. **323** Richard Adams, *Shardik* (Simon & Schuster, 1974) 303. **324** "full of gardens": Mary and Elizabeth Kirby, *Aunt Martha's Corner Cupboard* (Altemus, n.d.) 88; some older books say: e.g., *Harmsworth History of the World* (Carmelite House, 1908) vol. III, 2250. **325** Gibbon vol. II, 728. **328** "In Dilmun": Stephen Langdon, *Sumerian Epic of Paradise, the Flood and the Fall of Man* (UPenn Museum, 1919) 70. **329** Pausanias, *Guide to Greece* (Penguin, 1979) vol. I, 463–5; Muhammad would prophesy: Neal Robinson, ed., *The Sayings of Muhammad* (Ecco, 1998) 27; Plutarch: *Athens* 25; Carl Drews and Weiqing Han, "Dynamics of Wind Setdown at Suez and the Eastern Nile Delta" (2010), doi.org/10 .1371/journal.pone.0012481. **330** grudge against the sea: these examples are all from Carola Kloos, *Yhwh's Combat with the Sea* (Oorschot, 1986); Byron, *Poetic Works* 222, Sprengel. Donald Hopkins, *Princes and Peasants* 25. **331** Sayyid Saeed Akhtar Rizvi, *The Life of Muhammad the Prophet* (Darul Tabligh, n.d.), al-islam.org/life-muhammad-prophet-allamah-sayyid -saeed-akhtar-rizvi, "Year of the Elephant"; Procopius, *History of the Wars (Loeb)* (Heinemann, 1914) vol. I, 195; Lena Jayyusi, trans., *Adventures of Sayf Ben Dhi Yazan* (Indiana UP, 1996) 249. **332** Gibbon vol. II, 509. **333** "tarry a moment": Washington Irving, *Mahomet and His Successors* (Co-Operative, 1849) 88. **336** "an obscure citizen of Mecca": Gibbon vol. II, 912. **338** "the whole living world": Epiphanius Wilson, ed., *Sacred Books of the East* (Collier, 1900) 67. **339** St. Cyril: Jan Willem Drijvers, *Cyril Of Jerusalem* (Brill, 2004) 107.

18. AARON BURR

342 campaign song: Sam Haselby, *Origins of American Religious Nationalism* (Oxford UP, 2017) 307–8; 1864 pamphlet: *Abraham Africanus I: His Secret Life, As Revealed under the Mesmeric Influence: Mysteries of the White House* (J. F. Feeks, 1864) 10; Andy Soltis, "Post Readers: Hitler Was Most Evil," *New York Post* 11/17/99, nypost.com/1999/11/17/post-readers -hitler-was-most-evil; Tussaud: David Wallechinsky et al., *The Book of Lists* (Bantam, 1978) 1. **343** Lincoln: Edmund Wilson, *Patriotic Gore* (Norton, 1994) 3; "young and flippant":

Andrew Lang, "A Critical Taboo," *The Living Age* (July–Sept. 1892) 723. **344** Agnes Rep-
plier, *Points of View* (Houghton Mifflin, 1893) 75; 1920 comic strip: E. C. Segar, *Thimble
Theater* (1/15/1920); Uncle Tom–branded: Stephen Railton, ed., *Uncle Tom's Cabin and
American Culture*, utc.iath.virginia.edu/tomituds/toadsf.html; Harriet Beecher Stowe, *The
Minister's Wooing* (Houghton Mifflin, 1896) 168, 307. **345** *ib.* 170; Joseph B. Cobb, *Leisure
Labors* (D. Appleton, 1858) 77; debased and profligate character: Roger G. Kennedy, *Burr,
Hamilton, and Jefferson* (Oxford UP, 2000) 374; Matthew Livingston Davis, *Memoirs of Burr*
(Harper & Bros., 1837) vol. I, 91; "deliberate stab": Worthington Chauncey Ford, "Some
Papers of Aaron Burr," *Proceedings of the American Antiquarian Society* (AAS, 1919) vol.
XXIX, 86; "wonderful strength" Lyndon Orr, *Famous Affinities* (Harper & Bros., 1914) vol.
I, 82; classroom decorations: R. G. Kennedy 45 (*cf.* Gore Vidal, *Burr* [Random House, 1973]
51); George Lippard, *Washington and His Generals* (G. B. Zieber, 1847) 167; R. G. Kennedy
372. **346** Lincoln: Constance M. Rourke, *Trumpets of Jubilee* (Harcourt, Brace, 1927) 187;
other limericks: e.g., Gershon Legman, *The Limerick* (Citadel, 1979) 283 (#1373). **347** "God
forgive Christopher Columbus": Charles Edward Stowe, *Life of Harriet Beecher Stowe*
(Houghton Mifflin, 1890) 26; "Some of his sermons": *ib.* 406; pernicious effect: Edmund
Wilson, *Gore* 39; H. Stowe 156, 159. **348** James Wood, *The Irresponsible Self* (Farrar, Straus
& Giroux, 2005) 214; H. Stowe 417.

19. VIETNAM

349 Richard M. Nixon, *RN* (Grosset & Dunlap, 1978) 403; *id., The Real War* (Warner, 1980) 242.
350 Edmond Hamilton, *Crashing Suns* (Ace, 1965) 32 (Hamilton uses the etheric ray on a star,
not a planet, but there's no reason it shouldn't work on one as well as the other). **351** *Limits of
Oceans and Seas* (Imp. Monegasque, 1953) 4; Zhuang Zhou: *Chuang Tzu: Basic Writings* (Columbia UP, 1964) 35; *Saginaw*: A. D. Schenck, *The Rev. William Schenck, His Ancestry and His
Descendants* (Rufus H. Darby, 1883) 91. **353** the exotic name "Saigon": Henry Kamm, *Dragon
Ascending* (Arcade, 1996) 168–9. **355** Catherine the Great: Nixon, *RN* 54. **356** Philip Short, *Pol
Pot* 42, 27; "I like to hold": David Halberstam, *Ho* (Random House, 1971) 16. **357** downplayed
or suppressed: Michael Lind, *Vietnam: The Necessary War* (Free Press, 1999) 86ff.; Zhuang 51.
360 Lydia Saad, "Gallup Vault: Hawks vs. Doves on Vietnam," news.gallup.com/vault/191828
/gallup-vault-hawks-doves-vietnam.aspx. **363** medical experiments: Ben Kiernan, *The Pol
Pot Regime* (Yale UP, 1996) 439; Laurence Picq, *Beyond the Horizon* (St. Martin's, 1984) 152;
Johnson's advisers: Lind 41. **364** Twiggy: Jane and Michael Stern, *Sixties People* (Knopf, 1990)
11; Mamas and the Papas: Andy Wickham, *If You Can Believe Your Eyes and Ears* liner notes
(1966). **366** Susan St. James: *Kate and Allie* S05E02 "The Dilemma With Emma." **367** cases of
drugs: Art Linkletter, *Drugs at My Door Step* (Word Books, 1973) 40.

20. GLOBAL THERMONUCLEAR WAR

369 Nixon: Ron Rosenbaum, *How the End Begins* (Simon & Schuster, 2011) 35; Art Linkletter, *Oops! or, Life's Awful Moments* (Doubleday, 1967) 86. **370** Cartmill: Robert Silverberg,
"Reflections: The Cleve Cartmill Affair," *Asimov's Science Fiction Magazine* (Sept.–Oct.

2003); François Truffaut, *Hitchcock* (Simon & Schuster, 1967) 121 (but *cf.* Donald Spoto, *The Dark Side of Genius* [Little, Brown, 1983] 285). **371** Rosenbaum 62; Harold Hering: *ib.* 31. **372** Blair: William J. Broad, "Russia Has 'Doomsday' Machine, U.S. Expert Says," *NYT* 8/8/93, nytimes.com/1993/10/08/world/russia-has-doomsday-machine-us-expert-says.html. **373** Maxim: Adrienne LaFrance, "People Thought Machine Guns Might Prevent Wars," *Atlantic* 1/26/2016, theatlantic.com/technology/archive/2016/01/maxim-guns/428253; Hilaire Belloc, *The Modern Traveller* (Edward Arnold, 1898) 41; "pert little vigilant": Patrick Mac-Gill, *Soldier Songs* (Dutton, 1917) 33; Nobel: Martin Bayer et al., *On the Eve of the Great War* (Založba ZRC, 2015) 76; James Henry McLean, *Dr. J. H. McLean's Peace-Makers* (Baker & Godwin, 1880) 15, 150, 188 (*v.* also Bob Hohertz, "McLean's Peacemakers," rdhinstl.com /mm/mclpm.htm; my thanks to Osiris Oliphant for locating McLean's book). **375** Sherman: McPherson, *Battle Cry* 809; Oppenheimer: John E. Mueller, *Atomic Obsession* (Oxford UP, 2010) 17; Alex Wellerstein, "Oppenheimer and the Gita," blog.nuclearsecrecy.com/2014/05 /23/oppenheimer-gita. **376** General Advisory Committee: McGeorge Bundy, *Danger and Survival* 208; Oppenheimer: *ib.* 288; Mueller ix–x. **377** Eisenhower: Bundy 278; Churchill: Mueller 29; Rostow: *ib.* 30. **379** *Ren and Stimpy*: John Kricfalusi et al., "Space Madness" (August 25, 1991). **380** Rosenbaum 77; Brian Martin, "Critique of Nuclear Extinction," *Journal of Peace Research* vol. 19, no. 4 (1982), bmartin.cc/pubs/82jpr.html; Sagan: Frank D. Roylance, "Burning Oil Wells Could Be Disaster, Sagan Says," *Baltimore Sun*, 1/23/1991, articles.baltimoresun.com/1991-01-23/news/1991023131_1_kuwait-saddam-hussein-sagan. **381** R. F. Kennedy, *Thirteen Days* 23. **382** John Schilling, SSC Open Thread comment, slate starcodex.com/2016/04/11/ot47-openai/#comment-346878; Bundy 605. **383** "rocks!": Alice Calaprice, ed., *The New Quotable Einstein* 173; Gillette: Martin Gardner, *Fads and Fallacies in the Name of Science* (Ballantine, 1957) 55–6; Kichik Khan: *Baburnama* 120; Viktor Rydberg, *Teutonic Mythology* (Forgotten Books, 2012) 192. **384** Mircea Eliade, *Youth without Youth* (UChicagoP, 2007) 79 (of course, Eliade is an ironist; *c.g.s.*).

∞

387 Friedrich Nietzsche, *On the Genealogy of Morals and Ecce Homo* (Random House, 1989) 258; Cook: Nicholas D. Smith, ed., *Philosophers Look at Science Fiction* (Nelson-Hall, 1982) 53. **389** Arthur Platt, *Nine Essays* (Cambridge UP, 2015) 24; Lannes: Alan Schom, *Napoleon Bonaparte* (HarperCollins, 1997) 550; von Törne: Johan Ludvig Runeberg, *The Songs of Ensign Stål* (G. E. Stechert, 1925) 216, 223.

IMAGE CREDITS

Interior images from the British Library public domain digital collection except: **Chapter 1** telephone © Shutterstock. **Chapter 6** Sigmund Freud © Shutterstock. **Chapter 8** Europe 1939 map © Shutterstock. **Chapter 9** Constantinople © Shutterstock. **Chapter 10** Henry Wallace & nuclear bomb from Library of Congress (Harris & Ewing Collection). **Chapter 20** Jimmy Carter from Library of Congress; nuclear explosion © Shutterstock.